Corporate Social Responsibility

इश्वरो गुरुरात्मेति मूर्तिभेदविभागिने
व्योमवद् व्याप्तदेहाय दक्षिणामूर्तये नमः

CORPORATE SOCIAL RESPONSIBILITY

Ajith Sankar R. N.

Motilal Banarsidass Publications

MOTILAL BANARSIDASS
PUBLICATIONS
4741/23, Ansari Road, Daryaganj, New Delhi - 110002 (India)
Email: *mlbd@mlbd.com* | *sales@mlbd.com* | *exports@mlbd.com*
Website: *www.mlbd.com*

Corporate Social Responsibility
by
Ajith Sankar R. N.

First Edition Published in 2022

Published in India by Motilal Banarsidass Publications

ISBN : 978-93-91759-15-5 (HB)

Printed and bound in India

अविघ्नमस्तु

Avighnamastu...[1]

1 *'Vighna'* refers to obstacles, blockages, difficulties, hurdles, challenges, etc. *'Ishwara'* refers to the Lord, Deity, Supreme etc. Vighneshwara is an elephant-headed deity worshipped by the Hindus. So, does it mean that Vighneshwara creates difficulties for his devotees? He may, or, may not. The foresters and rangers will have stories to tell of how elephants had created blocks and hurdles on their paths, thereby saving these rangers from accidents and hazards. Lord Vighneshwara may create obstancles for his devotees to understand and decipher the nature of obstacles. Vighneshwara is also the *Siddhivinayaka* and *Ganapati*. Understanding a challenge, as it is, helps one to serve, and thus, lead. Vighneshwara is also *Vinayaka* (*nayak* = hero, leader). Vighneshwara's brother is Karthikeya, the commander of the forces that fights the demons. *A-vighnamastu...*

सरस्वती नमस्तुभ्यम्
वरदे ज्ञानविज्ञान रूपिणी
विद्यारम्भम् करिश्यामि
विनयद् भवतु में सदा[2]

2 In the work, *'Through the Looking Glass and what Alice found there'*, Lewis Carroll, through the character of 'Humpty Dumpty' mentions, "*... when I use a word*, it means just what I chose it to mean...". Seers, sages and scholars have delved into, or made attempts, to know about words and their meanings. Some say that a "form" (as in, a shape, or, a presence) may have a "sound" associated, referred to as *shabd* or *shabdam*. The *shabd* may express itself in a particular 'form', and a combination of sounds may manifest as formations. Sounds that are harmoniously expressed becomes music to our ears (*naad* or *naadam*). And thus our teachers, grand-parents, and well-wishers reminds us, "*Speak politely, do not be rude. Be respectful*". This *shabda-aakriti* relationship (*aakriti* – form, *kriti* – creation, *prakriti* – nature, *vikriti* – playfulness) is dependent or influenced by the essence or the quality of the mind – *bhaava*. Swami Tapovanam says, "Do all actions as the worship of the Lord... by *japa*, meditation, *keertans*, prayers and by doing good actions... the Lord becomes pleased... the Grace of the Lord is the only *Sadhana* to attain the fulfilment of all desires... Brahma *Jnaana*, which is the nearest step from the attainment of Brahma *Bhaava*, will also result gradually...

Confession[3]

Imagine yourself somewhere near the boundary of the 'solar system', after travelling years and years through the vastness of space. How would the earth look like? The size of a pebble, or that of a grain of sand? From earth, we are unable to see any of the distant planets of the 'solar system'. And we have so many such 'solar system's in our galaxy, and so many such galaxies in our visible universe. Our poets and writers have imagined existences even beyond this. One writes - "beyond the shores of this river of sky exists a thousand pillared marble hall, where a *gaandharva* arrives to sing, on every full-moon night". Even the cells of the body are not visible, forget about the molecules, atoms or the more minutiae. A bard from the *sierra* says, "If the Creator were to bestow a new set of senses upon us... we should never doubt that we were in another world." Indeed, ..."*the haunting and truly spectral unreality of realistic books.*"!

3 'Confession', from Latin, may mean 'to admit'. The first quote included in the above passage is a translation from a song written by K Jayakumar for the Malayalam movie '*Kunjaattakkilikal*'. '*Gaandharva*', as per the writings available in Indian literatures, are celestial beings. The second quote included above is from the journal entries of John Muir, dated Jan-May, 1869. The reference to books, made in the passage above, was made by Robert Louis Stevenson.

You may consider, whether 'now' is the moment to read this book...

If you may be reading this book through an electronic medium/ as an e-copy, etc., it may be noted that the radiations emanating from, and through, the electronic medium may be harmful and distorting. Please be gentle and kind to yourself.

CONTENTS

Chapter 1

INTRODUCTION

"Through His teachings, our first guru, Guru Nanak Dev Ji, explained that the world we humans create around ourselves is a reflection of our own inner state. So as we look around to our wasteful and polluting practices, we obtain an insight into the chaos within us. When the tenth master, Guru Gobind Singh Ji, founded the Khalsa in 1699, he charged Sikhs to challenge any force that threatened the well-being of others. He made us warriors with the responsibility to protect the vulnerable... Seva, the practice of selfless service, is a main tenet of Sikhism. Sikhs can perform seva by reducing our carbon footprints, recycling, investing in renewable energies, and being mindful about where our food comes from."

Excerpt from the 2014 'Sikh Declaration on Climate Change'[1]

On completion of reading the chapter, the reader may:

1. Understand the context related to the development of 'Corporate Social Responsibility'.

2. Recognise the evidences that indicate the mainstreaming of Corporate Social Responsibility.

3. Explain and appreciate the varied definitions and synonyms associated with Corporate Social Responsibility.

Legends are that in ancient India, there lived a king, *Amarashakthi*, who had three sons, with their names as *Bahushakti*, *Ugrashakti* and *Anantshakthi*, thereby epitomising a nature of grandeur in them. (*Bahushakti* – manifold strength, *Ugrashakti* – fierce strength, *Anantshakti* – infinite strength), While their names were majestic, these three princes were as meek as mice. They did not display any enthusiasm, talent, skill, manners fit for the royals, curiosity for higher knowledge, valour, leadership, etc., which would have made any parents proud. They earned laurels such as 'dull-witted' and 'blockheads'. '*How will they administer the kingdom in the future*', the king was worried.

'*Seek the help of Vishnusharma*', someone told the king. Vishnusharma was a teacher who has earned respects. The king called for 'Vishnusharma'. On his arrival, the king conveyed his worries to Vishnusharma and offered him a hundred villages, if he agrees to be the tutor for the princes. Vishnusharma

1 http://www.ecosikh.org/first-sikh-statement-on-climate-change-presented-by-ecosikh/, Accessed on September 30, 2020.

told the king that imparting knowledge is not such a transaction. However, he took up the challenge of nurturing these princes. Thus was born, the '*Panchatantra*', the collection of stories, which introduced the princes to the realm of statecraft, ethics and discrimination ('*Pancha*' - five). These stories portrays animals who talk in a human language. Many stories in *Panchatantra* was also a medium for imparting moral education for children. A survey[2] about the texts and versions of '*Panchatantra*' records that one of the earliest versions of *Panchatantra* is known as the *Tantrakhyayika* (*akhyayika*[3] - narrative, tale, book, lexicon, treatise, etc.).

Yet another survey[4], this on the consumer attitudes that are contemporary, done in 2015, amongst 30,000 consumers in 60 countries, indicated that 66% of the respondents were willing to pay extra for products and non-product business from companies that are committed to social and environmental responsibility. For a similar survey conducted in 2014, the percentage of such customers was 55%, while it was 50% and 45% in 2012 and 2011. This indicates that increasing number of consumers are giving importance to social and environmentally responsible practices. "*When you buy an animal skin product..., it encourages a seller to restock his wares... when the buying stops, the killing will stop too...,*" says Mike Pandey, whose films has won Green Oscars.

To ascertain whether consumer sentiment that supports responsibility practices is resulting in purchase decisions, the survey ascertained the sales performance of products that had sustainability attributes. This was compared with the sales performance of those products that did not have sustainability attributes. The survey states that "*sales of consumer goods from brands with a demonstrated commitment to sustainability have grown more than 4% globally, while those without, grew less than 1%.*" It can be concluded that consumers are rewarding companies that support responsibility practices. In addition to consumers, other stakeholders are also supporting this

---

2 Johannes Hertel, The Panchatantra-text of Purnabhadra: Critical Introduction and List of Variants, Harvard University, 1912.

3 '*Tantra*', may mean, that which helps in recognising that one is not just the physical body. '*Tantra*' may also be that which helps one to move beyond one's identiication with the physicality. '*Tantra*' may also refer to 'tact', 'strategy', 'method'. 'process' etc. '*Rajyatantra*', for example, deals with managing a kingdom ('*Rajya*' means place, state, nation, the region that is ruled, etc.). With reference to the writings of Adi Shankara, Arthur Avalon says that *Tantra Shastra* is a sadhana shastra, and "the object of it is to reach the highest Truth...".

4 http://www.nielsen.com/in/en/press-room/2015/consumer-goods-brands-that-demonstrate-commitment-to-sustainability-outperform.html, Accessed on July 21, 2016.

sustainability trend. 67% of those who responded to the 2014 survey said that they prefer to work for a socially responsible company.

Similar sentiments are being echoed elsewhere. A report[5] states, "*...increasingly important stakeholder is the community, and many companies have started realising that the 'licence to operate' is no longer given by governments alone, but communities that are impacted by a company's business operations.*"

Such studies can be influential. In India, some of the tube-light manufacturers attest for a lifespan "upto 18,000 hours", "upto 21,000 hours", etc. (Using a tublight for three hours daily for 10 and 15 years results in a usage of approximately 11,000 and 17,000 hours, respectively). Such studies may influence consumers to search for tube-lights that lights even more than 21,000 hours, at a lower price, while being energy-efficient, and adhering to better standards of e-waste management.

Much discussion has happened about the social responsibility of organisations. As per ISO 26000:2010, social responsibility of an organisation is defined as the responsibility of an organization for the impacts of its decisions and activities on society and the environment, through transparent and ethical behaviour that (a) contributes to sustainable development, including health and the welfare of society (b) takes into account the expectations of stakeholders (c) is in compliance with applicable law and consistent with international norms of behaviour, and (d) is integrated throughout the organization and practised in its relationships[6]. While the word 'corporate' in Corporate Social Responsibility (CSR) indicates that the word pertains to a for-profit organisation, the usage of this word has been pervasive that it is being used by not-for-profit organisations and institutions. 'International Labour Organisation' (ILO) explicitly mentions that social responsibility also includes economic responsibility[7].

OPERATIONAL TENETS OF CSR

Rumi has said[8],

5 http://www.pwc.in/assets/pdfs/publications/2013/handbook-on-corporate-social-responsibility-in-india.pdf, Accessed on May 24, 2015.

6 https://www.iso.org/obp/ui/#iso:std:iso:26000:ed-1:v1:en, Accessed on April 16, 2015.

7 http://www.ilo.org/legacy/english/integration/download/publicat/4_3_285_wcsdg-wp-27.pdf, Accessed on June 8, 2015.

8 As mentioned in 'The Essential Rumi', Translated by Coleman Barks, Harperone, 2013. Jalāl ad-Dīn Muhammad Rūmī, also known as Jalāl ad-Dīn Muhammad Balkhī, lived between 1207 and 1273, and was a native of the Central Asian region.

Fasting says, I have not eaten
even what is permitted. I must want no connection
to what is not. Giving to the poor says,
I am distributing my own property,
Certainly, I will not steal from others.

CSR may incorporate some or all of the following tenets depending on the maturity and sincerity of the CSR practices in an organization:

a. Engaging in socially and environmentally beneficial endeavours that may go beyond an organisation's operations.

b. Infusing responsibility practices into an organisation's operational DNA.

c. Love, expressing itself as service.

d. Practice of 'Ceilings on Desires' by the members of the organization, and sharing the saved time, energy, money and other resources for the well-being of all.

e. Sharing a portion of the profits with the community.

f. Channelizing the competencies of an organization for the greater common good of all.

g. Equitable distribution of wealth with those who contributed to wealth-creation.

h. Creating a work culture in the organisation that acknowledges that (i) the organisational wealth belongs to all, including generations that are yet to be born (ii) while profits are necessary to sustain the organization, it is only one of the attributes of success in an organisational endeavour.

i. Purity and unity of thought, word and deed.

DEFINITONS AND SYNONYMS FOR CSR

Corporate Social Responsibility can be defined as the ethos and practice of discovering[9], invoking[10], infusing[11], evoking[12] and radiating[13] the human

9 dis-cover.

10 to call (as in, "invoking the presence of a spiritual master, deity, higher power, a human value etc. during a prayer").

11 to inspire, instil, impart, etc.

12 to shine, illuminate, emit, spread, etc.

13 http://www.wbcsd.org/Pages/EDocument/EDocumentDetails.aspx?ID=83&NoSearchContextKey=true, Accessed on April 5, 2015.

values of righteousness (*Dharma*) and love (*Prema*) in an organisation's interactions with its stakeholders. Stakeholders of an organization can include its customers, employees, shareholders, society, natural environment, business associates, regulatory agencies etc.

> *Corporate Social Responsibility can be defined as the ethos and practice of discovering, infusing, evoking and radiating the human values of righteousness (Dharma) and love (Prema) in an organisation's interactions with its stakeholders.*

CSR has also been defined as:

a. The commitment of business to contribute to sustainable economic development, working with the employees, their families, the local community and society at large to improve their quality of life (World Business Council for Sustainable Development (WBCSD))[14].

b. The responsibility of enterprises for their impacts on society (European Commission)[15].

c. A management concept whereby companies integrate social and environmental concerns in their business operations and interactions with their stakeholders (UNIDO)[16].

d. Ethical behaviour of business towards its constituencies or stakeholders (International Labour Organization (ILO))[17].

Attempts have been made to communicate that CSR is not just charity. The idea that *"It is about how you do business and not how you give away or utilize the profits you make from that business"*[18] has been lived by some companies, and is reflected in their perspectives about CSR. Patagonia, an adventure-sportswear company, defines 'Corporate Responsibility' as a *"broad-based movement in business that encourages companies to take responsibility for the impact of their activities on customers, employees, communities and the environment."*[19]

14 http://www.wbcsd.org/Pages/EDocument/EDocumentDetails.aspx?ID=83&NoSearchContextKey=true, Accessed on April 5, 2015.

15 http://eur-lex.europa.eu/LexUriServ/LexUriServ.do?uri=COM:2011:0681:FIN:EN:PDF, Accessed on April 16, 2015.

16 http://www.unido.org/index.php?id=413#pp1[g1]/0/, Accessed on April 16, 2015.

17 http://www.ilo.org/legacy/english/integration/download/publicat/4_3_285_wcsdg-wp-27.pdf, Accessed on June 8, 2015.

18 http://www.livemint.com/Companies/lndzy4W8IBYZrzjqkj5BLJ/CSR-is-about-responsibility-Richard-Welford.html, Accessed on May 9, 2016.

19 http://www.patagonia.com/us/patagonia.go?assetid=67372, Accessed on July 1, 2015.

CSR may also be considered as a subset of a broader 'Corporate Responsibility' or sustainability movement. 'Tata Sustainability Group' says, *"The way we look at sustainability is that it must have many components to it. The first one is how you do your business, what are the kinds of issues you deal with specially on the ethical front, the social impact your business has and the environmental impact. The second part is what you do with your profits. All these taken together are an important part of sustainability. CSR just deals with what you do with your profits..."*[20]

> *CSR is not just about how an organization distributes its profits, it is also about how an organization generates its revenue.*

CSR has also been known as 'Corporate Social Responsiveness', 'Corporate Social Performance', 'Corporate Social Accountability', 'Corporate Citizenship', 'Responsible Business', 'Corporate Social Opportunity, 'Corporate Responsibility' etc.

Etymology of 'Corporate Social Responsibility' may be detailed as below:

Word	Word origin and meaning
'Corporate'	Corpus (Latin) - body, senses
'Social'	Socius (Latin) – comrade, companion, associate
'Responsibility'	Re + Spondee (French) – to pledge, offering

> ***To read, even a few pages, is itself an achievement.***
>
> ***You may take a break...***

OBJECTIVES, NATURE AND SCOPE OF CORPORATE SOCIAL RESPONSIBILITY

In 1931, Mohandas Karamchand Gandhi visited England to attend the second round-table conference related to the future of India within the British dominion. He was one among the many dozens of people who represented various interest groups from India – princes, industrialists, trade-unionists, etc., and Gandhi remarked that the conference do not find representation from the peasants of India, who made the vast majority

20 http://www.livemint.com/Companies/bUU22fyh56wZSmcaUihBeO/CSR-is-a-subset-of-sustainability.html, Accessed on May 9, 2016.

of the Indians. A British government representative mentioned that that he (the government representative) sincerely believed that Indians were unfit for complete self-government[21]. While the talks did not find much progress, this visit to England made Gandhi to visit the textile town of Darwen in Lanchashire. This region was economically affected, also due to the freedom movement in India, which emphasised self-reliance and hand-spun cotton (*khadi*, using *charkha*), resulting in a loss of business for the textile-mills in England. Gandhi was invited to the town by the Davies family, the owners of a textile mill, who wished Gandhi towards a direct experience of the place and its people, and how they were affected. *"The Davies family were prominent Socialists and Quakers, and they firmly believed that the Mahatma might understand the suffering through mill towns such as Bolton, Oldham, Burnley and Blackburn"*[22], says Harold Heys, a historian of Darwen. Gandhi was given a hearty welcome by the people. It is also remarked that many people regarded him with a curiosity, rather than as someone with the statu(r)e of a leader. Gandhi said that the boycott of foreign goods will continue[23][24] in India, and mentioned, *"You have three million unemployed, but we have nearly three hundred million unemployed. Your average unemployment dole is seventy shillings a month. Our average income is seven shillings and six pence a month."*[25] When some of the workers sought attention to how the town was economically affected, he replied: *"...you have no idea what poverty is."*[26] Gandhi stayed among the poor, also slept on roofs and balconies[27], traveled second-class, ate simple food, fasted and meditated, and his

21 http://www.mkgandhi-sarvodaya.org/biography/rndtable.htm, Accessed on October 1, 2020.

22 https://www.bbc.com/news/uk-england-lancashire-15020097, Accessed on October 1, 2020.

23 https://www.wcml.org.uk/our-collections/object-of-the-month/gandhi-in-darwen-september-1931/,Accessed on October 1, 2020.

24 John Keay, an author, writes, "Like *Satyagaraha*, he (Gandhi) interpreted Swaraj in a personal as well as a national sense. It could as well be translated as 'self-control' or 'self-reliance' as 'self-rule'. Political emancipation lay through economic emancipation from dependency on manufactured and imported products, through ideological emancipation from the materialism of the West, and through individual emancipation from... the violence of desire. His obsession with spinning, ...distribution of spinning wheels, ...wearing of homespun khadi looked to many like a wildly eccentric distraction... Gandhi, though, saw in it, the discipline and the dignity of a more profound and universal resurgence."

25 https://virily.com/culture/gandhis-visit-to-england-in-1931/, Accessed on October 1, 2020.

26 https://www.bbc.com/news/uk-england-lancashire-15020097, Accessed on October 1, 2020.

27 https://heritagephotoarchive.co.uk/p884949884/h43864CD6#h43864cd6, Accessed on October 1, 2020.

dressing consisted of a tunic and sandal. Acknowledging the warmth he received from the people, Gandhi said that he felt as one amongst them.

Another textile-town in England was Manchester. In mid 2010s, the city instituted a statue of Gandhi. A few centuries earlier, following the onset of the 'industrial revolution', the town became the all-famous textile town of England – in textile manufacturing, textile trade and related industries[28]. So famous, that textile towns in other parts of the world started calling themselves as the Manchester of that region. Manchester is also the home-turf of the football (soccer) club, 'Manchester United', whose jersey has been worn by players such as Cristiano Ronaldo, Bobby Charlton and David Beckham. This football club had its beginnings in 1878, At its home-stadium at Old Trafford, 'Manchester United' reserves some of the most-prized-seats in the stadium during the football matches, to be gifted free of cost for witnessing the football matches, to the physically challenged or the hearing impaired.

Why CSR?

For-profit organisations aims to generate wealth. This wealth is generated from the planet, which belongs to all. The organisation's primary accountability is thus to the society/ planet. Also, organisations cannot exist independently. To generate wealth and to sustain itself, an organisation seeks services from external entities. There is interdependency. Businesses cannot exist without a healthy planet and acknowledgement

28 Referring to '*The Highlands of Central India*' (1920), Captain J Forsyth wrote, "*...With few exceptions, the civil officers of those days never dreamt of penetrating the hilly portions of their charges; amd the writer is acquainted with one district containing some 3000 square miles of forest country, and inhabited by between 30,000 and 40,000 aborigines, in which one officer held charge for eleven years without once having put foot within this enormous territory. All accounts of such tracts were filtered through Hindu or Mahomedan subordinates, whose horror of a jungle, and its unknown terrors of bad air and water, wild beasts, and general discomfort, is such as to, ensure their painting the country and its people in the blackest of colours. But a new era dawned on these dark regions, when the conscience of the British rulers of India was awakened to the wants of their great charge, after a rebellion which nearly ousted them from their seat. Along with many more important provinces, this secluded region felt the benefit of the impulse then given to the administration of the empire. That great civiliser of nations - the iron road - was to be driven through the heart of its valleys; and Manchester had prophetically fixed an eye on its black soil plains as a future field for cotton...*" The "rebellion" here refers to 1857, known variously as "sepoy mutiny", "*war of independence, etc. Another observation made by the author in the book includes, "Large gangs of aboriginal Gonds from the nearer hill tracts were labouring on the railway works. The really wild tribes of the interior of the hills were not yet attracted by the labour market in the plains, preferring a dinner of jungle herbs and their squalid freedom, to [the] plenty earned by steady toil under the eye of the foreign taskmaster*".

of this interdependency. *Business is a fully owned subsidiary of the natural environment.*

Speaking about fossil-fuel based pollution, Al Gore, who won the Nobel Peace Prize for his efforts to create awareness about global warming, says, *"Companies are insisting on their right to use our atmosphere as an open sewer"*[29]. Such practices have resulted in planetary incongruence (**Refer Figure 1.1**) - visible in varied forms, be it water pollution or diseases.

Figure 1.1[30]

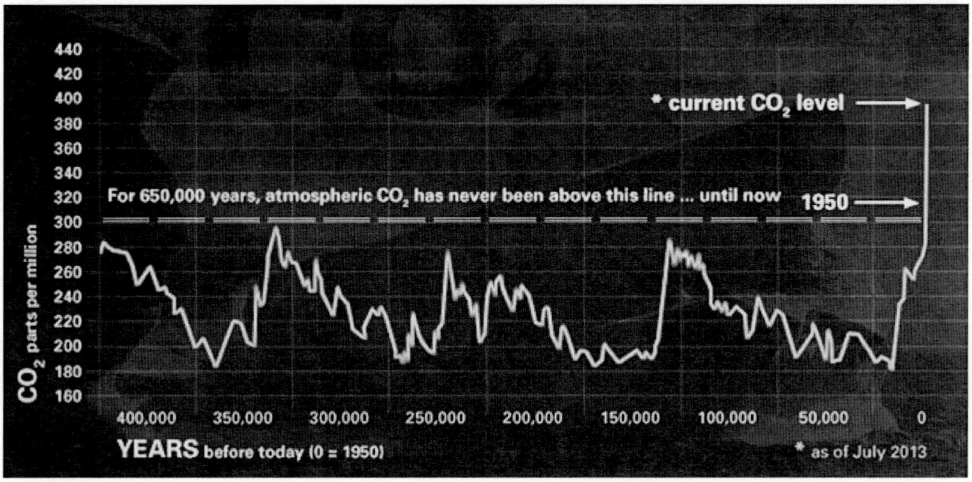

Critique is being done about the relentless obsession with growth. An entrepreneur ponders on this, *"Is it possible to consciously run a company with a broader definition of growth and move away from the demands of the 'grow forever' paradigm? The human toll of attempting a never-ending growth strategy are obvious and all around us every day... Growth isn't bad. But a focus on just one area of growth and requiring it to do so continuously is unrealistic and frankly inhumane."*[31]

While there are organisations that believe that their primary purpose is wealth generation, there are also business leaders who looks at work as an opportunity to explore ethics and service. A former senior executive with a

29 http://www.theguardian.com/sustainable-business/2015/jan/21/al-gore-lord-stern-oil-companies-fossil-fuels-climate-change, Accessed on June 4, 2015.

30 https://en.wikipedia.org/wiki/File:Evidence_CO2.jpg, Accessed on July 8, 2016.

31 http://www.huffingtonpost.com/jason-grahamnye/grow-grow-grow-and-then-w_b_7447492.html, Accessed on June 4, 2015.

telecommunications company, says, "*Financial and productivity goals used to have a huge priority for me. In the past I measured my success on reaching those goals. Today they do not have as much priority for me. I am productive and I do reach for goals – I do perform monetarily because that is expected of me – but I don't do it at the expense of doing things that are wrong.*"[32]

When society started noticing that for-profit organisations are not contributing to well-being of the planet and its inhabitants, and instead, they are causing harm, regulations may become more stringent. Consider the example of the plastic packaging industry. A 2016 report states, "*Plastic packaging generates significant negative externalities, conservatively valued by UNEP at USD 40 billion and expected to increase with strong volume growth in a business-as-usual scenario. Each year, at least 8 million tonnes of plastics leak into the ocean - which is equivalent to dumping the contents of one garbage truck into the ocean every minute. If no action is taken, this is expected to increase to two per minute by 2030 and four per minute by 2050. Estimates suggest that plastic packaging represents the major share of this leakage. The best research currently available estimates that there are over 150 million tonnes of plastics in the ocean today. In a business-as-usual scenario, the ocean is expected to contain 1 tonne of plastic for every 3 tonnes of fish by 2025, and by 2050, more plastics than fish (by weight).*"[33] Such destructive practices and societal awareness of this destruction has resulted in increased scrutiny of the plastic industry. This may also result in citizen boycott – for example, citizens deciding not to buy products with excessive and wasteful packaging.

CSR is also a business need. The total electricity consumption of an online social media company in 2018 amounted to 3,427,000 MWh, of which its data centres had a share of 3,245,000 MWh. Its water withdrawal and water consumption amounted to 2,367,000 and 1,279,000 cubic metres respectively. As per an internet-search company, its total electricity consumption in 2018 amounted to 10,104,295 Mwh. Its water consumption for the year amounted to 4,170 million gallons. If rural homes in India consume approximately 1000 KWh annually, it may be derived that the electricity consumed by the social media company[34] and the internet

32 Quotations extracted from the public knowledge base of the "Spiritual Based Leadership Research Programme" are © 2006 by the Global Dharma Center (GDC). GDC retains the copyright to all excerpts from this knowledge base.

33 World Economic Forum, Ellen MacArthur Foundation and McKinsey & Company, The New Plastics Economy — Rethinking the future of plastics (2016, http://www.ellenmacarthurfoundation.org/publications).

34 https://sustainability.fb.com/wp-content/uploads/2019/08/2018-Sustainability-Data-Disclosure.pdf, Accessed on February 5, 2020.

search company[35] is equivalent to providing electricity to almost 34 lakh (3.4 million) and one crore (ten million) homes in rural India, respectively. Or, to almost 68 lakh (6.8 million) and two crore (twenty million) homes, respectively, if homes in rural India consumes approximately 500 KWh annually. These two companies are amongst the thousands of technology-based global corporations that emerged in the past two decades. (Coal[36] production of a company in India has increased from 379 million tonnes in 2007-08[37] to 567 million tonnes in 2018[38].). Oliver Wyman, a consulting company, foresee an altered business environment in the next ten years, and the business environment will have the following characteristics[39]:

- Environmental taxes will become widespread across most industries and geographies; the cost base for companies with high carbon dioxide emissions, high energy/ water requirements, or high waste disposal volumes will increase substantially.
- Regulation at all levels will become more prevalent, particularly where industries have not been proactive.
- Prices for natural resources will continue to rise, with increasing resource scarcity as population increases and industrialization spreads.
- Investors will make sustainability a standard component of their investment criteria.
- Clean tech solutions will partially or completely disrupt a wide range of industries; those who have failed to adapt will experience diminishing relevancy and competitiveness.
- Business customers and end consumers will require sustainability as key purchasing criterion; non-sustainable companies also will have difficulty recruiting and retaining talent.
- Local and regional stakeholders will exert increasing pressure on non-sustainable industries and hold them accountable for their impacts on the local community.

---

35 https://services.google.com/fh/files/misc/google_2019-environmental-report.pdf, Accessed on February 5, 2020.

36 Coal, due to pollution, is amongst the least preferred sources for generation of electricity.

37 https://www.coalindia.in/DesktopModules/DocumentList/documents/Directors%20Report%202008-09.pdf, Accessed on February 6, 2020.

38 https://www.coalindia.in/en-us/performance/physical.aspx, Accessed on February 6, 2020.

39 http://www.oliverwyman.com/content/dam/oliver-wyman/global/en/files/insights/sustainability-center/2014/Jan/From%20Green%20to%20Sustainable_web_2.pdf, Accessed on August 11, 2015. Included with permission.

- Climate change will continue to be a "risk multiplier"; businesses that fail to plan ahead will see supply chain and operational disruption.

CSR as the focus on triple bottom-line

Conventionally, top-line referred to the revenue generated by the company, while bottom-line referred to the net-profit. They were referred such, considering that revenue was mentioned on the top of a financial statement[40]. An organisation focusing on triple bottom-line attempts to create financial surplus, enhancement of planetary well-being and improvement in the quality of life for people. Organisations that focus on these three parameters are referred to as triple-bottom-line organizations. Earlier, for most organizations, the focus was only on creating financial surpluses. However, this concept no longer holds true for many organizations. Peter Senge[41] says, "*Years ago, during the dot-com bubble*[42], *C. K. Prahalad*[43] *moved from the University of Michigan to the West Coast*[44] *because he wanted to be in the middle of the entrepreneurial environment. I asked him then whether he believed entrepreneurs there were motivated by the opportunity to make money. He responded, 'Oh, I think that's absolutely true - for all the mediocre entrepreneurs.'*"[45] As can be inferred from this perspective, making money is no longer the sole parameter that drives business entrepreneurship for many. Traditionally, one can discover the belief across cultures that gifting of wealth generated through noble and righteous means benefits both the giver and the receiver.

CSR coverage

CSR activity usually encompasses the below three areas:

a. To minimise the negative footprint of a for-profit organisation on its

---

40 The practice of net profits occupying the bottom space of a financial statement has almost become extinct with indicators such as 'Earnings per Share' gaining attention.

41 Peter Senge is the author of 'The Fifth Discipline' and Director, Center for Organizational Learning, Sloan School of Management, Massachusetts Institute of Technology (MIT).

42 Dot-com bubble happened in the late 1990s and early 2000s. The bubble period was known for its euphoric valuations for technology and internet stocks, even for companies that were not making profits.

43 CK Prahalad was a professor of business strategy at University of Michigan.

44 The West coast or Pacific coast of the United States has some of the entrepreneurial centres such as Silicon Valley. Within the USA, this region has a larger proportion of green cities.

45 Tricia Bisoux, Reshaping Business, BizEd, May/ June 2010. http://www.bizedmagazine.com/~/media/BizEd%20Magazine/Archives/2010/MayJun/fullissue.ashx, Accessed on March 5, 2016.

stakeholders. The underlying theme is "Do No Evil". A company may undertake a number of measures to minimise its detrimental impacts. Examples may include adoption of technologies that are less polluting, building schools and housing for the local community that would have been affected by the organization's business practices, etc.

b. To enhance the well-being of its stakeholders. An organization may do this through research, development and launch of a new product or non-product business that improves the quality of life for all stakeholders from a full-life-cycle perspective. Practising business legally and ethically also contributes to stakeholder well-being.

c. Discussion, Dialogue and Disclosure – An organization engages in discussion and conversation with its stakeholders to assess its reason of existence, and communicates accountability through performance reporting. Organisational contemplation helps an organisation to discover its purpose of existence.

Is CSR necessary?

And there comes a time when one must take a position that is neither safe, nor politic, nor popular, but he must do it because Conscience tells him it is right.

Martin Luther King[46]

There have been discussions on whether CSR endeavours are necessary. Some of the arguments put forward that challenges and questions the genuineness and merit of CSR practices are as below:

- *Avoiding accountability and societal regulation.* CSR may be adopted by companies to avoid regulation and accountability to an independent regulator. For example, media companies, as part of their CSR practices, may fund and launch a self-regulating organisation that claim to regulate misleading advertisements. Such a self-regulation may be a ploy to avoid more stringent accountability to an independently-funded third party organisation that has the legal and executive powers to impose stringent punishments.
- *Only enlightened self-interest.* For example, a Fast Moving Consumer Goods (FMCG) company may launch an educational program to inculcate hygiene habits amongst rural population. By doing so, the company hopes that, in the long-term, there will be increased spend on hygiene related products by rural population, which will result in increased revenue for the company.

46 Remaining awake through a great revolution, March 31, 1968.

- *An image building tool.* CSR may be a public relations gimmick adopted by companies to create a better image amongst consumers, while not committing to any long-term benefits for the society. For example, an automobile company may offer "free pollution check" to vehicles, while not campaigning for healthier emission standards or making significant investments in research related to environmentally-friendly technologies. The automobile company may also 'greenwash' their advertisements, while not encouraging sustainable mobility solutions and public transportation.
- *A channel for passive exploitation.* CSR activities of a company may also influence the stakeholders to overlook some of the unethical practices done by the organization. CSR may be used as a facade to retain and increase loyalty and commitment towards the organisation from its stakeholders such as employees and consumers.
- *Avoiding taxation or higher taxation.* There is a demand from the society on increasing the taxation on for-profit organisations. Engaging in CSR practices helps such companies to communicate that they are contributing to the welfare of the society, and imposing higher taxation may not be necessary. CSR practices also help organisations to claim exemptions from tax payments.
- *Focus on profits.* There are perspectives that social responsibility and environmental responsibility practices are the role of governmental organisations and not-for-profit organisations. There have also been discussions that the role of business is to generate profits. Milton Friedman, Nobel Prize winner in Economics in 1976, mentions, "*...there is one and only one social responsibility of business - to use its resources and engage in activities designed to increase its profits so long as it stays within the rules of the game, which is to say, engages in open and free competition without deception or fraud.*"[47]

Managing a business with honesty and integrity, while not harming the planet, is itself CSR.

- *The honest harmless business* – Managing a business with honesty and integrity, while not harming the planet, is itself CSR. Such a company need not engage in any additional philanthropic or humanitarian activities.
- *Influencing law enforcement agencies.* Engaging in CSR practices may help a firm during criminal prosecution. It has been found that

47 Milton Friedman, The Social Responsibility of Business is to Increase its Profits, The New York Times Magazine, September 13, 1970.

companies with the most comprehensive CSR initiatives received lesser punishments from law enforcement authorities. "*We estimate that either eliminating a substantial labour-rights concern, such as child labour, or increasing corporate giving by about 20% results in fines that generally are 40% lower than the typical punishment for bribing foreign officials,*" said Mr Harrison Hong, Professor – Economics and Finance, Princeton University.[48] A freelance journalist commented, "*The last thing I want is for companies to create CSR programs just to improve their likelihood of escaping prosecution for other crimes. And not just because this is a bad for society, but, frankly, it isn't good CSR either.*"[49]

- *Distribution of the loot, and equitable distribution of the after-effects of looting*!

Changing expectations about CSR

Expectations about businesses and their CSR practices have been changing. "*Earlier, every company existed only to enhance shareholder value, which means maximum profits for shareholders. That situation has evolved today and now firms are talking about stakeholder value. There is clear empirical evidence that those companies that have contributed and concentrated on stakeholder value have benefited in the long run,*" says the CEO of an accounting firm[50]. Societal stakeholders are expecting CSR initiatives undertaken by the company to be authentic and sincere.

Many companies engage in CSR initiatives as a marketing opportunity. This resulted in such initiatives being considered as a hyperbole or 'greenwashing'. An example for green-washing include financial-services companies asking customers to opt for e-updates, instead of paper based updates (for example, mobile or e-mail based e-statements for banking transactions, instead of recording the transactions on a passbook) with the message that opting for e-statements can save paper and trees. To save on paper is a planet-friendly practice. However, some financial-service companies opted for such practices as a cost-control and risk-mitigation measure, rather than due to planetary commitment. The customers were thus doubtful about the genuineness of such initiatives, as only some companies extended such responsibility practices in a comprehensive manner. Non-funding of projects generating attractive financial returns,

48 http://www.economist.com/news/business/21656218-do-gooding-policies-help-firms-when-they-get-prosecuted-halo-effect, Accessed on August 11, 2015.

49 http://www.triplepundit.com/2015/07/halo-effect-csr-allows-companies-get-away-corruption/, Accessed on August 11, 2015.

50 http://www.livemint.com/Companies/dBCf5yVBdOLMvIVEFk8WlO/CSR-rules-need-flexibility-incentives-and-foresight-Richar.html, Accessed on May 9, 2016.

however, at a societal and environmental cost, could have been a genuine way for an investment management company to be socially responsible. Another example for a financial services company to be socially responsible may include the willingness of the company to wait for an extended time for generating financial returns, on projects that demonstrate better societal and environmental standards.

An article in *The Economist* comments, *"Many corporate 'sustainability plans'... ...focus on saving energy, cutting waste and streamlining logistics. Nothing wrong with that: these things reduce operating costs while benefiting the environment. They help explain why sustainability efforts tend to increase profits, not reduce them... ...However, there are drawbacks to such plans. For one thing, they are misnamed: these are efficiency policies, not sustainability ones. Companies ought to want to save energy or cut waste anyway, regardless of the impact on the environment..."*[51].

In 2016 and 2017, the CEO of an information-technology company communicated to its employees about the company's no-alcohol policy at office premises[52][53]. While this decision can be due to CEO's consideration for the well-being of employees[54], it may also be due to the risk associated with such practices. A professor at a management school opined that *"Employers are rightly concerned about legal liability for actions that their employees take either at work or after hours when they have been drinking alcohol provided by the employer. If I'm injured by a drunk employee, I'm likely to sue their employer because the employer has more money."*[55]

Advantages and disadvantages for companies in engaging with CSR practices

Advantages:

- A direct opportunity for the company to contribute to the well-being of the society.

51 http://www.economist.com/news/business/21614152-few-pioneering-businesses-are-developing-sustainability-policies-worthy-name-new, Accessed on July 6, 2015.

52 https://www.cnbc.com/2017/11/01/salesforce-ceo-marc-benioff-reminds-employees-of-no-drinking-policy-alcohol-is-a-drug.html, Accessed on September 29, 2018.

53 https://twitter.com/benioff/status/739689690811375616?lang=en, Accessed on September 29, 2018.

54 https://www.drugabuse.gov/related-topics/trends-statistics, Accessed on September 29, 2018.

55 https://www.cnbc.com/2017/11/01/salesforce-ceo-marc-benioff-reminds-employees-of-no-drinking-policy-alcohol-is-a-drug.html, Accessed on September 29, 2018.

- Societal attention will be drawn towards the company.
- Societal goodwill towards the company.
- Consumers may prefer to purchase products from those companies that engage in social responsibility practices. This can contribute to increased revenue for the company.
- Inspired employees.
- Employees will be motivated to participate in efficiency practices within the company.
- Regulatory authorities/ governmental agencies will have a positive view about the company.
- Increased opportunities for a company to create meaningful engagement with the society.
- CSR practices can deepen and broaden the perspectives of the company management and employees about society. This may result in the creation and development of new business involving products and non-products and markets.
- CSR practices can help the company to better understand its 'Strengths, Weaknesses, Opportunities and Threats'.

Disadvantages:

- Any communication about CSR practices to the public may generate public attention towards the company. Increased attention may result in increased scrutiny.
- CSR practices may increase spending.
- Discussion about CSR practices may result in exchange of ideas that may be uncomfortable to some stakeholders.
- A company may corrupt the genuineness of the CSR project and use the project for narrow gains. Such an attitude may spread through the organization, affect.
- There may be a tendency to derive brand mileage from a CSR practice, rather than focusing on strengthening the CSR practice.
- Dilution in the quality and focus on the genuineness of CSR practices may not be appreciated by the society.

To read, even a few pages, comprehending the non-comprehended, is itself a great achievement....

You may take a break...

HISTORICAL EXAMPLES OF CSR AND PHILANTHROPIC PRACTICES

Shri Ganesh Shrikrishna Khaparde was a lawyer of Amaravati, in central India. Well-versed in Marathi and Sanskrit, he was an eloquent speaker, a member of the Central Legislative Assembly, and was also an aide of Bal Gangadhar Tilak. Khaparde and his wife were devoted to Sai Baba of Shirdi, who was a fakir, and a *Sadhguru* for his devotees. Experiences of miracles, and parables that he communicated, also attracted people to Shirdi Sai Baba. Khaparde, through the daily entries of his diary, reminisces about the remarks made by Sai Baba (whom Khaparde refers to as *Sayin Maharaj*) during one of his visits to Shirdi (December 1911). *"The prayer this morning was very very pleasant and after it, I felt quite elevated. Then i started explaining the first few verses of Panchadashi to Dattatraya Chitnis. He is a very nice man. Then we visited Sayin Maharaj, both as he went out, and after he returned. He gave me the Chillam very often and grapes that Radhakrishnabai had sent. He gave the grapes twice to my son Balwant. In the afternoon i heard that he was cleaning the musjid. So i did not attempt to go that side. All the people brought a deputation to Sayin Maharaj to get rid of the plague. He advised them to clean the roads, sweep the tombs and burning and burial ghats, and to feed the poor...."*[56]

Mahatma Gandhi mentioned, *"We want freedom for our country, but not at the expense or exploitation of others... I want the freedom of my country so that other countries may learn something from my free country, so that resources of my country might be utilised for the benefit of mankind"*[57]. This humanity can be witnessed in many industrialists.

A notable historical example of CSR leadership in India belongs to the social commitment of Tata Steel. The first private iron and steel company (TISCO, or, Tata Iron and Steel Company) in India was started by Dorabji Tata in Jamshedpur, in 1907. This industrial unit was envisioned by Jamsetji Tata, father of Dorabji Tata. Tata Steel contributed much to the economic and civic life of Jamshedpur. The township construction started in 1908. The Tata group contributed to the township through educational institutions, football academy, archery academy, sports complexes, parks, hospitals, etc. The city of Jamshedpur (from the name 'Jamset'ji) is referred to as "Tata" by many people, and the Jamshedpur railway station had been named as Tatanagar.

---

56 *Shirdi diary of the the Hon'ble Mr. G. S. Khaparde*, Shri Sai Baba Sansthan Shirdi, 1997.

57 Mahadev Desai, Gandhiji in Indian Villages, S Ganesan, 1927.

> *"We want freedom for our country, but not at the expense or exploitation of others... I want the freedom of my country so that other countries may learn something from my free country, so that resources of my country might be utilised for the benefit of mankind."*

Jamsetji Tata, the founder of the Tata Group of Companies, also initiated the creation of Indian Institute of Science, Bangalore (IISc). Jamsetji Tata met Swami Vivekananda on the trip to Chicago in 1893, and years later, invited Swami Vivekananda to lead this institution. Through the years, the Tata Group has contributed to the creation of a number of social-benefit-organisations such as Tata Institute of Social Sciences (TISS), Tata Institute of Fundamental Research (TIFR), National Centre for Performing Arts (NCPA) and more.

The commitment to societal well-being, as lived by Jamsetji, was replicated by many in the Tata group, including JRD Tata. JRD Tata was the Chairman of the Tata Group for five decades beginning 1938. He was once approached by colleagues about tax payment. *"On one occasion a senior executive of a Tata company tried to save on taxes. Before putting up that case, the chairman of the company took him to JRD. Vyas* (a tax consultant) *explained to JRD: 'But sir, it is not illegal.' JRD asked, softly: 'Not illegal, yes. But is it right?'*[58,59] (In 1992, JRD Tata was conferred with Bharat Ratna, the highest award in India given by the government. On this occasion, he is reported to have said, *"I don't want India to be an economic superpower. I want India to be a happy country."*[60,61])

---

58 RM Lala, The Creation of Wealth: The Tatas from the 19th to the 21st Century, Portfolio Penguin, 2004.

59 Nicholas Lord, Senior Lecturer, University of Manchester, says, *"The ethics of reducing tax liabilities becomes problematic when it is aggressively avoided through creative schemes that are not intended or authorised by the state – but which do abide by the letter of the law. It is here we see what is referred to as 'tax avoidance'. This is formally legal but highly questionable, seriously harmful and often unethical."* (http://www.manchester.ac.uk/discover/news/tax-avoidance-legal-ethics/, Accessed on November 14, 2017.) Vyas remarked that not in his decades of professional work had anyone asked him a question similar to the one posed by JRD. He also wrote in an article, "JRD would have been the most ardent supporter of the view expressed by Lord Denning: 'The avoidance of tax may be lawful, but it is not yet a virtue',"

60 http://www.tata.com/htm/remembering-jrd/index.html#7thPage, Accessed on June 10, 2017.

61 http://www.tata.com/aboutus/articlesinside/F9V5lfjQy5I=/TLYVr3YPkMU=, Accessed on June 10, 2017.

India's influence and contribution to philanthropy and social responsibility of businesses

Many of us, utterly overcome by Tamas, the dark and heavy demon of inertia, are saying nowadays that it is impossible, that India is decayed, bloodless and lifeless, too weak ever to recover; that our race is doomed to extinction. It is a foolish and idle saying. No man or nation need be weak unless he chooses, no man or nation need perish unless he deliberately chooses extinction.

Sri Aurobindo, *Bhawani Mandir*, 1905

India has interested many. The Austrians, Dutch, English, French, Portuguese, Swedes - each had their "East India Company". Even prior, trade flourished between regions in India and other regions. An entrance to Alexandria, Egypt, had its name as "Pepper Gate". Pepper, a spice from the veins indigenous to the forests of Malabar and Travancore, has its name derived from the Sanskrit *Pipalika.* Referring to cucumber, an ingredient in many salads and sandwiches, it is said, "*Originating in the foothills of the Himalayas, where it once grew wild, the cucumber has been cultivated in India for more than 3000 years. It was introduced into Egypt and carefully cultivated by the Hebrews in Galilee*"[62].

Cosmas, a Greek merchant of the sixth century (550 AD), wrote a treatise titled '*Christian Topography*' in Slav language (ancient Greek). He was also referred to as "*Indicopleustes*" (*Indicoplov*) – an honorary title given to those who've travelled to the distant India. As a merchant, Cosmas traveled to many countries on trade, and later became a hermit. Eurasians contributed to the fascination about India – represented as a place where ants digged gold[63]. It was told that people of a tribe in India was of single leg, with which, they hopped and jumped. During rains, they raised their leg and held it above their head, as an umbrella. There were also people with heads of dogs, and legs of horses. And at the Ganges basin, there was an unfortunate tribe without mouth. They lived through sniffing. During distant travels, they kept an apple, and smelling it, they alleviated their hunger[64].

---

62 *Larousse Gastronomique*, 1988.

63 *"They get the gold from ants. These creatures are larger than foxes, but are in other respects like the ants of our own country. They dig holes in the earth like other ants. The heap which they throw up consists of gold the purest and brightest in all the world. The mounds are piled up close to each other in regular order like hillocks of gold dust, whereby all the plain is made effulgent. It is difficult, therefore, to look towards the sun, and many who have attempted to do this have thereby destroyed their eyesight."*

64 A Tomilin, *How people discovered the shape of the Earth*, Raduga Publishers, 1986.

Indus Valley excavations indicated the existence of what could possibly be one of the earliest dockyards of the world that is available to the humanity as an archeological remnant. The navigators steered ships through the Red Sea, trading between India and regions near Egypt. Further, with the help of monsoon winds, ships sailed *through* the Arabian Sea, rather than moving along the coast, also implying that the navigators had the knowledge of India extending north-south into the ocean.

For many Europeans, any region west of the African continent was India. Being conduits of trade between the Orient and Europe, there was the flourishing of cities, regions and land travel paths. Referring to the city of "Baldach" or "Bagadet"[65] of the tenth century, it was mentioned, "*Almost all the pearls brought to Europe from India have undergone the process of boring, at this place... It is the noblest and most extensive city to be found in this part of the world*". Some of the visitors to India had qualities that went beyond trading-interests. Enrichment resulted, in ways expected and unexpected - be it a *'catamaran'* and a *'dhow'*, or, a *'curry'* and *'chutney'* (**Refer Figure 1.2**).

Amongst all exchanges, the esoteric was something special. A *'guru'* and *'pundit'* earned more respect than a *'maharaja'*, though emperors such as King Ashoka, more than 2000 years ago, publicised codes that considered the well-being of all, including the non-human. A 'half-naked *fakir'* elevated struggles - including the political - to the path of self-liberation, while the lives of gymnosphists[66] became a reference for study for many scholars (and their lineage) in Eurasia.

Known for its religious fervour, India reflected the divine in the mundane, 'at least, as a ritual'. William Logan (*Malabar*, 1887) provides examples for this in the 'deed' documents (in land, property, benefit distribution rights etc.) - one deed mentions *'Vilwaadrinathan'*[67] and *'Vadakkumnathan'*[68] as witnesses, while there were deeds with a span "*till stones and Cavery and grass and the earth exist*" or "*for the time that sun and moon shall last*". A few deeds bordered on the daring – a deed was "*written by the god's accountant*"! In the contemporary times, one of the political parties in a state of India

65 Referring to the city, it was remarked that Mahometan law is regularly studied there, "*as are also magic, physics, astronomy, geomancy and physiognomy*".

66 A term used to refer to the non-clothed ascetics that the Eurasian travellers and traders, royals and administrators, etc., met and heard about, during their travel to the "East".

67 A reference to 'Vilwadrinatha' of Vilwadrinatha Temple, in Thiruvilwamala, Kerala. 'Vilwadrinatha' may also mean the 'Lord of the Vilwadri'. The hills in the region are referred to as the Vilwadri hills.

68 A reference to 'Vadakkumnatha' of Vadakkumnatha Temple, Thrissur, Kerala. 'Vadakkumnathan' may also mean the 'Lord of the North'.

promised to distribute TVs, free of cost, to voters, if the party is elected to power. They were elected, and some of the voters received more than a single TV. *"God has given, we have taken"* was their motto.

Figure 1.2[69]

Pictured above is a 1953 postage stamp. Many regions of the Middle-East (including Oman and Yemen) were known for making 'dhow's. These were usually built with wood (teak, mango) from Malabar. Coir was also sourced from the coastal south of India.

(Also, the architectural ethos in some of the Arab regions is that a building may not be higher than that of the nearby mosque. The mosque, meanwhile, may not be higher than the nearest hill or mountain. Similar expressions may be found amongst the Hindus - that the height of a construction may not surpass the height of the nearby temple.).

69 Source: https://commons.wikimedia.org/wiki/File:Aden_1953–35c.jpg, Accessed on September 14, 2019. Image available in the public domain.

Initiatives of charity and philanthropy in India are significantly associated with religion, and religious practices. *Dharamshala* is an example. Historically, these infrastructures, which provided food and accommodation free of cost or at a subsidised rate, for pilgrims, were available at many pilgrimage locations. Construction and sustenance of these *Dharamshalas* is a tradition in India, and practitioners of religions such as Hinduism, Jainism and Buddhism (**Refer Figure 1.3**) are known for providing sustenance to such *Dharamshalas.*

Figure 1.3[70]

"A Daramsalla in Tibet"

India cannot claim breadth and depth in baking and bakery-practices, while, cultural adaptations to these institutions and enterprises resulted in "Iyyengar bakeries", one of them being in Bangalore, with its origins in 1898. These bakeries provided food products that are eggless. In 2010, the "Guinness World Record" for the largest buffet was a buffet that was fully vegetarian. The record certificate stated that this buffet consisted of 5612 dishes in an event organised by the Art of Living Foundation (India) at Sri Sri Dham, Ahmedabad, on 2 November 2010.

70 "Daramsalla mountain shelter in Tibet" by w:Arnold Henry Savage Landor - "Tibet and Nepal" as digitised by the Internet Archive's text collection.. Licensed under Public Domain via Wikimedia Commons - https://commons.wikimedia.org/wiki/File:Daramsalla_mountain_shelter_in_Tibet.jpg#/media/File:Daramsalla_mountain_shelter_in_Tibet.jpg, Accessed on June 25, 2015.

Despite being a country that inherited the richness of a vegetarian diet – ancient travelogues refers to monastic centres in India where even milk and butter is not used, and even the non-monastic people avoid onion and garlic - the oldest vegetarian restaurant of the world is not located in India. This was, possibly, because, to charge money for food and stay was a cultural taboo, and almost, a sin, in India. Even the first luxury hotel in India started only in 1903, many decades after the commencement of such structures in other parts of the world, and despite the cities of India being major trading stations and transit-points for international trade.

Travellers were mostly merchants and pilgrims. For an Indian pilgrim, there was 'Kashi', and then, there was both 'Dakshin Kashi' and 'Uttar Kashi'. Simple in taste, they carried food or food ingredients. Merchant groups also contributed to the building of facilities that offered food and stay, for their own benefit and pilgrims.

Hieun Tsiang, the Chinese traveler of AD 600s, mentions about the existence of "house of mercy" (or, "Punyashala"), in multiple kingdoms of India. These houses of mercy provided shelter to the poor and sick, as also food, clothing, medicine, and other necessities. Many spiritual-religious-charitable organisations in contemporary India are engaged in providing services that benefits humanity. It is common for a devout Sikh to serve in a 'Gurudwara', especially at the langar. These langars offers a simple and nourishing meal to the hungry[71]*.*

Swami Vivekananda has influenced many industrialists towards endeavours of greater common good. Jamsetji Tata, who made pioneering contribution towards the creation of Indian Institute of Science (IISc), Bangalore, wrote in a letter to Vivekananda[72], *"I trust you remember me as a fellow-traveller on your voyage from Japan to Chicago. I very much recall at this moment your views on the growth of the ascetic spirit in India, and the duty, not of destroying, but of diverting it into useful channels. I recall these ideas in connection with my scheme of the Research Institute of Science for India, of which you have doubtless heard or read. It seems to me that no better use can be made of the ascetic spirit than the establishment of monasteries or residential halls for men dominated by this spirit, where they should live with ordinary decency, and devote their lives to the cultivation of sciences - natural and humanistic. I am of opinion that if such a crusade in favour of an asceticism of this kind were undertaken by a competent leader, it would greatly help asceticism, science, and the good name of our common country: and I know not who would make a more fitting general of such a campaign than Vivekananda. Do you think you would care to apply yourself to this mission of galvanising into life our ancient traditions in this respect?"* This letter was written by Jamsetji Tata in 1898. The institute that Jamsetji Tata

71 Ambika Gupta, visiting the *langar* at Golden Temple, Amritsar, writes, *"...I doubt i'll ever again see such a huge collection of plates – they were stacked to twice my height and passed between hands in a hypnotic assembly-line..."*

72 http://icast.org.in/news/2004/jul04/jul24aa.html, Accessed on September 1, 2016.

envisioned, was established in 1909, five years after the passing away of this philanthropist.

Anaatha Pindika's donation of Jetavana

One of the earliest recorded instances of philanthropy and generosity practised by a businessperson may be that of AnaathaPindika, a disciple of Gautama Buddha. AnaathaPindika engaged in the business of banking. His charitable initiatives made people to call him 'Anaathapindika', which means, the provider (of food and other material necessities) to the forlorn or the homeless. His former name was Sudatta. Being a contemporary of Gautama, The Buddha, AnaathaPindika's existence can be between sixth and fourth century BCE.

Anaathapindika was known for his donation of Jetavana (**Refer Figure 1.4**), a Buddhist monastery located at Shravasti, Uttar Pradesh. He invited Gautama Buddha to Shravasti, and was searching for a place where Buddha can stay and teach. A park, 'Jeta Vana', existed there, and this was recognised to be a convenient location for a monastery, *vihara*. Anaathapindika went to 'Jeta', the owner of the park, for purchasing the park. However, Jeta demanded a sum that was discouraging.

Yet, Anaathapindika, knowing the importance of the cause, covered the ground of the park with gold. Impressed with the earnestness of Anaathapindika, Jeta not only agreed to the sale of the park, but also donated the wealth received from Anaathapindika, towards park improvement and for the necessary constructions in the park.

With changing times and fortunes, Anaathapindika did not have monetary wealth that can be contributed. Yet, he continued the practice of giving. He used to collect handfuls of high quality soil from the various places he visited. Whenever he visited the monastery at Jetavana, the collected soil was deposited on the monastery grounds, so that the monastery grounds are fertile, and many will benefit.

Figure 1.4[73]

A sculpture found in Bharhut, Madhya Pradesh, indicating Anaathapindika's role in the purchase of Jetavana.

Fa-Hien[74]*, who started his travel to India from China in 399 AD, mentions,* "Leaving the city (*of Sravasti*) by the south gate and proceeding 1200 paces on the road, on the west side of it is the place where the lord Sudatta built a *vihara*. This chapel opens towards the east. The principal door is flanked by two side chambers,

73 https://commons.wikimedia.org/wiki/File:Jetvan_bharhut.JPG, Accessed on May 20, 2016.

74 Also known as *Sakyaputra* Fa-hien or *Shii* Fa-hien, he was a native of Wu-Yang, of the district of Ping-yang, in the Chinese province of Shan-si. It was common for mendicant priests of that age, to add the title *Sakyaputra* or *Shii* to their names, during their time of ordination, adopting the Buddhist faith. Time, distance and speed may have corrupted many of the Buddhist scriptures, as available in China then. Fa-hien mentions that he "*regretted the imperfect condition of the Vinaya Pitaka*", a Buddhist text. Along with other priests, he traveled westwards towards India, from Chang'an, and returned after fourteen years, following which, he, with Buddhabhadra, translated many Indian scriptural texts to the Chinese language.

in front of which stand two stone pillars. On the top of the left-hand one is the figure of a wheel, and on the right-hand one the image of an ox. The clear water of the tanks, the luxuriant groves, and numberless flowers of variegated hues combine to produce the picture of what is called a *Jetavana vihara.*"[75]

The life and contribution of Jamnalal Bajaj and Prafulla Chandra Ray

Jamnalal Bajaj founded the Bajaj group of companies in 1926. Born in 1889, Jamnalal Bajaj was known for his association with Mahatma Gandhi and for his active participation in India's freedom struggle and social reforms. Jamnalal Bajaj opened their family temple to Harijans, who were earlier not allowed inside temples. He also promoted the usage of *khadi*, women's education, and caring and service for cows. Jamnalal Bajaj says, "*Business should be pursued with a view to benefit the poor, not just to become a millionaire or a billionaire*". His life indicates his message of "*Truth and Integrity form the bedrock of prosperity in business*"[76]. The Bajaj group has named their foundation as 'Jamnalal Bajaj foundation'. While the British government bestowed Jamnalal Bajaj with the titles of 'Honorary Magistrate' and 'Rai Bahadur', he renounced them due to his involvement in India's freedom movement and his endeavours to understand the soul of India[77].

Considered as the father of Indian pharmaceutical industry, Prafulla Chandra Ray (**Refer Figure 1.5**) was a teacher and philanthropist. Some of the contributions and achievements of P C Ray were:

- In 1901, he founded the Bengal Chemicals and Pharmaceutical Works Ltd., India's first pharmaceutical company.
- Founded the Bengal Salt Corporation and a cotton mill at Khulna, in Bangladesh.
- 'Emeritus Professor' at Calcutta University.

---

75 SI-YU-KI. Buddhist Records of the Western World. (Translated from the Chinese of Hiuen Tsiang), Samuel Beal, Trubner & Co., 1884.

76 From the booklet published by Jamnalal Bajaj Foundation, as part of the 125th birth anniversary of Jamnalal Bajaj.

77 During the Independence movement in India, many renounced such titles. Examples also include that of Subhash Chandra Bose renouncing the 'Rai Bahadur' title, Mahatma Gandhi and Sarojini Naidu renouncing the 'Kaiser-e-Hind' title, Rabindranath Tagore renouncing the knighthood etc. Following the Jallianwala Bagh tragedy, Tagore wrote to Lord Chelmsford, the Viceroy of India, "*...The time has come, when badges of honour make our shame glaring in the incongruous context of humiliation, and I for my part wish to stand, shorn of all special distinctions, by the side of those of my countrymen, who, for their so-called insignificance, are liable to suffer a degradation not fit for human beings...*"

- Prolific writer in English and Bengali. One of the works includes *'A History of Hindu Chemistry from the Earliest Times to the Middle of Sixteenth Century AD'*. Published a number of scientific papers.
- Known for philanthropic contributions to various service endeavours, which included social service projects and projects related to the promotion of science, especially chemistry. At the age of 60, he donated, in advance, all his salary from the university towards the development of chemistry department and for creating two research fellowships[78]. While introducing Ray to Gandhi, Gopal Krishna Gokhale says, "*This is Professor Ray, who, having a monthly salary of Rs 800, just keeps Rs 40 for himself and devotes the balance to public purposes. He is not, and does not want to get, married.*"[79]
- Worked towards the popularisation of *khadi*, supported the entry of Harijans to temples, and was against distribution of any state favor based on communal grounds[80].

Figure 1.5[81]

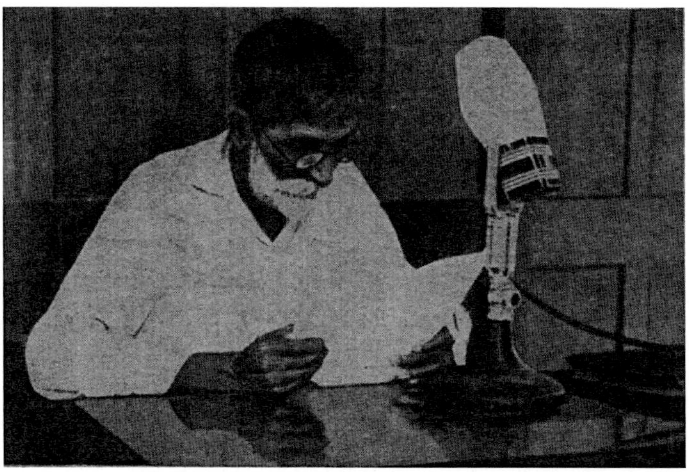

78 http://www.tifr.res.in/~outreach/outreach/scientists.pdf, Accessed on May 11, 2016.

79 As quoted in the autobiography of Mahatma Gandhi.

80 http://www.insa.nic.in/writereaddata/UpLoadedFiles/IJHS/Vol46_3_6_SKMajumdar.pdf, Accessed on May 11, 2016.

84 https://commons.wikimedia.org/wiki/File:%E0%A6%86%E0%A6%A4%E0%A7%8D%E0%A6%AE%E0%A6%9A%E0%A6%B0%E0%A6%BF%E0%A6%A4_%28%E0%A6%AA%E0%A7%8D%E0%A6%B0%E0%A6%AB%E0%A7%81% E0%A6%B2%E0%A7%8D%E0%A6%B2%E0%A6%9A%E0%A6%A8%E0%A7%8D%E0%A6%A6%E0%A7%8D%E0%A6%B0_%E0%A6%B0%E0%A6%BE%E0%A6%AF%E0%A6%BC%29_010.tif,Accessed on May 11, 2016.

A research-paper about him states, "*He became the guru of the first research school of chemistry in the country, the first historian of chemistry in ancient and medieval India, a champion of the Indian Chemical Industry and the founder of the Indian Chemical Society.*"[82] PC Ray retired at 75. Mahatma Gandhi says, "*Great he undoubted is: But goodness from Indian standpoint is greater than greatness and Acharya Ray is even more good then he is great. And it is his goodness - his childlike simplicity, his suavity of manners, his ready accessibility, his unblemished purity, unostentatious charity, his voluntary poverty with plain living and high thinking, his enthusiasm and optimism, his innate spirit of self-denial, his incurable habit of always taking a back seat, his sturdy independence, his inflexible incorruptibility... in a word, his nobility of nature made him idol of the people. Service and sacrifice were his watch-word...*"[83]

Vinoba Bhave and the Bhoodaan movement

Vinoba Bhave is popularly associated with the *Bhoodaan* (The Gift of Earth) movement, a voluntary land distribution movement in India that started in the early 1950s. The contemporary India has referred to him as a "*leading social entrepreneur*"[84]. Also referred to as *Acharya* Vinoba Bhave, he was jailed many times for participation in India's freedom movement.

In the Bhoodaan movement, wealthy land-owners were persuaded to give a portion of their land to landless. Those who receive this land can use it for growing food, while also settling down there. However, the land cannot be resold or cannot be used for non-agricultural purposes. Vinoba Bhave walked across India requesting people to consider him as one of their sons and to donate him one-sixth of their land, which was re-distributed to the landless poor. Speaking about Vinoba Bhave, Nipun Mehta, Founder - ServiceSpace, says, "*He decides to go on a walking pilgrimage. He goes from village to village. He tells the rich landowners to donate one-sixth of their land to the poor land-owners. No coercion, no compulsion; just purely for the spirit of generosity. He appeal to their inner transformation. He ended up walking 70,000 kilometres. And, through those 70,000 kilometres, more than 5 million acres of land was donated. That's bigger than the size of Kuwait, twice the size of Lebanon,*

82 Animesh Chakravorty, The Chemical Researches of Acharya Prafulla Chandra Ray, Indian Journal of History of Science, 2014. Also available at http://www.insa.nic.in/writereaddata/UpLoadedFiles/IJHS/Vol49_4_3_AChakravorty.pdf

83 http://www.insa.nic.in/writereaddata/UpLoadedFiles/IJHS/Vol46_3_6_SKMajumdar.pdf, Accessed on May 11, 2016.

84 http://india.ashoka.org/who-social-entrepreneur, Accessed on August 9, 2016.

almost as big as Israel... It ended being the largest peaceful transfer of land in human history."[85]

Speaking about his travels by foot, Vinoba Bhave says, *"Why not a train, people will surely ask, or even an aeroplane?... ...But there is a place for everything. Spectacles may be of very great service, but they cannot take the place of eyes. In the same way, aeroplanes and other speedy means of travel certainly have their uses, but it is still important to have legs. Walking has advantages which aeroplanes cannot provide."*[86][87] He was also the first recipient of the Ramon Magsaysay Award for Community Leadership (in 1958).

Vinoba Bhave and the Bhoodaan Movement continue to be a source of inspiration for many, including 'Karma Kitchen', where guests can choose how much to pay for their meal (**Refer Figure 1.6**).

Figure 1.6

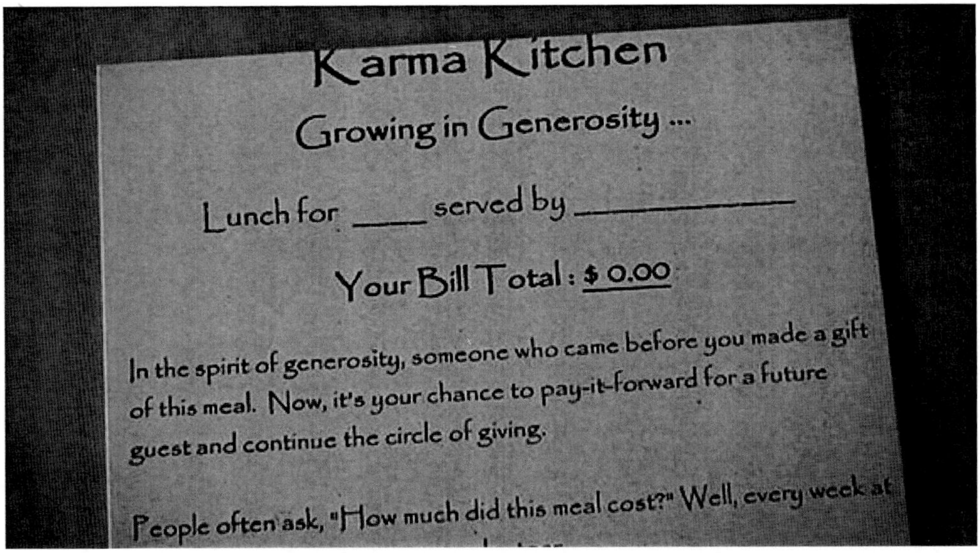

The bill given to the guest at 'Karma Kitchen' (karmakitchen.org), Berkeley.[88]

---

85 http://tedxtalks.ted.com/video/TEDxBerkeley-Nipun-Mehta-Design, Accessed on August 13, 2016.

86 http://www.mkgandhi.org/movedbylove/chap11.htm, Accessed on August 9, 2016.

87 Similar to Vinoba Bhave, Nipun Mehta has also been on a walking pilgrimage. Many luminaries have preferred to walk, though transportation options (motorised and non-motorised) were available. This practice also guides those observing the ideals of Dharmic religions.

88 Included with permission.

The CSR Chronology

Early 1400s – Port of Malacca, in South East Asia, built by Prince Parameshwara, The name may have its origins to the *Malaka* tree (Sanskrit), or, to the Arabic *malakat* (market).

1450-1550 – The flourishing of the Inca civilisation, and their destruction. The Inca people cultivated a wide variety of potatoes, which, through the Spanish and Portuguese traders, became common, almost anywhere in the world. Peruvian legends are that, faced with the near-certain defeat from the invaders, the Incas destroyed the paths and trails leading to their shrines and sacred locations, which, (as per legends) housed vast amount of wealth.

1534-35 – The Pope of Rome accords Michelangelo Buanarroti with a life-time pension of a hundred ducats every month, of which, fifty ducats will be from the Papal treasury, while fifty ducats will be from the ferry over the Po river at Piacenza.

16th century - Cultivation of cashew begins in India. Cashew has its origins in South America.

Early 1600s – Founding of the 'Dutch East India Company'. This company becomes the first company to issue its shares to the public ("IPO") and also plays a major role in the first "stock market crash".

1701-1718 – 'His Majesty's College of Connecticut' (Yale Collegiate School, Saybrook) benefits from a large collection of books sent to them by a philanthropist, Elihu Yale. Elihu Yale also sends other valuables, which on an auction at Boston, provides the money for constructing a building that was to become Yale College (New Haven, Connecticut). Elihu Yale, an American who joined the 'British East India Company' as a clerk, rose through the ranks, and retired as a governor at Fort St George, Madras. On retirement, he remained in the city for another two decades, as a spice merchant, before returning to England in 1699.

1714 - *De Pelikaan* ("The house of Pelican") was built at Bruges (Belgium). This building also served the purpose of being an alms-house that housed and supported elderly widows. Beginning 14th century, many such buildings emerged in the Bruges region, supporting elderly, physically challenged, etc. Wealthy families and guilds contributed to the construction and sustenance of these alms-houses.

1762 – Completion of *Fontana di Trevi*, a fountain in Rome. Almost three decades it took, to complete this work. This new fountain replaced an earlier fountain that existed there. The water in the fountain was from an aqueduct that supplied drinking water to the people of Rome. Barrels and barrels of water from the Trevi fountain was taken to Vatican every week. *'You may toss a coin at this fountain'*, the visitors to Rome are told, *'and you'll return to Rome'*, so say the legends.

1773 – "Boston Tea Party" becomes the precursor for similar revolts that involved tea.

1600s-1800s - The notorious 'triangular trade'. Molasses and sugar collected from the Carribean islands ("West Indies"), shipped to "New England" (North-eastern region of the present USA), where it was distilled into 'Rum', which was shipped to Western Africa, in exchange for slaves, to work in plantations in the Carribean, In 1865, the thirteenth amendment to the constitution of America abolished slavery.

Figure 1.7[89]

A map made in 1513, indicating regions of South Asia and South-East Asia

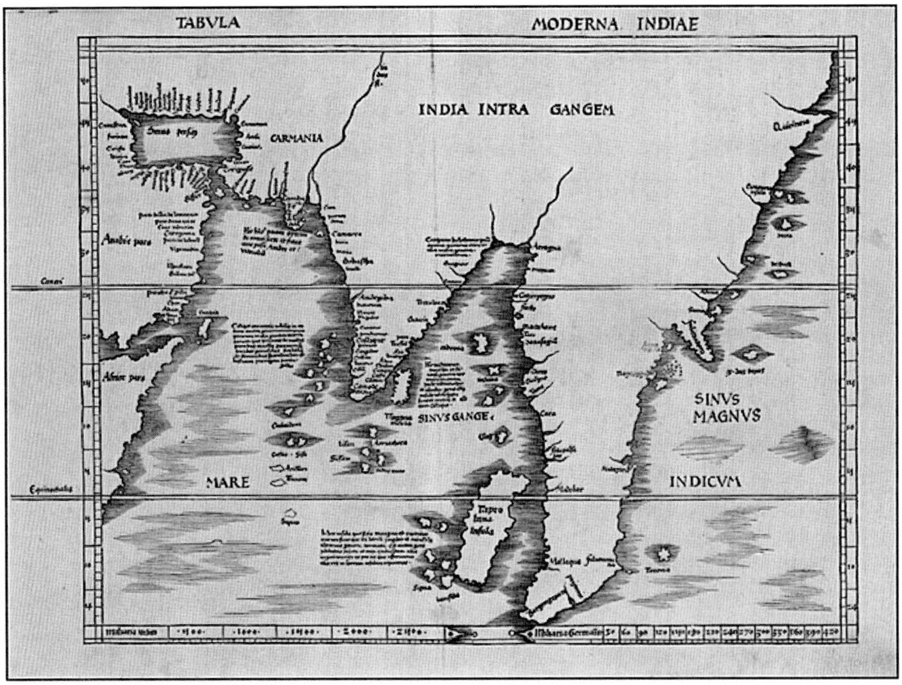

The break in the landmass, as can be found in the middle of the left hand side of the map above, indicates the meeting of the 'Red Sea' with the 'Arabian Sea'. Navigating through

89 https://commons.wikimedia.org/wiki/File:1513_map_of_South-_and_Southeast_Asia_by_Martin_Waldseem%C3%BCller.jpg, Accessed on September 5. 2020.

the 'Red Sea', the traders reached the Suez canal (not visible in the map) and further, the Mediterranean. Prior to the opening of the Suez Canal, sea-farers between Europe and Asia-Pacific circumnavigated the African continent. In 1499, Vasco da Gama returned to Portugal, after his voyage to India, with a cargo valued sixty times the monetary cost of the expedition.

1869 – Opening of the Suez Canal, enabling direct sea route between Europe and the Asia-Pacific (**Refer Figure 1.7**). The Suez Canal Company was an Egyptian joint-stock company, head-quartered in Paris. The company's initial board (of directors) had representation from 14 countries. In 1949, it was agreed that Egypt would be allotted seven percent of gross profits, 90 percent of new clerical jobs and 80 percent of technical appointments. The company was also to provide amenities such as hospitals and schools. In 1956, the canal was nationalized by the Egyptian government, under President Gamal Abdel Nasser.

1880s-1920s – Tens of thousands of labourers[90] from India works on laying railway tracks from the east coast of African continent to the heartland of the "dark continent", with railway works intermittent, due to the death of labourers and lions, as the latter insisted on not ceding their territory.

1880s - Trubner & Co., London, publishes books related to Orient, known as "*Trubner's Oriental Series*". For *Times*, 'oriental' also included works in Sanskrit, "*the language and sacred books of Zorastrians*", "*Egyptian, Assyrian, and other records of the remote past*", scholarly opinion and references to the "*more recondite Accadian and Hittite monuments*", etc. Referring to these works related to "*Oriental literature, philosophy and religion*", the *Times* stated that "*...the results of all the scholarship that has been devoted to these subjects have been almost inaccessible to the public because they were contained for the most part in learned or expensive works or scattered throughout the numbers of scientific periodicals. Messrs. Trubner & Co., in a spirit of enterprise which does them infinite credit, ...*" provided this knowledge to the world, in a comprehensive form.

Late 1880s – The detective stories featuring Sherlock Holmes, written by Arthur Conan Doyle, starts gaining popularity. These stories provided

90 These labourers were known as *'coolies'*, a term that entered the Indian psyche in various ways. People who carried passenger luggages from transit points were also known as coolies. The lakhs of Indian soldiers (more than 20 lakh or two million) who fought outside India, for the British empire, during World War II, were known as "coolie soldiers". "Coolie" was soon to be a popular theme for the Indian movies. A Bollywood move had the title "Coolie No. 1", while Jayan, a popular hero of the Malayalam movies of the 1970s conveys, "*...maybe we are poor..., coolies..., trolley pullers..., but we are not beggars.*".

glimples into the nature of professional practices in London, and elsewhere. Examples included characters who "fattened fowls for the market" (especially goose, during Christmas), characters engaged in professional beggary and saved considerable sums of money, while growing ambitious as they grew richer, characters who were highway robbers of the 1860s Australia, characters who were members of a deadly secret society, etc. Being detective stories, many professions in these writings featured an element of the bizzare, the peculiar, the strange, and occasionally, criminal. Alas, there are not enough Sherlock Holmes'es now-a-days to employ cold reasoning, towards deciphering their hideous plans, and nabbing the latest versions of these professionals!

1917 – 'Red Cross' receives the Nobel Peace Prize.

1936 – 'Modern Times', a Charlie Chaplin movie, becomes a popular film in Britian.

1945 – '*Sahithya Pravarthaka Sahakarana Sanghom*', the first writer's co-operative in India, starts in Kerala. They paid a royalty rate of 30% to its author-members and 20% to authors who are non-members (the usual royalty rate usually being paid to most authors being 10% of the retail price of a book).

1953 – The Ascent of Mount Everest.

Frank S Smythe wrote, in 1937, in "*The Valley of Flowers*": "*The ascent of Mount Everest has become a duty, perhaps a national duty, comparable with attempts to reach the Poles...*". He also mentions that "*Mountaineering in the Garhwal and Kumaon Himalayas more nearly resembles mountaineering in Switzerland, for here are mountains and valleys like Swiss mountains and valleys but built on a greater scale. But, unlike parts of Switzerland, the country is unspoilt by commercialism. There are no railways, power lines, roads and hotels to offend the eye and detract from the primitive beauty and grandeur of the vistas, and there are peaks innumerable, unnamed and unclimbed, of all shades of difficulty, and valleys that have never seen a European, where a simple kindly peasant folk graze their flocks in the summer months.*"

1977 – 'Amnesty International' receives the Nobel Peace Prize.

1986 - The explosion of a nuclear reactor in Chernobyl in 1986. It takes another three decades before the tourism industry and official authorities were able to welcome tourists to this area, with one of the tourist attractions being a giant-wheel scheduled to open a few days after the burst of the reactor. Despite the tourism initiatives, warnings and cautionary messages to tourists remain - due to the threat of varying radiation and collapsing buildings.

1986 – As part of the 'Statue of Liberty' weekend, a musical performance orchestrated by the 'New York Philharmonic[91]', was attended by tens of thousands of people at the Central Park, New York. The musical was conducted by Zubin Mehta and was a free-of-cost open-air concert.

1992 – The Sultanate of Oman mandates that new buildings being constructed in Muscat, the capital city of Oman, has to reflect the traditional architectural ethos[92]. Maps made in the early 1900s or earlier, indicates places such as 'Basra' (Iraq), 'Eden' and 'Muscat'.

1993 - Jack Hawley authors the book *"Reawakening the Spirit in Work: The Power of Dharmic Management"*.

1997 – 'International campaign to ban landmines' receives the Nobel Peace Prize.

Late 1990s - 'Federal Communication Commission' (FCC) of USA recommends and mandates a SAR value of 1.6 W/kg as the upper limit of radiation in mobile-phones. In the years that followed, FCC starts working on assigning upper limits for radiation from other electrical-electronic products. Research articles focus on the importance and necessity for improvising the methodology/ selection of parameters that results in the SAR value, and questions whether SAR value can be considered as the appropriate value for user-safety and health, especially in instances where an electrical-electronic product has an extended usage - in time, levels of radiation, area impact etc. Meanwhile, discussions happen about creating and sustaining "wave-free" areas, as in, areas where artificially created RF waves (radio-frequency waves) do not exist.

---

91 'Philaharmonic' is a title adopted by a band or an organisation that has many musicians and a range of musical instruments. A society that appreciates and reveres music may also adopt this title. In 1990-91, the 'New York Philaharmonic' orchestra consisted of almost 150 members. Some of the acclaimed "philharmonic"s include the 'Vienna Philharmonic', "Berlin Philharmonic", etc.

92 *A 2017 study done in London indicated that electricity usage in office buildings of 20 or more storeys, is more than double, in comparison with buildings that are six storeys or lesser. This study was done based on energy consumption data from 610 office buildings in London. In 1984, a writer, observing the growth of tall buildings in American cities, mentioned, "After an absence of some years, anyone who returns to an American city is inevitably surprised hy the radical change that has occurred in its skyline. Indeed, the skv line of every major American city..., has been completely changed over the last 20 vears by the construction of large numbers of high-rise office buildings."*

1999 – 'Medicine Sans Frontiers' receives the Nobel Peace Prize.

2003 – The 21st meeting of the Inter-Agency Space Debris Coordination Committee (IADC) hosted by Indian Space Research Organisation (ISRO) at Bengaluru during March 10-13. On May 11, 2020, a space-debris weighing nearly 18 tonnes, an empty core stage from a 'Long March - 5B Rocket', fell into the Atlantic Ocean. The CNN reported, *"for a few tense hours, its re-entry path and eventual landing site were a mystery to those tracking its fall."* Millions of pieces of man-made space debris (also known as "space junk", "space trash", "space litter", etc.) floats around the earth. Of these, a few tens of thousands of the larger sized debris are/ can be tracked. Some of these debris may be moving at a speed of more than 17,000 miles per hour (or, more than 25,000 kilometres per hour).

2005 - The Pumalin Park in northern Patagonia, Chile, is designated a 'Nature Sanctuary'. The sanctuary had its beginnings when Douglas Tompkins, who founded the 'North Face' company, started buying semi-abandoned plots in 1991. By 2020, the Tompkins Conservation Foundation donated a million acres to the Chilean government for conservation endeavors, With the Chilean government earmarking an additional ten million acres, this partnership has created the 'Route of Parks', a 17-park network in Chile stretching from Puerto Montt to Cape Horn.

2013 - India mandates for-profit companies to channelise two percent of their profits toward CSR initiatives (Refer Chapter 4, for details).

2016 - A constitution bench of the Supreme Court of India mentioned that *"Education is... ...a noble 'occupation'... those who establish and are managing the educational institutions are not expected to indulge in profiteering or commercialise this noble activity."* The Supreme Court also mentioned that *"...that the occupation of education cannot be treated at par with other economic activities."*.

2017 – 'Air India' avoids non-vegetarian food in economy-class, in flights operating within India.

> ***To read, even a few pages, by caring for your eyes and mind, is appreciable....***
>
> ***You may take a break...***

CSR: RESPONSE TO THE BUSINESS ENVIRONMENT

SK Pottekkatt, a writer in Malayalam language, mentions about the Kedar region of the Himalayas in one of his travellogues.[93] Contextually, he refers, *"...We've already heard about Phalhaari Baba, a permanent resident at Kedar. In the winter, not a single living being is found in Kedar (Even 'Kedarnath', the deity of Kedar, is shifted to Okhimath, 30 miles below). But even during the toughest seasons, there is a monk who stays alone at Kedar: Phalhaari Baba. Within a stone-made room, warmed by burning wood, and eating only dry fruits, this Baba spends months together (The Baba got his name 'Phalhaari' as he lives on fruits only.). As we went there, Baba – dark, lean, old, with a long beard as white as snow, was conversing and discoursing with those who've visited him. His philosophies did not evoke any feel of unique or novelty. Yet, one cannot but appreciate his forbearance, of living alone fighting the harshy coldness of Kedar."*

There has been a time when living on a fruit-based diet, a plant-based diet, etc., were associated with only those who lives secluded in mountains such as the Himalayas. It is no longer so. In 2018, a company providing shared workspaces[94], announced that it will not serve red meat, poultry and pork in the staff events funded by the company, and will also not reimburse spending made by staff on such items. The company mentioned that one of the reasons for this decision is an aim to reduce carbon-dioxide emissions. Citing carbon-emission-reduction as a reason for avoiding animal-based items, a reason that would have been unheard of till a few decades ago, may also have been supported by discussions about such a necessity[95] (**Refer Table 1.1**).

93 Excerpt from S K Pottekkatt's *'Himaalaya Saamraajyathil'*. The English translation included in this page is made by the author of the book on CSR, and may not be conveying the original meaning.

94 http://fortune.com/2018/07/13/wework-no-longer-allow-6000-employees-expense-meals-meat/, Accessed on May 7, 2019.

95 https://www.sciencedirect.com/science/article/pii/S0959652616303584?via%3Dihub, Accessed on October 13, 2018.

Table 1.1[96]

GHG (green house gas) emissions of various ingredients

1	Sugar	0.1	28	Tea	1.9
2	Potatoes	0.4	29	Soyabeans	2
3	Starchy Roots	0.4	30	Coconut Oil	2.1
4	Onions	0.5	31	Cream	2.4
5	Lemons, Limes	0.6	32	Pepper	2.5
6	Oranges, Mandarines	0.6	33	Pimento	3.2
7	Apples	0.7	34	Vegetable Oils	3.2
8	Maize	0.7	35	Palm Oil	3.3
9	Beans	0.8	36	Pulses	3.3
10	Grapefruit	0.8	37	Sunflowerseed Oil	3.3
11	Grapes	0.8	38	Cocoa Beans	3.4
12	Groundnut Oil	0.9	39	Barley	3.8
13	Honey	1	40	Rice (Milled Equivalent)	3.9
14	Oats	1	41	Sesameseed	4.2
15	Rye	1	42	Sesameseed Oil	4.2
16	Wheat	1	43	Olive Oil	4.5
17	Dates	1.1	44	Olives	4.5
18	Peas	1.2	45	Eggs	4.9
19	Bananas	1.4	46	Fish, Seafood	5.4
20	Groundnuts (Shelled)	1.4	47	Freshwater Fish	5.4
21	Tomatoes	1.5	48	Marine Fish, Other	5.4
22	Plantains	1.6	49	Poultry Meat	5.4
23	Vegetables	1.6	50	Pigmeat	7.9
24	Butter, Ghee	1.8	51	Coffee	10.1
25	Milk	1.8	52	Mutton & Goat Meat	64.2
26	Soyabean Oil	1.8	53	Bovine Meat	68.8
27	Pineapples	1.9			

GHG emissions are in kgCO2e/kg, for UK, considering production in UK and imports[97].

Pizza is popular globally. Naples, in Italy, has been considered as the home-ground of pizza. Prior to its adaptations, the pizza was an expression of austerity, simplicity and

96 Peter Scarborough, Paul N. Appleby, Anja Mizdrak, Adam D. M. Briggs, Ruth C. Travis, Kathryn E. Bradbury, Timothy J. Key, Dietary greenhouse gas emissions of meat-eaters, fish-eaters, vegetarians and vegans in the UK, Climatic Change, 2014, Volume 125, Number 2, Page 179.

97 For a detailed listing, visit, https://link.springer.com/article/10.1007% 2Fs10584-014-1169-1

subtlety. The Neopolitan pizzas are cooked in wood-fired ovens. It was in 1889 that the now popular 'Margherita' pizza was born, in which was added Mozzarella cheese. However, a few decades prior, the 'L'Antica Pizzeria Da Michele' was serving the 'marinara' pizza, an almost circular thin bread, topped with a puree of locally grown tomatoes, garlic, oregano and olive oil. "Grass-fed cows" and "thorn-hedged pastures" were the norm and the usual during those times.

A chef known for Italian cuisine, says, when introduced to the dietary practices of Jains, "I'd heard of vegetarians and vegans, but never of people who don't eat vegetables that grow beneath the ground like garlic and onion!"

> *CSR has emerged in a context where wealth creation is towards the optimal benefit of all stakeholders - including shareholders, employees, customers, community, nature, society, and future generations*

CSR has also been considered as a trend driven by consumers voicing their preference for dealing with companies that act as ethical stewards for the good of the larger whole, and has emerged in a context where *"wealth creation is towards the optimal benefit of all stakeholders - including shareholders, employees, customers, community, nature, society, and future generations"*[98].

Another example where businesses are adopting new business practices in response to the changing business environment has been with reference to the usage of electronic gadgets. In 1999, almost none had a mobile phone in India. In 2019, almost everyone had a mobile phone in India, a country with a billion-plus population. Even toddlers, infants and children have access to gadgets such as television and mobile phone. While so, businesses have been recommending caution and responsible usage of these gadgets.

Companies such as Sodexo have been educating citizens about priority to safety while using a mobile phone (**Refer Figure 1.8**). It has been found that increased interaction with technology may be causing some students to display borderline autistic behaviour[99]. Studies have also discovered that *"adolescents spent a large amount of time during the day and at bedtime using electronic devices"*, and usage of electronic devices results in *"an increased risk of short sleep duration, long sleep onset latency and increased sleep deficiency"*[100]. Authors such as Devdutt Pattanaik has made observations

98 http://www.globaldharma.org/Files%20-%20Adobe%20Acrobat/SBL/Spirituality.%20Emerging%20Context%20for%20Bus.%20Ldrship%20UPDATED%20Oct08.pdf, Accessed on September 29, 2018.

99 https://www.telegraph.co.uk/education/educationnews/11553012/Smartphones-making-children-borderline-autistic-warns-expert.html, Accessed on September 29, 2018.

100 https://bmjopen.bmj.com/content/5/1/e006748, Accessed on September 29, 2018.

about the long-term cultural impact of technological applications such as television[101]. Considering the erosion of etiquette values, some of the food service outlets in UK refused to serve customers who use mobile phones in their premises[102][103][104].

Figure 1.8[105]

Gadgets and related applications may interfere with ignition and navigation systems, also have security implications[106][107][108][109][110] *hazards related to health*[111][112][113]*, etc. Keeping*

101 https://www.youtube.com/watch?v=zciGzB-XXpw, Accessed on November 27, 2018.

102 http://www.edp24.co.uk/news/norwich-market-coffee-seller-refuses-to-serve-customers-who-order-while-talking-on-mobile-phones-1-1345284, Accessed on September 29, 2018.

103 https://www.bbc.co.uk/news/av/uk-england-coventry-warwickshire-35317390/chef-bans-mobile-phones-at-leamington-spa-restaurant, Accessed on September 29, 2018.

104 https://www.bbc.co.uk/news/av/uk-35321122/restaurant-in-leamington-spa-bans-mobile-phones-at-dinner-table, Accessed on September 29, 2018.

105 Included with permission from Sodexo.

106 https://indianexpress.com/article/technology/social/defence-ministry-to-indian-armed-forces-uninstall-these-42-apps-including-mi-store-wechat-truecaller-4962876/, Accessed on June 5, 2019.

107 https://indianexpress.com/article/technology/social/we-are-not-malware-says-truecaller-after-reports-of-being-banned-for-indian-armed-forces/, Accessed on June 5, 2019.

108 https://www.iiitb.ac.in/files/CITAPP/Dhwani-Privacy.pdf, Accessed on June 5, 2019.

109 https://advertisers.truecaller.com/brand-stories, Accessed on June 5, 2019.

110 https://yourstory.com/2019/05/instagram-celebs-private-data-leaked, Accessed on June 5, 2019.

111 https://www.ncbi.nlm.nih.gov/pubmed/27454111, Accessed on August 22, 2019.

112 https://bioinitiative.org/research-summaries/, Accessed on August 22, 2019.

113 https://www.ncbi.nlm.nih.gov/pmc/articles/PMC5376454/, Accessed on August 22, 2019.

the electrical and electronic appliances switched-off may not only result in financial savings[114]*, it can reduce negative environmental impact.*

As per a branch of Indian philosophy and practice, a human being is a constitution of 'Annamaya Kosha', 'Manomaya Kosha', 'Praanamaya Kosha', 'Vigyanamaya Kosha' and 'Aanandamaya Kosha'. Current researches, based on an objectively verifiable methodology, usually, study the impacts of electronic-electrical technology at the level of visible body (including those visible by precision instruments) and also at the level of the subjective mind. Electronic-electrical technology may also be interfering with the 'praanamaya kosha', the effects of which may be difficult to predict and foresee.

The textbooks pf physics informed us that 'matter' is 'wave', while being uncertain about the implications of the booming interferences and impulses in the wave-space and the spaces-in-waves, and how these may impact earth-related phenomena and the health of organisms on the earth.

While visiting a region affected by left-wing disturbances and extremism, a writer was told by the chief of police of that district, *"...frankly speaking this problem can't be solved by us police or military. The problem with these tribals is they don't understand greed. Unless they become greedy, there is no hope for us. I have told my boss, remove the force and instead put a TV in every home. Everything will be automatically sorted out."*

Pollution is an indicator of disharmony in existence. Even renowned characters such as Sherlock Holmes had existential challenges. Referring to this, Eoin Colfer writes, *"The cases were his life, and when there was no mystery to be examined, Holmes often sank into drug-fuelled depression..."*[115]. Yet, a reader may not be able to withhold a glint of admiration towards Holmes when he says, to a lady who approaches him for help, while not immediately having the financial resources to pay Homes, *"...I can only say, madam, that i shall be happy to devote the same care to your case as i did to that of your friend. As to reward, my profession is its own reward; but you are at liberty to defray whatever expenses i may be put to, at the time which suits you best."* An increase in the tendency to possess - an increase in the levels of pollution. Decrease in 'wants' and 'needs' - decrease in pollution. *"The Lankavatara Sutra*[116] says, *"...In the worldly life where one is still holding tenaciously to the*

114 The financial savings is usually negligible as the electricity charge usually do not reflect the societal and environmental costs involved in the generation and distribution of electricity.

115 In the 'Introduction' to *The Adventures of Sherlock Holmes*, Scholastic India, 2006.

116 Dwight Goddard, *Self-Realisation of Noble wisdom*, 1932. 'The Lankavatara Sutra' is a collection of Buddhist teachings. This *Sutra* is associated with Boddhidharma, a monk of the 'Shaolin Temple'. For many martial-art enthusiasts and practitioners, the Shaolin Temple is a revered shrine and space, and Boddhidharma their 'patron saint'.

notions of an ego-soul and what concerns it and holding fast to the discriminations of dualism, if only for worldly benefits, one should cherish ideals of charity, good behavior, patience, zeal, thoughtfulness and wisdom. Even in the worldly life the practice of these virtues will bring rewards of happiness and success...".

Benares. Amongst the oldest living cities of the world. The Jain *Theerthankara* Parshwanath was born here – that was a few centuries before Gotama Buddha. This Theerthankara was also known as '*Kalpavruksha*'. Benares is also home to one of the schools of the Hindustani classical music – the *Benaras Gharana*. It is at Benares, also known as *Kashi*[117] or *Varanasi*, that the 'Dhrupad Mela' is held. This *mela* (fair, with stalls, etc.) is known for its musical nights – dusk to dawn – lasting for multiple days, and thus, also known as *Dhrupad Mahotsav* or *Dhrupad Samaroh*. During the temple festivals of India, one can discover, hordes of children and adolescents, testing their steps. Inspirational, it may not be, yet, educational, for many. Well, no admission-fee is charged! Drupad is a vocal rendering, tracing its roots to Swami Haridas and Tansen[118]. A singer and supporter of *Drupad Mela* mentions, "*...considering that Dhrupad's themes mostly revolve around deities, it is only natural that the festival would begin here as an ode to Mahashivrathri...*" They perform in the banks of Ganges, at the *Tulsi Ghat*, where Sant Tulsi Das composed the *Ramcharitmanas* and the *dohas*. "Dhrupad is *Vipassana*, performed out of love... the musicians who sing here do so out of generosity and not for money."[119]

Chapter Summary

1. Corporate Social Responsibility (CSR) has multiple definitions.
2. CSR is defined as the ethos and practice of discovering, infusing, evoking and radiating the human values of righteousness (*Dharma*) and love (*Prema*) in an organisation's interactions with its stakeholders.
3. 'Corporate Social Responsibility', 'Corporate Social Responsiveness', 'Corporate Social Performance', 'Corporate Social Accountability',

117 Fa-Hien mentions, *"...still keeping along the course of the Ganges and going west twelve yojanas, we arrive at the country of Kasi and the city of Banaras. about ten li or so to the north-east of this city is the chapel of the deer park of the Rishis. This garden was once occupied by a Pratyeka Buddha. There are always wild deer reposing in it for shelter."* (SI-YU-KI. Buddhist Records of the Western World. (Translated from the Chinese of Hiuen Tsiang), Samuel Beal, Trubner & Co., 1884.)

118 Swami Haridas was a saint associated with the lineage of the philosopher Nimbarka. Stories related to Tansen are 'legendary' in India.

119 Simar Preet Kaur, The Musical Sounds of Kashi, National Geographic Traveller India, April 2013.

'Corporate Citizenship', 'Responsible Business', 'Corporate Social Opportunity', 'Corporate Responsibility' etc. may be used as synonyms.

4. How an organisation generates its wealth (the way) is as important as how an organisation distributes its profits (the goal).
5. CSR has emerged as a business need.
6. There is a linkage between CSR and a focus on the triple bottom-line, which is about creating financial surplus, enhancement of planetary well-being and improvement in the quality of life for people.
7. Critique has been made about the genuineness and merits of CSR practices.
8. Practice of CSR provides an organisation with varied advantages.

Keywords

Social Responsibility, Environmental Responsibility, Corporate Social Responsibility, ISO 26000:2010, Corporate Social Responsiveness, Corporate Social Performance, Corporate Social Accountability, Corporate Citizenship, Responsible Business, Corporate Social Opportunity, Corporate Responsibility, Bhoodaan Movement, Pay as you wish

Multiple Choice Questions

1. *'...the ethos and practice of discovering, infusing, evoking and radiating the human values of righteousness (Dharma) and love (Prema) in an organisation's interactions with its stakeholders.'*. To which of the following terms has the textbook given this definition to:
   (a) Corporate Social Responsibility
   (b) Marketing Management
   (c) Financial Management
   (d) Business Accounting
   (e) Data Analytics
2. Which of the following is considered a guiding parameter for all organisations focusing on triple-bottom-line
   (a) sending people to Mars
   (b) enhancement of planetary and community well-being
   (c) making an 'Initial Public Offering' (IPO)

(d) getting featured on the cover page of prominent business magazines
(e) ordering pizza for employees working overtime

3. Anaathapindika lived in the times of which of the following spiritual leaders
   (a) Saint Francis of Assissi
   (b) Gautama, the Buddha
   (c) Mahaveera
   (d) Adi Shankara
   (e) Confucius

4. Which business leader was associated with initiating and popularising the idea of establishing a research institution related to science, which later came to be known as Indian Institute of Science?
   (a) Tata Bye-bye
   (b) JRD Tata
   (c) Ratan Tata
   (d) Noel Tata
   (e) Jamsetji Tata

5. Name the business leader who renounced the titles of 'Honorary Magistrate' and 'Rai Bahadur' bestowed on him by the British government
   (a) Jamnalal Bajaj
   (b) Janamlal Bajaj
   (c) Bhajanlal Bajaj
   (d) Purushottam Bajaj
   (e) None Of The Above

6. Name the Bengali teacher-entrepreneur-philanthropist who is considered as the father of Indian pharmaceutical industry
   (a) Prafulla Chandra Ray
   (b) Bankim Chandra Chatterjee
   (c) Saurav Ganguly
   (d) Sathyendranath Bose
   (e) None Of The Above

7. About whom did Mahatma Gandhi made this reference *"Great he undoubted is: But goodness from Indian stand point is greater than greatness and --------- is even more good then he is great. And it is his goodness - his childlike simplicity, his suavity of manners, his ready accessibility, his unblemished purity, unostentatious charity, his voluntary poverty with plain living and high thinking, his enthusiasm and optimism, his innate spirit of self-denial, his incurable habit of always taking a back seat, his sturdy independence, his inflexible incorruptibility... in a word, his nobility of nature made him idol of the people. Service and sacrifice were his watch-word..."*
   (a) Prafulla Chandra Ray
   (b) JRD Tata
   (c) Jamnalal Bajaj
   (d) Sathyendranath Bose
   (e) Vinoba Bhave

8. Name the person associated with Bhoodan movement, and is now referred to as one of India's leading social entrepreneurs:
   (a) Nipun Mehta
   (b) Vinoba Bhave
   (c) Mohammed Yunus
   (d) Kailash Satyarthi
   (e) Dr Govindappa Venkataswamy

9. Which amongst the below, from Berkeley, California, offers food to guests on the basis of 'Pay as you wish'?
   (a) Komala Vilas
   (b) A2B
   (c) Karma Kitchen
   (d) Annalakshmi
   (e) Haus Hiltl

10. Name the textile town in Lanchashire, England, that was visited by Mohandas Karamchand Gandhi in 1931:
   (a) Doorman
   (b) Darwin
   (c) Darwen
   (d) Darewin
   (e) Windor

Short Answer Questions

1. Provide any two definitions for Corporate Social Responsibility.
2. Mention any three terms that are used as synonyms for Corporate Social Responsibility or CSR.

Long Answer Questions

1. Mention any three advantages and disadvantages for a company to engage in CSR practices.
2. Examine the arguments put forward to ascertain the merit and genuineness of CSR practices. Do you have any arguments to contribute to this discussion?

Reflective Questions

1. Refer to Mahatma Gandhi's quote about Prafulla Chandra Ray. Have you seen people living such ideals? Did you feel towards including any of their qualities in your living? If yes, how may this be done, or, how were this included in your life?
2. How may such qualities contribute to ennobling an organisation and its interaction with stakeholders such as customers, employees, shareholders, civil society, etc.?
3. If you are an investor, what are the ways through which you can avoid investing in businesses that harm people, planet and its creations?
4. If you have an account with a financial services company, for example, a savings account with a bank, you receive the after-effects of that investment through a financial return [a dividend, monetary financial interest, etc. Would you be willing to receiving the other after-effects of your investment, if you know that, the financial investments made by this financial services company is also investing in businesses that harm people and their health, inflict violence on non-human creations, and degrade the natural environment?

About the chapter:

1. Learning from the chapter, if any:

2. Topics, concepts, themes, etc. that you may be interested to research/ refer/ study/ ponder upon:

3. Applications in daily life, if any:

Notes:

Chapter 1 completed... You may take a break...

Pictured above is the first electric train in India that started in 1925, between VT (now, CST) and Kurla[120]. A century later, non-air-conditioned travel in Mumbai suburban railway is one of the most environment-friendly[121] motorised transportation options in the world, though these trains are over-crowded to danger levels during peak-hours. In the pre-independent India, the trains were operated by the 'Great Indian Peninsular Railway' (later, part of the 'Central Railway' of Indian Railways). The non-air-conditioned Mumbai suburban railway was also referred to as the "local" and was the original "metro" of the city.

Referring to a railway route in USA, Jules Verne mentioned in his fictional classic, 'Around the world in eighty days', *"There were few or no bridges or tunnels on the route. The railway turned around the sides of the mountains, and did not attempt to violate nature by taking the shortest cut from one point to another."* [122]

---

120 http://cr.indianrailways.gov.in/view_photo.jsp?fileid=104&filename=1297161849388-FirstEMU1925Feb3.jpg, available in public domain.

121 CO_2 emissions for Indian Railways would be approximately 10g per passenger per kilometre. Emissions for travel by air would be approximately 100g per passenger per kilometre. A passenger car would result in a CO_2 emission of approximately 20g per passenger per kilometre, only if the car operates at maximum occupancy. Reduction in the number of passengers in the car will increase its per passenger emission.

122 Chapter XXVII

Chapter 2

A THEORETICAL EXPLORATION

"To have compassion means to have passion for all things, not just between two people, but for all human beings, for all things of the earth, the animals, the trees, everything the earth contains. When we have such compassion we will not despoil the earth as we are doing now, and we will have no wars."[1]

—Jiddu Krishnamurti

On completion of reading the chapter, the reader may:

1. Identify and explain the reasons that contributed to the prevalence of CSR practices.

2. Examine the modes of practising philanthropy

3. Explore the possibility and prevalence of human values and spiritual values being the foundation for CSR practices

3. Analyse and Critique the reasons put forward for an organisation to practice CSR

Voluntary blood-donation and organ-donation are practices that affirm nobility and humaneness (**Refer Figure 2.1**). Organisations conduct blood-donation events as a CSR endeavor. In 2013, a Guinness world record was set for maximum participation for a blood donation service, supported and coordinated by a banking company operating in India. More than 60,000 individuals, mostly students belonging to educational institutions, donated blood at more than 700 locations.

Mickey Lemle directed two documentaries about the 14th Dalai Lama, the monastic and spiritual leader of Tibetan Buddhism. Referring to his initial discussion with the Dalai Lama on the first documentary, Mickey says,

"...He was spending a couple of days at a monastery in New Jersey. He listened very carefully and at the end, he said, "Do you think this is [a] worthwhile undertaking?" And I said, "Your Holiness, if I didn't think it was worth undertaking, I wouldn't spend my time doing it." And he looked at me with those wonderful eyes and he said, "That's a very American way of looking at it."

After spending years with Tibet and Buddhist friends, I learned that the most

1 From the talks given by Jiddu Krishamurti in Saanen, Switzerland, 1974, http://www.jkrishnamurti.org/krishnamurti-teachings/view-text.php?tid=39&chid=5, Accessed on March 5, 2016.

important part of any action that you take is what's your motivation... So what he was asking me was, what was my motivation for wanting to do the film?[2]

Figure 2.1

The above photograph indicates 'Red Cross Singapore' facilitating an acknowledgement to the blood donors. Blood donation is usually unpaid and voluntary. The Guinness world record holder for being the oldest regular donor is aged 90 years, and donates blood every two months. Blood donation sustains because people feel to give. Every donation may help more than one individual.

DRIVERS OF CSR INITIATIVES

CSR initiatives may be due to the below reasons.

a) Environmental Reasons

b) Social Reasons

c) Employee Perspective and Well-Being

d) Governance Reasons

---

2 https://www.salon.com/2017/08/27/the-last-dalai-lama-documentary/, Accessed on May 15, 2020.

e) Ethical and Moral Reasons, and Development of Corporate Conscience
f) Governmental Policies
g) Practices of Peer Group
h) Consumer Demand
i) Sustainability Perspective
j) Interdependency Perspective/ System Perspective
k) Managing Reputation
l) The "Business Case" for CSR

Environmental Reasons

> *"...space-time is not necessarily something to which one can ascribe a separate existence, independently of the actual objects of physical reality. Physical objects are not in space, but these objects are spatially extended..."*
>
> —Albert Einstein[3]

A *"mandala"*, in the religions of Buddhism, Hinduism and Jainism, is a geometrical representation. As per Vajrayana Buddhism, as practised in Tibet, a *mandala* is a pure realm of a Vajrayana deity. Further, the Tibetans may also consider a *Mandala* as "a symbolic representation" of the Universe for the purpose of making an offering to the Three Jewels"[4] of *Buddha, Dharma* and *Sangha*. Travel down south, to Sabarimala in southern India, and the devotees of the deity there, has to live a life of penance for a *mandala* (considered as a minimum of 41 days, in that region), before their pilgrimage to the temple.

It is common in certain cultures to view the physical dimension of distance through the lens of time. So was mentioned by Frank S Smythe, during his treks to the Himalayas, "*Beyond were numerous hamlets whose inhabitants were working industriously on their small terraced fields of grain and vegetables. I asked one of them how far it was to Joshimath, and he replied two miles, but it was more like four or five; these people have small regard for distance, and measure it in time rather than mileage.*"[5].

The industrial mind considered planet earth as a resource to be exploited. This resulted in the plundering of the planet to an extent that most of its life-

---

3 As written in the 'Note to the fifteenth edition' (June 9, 1952) of '*Relativity: The Special and the General Theory*'.

4 Lama Jampa Thaye, *Way of Tibetan Buddhism,* Thorsons, 2001.

5 *Valley of Flowers.*

supporting systems are on peril. As a former vice-chairman of a Switzerland based co-operative retail organisation mentioned, "*The ecological footprint of today's industrialized food production is far too large, and almost totally dependent on oil and chemical derivatives. The negative implications for our planet are massive. If we want to continue to generate continued economic growth, as well as maintain bio-diversity, all while protecting our water resources and fertile soils, we need a fundamental re-think..*"[6] The focus on the natural environment is not just because of the respect for the planet, it is also because of the need for the sustenance of business - a healthy planet is a pre-requisite for the survival of business organisations.

Figure 2.2[7]

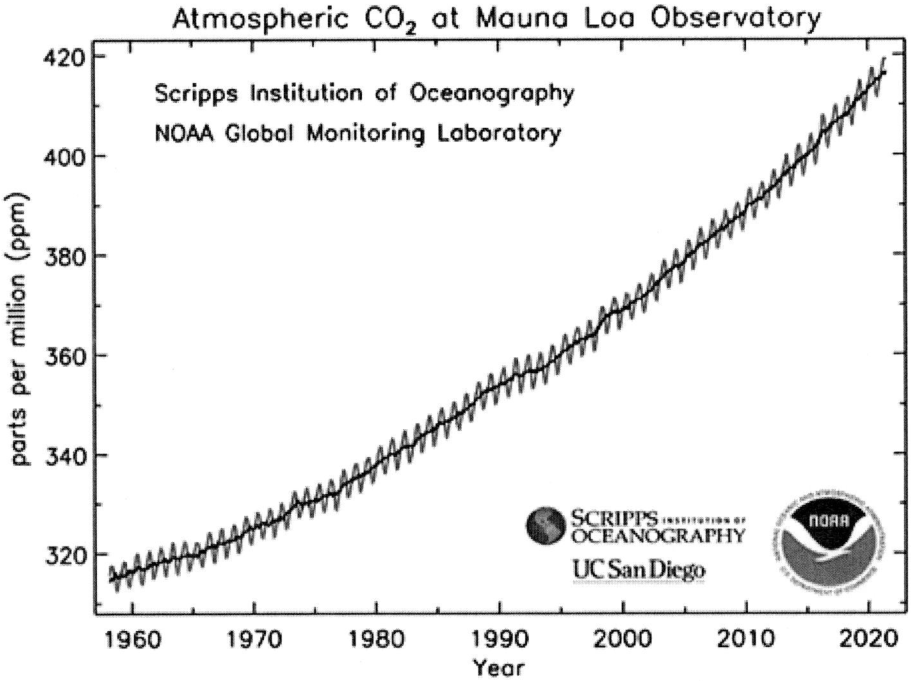

The "fundamental re-think" can happen by conscious choices or sudden jolts. **Figure 2.2** indicates how the lifestyles of human beings are surpassing planetary thresholds. Media reported that commercial shipping tankers

6 http://www.oliverwyman.com/content/dam/oliver-wyman/global/en/2014/jul/2013_OW_Sustainability_4.pdf, Accessed on July 9, 2015.

7 http://www.esrl.noaa.gov/gmd/webdata/ccgg/trends/co2_data_mlo.png, Information provided in the website of ESRL are "provided as a public service" and "are in the public domain". For details, https://www.esrl.noaa.gov/gmd/about/disclaimer.html, Accessed on September 3, 2019.

were travelling through the Arctic waters ('Northern Sea Route') during 2017-18. Citing these, a 'World Economic Forum' article mentioned, *"Unfortunately, the increasing ease with which ships can cross the Northern Sea Route during winter points directly toward the alarming effects of climate change... While thinning ice volumes does present opportunities for increasing trade, perhaps the drawbacks outweigh the benefits."*[8]

The above chart (Figure 2.2) provides a perspective on a global scale. Environmental degradation is affecting all - waste dumps, polluted water bodies and dust infested air. Business organisations will increasingly find it difficult to operate, without considering the factors that affect the natural environment. Regulatory organisations and citizens will increasingly and stringently intervene in organisational projects, if these projects are not contributing to meaningful living. For example, in 2016, the National Green Tribunal (NGT) in India imposed a fine of Rs 25 crore on a port company for carrying out port related work at Hazira without acquiring environmental clearance. In the same year, NGT imposed a fine of Rs 100 crore on three shipping companies for an oil spill near Mumbai coast[9]. In 2015, a Berlin based global automobile manufacturer had to incur millions of dollars in fines and financial losses for cheating regulatory agencies and consumers on emission related parameters by installing a "defeat device" software in its diesel cars.

While many business organisations have started incorporating environmental parameters into their peripheral activities, there are also business organisations that have made "green" the core of their business strategy. For Dalai Lama, a "universal responsibility" refers *to the responsibility that we all have for each other and for all sentient beings and also for all of Nature.*

Social Reasons

Technology attempts to make life easy. In India, online ticket booking for train travel helped a passenger to avoid visiting the ticket booking counter at the railway station or other places, thereby avoiding hassles related to travel, waiting on queues, expenses on travel, and almost half a day or a full day's time. A few other advantages included saving on fuel and lesser travel related pollution, access to information, and saving oneself from involuntary corruption. However there are other effects too. Booking

8 https://www.weforum.org/agenda/2018/02/tanker-crossed-arctic-in-winter-unassisted-first-time, Accessed on February 19, 2017.

9 http://www.financialexpress.com/industry/companies/ngt-slaps-rs-100-cr-damages-on-shipping-firm-for-oil-spill/355404/, Accessed on August 23, 2016.

of travel tickets through wireless technologies required installation of communication towers, requirement of electronic devices, etc. The image below (**Refer Figure 2.3**) indicate a source for Lithium extraction. Lithium is a mineral used in batteries of mobile phones and computers, e-book readers, electric cars, space rovers, etc.

Figure 2.3[10]

Salar de Uyuni, in south-western Bolivia. At approximately 3500 metres (or, approximately 11,000 feet) above sea level, this mountain range salt-flat is one of the landmarks of Bolivia. Advancement of technology and its adoption has made this region one of the coveted locations for Lithium extraction. An article, published in 2015[11]*, mentions, "Previously, on travelling across the blinding white surface, one could expect to come across mirages, multi-coloured lakes and even flamingos or geysers. This time there are no flashes of light or oases on the world's largest salt flat, just an inestimable number of artificial lakes, clunking machinery and workers."*

10 Image Source: https://commons.wikimedia.org/wiki/File:Salar_de_Uyuni_3.jpg, Accessed on January 11, 2021. Lion Hirth (User:Prissantenbär), Public domain, via Wikimedia Commons.

11 https://dialogochino.net/en/extractive-industries/3459-bolivias-lithium-boom-dream-or-nightmare, Accessed on January 10, 2021.

When a company mines minerals, that mineral wealth do not just belong to the company, but belongs to all, including generations that are not yet born. A consultative document from Government of India mentioned about "*inter-generational equity*" and stated that "*...natural resources, including minerals, are a shared inheritance where the state is the trustee on behalf of the people to ensure that future generations receive the benefit of inheritance...*"[12]. Expressions of equitable sharing by a company may take forms such as job creation, providing jobs to people who are physically challenged, provision for educational facilities and medical care, paying taxes to the government, caring for the environment that includes the various species, and considering the difference between 'needs' and 'wants', so that there are reserves to benefit unborn generations.

Business has been viewed as "*the conversion of matter, energy, and knowledge into useful products and services for customers through the power of mind and spirit*"[13]. Renewal of operational licences for business organisations are provided by the society with the the expectation that the organization will provide these useful products and non-products. Michael E Porter and Mark R Kramer writes, "*Not all profit is equal... profits involving a social purpose represent a higher form of capitalism...*"[14].

There are business leaders who pro-actively share their wealth. The founder of 'The Body Shop', an international cosmetic company, says, "*My spiritual theme is kindness: Kindness is my religion. With profits, the purpose of business is to do something remarkable within the community, because it is the community of your customers that gives you your wealth.. There is no value in accumulating wealth; accumulated wealth is like water in a vase that has gone rancid.*"[15]

Employee Perspective and Well-Being

In the mid 1930s, Bertolt Brecht (Eugen Berthold Friedrich Brecht), a German playwright and poet (1898-1956), wrote '*A Worker Reads History*', with its initial verses being,

12 http://www.indiaenvironmentportal.org.in/files/file/draftnationalmineralpolicy2018.pdf, Accessed on March 25, 2018.

13 http://www.globaldharma.org/Files%20-%20Adobe%20Acrobat/SBL/Spirituality.%20Emerging%20Context%20for%20Bus.%20Ldrship%20UPDATED%20Oct08.pdf, Accessed on July 21, 2016.

14 Michael E Porter, Mark R Kramer, Creating Shared Value, Harvard Business Review, January-February 2011.

15 http://www.globaldharma.org/Files%20-%20Adobe%20Acrobat/SBW/Basics%201.23%20The%20Wealth%20of%20Life.pdf, Accessed on July 21, 2016.

Who built the seven gates of Thebes?

The books are filled with names of kings.

Was it the kings who hauled the craggy blocks of stone?...

Employees know that they are contributing to organizational wealth, and would like the organization to share that organizational wealth. Organisational involvement in CSR endeavours can contribute to organizational commitment from employees, organizational performance and more[16][17][18].

A CEO of a US based hospital speaks of the path of wisdom, "*Every answer will not be on a spreadsheet. It all comes from a position of love. I truly love my work and the people i work with. I treat them first and foremost with love...*"[19] Many organizations provide opportunities for employees to contribute to the greater common good. 'Patagonia' has a paid two month 'Environmental Internship Program', which provides opportunities for employees of Patagonia to volunteer full-time with various not-for-profit organisations for two months[20]. There are many organizations where employees contribute a percentage of their salary to a common pool, and the organisation adds an amount equal to that collected amount, known as a 'matching gift'. This is contributed to a noble cause. Employee contributions and "matching gifts" has been one of the major contributors to Wikipedia.[21]

Organizations engaging in values-driven initiatives attract better talent. A former country manager (El Salvador) for Nabisco says, "*At a certain time, we decided to do some combined publicity for the company and human values training. We went to local high schools and offered them an opportunity for the students to come to the plant. We had an auditorium, and I had each of my managers talk about one of the five human values, truth, right conduct, peace, love*

---

16 Imran Ali, Kashif Ur Rehman, Syed Irshad Ali, Jamil Yousaf, Mariz Zia, Corporate social responsibility influences, employee commitment and organizational performance, African Journal of Business Management, Vol 4(12), pp. 2796-2801, October 4, 2010.

17 http://www.vanessaburbano.com/uploads/2/5/0/4/25049117/burbano_jobmarketpaper_updated.pdf, Accessed on July 13, 2017.

18 Stephen Brammer, Andrew Millington, Bruce Rayton, The International Journal of Human Resource Management, Volume 18, Issue 10, pages 1701-1719, 2007.

19 http://www.globaldharma.org/Files%20-%20Adobe%20Acrobat/SBW/Practice%202.12%20See,%20Savour,%20and%20Serve%20the%20Divine.pdf, Accessed on July 21, 2016.

20 http://www.patagonia.com/environmental-internship-program.html, Accessed on February 29, 2018.

21 As mentioned by Wikipedia, during its fifteenth birthday celebration. For details, visit https://15.wikipedia.org/contributors.html, Accessed on January 21, 2015.

and non-violence, and how it affected his area. The Controller would talk about truth, how truth is important in doing the bookkeeping, the accounting, paying the taxes, etc. The Sales Manager would talk about right conduct, how you have to treat the customers correctly. The Plant Manager talked about love, because he had to keep everybody in harmony, so the production would be good. The Quality Control Manager would talk about peace, that if you do your work right, you will be tranquil, because you'll know that the quality of all the products is fine. The Maintenance Manager would talk about non violence, that if you weren't polluting and contaminating, then you would have non-violence. The amazing thing was that the students would come in batches of a hundred, filling the auditorium. The managers were the ones who benefited the most, because they had to learn about these values to talk about them. Then they started seeing how the values worked in their job. The students would also understand the values in relation to a work ethic. After the talks we would take them on a tour of the plant and give them free cookies and so on. We did it frequently to have an outreach to the high schools, and as a result, the young people would apply to work with us, because they liked what they saw, so we had a good pool of resources."[22]

Governance

Investors are asking the senior management of a company and the board members to focus on long-term value creation, and be increasingly transparent with the organisational practices and policies[23]. The members of the board also feel that addressing societal issues helps an organisation to mitigate risks and develop clarity about long-term value creation.

In *Jyotisha*, the system of astrology prevalent in India, there is a practice of asking people to engage in pious practices to offset the sin caused by their forefathers, sins committed by oneself during previous births and the life-ongoing. These practices may include pilgrimage, propitiation of elements of nature, caring for non-human creatures, providing food and shelter to the needy, engaging in charitable initiatives etc. Practising these with piety may result in a person being mindful about the impact of their living on others and future generations. These practices are also advised as a method to avoid harm that may fall upon oneself and also to bring auspiciousness in one's life.

Similarly, an organization conducting outreach activities and endeavours

22 Quotations extracted from the public knowledge base of the "Spiritual Based Leadership Research Programme" are © 2006 by the Global Dharma Center (GDC). GDC retains the copyright to all excerpts from this knowledge base.

23 https://www.businessinsider.com.au/blackrock-ceo-larry-fink-letter-to-sp-500-ceos-2016-2, Accessed on February 20, 2019.

of greater common good may develop insights about long-term sustenance. For example, employees of an automobile company volunteering in medical camps and medical care facilities may understand the impact of pollution on people and develop sensitivity towards others. This may lead them to make use of renewable energy, channelise higher investments towards no-pollution technologies, increasingly use recycled and recyclable material during manufacturing, focus on safety aspects, adopt public-transportation, etc.

Ethical and Moral Reasons, and Development of Corporate Conscience

Cricket is a popular game in the Indian sub-continent and emotions can reach feverish levels during international matches. There are occasions in the game of cricket when a batsman knows about the certainty of their dismissal (being "out"), though other players or the umpire may not have observed the reasons contributing to the dismissal, or remain unsure whether the batsman needs to be dismissed. "Walking", is when a batsman walk off the pitch, as a self-acknowledgment to their dismissal, even when the umpire may give a judgement favouring the batsman - to continue on the field. 'Walking' is not a common practice, as, to continue on the field is beneficial for the player and the player's team.

However, 'walking' does happen, as when Sachin Tendulkar from the Indian cricket team 'walked' during a match with West Indies in the 2011 World Cup. Earlier, in the 2003 world cup, Adam Gilchrist from the Australian cricket team did a 'walk' during the semi-final match with Sri Lanka. Gilchrist mentions, "*Of course, the guys back in the viewing room were a bit stunned at what I'd done. Flabbergasted, really, that I'd do it in a World Cup semi. While I sat there, thinking about it and being asked about it, I kept going back to the fact that, well, at the end of the day, I had been honest with myself...*"[24]. Commenting on the match, Wisden, the cricket reference guide, mentioned, "*This was Gilchrist's match, not for what he did with bat or gloves but for his decision to walk...*"[25]

There are ethical and moral reasons for responsibility practices.

- The owners of business may have a genuine feeling to share and return

24 https://www.smh.com.au/articles/2003/10/26/1067103274199.html, Accessed on July 4, 2018.

25 John Stern and Marcus Williams (Eds), The Essential Wisden: An Anthology of 150 Years of Wisden Cricketers' Almanack, Bloomsbury, 2013, page 567.

to the society, what they have benefited or received from the society, popularly referred to as "giving back".

- Society provides the businesses with a licence to operate, with the expectation that businesses will serve the society. Moral reasons entail the businesses to respect this expectation.
- *"Work is love made visible"*[26]. Business leaders who operate from a context of love naturally feels to serve all, through their businesses. This attitude to serve is reflected in the policies and practices of the company, including CSR.
- For many, work is a spiritual practice. In India, it is said, *"Paropakaaraartham Idam Shareeram"* - this body is meant for the service of others or for the higher ideals. Bhagavad Gita states, *"Yagnayacharatah Karma"*, indicating that work has to be done in a spirit of sacrifice (Sacrifice, from its Latin roots, meant, to make things holy or sacred.). Many people also consider *"Atmano mokshartham jagat hitayacha"* as a work value that they live by. This credo communicates that what is done for one's spiritual fulfilment may also contribute to the good of the world. This statement can also be interpreted this way: we need to ascertain, on whether the actions that we engage in for our well-being, also contribute to the well-being of the world. For those who live by these values, responsibility practices are a natural outcome.
- There is increasing respect for the inherent worth of every being.
- It has been noted that many successful leaders operate from a context of integrity. For them, one of the key parameters of measuring their success is *`Trikaranasuddhi'* (purity and unity of thought, word and deed). When a business leader attempts *'Trikaranasuddhi'* in their life, it also get expressed in their work practices, including responsibility practices in the organization.

'Sathyam, Shivam, Sundaram', translated as 'Truth, Auspiciousness (Goodness), Beauty' is a principle adopted by the magazine *'Resurgence'* to choose articles for their editions. Satish Kumar, who was the editor-in-chief of that magazine says, *"With our head, with our thinking and intellect, we comprehend truth; with our heart we experience goodness and with our hands we create beauty. Unfortunately our educational and economic systems place undue importance on the head, above heart and hands... Our society needs a bigger picture—a holistic vision. The hallmark of a balanced society is to honour and respect mental work and manual work equally. We need both. Only then we can develop our head, heart and hands in total harmony; science, spirituality and the*

26 Khalil Gibran, The Prophet, Alfred A Knopf, 1923.

arts need to be in complete coherence leading to the trinity of TGB - truth, goodness and beauty - as an integrated whole."[27]

Vijay Sweets, Coimbatore (**Refer Figure 2.4**) prepares sweets and snacks that are fully plant-based. For example, its '*mysorepak*'[28] (avoiding ghee) is made from coconut milk, chickpea flour, palm jaggery, sugar and cardamom, while it has a 'wheat halwa' made with wheat milk, jaggery, coconut oil, cardamom and watermelon seeds. Vijay Sweets also prepares 'Ragi Halwa', 'Spinach Seed Laddoo' etc.

Figure 2.4[29]

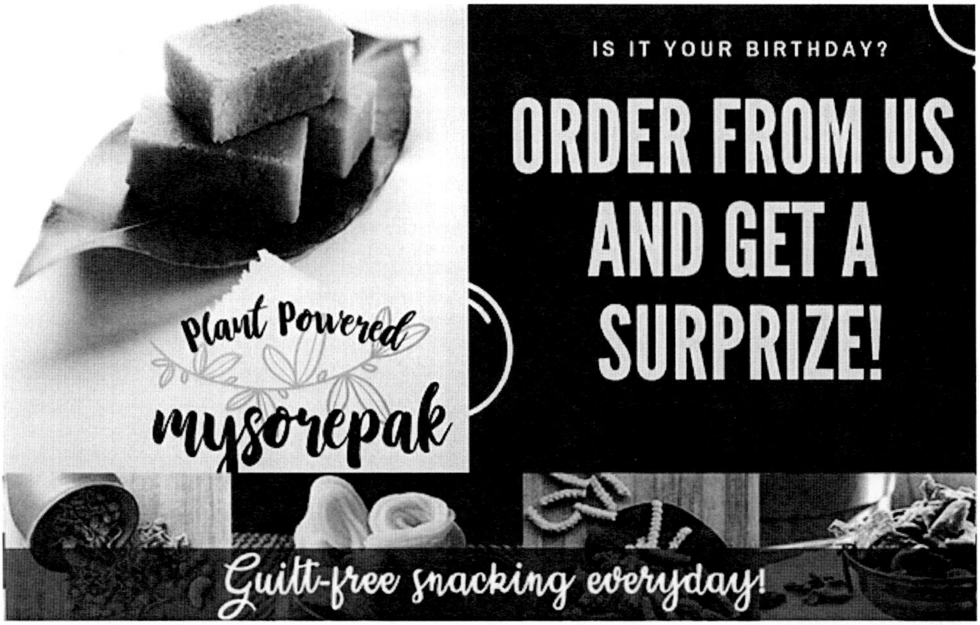

Aravindan from Vijay Sweets (www.vijaysweets.com) says, *"It's a family business. We have been selling sweets and namkeens for the past 30 years. When I quit my job I knew I wanted to take up my family business... I didn't want to earn money by running a business that used animal products. I started experimenting with ingredients..."*.[30]

27 http://www.resurgence.org/magazine/article4136-truth-goodness-and-beauty.html, Accessed on February 11, 2016, included with permission.

28 A sweet preparation popular in Southern India.

29 Included with permission.

30 http://messycookingalwaysvegan.blogspot.com/2018/05/the-vegan-mysore-pak-story-aravindan-v.html, Accessed on February 10, 2019.

Governmental Policies

1866. Prussia defeats Bavaria, making the King of Bavaria (King Ludwig II) withdrew further to himself, and to his interests – of music and castles. This was much before Walt Disney Company started building castle-like play-areas or included a castle in the company logo. Forts are historic. Castles, almost fairytaleish. Aragon, after successful battles and adventures of the ring fellowship, was crowned the king at *Minas Tirith*. Splendorous the castles were, and they had stories to tell. King Ludwig II, the Bavarian king, may not have won the battle, though that did not erode the regards and respects the people of Bavaria had for him. There were times when the king used to be seen walking alone in the mountains, and the king would visit the peasants' home, unannounced, for tea. The king's travels on his horse-drawn-sledge – a convenient transportation for the snowy Bavarian Alps – was also remarkable, with the sleigh carrying loads of presents to be gifted to his subjects. The Bavarian king's castles were indeed castles – towering and majestic – that even the tremors and trembles associated with the politics of 1930s' Germany did not deter Walt Disney from visiting Ludwig's Neuschwanstein castle.

While generation and equitable sharing of wealth is one of the prime responsibilities of businesses, the inequality in wealth distribution is on an increase. An Oxfam report, of 2016, indicated that the wealth of the richest 62 people of the world equals that of the poorest half of the world's population[31]. In 2014-15, the CEO pay of few of the Indian companies was more than 400 times the median employee salary of that company[32][33].

Irresponsible businesses make a significant negative impact on the society, including financial costs. For example, the total annual healthcare related costs due to the usage of alcohol and tobacco. In the USA, direct medical care for adults due to the ill-effects of tobacco usage amounts to almost $170 billion, while lost productivity amounts to more than $150 billion[34]. The

---

31 https://www.oxfam.org/en/pressroom/pressreleases/2016-01-18/62-people-own-same-half-world-reveals-oxfam-davos-report, Accessed on February 11, 2016.

32 http://qz.com/445350/heres-how-much-indian-ceos-make-compared-to-the-median-employee-salary/, Accessed on February 11, 2015.

33 Aldous Huxley asks, "*What is the degree of economic inequality that should be allowed to exist in any community?*" He comments that obtaining complete equality of income is probably impossible, perhaps even undesirable, and there can be no universally valid answer. Acknowledging the individual differences, he mentions, "*I simply cannot imagine what it feels to be a genius at chess, a great mathematician, a composer...*". Yet, he is of the opinion of the necessity of taking certain steps in the direction of equalization.

34 http://www.cdc.gov/tobacco/data_statistics/fact_sheets/fast_facts/, Accessed on July 21, 2016.

financial costs of excessive alcohol consumption in USA amounted to more than $220 billion dollars on an annual basis[35]. Lord Holme of Cheltenham CBE says, "*...if companies behave irresponsibly, in social or environmental terms, then no amount of good-cause giving will tilt their overall contribution to society back from the negative to the positive. A pirate throwing a few doubloons to a beggar may claim to be a philanthropist, but that hardly makes him a responsible businessman.*"

As governmental policies evolve in consonance with changing societal needs, governments across the world are evolving policies that favours social responsibility practices. Few examples are as below:

a) In 2014, the Government of Kerala announced a 10 year phased prohibition of alcohol, while the Bihar government announced a total prohibition in 2016. The state's (Kerala) finance minister stated that the health of people and families were more important than the income generated by the state through the taxes from the sale of alcohol.

b) Responding to the need for increased transparency, flexibility, and fairness, Government of India, in 2014, indicated that it will "*encourage the formal adoption and usage of Open Source Software*"[36] amongst governmental organisations. While usage of Free and Open Source Software (FOSS) has been promoted by many during the past few decades, governmental recognition and promotion of FOSS is on an increase in the recent times.

c) In India, the concept of a 'business sustainability report' or a 'responsibility report' only started in the beginning of 2000s. In a decade, issuance of a business responsibility statement became a mandatory practice for large, listed companies[37].

d) People make choices related to the usage of '*atta*' (also referred as 'wheat flour' or 'whole wheat flour') and '*maida*' (also referred as 'refined wheat flour') in food products for various reasons. Some people prefer 'Whole wheat flour' for health reasons[38][39] (**Refer Table 2.1**), whereas some may be including 'refined wheat flour' as an ingredient in certain

35 http://www.cdc.gov/features/alcoholconsumption/, Accessed on July 21, 2016.

36 http://deity.gov.in/sites/upload_files/dit/files/policy_on_adoption_of_oss.pdf, Accessed on January 9, 2015.

37 https://www.sebi.gov.in/legal/circulars/nov-2015/format-for-business-responsibility-report-brr-_30954.html, Accessed on March 25, 2018.

38 https://www.hsph.harvard.edu/nutritionsource/what-should-you-eat/whole-grains/, Accessed on July 2, 2019.

39 http://www.berkeleywellness.com/node/2929, Accessed on July 2, 2019.

food products. In 2019, the Food Safety and Standard Authority of India (FSSAI) mandated the specificity in the 'ingredient listing' when ''*atta*' or '*maida*' is included in a food product[40][41][42].

Table 2.1

	Atta or 'Whole-wheat Flour'	*Maida or* 'Refined Flour'
Calories	340 kcal	364 kcal
Total Fat	2.50 g	0.98 g
Saturated Fat	0.430 g	0.155 g
Carbohydrate	71.97 g	76.31g
Sugar	0.41g	0.27g
Dietary Fibre	10.7g	2.7 g
Protein	13 g	10.33 g
Vitamin E	0.71 mg	0.06 mg
Vitamin K	1.9 mcg	0.3 mcg
Thiamin	0.502 mg	0.120 mg
Riboflavin	0.165 mg	0.040 mg
Niacin	4.957 mg	1.250 mg
Vitamin B6	0.407 mg	0.044 mg
Iron	3.60 mg	1.17 mg
Magnesium	137.00 mg	22.00 mg
Phosphorous	357.00 mg	108.00 mg
Potassium	363.00 mg	107.0 mg
Sodium	2 mg	2 mg
Zinc	2.60 mg	0.70 mg
Copper	0.410 mg	0.144 mg
Manganese	4.067mg	0.682 mg
Selenium	61.8 mcg	33.9 mcg
Calcium	34 mg	15.00 mg

The above information considers 100g of the ingredient. Data included in the table is

40 https://foodsafetyhelpline.com/2019/02/fssai-issues-directions-regarding-english-nomenclatures-for-atta-and-maida/, Accessed on July 2, 2019.

41 https://fssai.gov.in/dam/jcr:09bddace-8ca4-4621-80fc-e798f9a2cad6/Order_Wheat_Flour_01_02_2019.pdf, Accessed on July 2, 2019.

42 https://fssai.gov.in/dam/jcr:d4f4fc52-adac-476a-9354-0ddf059ea9d0/Direction_Wheat_01_05_2019.pdf, Accessed on July 2, 2019.

based on USDA National Nutrient Database[43][44]. *Comparison is made between* "Wheat flour, whole-grain" *(, which is similar to "atta") and* "Wheat flour, unenriched, all-purpose, white"*(, which is similar to "maida"). 'Bleaching', which may be done during "refining", is harmful for health.*

A 'galette' *is a cake, which is made from whole grain flours - oats, wheat, rye, barley (sweetened with honey), etc. The* 'Galette des Rois', *also known as the 'King's cake', is popular in France, especially during the Epiphany, signifying the arrival of 'the three wise men from the East', during the birth of Jesus. In the cake distributed among family members, a bean is kept hidden – kept when the cake is made. The person who receives the slice with the bean becomes the "Baby Jesus", and is crowned as the king or queen of the evening. It was a tradition to give a portion of the "Twelfth-night" Galette des Rois to the poor.*

Maybe a strict regimen, but the food for the first day of the seven days of 'Passover', allows the Jewish community to know taste – as they prepare foods without the addition of salt, sugar, spices or fat. During all the seven days of the 'passover', Jews do not add yeast during the preparation of bread.

For various reasons (religious, ethical, humane, personal choices, health, etc.), many people prefer breads, cakes, dumplings and other food to be prepared without the addition of yeast. Breads made without the addition of yeast is referred to as unleavened breads.

Usage and popularisation of 'refined flour' happened in the past few centuries, prompting and alerting many nutritionists, for example, Sylvester Graham (1794-1851), and chefs to communicate the essentiality of using only whole-grain-flours in the preparation of food[45]. *Indian cuisine offers many unleavened flat-breads made from whole-grain flours. They are also eggless.*

Practices of Peer Group

Scott Beaudoin, global practice director, corporate and brand citizenship,

---

43 https://fdc.nal.usda.gov/fdc-app.html#/food-details/168893/nutrients, Accessed on November 17, 2019.

44 https://fdc.nal.usda.gov/fdc-app.html#/food-details/169761/nutrients, Accessed on November 17, 2019.

45 In 'Return to Nature!' (1899, fourth edition), Adolf Just, a practitioner of natural healing, mentions that (as translated by Benedict Lust) "...The Bible shows how civilized mankind has gone astray. In the beginning men lived in a state of paradise; thev lived on the fruit which nature yielded spontaneously. The first fall from nature was the beginning of the chase, and the fall of man was the chase... ...Now they fell sick, an inner restlessness made itself felt, just as the horse that is fed on ripe oat kernels, instead of on its natural food (grass), becomes restless, and must be put to hard work. Men likewise had to begin to work now, and cleared the forests ; the age of agriculture began... ...Alter agriculture came grape-culture, and alcohol with its disgusting consequences made its appearance... Then came the trades and the arts... ...The art of building was also introduced. The tower of Babel was begun. And row arose the various languages... But misery steadily increased, men were plunged more and more deeply into error...".Perspectives of Adolf Just can also be found in two footnotes of Chapter 6.

MSLGroup says, *"Profit and purpose are no longer mutually exclusive. For everyone around the globe, that is increasingly becoming the prevailing belief. The question then becomes how to make profit in a purpose-driven way."*[46] It has been suggested that the adoption of CSR practices by an organization (firm) *"can affect its peer firms' strategies and market valuation."*[47] An organization that is driven by human values influences and improves the practices of the peer group. Similarly, a business environment that respects ethical behaviour influences organizations operating in that environment to behave ethically.

Belu Water, operating in UK, is considered a responsible brand. It is UK's first carbon-neutral bottled water brand. The company also gives 100% of its profits to WaterAid, an international not-for-profit organisation working towards providing people with clean water, safe toilets and hygiene education. Belu Water has also made a conscious decision not to export its products to other countries, as exports will result in a higher environmental impact due to transportation related emissions. Such practices have resulted in the company being the preferred bottled water brand amongst many hotels and other places.

> *'Belu Water' is UK's first carbon-neutral bottled water brand. The company also gives 100% of its profits to an international not-for-profit organisation working towards providing people with clean water, safe toilets and hygiene education. Belu Water decided not to export its products, thereby reducing its environmental impact, due to transport-related emissions.*

Bridgeway Capital Management (Bridgeway) is a Houston (Texas, USA) based investment management company. This company donates 50% of its profits to not-for-profit organisations.

Harbour Air is a Canada based airline company that is carbon-neutral.[48] Beginning 2007, the company has offsetted more than 73,000 tonnes CO2e. The company website mentions that *"For those emissions that can't be reduced, we invest in carbon offsets to moderate our collective impact"*.[49]

The presence of brands such as Belu, Bridgeway and Harbour Air, makes

46 http://www.prweek.com/article/1345238/csr-roundtable-purposeful-pursuit-extended, Accessed on June 7, 2015.

47 https://corpgov.law.harvard.edu/2015/09/21/peer-effects-of-corporate-social-responsibility/, Accessed on July 21, 2016.

48 https://www.harbourair.com/media/509481/Offsetters_HarbourAir_2017Infographics_Timeline_outlines_V7%20(dragged).pdf, Accessed on March 25, 2018.

49 https://www.harbourair.com/about/carbon-neutral/, Accessed on March 25, 2018.

the peer group take notice about the uniqueness of such brands, and possibly, include socially responsible business practices in their businesses too.

> ***To read, that which do not degrade oneself, is an exercise in alertness...***
>
> ***You may take a break...***

Consumer Demand

A professor of social enterprise says, "*...Today, people look to use their commercial involvement to promote the causes that matter to them. Furthermore, consumers are using their shopping carts to change society.*"[50] Ecosia.org is a web-search site based in Berlin, Germany, that became a global brand based primarily on its environmental responsibility credentials. In the initial years, the company contributed a significant amount (80%) of their "surplus income" to projects that supported afforestation. The sustainability credo of the company was recognised by the internet users and this led to the popularity of the company, and its growth – the number of full-time employees in the company increased to more than 30 full-time employees in January 2019, while the company had less than ten full-time employees in January 2015.

Consumers are also becoming more concerned about their personal health and environmental health. Considering the ongoing debate about including genetically modified ingredients in food products[51], Chipotle, a US based restaurant chain decided to use only ingredients that are not genetically modified. India is witnessing the emergence of a large number of food and ingredient suppliers that cater to the health, social and environmental responsibility parameters. The below photo (**Refer Figure 2.5**) indicates the operational parameters followed at *Aruvi*, a nature food restaurant at Kochi. Some of the practices at this restaurant include the avoidance of artificial colors and preservatives, ajinomoto[52], red chilles, *maida* (refined flour), coffee, tea, fried items etc. This is a restaurant where food is not

50 http://www.prweek.com/article/1345038/csr-roundtable-purposeful-pursuit, Accessed on June 7, 2015.

51 http://www.ensser.org/fileadmin/user_upload/EN_PR_no_consensus_ENSSER_LV.pdf, Accessed on July 22, 2016.

52 Ajinomoto is a Japanese company manufacturing pharmaceutical products, taste enhancers, detergents, etc. The company produces mono-sodium-glutamate (MSG), a taste-enhancer.

reheated and refrigerated, and food is prepared in earthen and bronze vessels.

Figure 2.5[53]

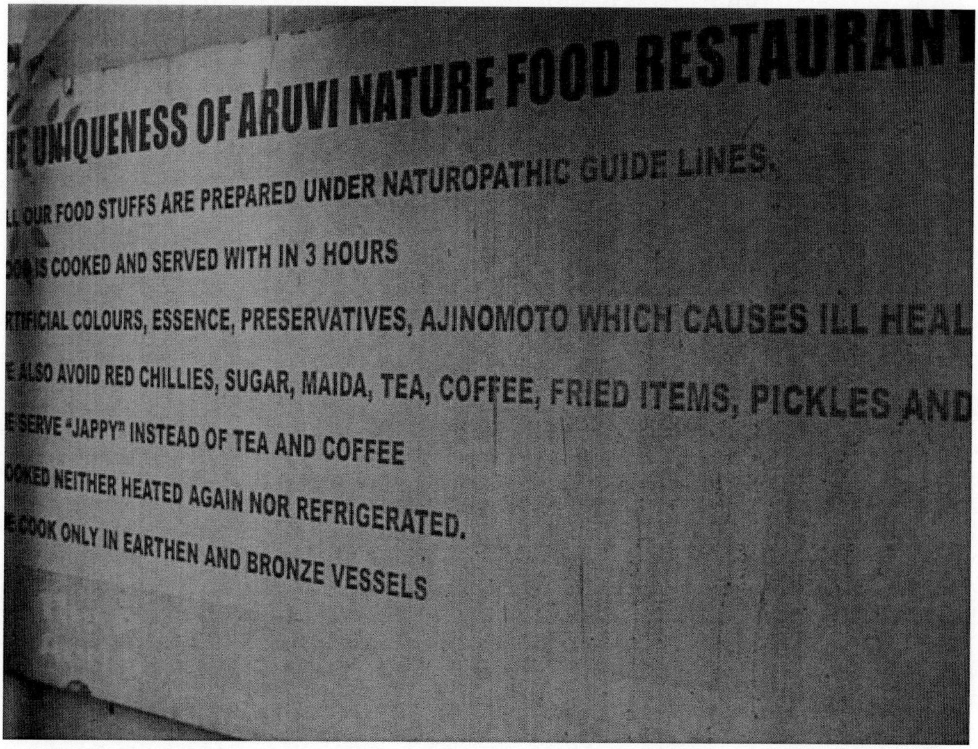

There are consumers who would like to vote with their wallet and reward companies that are engaged in practices that set higher standards in responsibility. A former vice-chairman for a Switzerland based co-operative retailing organisation says, "*Sustainability is a theme which already resonates strongly with our customers – and will continue to grow in importance. Consumers care today, and will care even more tomorrow.*"[54] Many are willing to purchase products that carry social or environmental responsibility labels or are associated with practices of environmental and social responsibility, though these products may be priced relatively higher.

Sustainability Perspective

Many organisations exist with the belief that they may live in perpetuity.

53 Photograph by author and made available to the public domain.

54 http://www.oliverwyman.com/content/dam/oliver-wyman/global/en/2014/jul/2013_OW_Sustainability_4.pdf, Accessed on July 9, 2015.

Organizations thus need to assess their business practices from a long-term perspective rather than a perspective that is short-term. 'Extract'ing resources from the planet may result in huge short-term gains and immediate economic growth. However, it has serious consequences for the long-term (**Refer Figure 2.6**).

Figure 2.6[55]

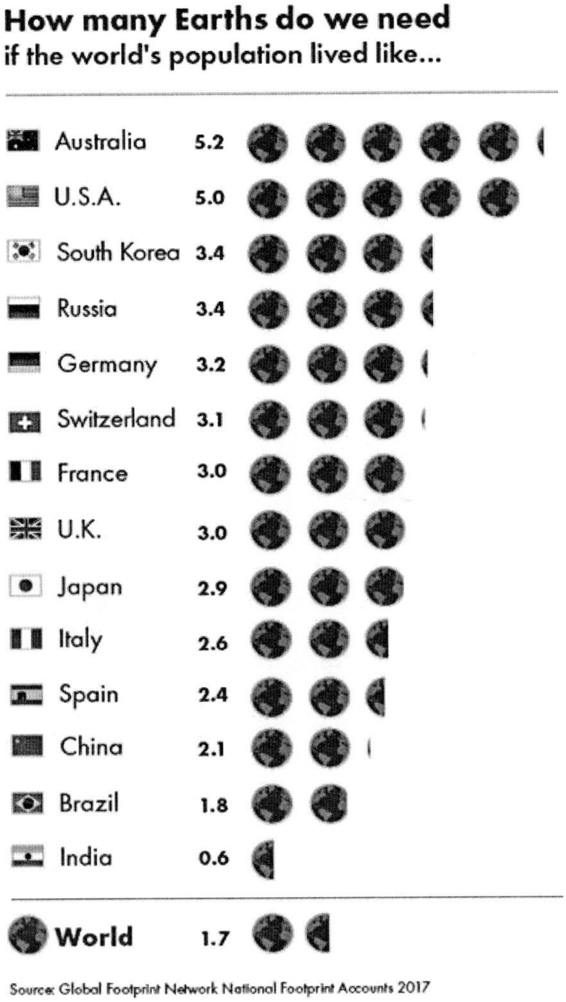

There are countries with an ecological footprint higher than that of Australia, which is listed above. There are also countries with an ecological footprint lower than that of India, which is listed above. Countries with an ecological footprint lower than that of India

55 Image included with permission from Global Footprint Network (www.footprintnetwork.org).

includes Rwanda, Malawi, Eritrea, Tajikistan etc. Economic poverty amongst some of the citizens is also a reason for the low ecological footprint of these nations, including that of India. However, this low footprint is also due to many of its citizens choosing 'voluntary simplicity'/ 'holy simplicity'[56]*. The ideal of 'noble thinking and simple living' respects the planet*[57]*.*

Ecological footprint of a country is an average of the individual ecological footprints of the people living in that country. Depending on lifestyle, there will be differences in individual ecological footprints of people, within a country. An individual, who lives a life of reverence to nature and its living-beings, even while living in a country with a higher ecological footprint, may have an individual footprint that is comparable, or, even lower than the average ecological footprint of a country, with a lower ecological footprint.

An 'Overshoot Day' indicates the day on which the needs (consumption) of the population (of a region, or, the planet) exceeds the bio-capacity (of a region, or, the planet). The below are the overshoot days for some of the countries of the world:

Country	Overshoot day	Country	Overshoot day	Country	Overshoot day
Qatar	Feb 9, 2021	Luxembourg	Feb 15, 2021	United Arab Emirates	March 7, 2021
Bahrain	March 9, 2021	Canada	March 14, 2021	United States of America	March 14, 2021
Kuwait	March 14, 2021	Oman	March 22, 2021	Australia	March 22, 2021
Denmark	March 26, 2021	Belgium	March 30, 2021	Korea, Republic of	April 5, 2021
Sweden	April 6, 2021	Austria	April 7, 2021	Brunei Darussalam	April 8, 2021
Kazakhstan	April 8, 2021	Singapore	April 10, 2021	Cayman Islands	April 10, 2021
Finland	April 10, 2021	Norway	April 12, 2021	Saudi Arabia	April 12, 2021

56 Among various references, 'Holy Simplicity' also finds mentions in the English translation (by E J Strickland) of the *'Abandonment to Divine Providence'*, written in French by Jean-Pierre de Caussade, who lived in the 1700s. One of those mentions include, *"I am aware that my direction is considered rather too simple, but what does that matter? This holy simplicity hated by the world is, to me, so delightful that I never dream of correcting it. Everyone to his taste. I respect those who are wise and prudent, but content myself with remaining one of those poor, simple and little people of whom Jesus Christ speaks..."*.

57 An ecological footprint quiz/ calculator is available at www.myfootprint.org that helps individuals to ascertain their ecological footprint. Ecological/ environmental footprint assessment is an evolving area of study.

Israel	April 16, 2021	Russian Federation	April 17, 2021	Czech Republic	April 17, 2021
Netherlands	April 27, 2021	Ireland	April 27, 2021	Poland	May 4, 2021
Germany	May 5, 2021	Japan	May 6, 2021	France	May 7, 2021
Switzerland	May 11, 2021	Italy	May 13, 2021	Portugal	May 13, 2021
Bhutan	May 14, 2021	New Zealand	May 15, 2021	United Kingdom	May 19, 2021
Greece	May 22, 2021	Spain	May 25, 2021	Malaysia	May 30, 2021
China	June 7, 2021	Hungary	June 8, 2021	Bulgaria	June 10, 2021
Bahamas	June 10, 2021	Turkey	June 16, 2021	Romania	June 21, 2021
Lebanon	June 25, 2021	Argentina	June 26, 2021	Iran, Islamic Republic of	June 30, 2021
South Africa	July 4, 2021	Paraguay	July 8, 2021	Bolivia	July 9, 2021
Mauritius	July 10, 2021	Brazil	July 27, 2021	Fiji	July 27, 2021
Botswana	August 1, 2021	Ukraine	August 8, 2021	Mexico	Aug 11, 2021
Thailand	August 15, 2021	Costa Rica	August 16, 2021	Algeria	Sept 11, 2021
Viet Nam	Sept 18, 2021	Peru	Sept 29, 2021	Namibia	Oct 5, 2021
El Salvador	Oct 21, 2021	Azerbaijan	Oct 23, 2021	Jordan	Oct 30, 2021
Colombia	Nov 2, 2021	Cuba	Nov 17, 2021	Iraq	Nov 20, 2021
Armenia	Nov 21, 2021	Egypt	Nov 24, 2021	Morocco	Nov 26, 2021
Dominican Republic	Nov 29, 2021	Nicaragua	Dec 2, 2021	Ecuador	Dec 7, 2021
Myanmar	Dec 8, 2021	Chad	Dec 16, 2021	Indonesia	Dec 18, 2021

The above table may, at its best, be indicative. The skyscrapers in megalopolises of the world have become so tall that it is difficult to fit them within the photo-frame of an ordinary lens. Some such sky-scrapers are constructed in regions where people, living their natural lifestyle, finds it difficult to source drinking water, or, to grow fruit-trees. Some of the Gulf countries (Middle-eastern region) have huge skyscrapers. The construction-labour for these skyscrapers, many-a-times, are people from nations that may be economically poor. Such expatriate population also contribute to the economic growth in their home-countries, through their remittances to their home countries. Within the Gulf population (including both natives and expats), there is, again, a huge disparity in lifestyle. Yet, none may find it surprising that water-desalination mechanisms powered ny petroleum, or, skyscrapers built by violating the sacrosanctness of the natural sea-and-land boundary are not without impacts.

The above table may be assessed considering the above and similar perspectives. Data collection, compilation and assessment of the data that goes into the above table may provide various possibilities of improvement. The above table, thus, may not be considered all-comprehensive and error-proofed, while, the table may be an indicator.

Increased consumption of "sea-food" has resulted in the plundering of ocean. Overfishing has resulted in declining fish catches. The declining fish catch near the shores makes people venture farther and deeper into the ocean, thereby resulting in further exploitation. With such practices, population of fishes in the deep ocean are also affected. Global fish catch has been on a decline since the 1990s[58]. Fishing also affects other marine organisms such as dolphins, corals, turtles etc. Overfishing, while beneficial in the short-term, has a negative impact for the long-term. A travel magazine mentions, "*The Andamans have not yet been acquainted with a modern fishing fleet...*", and (hence, the region's) "*...marvellously varied aquatic life has been largely left undisturbed...*". The countless reefs of the region has also not been a tourist's paradise, and hence the region witness the flourishing of "*coral, giant rays, sharks, ...*" and other living forms.

Will the goose that lays the golden egg be killed? Fritjof Capra says, "*If 'development' is used in the current narrow economic sense associated with the notion of unlimited quantitative growth, such economic development can never be sustainable, and the term 'sustainable development' would be an oxymoron. If, however, the process of development is understood as more than a purely economic process, including social, ecological, and spiritual dimensions, and if it is associated with qualitative economic growth, then such a multidimensional systemic process can indeed be sustainable. Many in business, government, and civic society now use the term 'sustainability' to examine these issues, along with hundreds of new academic programs and consulting firms. For example, an automobile company*

58 http://www.nature.com/articles/ncomms10244, Accessed on September 27, 2018.

should realize that it is not necessarily in the business of selling cars but rather in the business of providing mobility, which can also be achieved, among many other things, by producing more buses and trains and by redesigning our cities."[59]

Interdependency Perspective/ System Perspective

The idea of inter-dependency has been in popular discussion through topics such as 'butterfly effect'. 'Inter-dependency' communicates that all are connected, no action can be done without making an impact on something else, and the impact of various decisions may not be immediately visible.

Figure 2.7

A harvestor-machine being employed in a rice-paddy-field in the state of Kerala (in India) in the early 2020s. It was in 2010s that a large-scale shift to harvestor-machines (from human labour) occurred in this southern state of India.

'Green revolution' may be cited as an example to evolve a perspective about inter-dependency. 'Green revolution' was aimed at eliminating hunger. Through "green revolution", or, in the name of 'green revolution', practices such as usage of pesticides and synthetic fertilizers, mono-culture, promotion of water-intensive-farming, development of seeds in the laboratories, construction of dams, etc. were encouraged. While 'green revolution' did provide benefits, it had its disadvantages. Water-intensive-farming required construction of channels of irrigation from dams.

59 http://www.fritjofcapra.net/qualitative-growth/, Accessed on June 10, 2015.

Synthetic fertilizers were produced from fossil fuels. Farming became energy-intensive and machine-based (**Figure 2.7**). Farmers used to procure seeds from the harvest in their fields. The focus on high-yielding varieties of seeds resulted in some farmers procuring seeds from third parties, thereby becoming dependent. It also resulted in non-usage and loss of traditional seed varieties. Usage of pesticides affected health of many life forms, including humans. Pesticides affected the food chains. Synthetic fertilizers took away the fertility that is inherent in the soil.

Yet this *(green) revolution* contributed to the growth of various areas - farm equipments and machines, petroleum and chemical based products, construction and irrigation, seed development and testing, transportation and storage of grains and agricultural produces, weather-forecasting, satellite-imagery and aerial-mapping, and the formation of governmental ministries, enterprises and specialised departments to manage all these. It is not uncommon to hear the remark that, 'In this equation of farming, the farmer was not considered'.

Many profit-making businesses are not only resource-depleting, but also resource-exploiting. The plastic packaging industry is an example. "*While delivering many benefits, the current plastics economy has drawbacks that are becoming more apparent by the day... A staggering 32% of plastic packaging escapes collection systems, generating significant economic costs by reducing the productivity of vital natural systems such as the ocean and clogging urban infrastructure. The cost of such after-use externalities for plastic packaging, plus the cost associated with greenhouse gas emissions from its production, is conservatively estimated at USD 40 billion annually - exceeding the plastic packaging industry's profit pool,*" says a report[60]. The ill-effects of plastic waste is well-known. While plastic packaging industry may be making profits, the negative effects of this business is paid by the society.

The impact of businesses are global. A smart-phone is made with materials sourced from multiple countries, manufactured in yet another country, and then, exported to another. There have been reports of how human dignity is not respected in this supply chain. A mobile phone may be purchased in China, and this purchase may contribute to an exploitation happening in an African country. In a similar manner, carbon emissions cause global warming, and the negative impacts of global warming are felt around the globe. Emissions from a coal fired power plant in India can contribute to

60 World Economic Forum, Ellen MacArthur Foundation and McKinsey & Company, The New Plastics Economy - Rethinking the future of plastics (2016, http://www.ellenmacarthurfoundation.org/publications).

increased frequency of hurricanes in USA. Automobile emissions in USA can contribute to extreme weather in South-east Asia. The increase in global trade causes increased movement through sea, causing marine pollution. It can thus be inferred that the moral permission to start a business operation has to be given by the global community, and not just by a licensing authority.

Cataclysmic changes in society (in the form of social unrest, terrorism, revolutions, etc.) and environment (through extreme and erratic climates) is not conducive for a prosperous business environment. For a business to exist sustainably, it is important that its practices are also sustainable.

There are companies that attempt to acknowledge this interdependency. Fairphone[61], an Amsterdam based social enterprise, designs smart-phones that do not contain "conflict minerals". Conflict minerals are those natural resources that have been mined or sourced from an area where conflicts occur, and the trade in these minerals are known to fund these conflicts. Smart-phones made by Fairphone are easier to repair and upgrade, thereby increasing the durability of the product. The company not only ensure that fair labor conditions are provided for its employees, it also ensures that such conditions are provided to all people working on the supply chain. A Fairphone factsheet says, *"We're making a positive impact across the value chain in mining, design, manufacturing and life cycle, while expanding the market for products that put ethical values first."*[62]

MANAGING REPUTATION

Liquified Petroleum Gas (LPG) is increasingly being used as a fuel for cooking. Traditional methods of cooking, especially, if done within closed spaces and without ventilation, is hazardous for human health, due to the smoke produced. LPG and related modern appliances reduces exposure to such pollution and helps to control and manipulate the output of heat. However, using LPG amd other forms of non-renewable fuels has its disadvantages too, whereas traditional methods has some advantages: The photograph below (**Figure 2.8**) indicates one such advantage – the replenishability of the fuel or material used for burning.

61 More details about Fairphone can be accessed in the section on case-studies/ caselets.

62 https://www.fairphone.com/wp-content/uploads/2016/01/Fairphone-factsheet-EN.pdf, Accessed on March 5, 2016.

Figure 2.8

Leaves of the coconut-tree are easily available in tropical regions.

Some of the parameters that may be considered to ascertain the suitability of a "cooking fuel" are:

(a) Ease of use.

(b) Replenishability and renewability of the fuel or material, which is used for burning.

(c) Availability and accessibility of the fuel or material, which is used for burning.

(d) Monetary cost or price of the fuel or material, which is used for burning.

(e) Transportation distance (from source of collection or extraction, to user-location), and its environmental impact.

(f) Method of collecting or extracting the fuel or material, and its environmental impact.

(g) Safety aspects, during transportation and burning.

(h) Pollution caused while burning (or cooking with) the fuel/ material, and its impact on human health.

(i) Maintenance expenses related to safety, optimum burning, etc.

Even after considering the above and other related factors, one may continue to prefer LPG for cooking, for various reasons, including impacts related to health. Those preferring traditional methods of cooking, application of simple technologies such as less-smokey "smokeless" stoves, choosing a non-enclosed open space as the place for cooking, cooking in an area where there is free-flow of air, not being in close physical proximity to the area of burning (and thus smoke), etc., has been found to be beneficial and helpful.

With increased availability of relevant information, the citizen is empowered to make and influence purchase choices. In this context, the reputation of a company can significantly affect the purchase decision of a buyer. Being and doing good is an important parameter for an organization to manage its reputation.

GoodGuide.com, an e-commerce website gives independent ratings to more than 250,000 products in its website on parameters related to health impact, environmental impact and social impact. This rating, ranging between 0-10, helps the consumer to purchase products that are friendly to health, society and environment (**Refer figure 2.9**)[63]. The firms that give focus on improving on these parameters receive a higher rating. A higher rating positively affects the reputation of the companies. GoodGuide.com is also an e-commerce site where the consumers can make online purchases.

Figure 2.8[64]

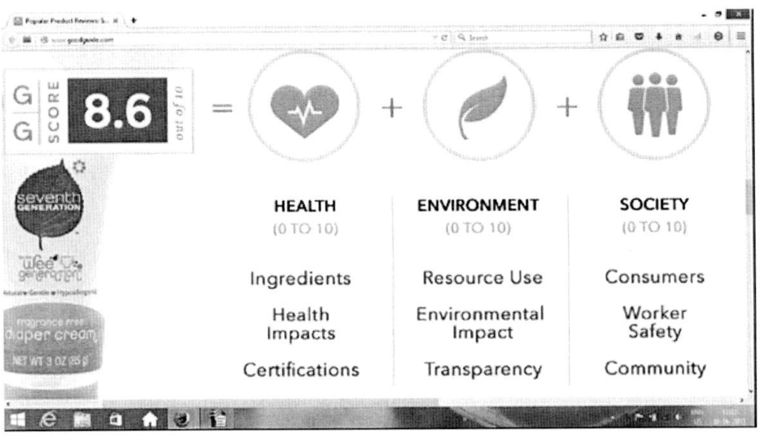

63 As of June 2017, GoodGuide has been focusing on the 'Health' parameter.

64 Included with permission.

The "Business Case" for CSR

Observations have been made that CSR activities can be due to 'enlightened self-interest'. The CEO of a Canadian paper company states, "*Paper and cardboard come from processing trees, using chemicals, energy and water. Recycling one product to make another reduces the pressure on natural resources. Our 'forest' is urban — it's in the recycling bin.*"[65]

Businesses are also looking at responsibility practices as a way to reduce operational costs. As per a survey, 87% of business organisations from India that participated in the survey, cited 'cost management' as one of the drivers to engage in responsibility practices[66]. At a global level, 67% businesses cited this as a reason.

There have been studies indicating that practices in Corporate Social Responsibility can result in better financial performance for the companies. Project ROI[67], a study undertaken to measure the benefits of environmental, social and governance (ESG) programmes to businesses, indicated that the corporate responsibility activities of large, publicly traded companies can provide the following benefits:

- Enhanced wealth creation for shareholders
- Increased stock market valuation
- Reduction in the cost of equity
- Reduction in share price risk
- Reduction in systematic risk
- Reduction in cost of debt
- Increased sales revenues
- Increased price premium
- Increased customer satisfaction and loyalty
- Reduced consumer defection
- A higher brand and reputation value
- Enhanced HR productivity
- Reduction in employee turnover
- Increased employee engagement

65 https://davidsuzuki.org/story/cascades-canadas-first-recycled-paper-products-company/, Accessed on January 13, 2017.

66 https://www.grantthornton.global/globalassets/1.-member-firms/global/insights/article-pdfs/2014/ibr2014_ibr_csr_web.pdf, Accessed on February 19, 2018.

67 Project ROI: Defining the Competitive and Financial Advantages of Corporate Responsibility and Sustainability, http://projectroi.com/, Accessed on March 5, 2016.

CSR initiatives can help the organization in a number of ways. However, those benefits may emerge only if the organization maintains high standards in other parameters such as quality of products, efficiency in operations etc. High standards in CSR practices, is a necessary while not a sufficient reason, for organizational excellence. The CEO of an investment management company says, "*Companies must benefit all of their stakeholders, including shareholders, employees, customers, and the communities in which they operate. Without a sense of purpose, no company, either public or private, can achieve its full potential...*"[68]

As per the survey mentioned earlier, 81% of the businesses in India cited 'right thing to do' as a key driver for sustainability practices, while in Japan it was 92%. The survey report states that "*The majority of businesses are prepared to take an altruistic leadership position on the adoption of more sustainable business practices.*"[69]

To read, for the well-being of all, is ennobling...

You may take a break...

CONCEPTS RELATED TO CSR

Aakashasya Sthithiryavad
yaavangca jagat sthithi:
Taavanmama sthithirbhooya
Jagad-dukhani nighnatha:
For as long as space endures,

and for as long as living beings remain,
until then may I too abide,
to dispel the misery of the world.

—Shantideva, an 8th century Buddhist scholar who studied at Nalanda[70].

Corporate Social Responsibility has been a topic that has generated academic

68 https://www.blackrock.com/corporate/en-no/investor-relations/larry-fink-ceo-letter, Accessed on February 19, 2018.

69 http://www.grantthornton.at/files/GTI%20IBR/corporate-social-responsibility-beyond-financials.pdf, Accessed on February 19, 2018.

70 Nalanda, located in the state of Bihar in India, had a thriving learning centre in ancient times, and had students from various regions of Asia.

and practitioner interest. It has been mentioned that businesses need to consider the economic, legal, ethical, and discretionary/ philanthropic responsibilities[71].

Creating Shared Value

In 2011, in the context of 'reinvent capitalism', Micheal Porter and Mark Kramer wrote about 'Creating Shared Value' (CSV)[72]. The authors are critical about the organizations' focus on short-term financial performance. They ponder, *"How else could companies overlook the well-being of their customers, the depletion of natural resources vital to their businesses, the viability of key suppliers, or the economic distress of the communities in which they produce and sell? How else could companies think that simply shifting activities to locations with ever lower wages was a sustainable "solution" to competitive challenges?"*

Porter and Kamer suggested CSV, which is about economic value creation in a manner that creates value for society by addressing the needs and challenges of the society. The authors communicate that CSV is not identical to social responsibility, philanthropy or sustainability, and also advocates that the purpose of a for-profit company can be re-defined as creating shared value, and not just profit per se.

Limits To Growth

The Worldwatch Institute states,

"With a global population of over 7 billion and growing, the need to preserve ecosystems is undeniable. Yet, for many products, the growth of consumption is reaching new levels:

- Global meat production has more than quadrupled in the last half century to over 308 million tons in 2013, bringing with it considerable environmental and health costs due to its large-scale draw on water, feed-grains, antibiotics, and grazing land.
- Coffee production has doubled since the early 1960s. However, an estimated 25 million coffee growers worldwide are at the mercy of extreme price volatility.
- For more than 50 years, global plastic production has continued to rise,

71 Archie B. Carroll and Kareem M. Shabana, The Business Case for Corporate Social Responsibility: A Review of Concepts, Research and Practice, International Journal of Management Reviews, 2010.

72 Michael E Porter, Mark R Kramer, Creating Shared Value, Harvard Business Review, January-February 2011.

with 299 million tons of plastics produced in 2013 alone. Recycling rates remain low, however, and the majority of plastics end up in landfills and oceans - polluting ecosystems, entangling wildlife, and blighting communities.

- *The world's fleet of automobiles now surpasses 1 billion, with each vehicle contributing greenhouse gases and reducing air quality."*[73]

The financial media discusses and debates multi-year plans of companies to accelerate growth in revenues and profits. However, the advocates of the idea of 'limits to growth' communicates that it may not be feasible to consider perpetual growth, considering the finiteness of planetary resources. "*Consumers often do not know the full footprint of the products they are buying, such as the embedded water in a t-shirt or steak, the pesticide exposure of cotton farmers, or the local devastation caused by timber companies cutting down forests to produce paper,*" says Michael Renner, Project Director - Vital Signs, Worldwatch Institute[74] (**Refer Figure 2.10**).

Figure 2.10

Cartoon by Alexandre Magnin - https://www.sustainabilityillustrated.com

The finite nature of many of the existing life supporting systems has led many to ponder on the concept of 'Limit to Growth'. There have been

73 http://www.worldwatch.org/global-consumption-trends-break-new-records, Accessed on May 17, 2016.

74 http://www.worldwatch.org/global-consumption-trends-break-new-records, Accessed on May 17, 2016.

calls for a relook at the prevalent economic systems, and to reorient economic systems that improve well-being, while restoring the planet's life supporting systems. Erik Assadourian, Senior Fellow - Worldwatch Institute, says, "*Degrowth is the intentional redirection of economies away from the perpetual pursuit of growth. For economies beyond the limits of their ecosystems, this includes a planned and controlled contraction to get back in line with planetary boundaries, with the eventual creation of a steady-state economic system that is in balance with Earth's limits.*"[75]

Such thinking calls for delinking economic growth from societal and individual well-being. From a 'corporate social responsibility' perspective, 'limits to growth' is about:

- acknowledging the finiteness of planetary resources,
- a re-orientation to quality of living, rather than quantity of consumption,
- an assessment on the optimal size for an organization,
- letting go the myth of perpetual organisational growth,
- on whether an organization needs to go dormant or discontinue its businesses, etc.

Triple Bottom-line

Triple Bottom-line is a reporting framework that measure social and environmental impact of a company, in addition to its financial performance. It is also referred to as TBL, 3BL, 'People, Planet, Profit' etc. An article in *The Economist* says, "*In some senses the TBL is a particular manifestation of the balanced scorecard. Behind it lies the same fundamental principle: what you measure is what you get, because what you measure is what you are likely to pay attention to. Only when companies measure their social and environmental impact will we have socially and environmentally responsible organisations.*"[76]

Table 2.2 have quotes from few companies indicating their triple bottom-line operating philosophy.

75 http://erikassadourian.com/wp-content/uploads/2013/07/The-Path-to-Degrowth.pdf, Accessed on May 17, 2016.

76 http://www.economist.com/node/14301663, Accessed on June 3, 2015.

Table 2.2

Name of the company	Quotes exemplifying triple bottom-line
Better World Books	"'Better World Books' is among a unique and growing group of triple bottom line companies who understand that *profit* is not the only way to measure business success. People also matter. And so does the planet on which we all live. For Better World Books, the triple bottom line comes in lots of forms. From helping to build a nursing library in Somaliland to offering customers carbon neutral shipping on every book they buy, doing good is not just a part of Better World Books' business - it *is* the business."[77]
One Earth Designs	"'One Earth Designs' seeks to create complete design solutions that integrate principles of social, environmental and financial longevity. We work towards creating positive impact in every stage of the product life cycle: from selecting high quality sustainable raw materials and working closely with responsible manufacturers, to maximizing product durability and recyclability, we strive to bring the greatest value of our products to users."[78]
Yes Bank	"'Yes Bank' has set new benchmarks in the Indian Banking sector, especially in the Triple Bottom Line accounting and reporting. As triple bottom line accounting becomes mainstream, the Bank believes that an integrated view on reporting – which looks at financial, human, social & relationship, natural, intellectual and manufactured capital, is the way forward."[79]

77 http://www.betterworldbooks.com/info.aspx?f=bottomlines, Accessed on May 25, 2015.

78 https://www.oneearthdesigns.com/about/philosophy-sustainability/, Accessed on May 25, 2015.

79 https://www.yesbank.in/banking-initiatives/responsible-banking/transparency-and-accounting/triple-bottom-line-sustainability-disclosure, Accessed on March 29, 2018.

Stakeholder Perspective

An important development in the corporate world has been the increased focus given to the needs of all stakeholders, rather than an exclusive focus on the needs of shareholders. There is increased acknowledgement that all stakeholders (such as employees, suppliers, customers) have a share in the prosperity of the company, and prominence need not be given to the investors. The emergence of this perspective has contributed to the increased popularity of employee stock options, social and environmental outreach activities, and public service campaigns.

Taking decisions from a stakeholder perspective involves looking at a scenario from varied perspectives. In a situation of decision-making, the decision-maker explore how decisions will made by varied entities (**Refer Figure 2.11**). This broadened vision helps the decision maker to make a decision that contributes to the greater common good.

Figure 2.11[80]

Decision-making from a stakeholder perspective

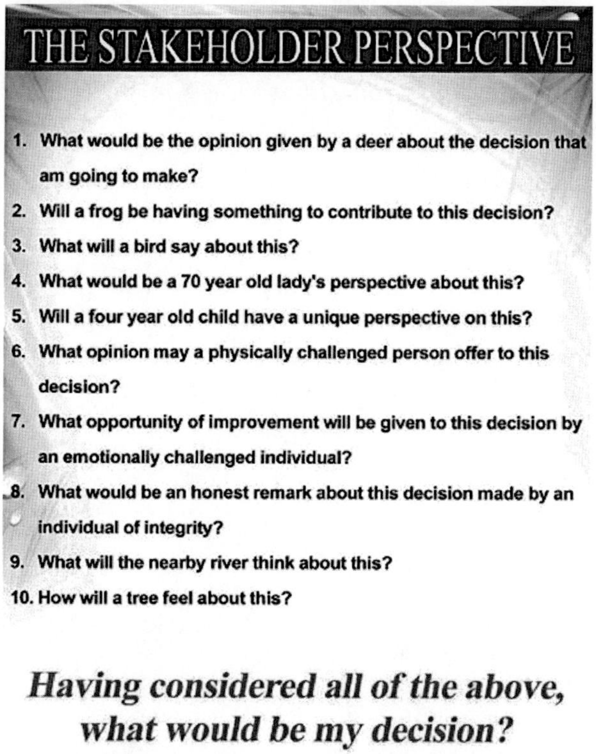

80 Image made available in the public domain by the author.

A stakeholder perspective will naturally emerge in organisation when there is an attitude to serve. Stephen Covey, author of the popular book, *'The 7 Habits of Highly Effective People'* and consultant, says, "*Spiritual-based leaders respect others and are guided by the fundamental ethic: service to others comes before serving one's self. From an existential perspective, the raison d'être of organisations is to serve human needs... Individuals and organisations grow when they give themselves to others. Relationships improve when there is a focus on serving the other, be it at the level of the individual, the family, the organisation, the community, the society, or all of humanity.*"[81]

A stakeholder perspective may include the well-being of non-human creations and, or, of the well-being of generations that are not yet born. For example, Compassionate Choices Pvt. Ltd. offers dairy-free ice-creams named 'White Cub' (www.whitecub.in), in varied flavours such as chocolate, butterscotch, strawberry, coffee, mango, hazelnut, blueberry etc.

Spiritual Values/ Human Values as the basis for leadership in CSR

Drawing attention to the connect between 'God' and 'Work', the executive director, Institute for Faith, Work & Economics, asks, "*What are companies and corporations for? Are they primarily vehicles for employment, or investment, or another purpose?*"[82]

People find meaningfulness in a number of endeavours - work related endeavours, interpersonal relationships, volunteering, engagement with societal causes etc. For many, spirituality is an important aspect of their lives. Yet, for varied reasons, they may not be inclined to the idea of an alignment between spirituality and business leadership. The co-founders of 'Global Dharma Center'[83] says, "*Many people see life as a pie, with different slices belonging to family, personal time, health, learning, work, and spirituality/ religion. We see it differently. We think of the pie of life as ALL spiritual, rather than spirituality being only one slice. Therefore family, personal time, health, learning, and work are all spiritual activities.*"[84] They also state that spiritual

81 Quotations extracted from the public knowledge base of the "Spiritual Based Leadership Research Programme" are © 2006 by the Global Dharma Center (GDC). GDC retains the copyright to all excerpts from this knowledge base.

82 https://tifwe.org/christians-in-business-the-triple-bottom-line-through-a-biblical-lens/, Accessed on November 20, 2018.

83 www.globaldharma.org

84 http://www.globaldharma.org/Files%20-%20Adobe%20Acrobat/SBW/!Book%201%20Put%20Your%20Spirituality%20to%20Work%20-%20The%20Basics.pdf, Accessed on July 26, 2016.

values are human values[85]. Considering spirituality and human values as the foundational, fundamental or being the essence of the varied activities (**Refer Figure 2.12**), contributes to a shift in an outlook about work.

Figure 2.12

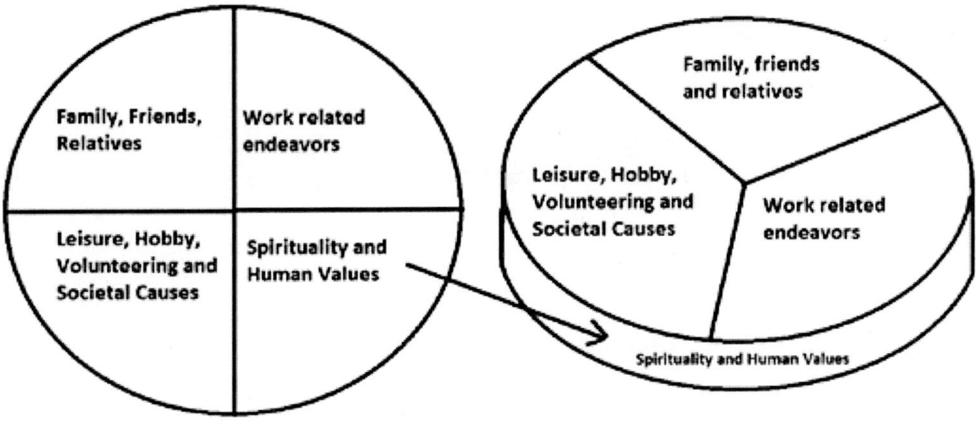

André Delbecq, Professor and Director of the Institute for Spirituality and Organizational Leadership at the Santa Clara University School of Business detail this by saying, *"I think a business exists to provide an innovative and compelling answer to a societal need in the form of a needed service or product... When this purpose is approached through a spiritual lens, it will be shaped differently in many ways... You become willing to let go of many trivial and opportunistic concerns, and instead increasingly put energy into important challenges. The transformational system you create to receive inputs and transform outputs will also shift, allowing greater attention to stewardship, justice and inclusiveness of the concerns of all stakeholders. The character of the organisation's culture will shift. The relational culture of the organisation will be more attentive to the gifts of all, and compassionate regarding each person's needs. Your own willingness as a business leader to endure the mystery of suffering will shift... You will see all the elements of business challenges as part of a calling to service. Because of this deeper perspective regarding the nature of business, a sense of patience and a greater willingness to endure hardship unfolds..."*[86]

85 http://www.globaldharma.org/Files%20-%20Adobe%20Acrobat/SBW/Basics%20 1.08%20Spiritual%20Values%20are%20Human%20Values.pdf, Accessed on March 29, 2018.

86 Quotations extracted from the public knowledge base of the "Spiritual Based Leadership Research Programme" are © 2006 by the Global Dharma Center (GDC). GDC retains the copyright to all excerpts from this knowledge base.

A similar perspective is shared by Stephen Covey. Covey speaks about universal principles as the basis and guiding factor in all the life dimensions of a leader. When spirituality/ human values/ universal principles becomes fundamental principles of a business practice, including leadership in CSR, *"the moral language of the mind witnesses the emergence of responsibility, the emotional language of the heart witnesses the emergence of love, and the spiritual language of the soul witnesses the emergence of compassion and unity."*[87]

The 'I-IT' and 'I-THOU' approach

Spiritual traditions have given clues on respecting the inherent worth of anything. In an article reminiscing about a disciple's experiences with Sathya Sai Baba, a spiritual teacher from India, the disciple writes, *"Once he asked me to shut the inner interview room door. I stretched myself, applied full force and shut the door. He at once reacted and said, '...why so much force? Excessive force is violence. Do not treat this as a door; it is nothing but consciousness. Remember, energy, food, money and time are God. You must learn to respect them.'"*[88]

The 'I-It' and 'I-Thou' concept was propounded by Martin Buber, a Jewish philosopher born in Austria. The 'I-It' and 'I-Thou' are expressions of how we relate. 'It' refers to an object, while 'Thou' means 'you', and is used in a sacred sense while referring to God, during prayers, etc.[89] When we relate to others, objectifying them as an instrument that we can make use of, such a relationship is referred to as an 'I-It' relationship. When we relate to others, respecting their divinity, such a relationship is referred to as an 'I-Thou' relationship.

One of the companies that attempted to evoke a 'I-Thou' relationship in business is 'Toms of Maine'. Toms of Maine was founded by Tom Chappell and his wife, Kate Chappell. The company was founded in 1970 and by early 1980s, it was growing at an annual rate of 25 percent[90]. However, Tom Chappell felt a yearning for a qualitative transformation in the way business was done. While on a sabbatical at 'Harvard Divinity School', he got introduced to the philosophy of Martin Buber, and the I-Thou

87 An adaption from a quote given by Peter Pruzan and Kirsten Pruzan Mikkelsen, available at https://www.lifepositive.com/the-spirituality-of-business/, Accessed on July 26, 2016.

88 http://www.theprasanthireporter.org/2013/06/baba-as-i-saw-him/, Accessed on June 15, 2016.

89 Thou' is usually used in prose related to Christian church. 'Thou' has similarities with the Sanskrit word 'Twam' (Twameva prathyaksham brahmaasi).

90 http://www.nytimes.com/1996/12/22/magazine/god-and-toothpaste.html, Accessed on June 20, 2016.

relationship. Tom Chappel started developing interest in creating an I-Thou culture at 'Toms of Maine'. Efforts of many years resulted in Toms of Maine emerging as a company admired by many.

The company do not test its products on animals or use animal ingredients.[91] Employees can give five percent of their work hours (12 days annually) towards volunteering and service activities. The company donate 10% of its profits to projects that benefit the planet and its inhabitants.[92] It also do not use any artificial colours, flavors, fragrance or preservatives in its products.[93] The company also shares details of ingredients in its products in the company website[94]. Tom Chappel says, "T*he ultimate goal of business is not profit. Profit is merely a means toward the ultimate aim of affirming the health and dignity of human beings and their families, affirming aspirations of the community and affirming the health of the environment -- the common good.*"[95]

Servant Leadership and the Inverted Pyramid Model

Servant Leadership is a leadership practice that focuses on service, in contrast to leadership practices that focus on exercising authority. Srvant leadership has been supported by religious scriptures, including Bible, which narrates the communication by Jesus Christ to his disciples emphasising the importance of service[96] (**Refer Figure 2.13**). Robert Greenleaf, who popularised the concept of Servant Leadership, mentions that an aspiration to lead, emerges from the practice and natural feeling to serve.

---

91 http://www.tomsofmaine.com/products/overlay/Product-Certification, Accessed on August 26, 2016.

92 http://www.tomsofmaine.com/goodness-report/community, Accessed on August 26, 2016.

93 http://www.tomsofmaine.com/products, Accessed on August 26, 2016.

94 http://www.tomsofmaine.com/products/ingredient-list, Accessed on August 26, 2016.

95 http://www.nytimes.com/1996/12/22/magazine/god-and-toothpaste.html, Accessed on June 20, 2016.

96 Mark 10: 42-45. The Amplifeid Bible says, "Calling them to Himself, Jesus said to them, "You know that those who are recognized as rulers of the Gentiles lord it over them; and their powerful men exercise authority over them [tyrannizing them]. But this is not how it is among you; instead, whoever wishes to become great among you must be your servant, and whoever wishes to be first and most important among you must be slave of all. For even the Son of Man did not come to be served, but to serve, and to give His life as a [a] ransom for many."".

Figure 2.13[97]

Nordstrom, a retail chain based in USA, has been known for its high quality customer service.[98] This company has also been known for its servant leadership practices. Ken Blanchard, author of many books related to leadership says, *"My daughter, Debbie..., ...worked at Nordstrom when she was in college. After she was there a week or so, she came to me and said, 'Dad, I have a strange boss.' When I asked what was strange about him, she said, 'At least two or three times a day he comes to me and asks if there is anything he can do to help me. He acts like he works for me.' And I said, 'That's exactly what he does. He sounds like a servant leader.' Nordstrom understands that their number one customer is their people - that's why Debbie's boss was acting as if he worked for Debbie. He was giving her the responsibility to serve their number two customer - people who shop in the store. Servant leaders know if they take care of their people and empower them, their people will go out of their way to take care of the customers."*[99]

Operationalisation of servant leadership model is reflected in the inverted pyramid operating model at Nordstrom where the customer comes on top of the pyramid (usually, in a hierarchical chart, the CEO occupies the top slot). Michelle de Haaff, writes in a blog, *"Tacked to the wall in the backroom of every store, the 'Inverted Pyramid' puts the frontline - those who interact with the customer every day - at the 'top' of the organizational hierarchy. Everyone at*

97 Included with permission. (c) SSCM, by Jeanne Ambre, SS.C.M. (www.sscm.org)

98 http://tompeters.com/columns/service-with-a-smile-and-for-a-profit/, Accessed on August 17, 2016.

99 https://howwelead.org/2016/04/27/understanding-servant-leadership-2/, Accessed on June 22, 2016.

Nordstrom starts at the 'top', including its executives. Even if you're a Nordstrom family member or a VP brought in with a particular expertise, you start on the floor, interacting with customers."[100] The next in the hierarchical pyramid are those people who serve the customer, which is, the sales personnel. This is followed by the employees who support them. Finally, at the bottom of the pyramid is the top management of the company. When an employee gets promoted at Nordstrom, they move down through the hierarchy.

An intern at Nordstrom, says, "*As a servant leader you wouldn't ask your team to do something you would never do... Nordstrom relies heavily on servant leadership in order to have a good team who is willing to provide excellent customer service."*[101] In the book *'The Nordstrom Way to Customer Service Excellence'*, Patrick McCarthy, who've been with Nordstrom for more than 30 years, say, *"Never judge a book by its cover, open it up. If you treat a kid who is buying a $19.95 belt the same as a businessman buying a $1,995 Oxford suit, you will be successful. That kid might become a customer for life"*.

To read, which ennobles oneself, is educative...

You may take a break...

STRATEGIC CSR

"Our responsibility as leaders is not about making the company survive for even the next few years. Our responsibility is to insure that the company will survive and thrive for the next 120 years. When you begin to think this way, you are really entering into the spirit of family, into the spirit of a multi-cultural environment, and into the spirit of humanity as a whole."[102]

Ramon Olle, President, Epson Europe

Strategic CSR refers to the practice of aligning CSR activities with an organisation's vision, mission and objectives. The firm thus identifies responsibility endeavours that go beyond the creation of goodwill and altruism. Creation of a CSR practice that is strategic and sustainable

100 http://blog.medallia.com/customer-experience/ceo-top-pyramid/, Accessed on June 9, 2015.

101 http://emilydonato.blogspot.in/2013/06/nordstrom-culture.html, Accessed on June 9, 2015.

102 http://www.globaldharma.org/Files%20-%20Adobe%20Acrobat/SBW/SBL%203.13%20Fuelling%20a%20Positive%20Future.pdf

invites a fundamental relook into the prevailing business models, and how organizations need to design innovative business models.

A SustainAbility report states, "*To date, many companies have realized the merits of modifying their products and processes to become more sustainable. Acknowledging the business benefits of improved product performance, some have revamped their offerings to be more effective, more efficient and produced with safer, 'greener' materials. Other companies have rethought their processes - for example, by utilizing renewable energy sources in production or enhancing performance and trust through various certifications. But, these innovations will only get us so far. What we need are not just better products and processes, but fundamentally different business models. We need companies and industries whose underlying structures are, at worst, zero negative impact, and at best, contributing to the regeneration and restoration of natural, human and social capital.*"[103]

Creating competitive advantage through CSR

Instant noodles have been a popular food product category. In India, through almost three decades, Maggi, a product from Nestle, became the prominent brand and had more than three-fourth of the market-share till 2015[104][105]. The mid 2010s witnessed the emergence of brands such as 'Patanjali Ayurved'.

Patanjali offered some of its products at a pricing lesser than the market leaders and mentioned that all their profits will go to charitable causes[106][107]. Patanjali Ayurved not only practiced 'cost leadership' over its competitors by keeping the price of its products lower, it also differentiated itself from competitors through communicating health benefits. For example, the attribute of Patanjali noodles containing more of wheat flour (*atta*, also referred to as 'whole wheat flour') and less of 'refined flour' (*maida*). Patanjali also produced biscuits that did not use 'refined flour' (*Maida* is

103 http://www.sustainability.com/library/model-behavior#.VYWJNEYpk3s, Accessed on June 20, 2015.

104 http://www.business-standard.com/article/companies/post-ban-maggi-noodles-still-no-1-despite-ceding-large-market-share-116022200412_1.html, Accessed on May 21, 2016.

105 http://www.livemint.com/Companies/XAJp4bSt3OwEWRl8D14soK/ITCs-Yippee-looks-to-step-in-to-fill-Maggi-void.html, Accessed on May 21, 2016.

106 http://economictimes.indiatimes.com/industry/cons-products/fmcg/how-baba-ramdev-has-built-a-rs-2000-crore-ayurvedic-fmcg-empire-plans-to-take-on-multinational-giants/articleshow/47657636.cms, Accessed on May 21, 2016.

107 http://www.thehindubusinessline.com/companies/baba-ramdev-the-monk-who-can-own-a-fleet-of-ferraris-but-wont/article7743772.ece, Accessed on May 21, 2016.

considered unhealthy[108]). Patanjali noodles used rice-bran oil instead of palm oil, though rice bran oil was costlier in comparison with palm oil.

The organization also popularised niche products such as juices of *amla* (gooseberry) and aloe vera. "*Humare yahaan crore ki salary paane waala koi vyakti nahee hai (We do not have any one earning crores as salary),*" says Baba Ramdev, the brand ambassador of Patanjali Ayurved[109]. Patanjali Ayurved is an example of how competitive advantage is created by an organisation through its social responsibility practices and communication. Social responsibility - in terms of healthy products, donating their profits to charitable causes, affordable pricing etc. - resulted in Patanjali Ayurved charting meteoric growth.

CSR can create competitive advantage in a number of ways:

- Increased mindshare amongst potential consumers, and this may result in increased market-share.
- A company that chooses not to exploit the consumers by overcharging on the product can create 'cost leadership'.
- Improvement in quality and processes can result in differentiation in products and non-product businesses.
- Attempts to recognise the needs of people, especially for groups that are not served by existing organizations, can lead to discovery of niche markets.

Effect of CSR on current and future regulatory practices

Less regulation in business environment facilitates operational freedom and space for innovation for businesses. When the stakeholders perceive that the organizations are not adding value to the society, they will strengthen their demand for regulation.

An example is the 'Occupy Wall Street' movement that started in 2011 in US, in the aftermath of the global financial crisis. This movement represented "*the 99% that will no longer tolerate the greed and corruption of the 1%*"[110]. With reference to the for-profit world of business, the goals of 'Occupy Wall Street' movement included a reduction in the influence of corporations

108 http://www.thehindu.com/news/cities/Madurai/parottas-loaded-with-danger-say-docs/article5014841.ece, Accessed on June 13, 2017.

109 http://www.businesstoday.in/magazine/corporate/baba-ramdevs-patanjali-ayurved-forays-into-indias-rs-5300-crore-instant-noodles-market/story/226011.html, Accessed on May 21, 2016.

110 http://occupywallst.org/, Accessed on May 24, 2016.

(for-profit organisations) on politics, and reforms in the banking sector. 'Occupy Wall Street' movement attracted media headlines and also resulted in discussions about financial regulation. Another example could be the increased demand for regulating the automobile industry. Emissions from automobiles are contributing to climate change and pollution, which is hazardous to health. Air pollution in Delhi and some of the cities in India has been amongst the worst in the world. In December 2015, Supreme Court of India temporarily banned the sale of diesel cars in Delhi region if these cars have an engine capacity of 2,000 cc or more. In May 2016, the National Green Tribunal (NGT) imposed a similar rule in Kerala.

Organizations that maintain the highest standards in responsibility practices have the potential to influence and inspire societal stakeholders. They may also be invited by regulatory authorities to give their perspectives when a new regulation is being created. A higher weightage and regard will be given to the perspectives of those organizations known for setting higher standards in greater common good. Their practices will soon become the norm for the industry.

Giving a "green" certification or an environment-friendly attribution to an airport is debated (imagine the power consumption of an airport – air-conditioning, lighting...)[111]. Yet, in 2015, Cochin International Airport Limited (CIAL) was showcased in the India pavilion at the Paris Climate Change Summit, COP21[112]. This was because CIAL is the first airport in the world to be full powered by solar energy. Similar initiatives, of generating and using solar based electricity, have now been replicated by many airports, and governmental authorities have been asking other airports to replicate the practice[113]. India has the largest number of carbon-neutral certified airports in the Asia-Pacific region. Kempegowda International Airport (Bangalore), Indira Gandhi International Airport (Delhi), Rajiv

111 During FY 2018-19, the total electricity consumption by Mumbai International Airport Limited (MIAL) amounted to 3,98,106.69 GJ (as reported in the 2020 sustainability report). This is equivalent to almost 110,585,277 kwh, which is the energy required to power more than a lakh rural Indian homes (110,585) annually, if the annual consumption of a rural Indian home is considered as 1000 kwh. If the annual consumption of a rural Indian home is considered as 500 kwh, then the power consumption equivalent to the power consumed by MIAL would be able to power more than two lakh homes. There are debates and discussions about the efficacy and effectiveness of green ratings. Platinum green ratings have been accorded to transportation projects involving underground construction and "deep excavation"s.

112 http://www.newindianexpress.com/cities/kochi/Kochi-Airport-Awaits-a-Paris-Recognition/2015/12/01/article3155125.ece, Accessed on May 24, 2016.

113 http://www.newindianexpress.com/cities/chennai/Chennai-Airport-set-to-go-Solar-shave-off-Rs-8-crore-from-power-bill/2016/05/19/article3439992.ece, Accessed on May 24, 2016.

Gandhi International Airport (Hyderabad), and the Chatrapati Shivaji International Airport (Mumbai) are carbon-neutral certified airports[114].

Conventional and Strategic Philanthropy

The word 'Philanthropy', from its Greek roots (*Phil, Anthropo*), means 'Love for Humans'. Philanthropy has been in existence for centuries (*Refer the section about Anaathapindika in Chapter I*). People have been engaged in philanthropy for a number of reasons. Charity has been promoted by rationalist and religious organisations. A quote by Robert Green Ingersoll, also popularised by Mother Theresa and Sri Sathya Sai Baba, *"Hands that help are holier than lips that pray"*[115], communicates the importance of service (**Refer Figure 2.14**).

Figure 2.14[116]

114 http://www.airportcarbonaccreditation.org/airport/participants/asia-pacific.html, Accessed on June 13, 2016. These airports (similar to some of the other international airports in other countries) were certified "carbon-neutral" by the "Airport Carbon Accreditation" programme of the 'Airports Council International Europe', which is part of 'Airports Council International', an association of airport operators. While the programme had its beginnings in June 2009, the websites (https://www.airportcarbonaccreditation.org/, https://airportco2.org/), as of September 2019, is yet to provide details of carbon-emission levels (pre-certification, on receiving certification, existing), reduction in CO2e emissions pre-and-post certification, carbon-offsets (quality standard, amount) etc., for each of the participating and certified airports.

115 http://infidels.org/library/historical/robert_ingersoll/stage_children.html, http://www.saibaba.ws/quotes/service.htm, http://nextbillion.net/cracking-the-code-on-affordable-health-care-part-1/, Accessed on July 28, 2016.

116 Copyright with Kevin Spear; Included with permission.

Business leaders acknowledge that there is more to life beyond the material. Richard Branson, an entrepreneur and investor, says, *"'Stuff' really is not what brings happiness. Family, friends, good health and the satisfaction that comes from making a positive difference are what really matters."*[117] An Indian-American businessman and philanthropist, says, *"Service to others seems the only intelligent choice for the use of wealth. The other choices especially personal consumption seems either useless or harmful."*[118] Philanthropic giving, many a times, was spontaneous and was more about fulfilment. Michael Bloomberg, founder and CEO of Bloomberg LP, a global financial data company, says, *"One of the senior managers at my company, Bloomberg LP, recently told me that part of his new hires recruiting pitch is to ask, 'What other company can you work for where the owner gives nearly all the profits to charity?' Nothing has ever made me prouder of my company than that one story"*[119].

In the recent times, there have been discussions and practices on linking philanthropy with specific societal goals that are measurable. David Rockefeller says, *"Philanthropists, at their best, try to address serious societal problems and occasionally come up with innovations that lead to enduring change."*[120] Organizational philanthropy is moving beyond the practice of just giving money. Lee Ballin, Head - Sustainable business programs, Bloomberg, says, *"We're at a tipping point for CSR where philanthropy is no longer just about giving money. It's about sharing the skills your company has inside its offices to help non-profits beyond financial empowerment."*[121] While many continue to find fulfilment in making a spontaneous contribution, some business leaders prefer to make planned decisions to their philanthropic giving and ask guiding questions. Eli[122] and Edythe Broad, in 'The Giving Pledge', writes,

"Before we invest in something, we ask ourselves three questions that guide our decision:

---

117 http://givingpledge.org/pdf/pledge-letters/Branson_Letter.pdf, Accessed on May 21, 2015.

118 http://givingpledge.org/pdf/pledge-letters/Bhargava_Letter.pdf, Accessed on May 21, 2015.

119 http://givingpledge.org/pdf/pledge-letters/Bloomberg_Letter.pdf, Accessed on May 21, 2015.

120 http://givingpledge.org/pdf/pledge-letters/Rockefeller_Letter.pdf, Accessed on May 24, 2016.

121 http://www.prweek.com/article/1345038/csr-roundtable-purposeful-pursuit, Accessed on June 7, 2015.

122 Eli Broad is the only person to build two Fortune 500 companies in two different industries.

1. Will this happen without us? If so, we don't invest.
2. Will it make a difference 20 or 30 years from now?
3. *Is the leadership in place to make it happen?*

Philanthropy is hard work. Many people think it's easy to give money away. But we are not giving money away. We want our wealth to make a measurable impact."[123]

A report from a consulting company mentions that *"Philanthropists cite a lack of accountability as the biggest obstacle to giving... Many HNWIs (High Net Worth Individuals) feel that there is a lack of easily available financial information about charitable organisations, leading to concerns about both inefficiency and misuse of their money. For new donors to increase their contributions, the need for improved accountability and financial transparency must be addressed."*[124] It was during the presence of Gandhi in South Africa that the 'Natal Indian Congress' was founded. Gandhi writes in his autobiography[125], *"...we always insisted on the receipts being given. Every pie was thus clearly accounted for, and i dare say the account books for year 1894 can be found intact even today in the records of the Natal Indian Congress..."*.

There are organisations that make available financial and operational information in the public domain. A case in example is *Akshayapatra*, a non-profit organisation known for providing mid-day meal scheme to more than 1.5 million children. Akshayapatra operates on the public-private partnership model and receives subsidies from the state governments and central government of India, and also receives donations from citizens. Akshayapatra, which complies with 'International Financial Reporting Standards' (IFRS) since 2008-09[126], has been inducted into the 'Hall of Fame' of 'Institute of Chartered Accountants of India' (ICAI) for winning ICAI Gold Shield Award for 'Excellence in Financial Reporting' for five consecutive years starting 2008-09[127].

It could be inferred that the words "conventional" or "strategic" do not indicate the superiority or inferiority of one practice with reference to the other. In conventional philanthropy, wealth is shared without any strings attached to it, while in strategic philanthropy, the giver looks into the

---

123 http://givingpledge.org/pdf/pledge-letters/Broad_Letter.pdf, Accessed on May 21, 2015.

124 http://www.bain.com/Images/REPORT_India_Philanthropy_Report_2012.pdf, Accessed on May 21, 2015.

125 The *story of my experiments with truth.*

126 http://www.akshayapatra.org/financial-reports, Accessed on June 13, 2017.

127 https://www.akshayapatra.org/five-time-winner-icai-award, Accessed on May 21, 2015.

giving as an investment on the society, with returns expected in the form of increased social good. Both forms of philanthropy have the potential to contribute to the well-being of the society.

Monetary philanthropy can be practiced in various ways, and some of them are listed below:

a) Making one-time donations or grants to individuals and not-for-profit organisations affiliated with noble causes. For example, providing funds to an NGO to improve the means and facilities towards feeding the hungry.

b) Providing 'patient capital'. This is similar to any conventional investment in a for-profit company. The provider of the capital expects the receiver to return the investment along with the interest. However, the provider is willing to wait for a considerably longer time, as compared to the time that one may give for generating returns from conventional investments. Usually, such 'patient capital' investments are made in for-profit social enterprises, who would require more time to generate financial returns.

c) Providing capital at below market rates. The provider of the capital will charge a lower rate of interest, or no interest at all, when making the investment.

d) Socially Responsible Investing – This can be an investment made in equities primarily to influence a company to bring about changes in its operational practices towards greater common good.

Subhash Chandra, who co-created the Zee television network in India, also considers *Vipassana*, an ancient Buddhist meditation practice, as one of the reasons for his success. In 1997, Subhash Chandra gifted a thirteen acre land in Gorai, a sea-facing suburb of Mumbai, on which was constructed a temple – a golden pagoda replicating the 2,000-year-old Shwedagon Pagoda in Yangon, Burma (Myanmar). *"I had benefited so much from Vipassana, I felt it was important for many more people to be able to share the experience... Vipassana*[128] *taught me how to maintain equanimity in all situations of life. This has helped me tremendously in business, more so in the tough times...,"*[129]

128 Vipassana courses are offered in multiple locations (dhamma.org) in many countries. The article (refer the following footnote) says, *"The courses are free and funded solely by donations from past students. Mastering this art of meditation begins with a ten-day residential course... Students meditate for ten hours daily, starting at 4 a.m., and are required to adhere to a strict moral code... They take a vow of silence..."*.

129 Naazneen Karmali, "Subhash Chandra: Transcendental Billionaire", Forbes Asia, March 15, 2012.

says Chandra. It took more than a decade towards the construction of the Gorai pagoda, and is one of the world's largest hollow stone dome constructed without any supporting pillars. It was made using traditional techniques, with interlocking blocks of red sandstone, bonded together with lime mortar.

The Giving Pledge

The Giving Pledge is a global initiative promoted by Warren Buffet along with Bill and Melinda Gates by inviting billionaires of the world *"to commit to giving more than half of their wealth to philanthropy or charitable causes either during their lifetime or in their will"*[130]. Azim Premji, on joining this initiative, mentioned, *"I was deeply influenced by Gandhi's notion of holding one's wealth in trusteeship, to be used for the betterment of society and not as if one owned it"*[131].

Issues in the "business case" of social responsibility

Focusing on the 'business case' of CSR practices may be helpful in communicating the need for responsibility practices to those who are focused on the monetary profits of businesses. Building the business case may also help in improving the efficiency of the CSR processes. However, one may be skeptical on whether too much attention has been given to the "business case". A Google search on "business case for CSR" resulted in more than 30,000 results. A similar search in Google Scholar, which contains research based documents, gave more than 2,000 results. Some of the issues related to the focus on "business case" may be as follows:

- Investments that are necessary for the public good may not happen, because a "business case" cannot be build to justify those investments. *"Making the business case for sustainable development may be seen as a pragmatic approach,"* says Lou Pingeot, policy adviser, Global Policy Form. Pingeot adds, *"This begs the question, however, of what to do when necessary efforts for the public good do not constitute a good investment for the private sector."*[132]
- "Business case" may dilute the genuineness and inherent goodness associated with philanthropy and CSR practices. Noble practices may be termed as "enlightened self-interest".

130 http://givingpledge.org/faq.aspx, Accessed on May 21, 2015.

131 http://givingpledge.org/pdf/pledge-letters/Premji_Letter.pdf, Accessed on May 21, 2015.

132 http://www.worldwatch.org/green-or-greedy-corporations%E2%80%99-role-global-sustainable-development, Accessed on May 19, 2016.

- Focus is moved towards monetary and non-monetary returns from the investment in CSR practices, rather than towards the quality and commitment given towards the CSR practices. The organisation may also witness a gradual increase in expectation on the returns from CSR practices.
- A "business case" may make the CSR practice yet another "fix-it" tool or a problem solving approach.
- A lack of stakeholder involvement, especially from the employees, may emerge if the giving is made as a "business case". "*Employees donate for deeply personal, often subconscious, reasons. On the other side, their employers are likely participating for largely commercial reasons. Beyond donations, people also give back through volunteering, and their motivations for giving their time are often more complex than donating dollars, involving deep social ties and personal relationships,*" says an article advocating a human-centered approach to corporate giving.[133]

Dalai Lama himself exemplifies the aspect of the intent related to an action. On the day of the Nobel Peace Prize announcement of 1989, Dalai Lama was in Southern California. The day before the announcement, Dalai Lama came to know that he and the former Czech President Vaclav Havel were the finalists, and the rumour was that Dalai Lama was the winner. Dalai Lama wished Havel to win, being known the work of Havel[134], and being impressed by the same. On the day of the announcement, Dalai Lama rose up early, as usual, offered his prayers, and then switched on the radio, to listen to the news of who the Nobel winner is. Initially, he was curious. Then, he switched off the radio. The next day, at a news conference, Dalai Lama was asked on whether he was excited, and he said, "*There was some excitement, in the morning, I turned the radio on, but i turned it off later*".[135]

The *Dukkhappattadigatha*[136] states, "*Danam dadantu saddhaya...*" (To give or be charitable - with devotion, care, attentiveness, respect, reverence etc.). Reminescing about his *Wanderings in the Himalayas* in the 1920s and 1930s,

---

133 http://www.fastcoexist.com/3059591/how-to-create-a-human-centered-approach-to-corporate-giving, Accessed on May 21, 2016.

134 Vaclav Havel was a poet, playwright and supporter or democratic reforms. In 1990, he became the President of Czechoslovakia, and later, the Czech republic.

135 As told by Rinchen Dharlo, member of a Tibetan family that exiled to India, from China, in 1959. He has represented the Dalai Lama and the Tibetan Government-in-Exile, for many years, in various roles, including that of being the representative to the Americas between 1987 and 1997. Dalai Lama has mentioned that winning the Nobel Peace Prize would mean much "to the people of Tibet, for it was they who were the real 'winners' of the prize".

136 A Buddhist text

Swami Tapovanam writes, "*... that was the day of being without food. Seeking bhiksha*[137] *in a nearby village did not yield any food. I sat under a tree, for quite a time, partaking the glory of the Himalayas, almost forgetting the need to continue with my walk to Gangotri*[138]. *An old Brahmin was passing by. A native to the mountains, he was sweating, with a heavy load on his shoulders. Tired, he sought rest near a water channel. He sat down and soon unfolded a food packet. Seeing me, he refolded the packet, and came near. Offering the whole packet, he requested me to take from it, as much as i wished. It was boiled potatoes. Respectfully, i took a little...*"[139].

CHAPTER SUMMARY

- A healthy planet is a pre-requisite for the survival of business organisations.
- CSR initiatives by an organisation could be for varied reasons.
- Reasons for CSR practices include environmental reasons, social reasons, employee well-being and commitment, governance reasons, ethical and moral reasons, governmental policies, practices of peer group, consumer demand, sustainability perspective, interdependency perspective or system perspective, managing reputation, and business related reasons.
- The moral permission to start and sustain a business operation has to be given by the global community, and not just by a licensing authority.
- CSR activities of large, publicly traded companies provide benefits such as (a) enhanced wealth creation for shareholders (b) increased

137 A Sanskrit word indicating the practice of monks seeking alms from householders, who consider it as their duty and responsibility to offer food and other essentials to the monks.

138 One of the sacred places in northern India. Revered through the centuries, Gangotri is located near the origin of the River Ganges (Ganga) and is usually visited by a person only after completion of their duties and responsibilities as a *Grihastha* (house-holder), while monks and nuns, also visit. In earlier times, not all places of pilgrimage in India were easily accessible. Despite the availability of modern and easier transportation options, many continue with the practice of walking pilgrimages.

139 Swami Tapovanam mentions that the potatoes were unsalted. The English translation included above is made by the author of this book (on CSR) and may not be conveying the meaning of the original writing by Swami Tapovanam. Swami Tapovanam's writings in Malayalam were initially published as an article series in the 'Manorama' newspaper in the 1930s. The articles, included together, was published in a book form, consisting of three volumes. The content included here is from the first part, and the first part was published in 1941. An updated version of the book, in Malayalam language, and also an English version, is available with Chinmaya Publications.

stock market valuation (c) reduction in the cost of equity (d) reduction in share price risk (e) reduction in systematic risk (f) reduction in cost of debt (g) increased sales revenues (h) increased price premium (i) increased customer satisfaction and loyalty (j) reduced consumer defection (k) a higher brand and reputation value (l) enhanced HR productivity (m) reduction in employee turnover (n) increased employee engagement.

- There have been indications that businesses are willing to engage in more sustainable business practices because 'its the right thing to do'.
- As per 'Creating Shared Value', the purpose of a for-profit company is about economic value creation in a manner that creates value for society by addressing the needs and challenges of the society, and not just profit generation.
- It may not be feasible to pursue infinite growth, considering the finiteness of planetary resources.
- The growth of consumption is reaching new highs, bringing with it, negative consequences on the planet and its inhabitants.
- Consumers can be ignorant of the footprint of the products they are buying.
- Triple bottom-line is a reporting framework that measure social and environmental impact of a company, in addition to its financial performance. It is also referred to as TBL, 3BL, 'People, Planet, Profit' etc.
- There has been discussion about the intentional redirection of economies, away from the perpetual pursuit of growth, and towards the creation of a steady-state economic system that is in balance with Earth's limits.
- A stakeholder perspective considers the needs of all stakeholders (such as employees, suppliers, customers), rather than an exclusive focus on the needs of shareholders.
- Servant Leadership is a leadership practice that focuses on service, in contrast to leadership practices that focus on exercising authority.
- In an inverted pyramid model of organisational hierarchy, the customer occupies the top slot.
- CSR can create competitive advantage for an organisation through differentiation and cost-leadership. CSR can lead to discovery of niche markets and increased market-share.

- Strategic philanthropy looks into giving as an investment on the society.

KEYWORDS

Matching Gift, Corporate Conscience, *Paropakaaraartham Idam Shareeram*, *Yagnayacharatah Karma*, *Atmano Mokshartham Jagat Hitayacha*, *Trikaranasuddhi*, Median Employee Salary, Free and Open Source Software (FOSS), Carbon-Neutral, Green Revolution, Organic Farming, Natural Farming, Conflict Minerals, Creating Shared Value (CSV), Capitalism, Economic Value Creation, Limits to Growth, Triple Bottom-line, Stakeholder Perspective, Human Values, Spirituality, Strategic CSR, Occupy Wall Street, Strategic Philanthropy, The Giving Pledge, International Financial Reporting Standards (IFRS)

MULTIPLE CHOICE QUESTIONS

1. Who said, "Not all profit is equal... profits involving a social purpose represent a higher form of capitalism..."?
   (a) Karl Marx
   (b) CK Prahalad
   (c) Dr Mahmohan Singh
   (d) Michael Porter
   (e) Amartya Sen
2. Name UK's first carbon-neutral bottled water brand.
   (a) Lalu Water
   (b) Velu Water
   (c) Belu Water
   (d) Balu Water
   (e) Value Water
3. Which Houston based investment management company donates half of its profits to not-for-profit organisations?
   (a) Calvert Investments
   (b) Bridgeway Capital Management
   (c) Parnassus Investments
   (d) Trillium Asset Management
   (e) Clean Yield Asset Management

4. What is the expansion of FOSS?
   (a) Fully Open Scam in Securities
   (b) Free and Open Source Software
   (c) Frequency of Operating System Shutdown
   (d) Flying Objects in Stellar Space
   (e) Fibre Optical System Software
5. Which state in India announced for a total prohibition of alcohol in 2016?
   (a) Assam
   (b) Karnataka
   (c) Chattisgarh
   (d) Delhi
   (e) Bihar
6. *Trikaranasuddhi* means:
   (a) Chanting of three prayers
   (b) The three reasons for human birth
   (c) Taking bath during morning, afternoon and evening
   (d) Purity and Unity of Thought, Word and Deed
   (e) Washing hands thrice a day
7. Which of the following about 'Conflict minerals' are true?
   (a) are those natural resources that have been mined or sourced from areas where conflicts occur
   (b) were known to have been used in mobile phones and other electronic gadgets
   (c) trade in these minerals have funded regional conflicts
   (d) Gold is considered to be a 'conflict mineral'
   (e) all of the above
8. Which smart-phone producer has been known to have pioneered and popularised the non-usage of conflict minerals?
   (a) Fairphone
   (b) Apple
   (c) Samsung
   (d) OPPO
   (e) BSNL

9. Name the Jewish philosopher who has propounded the expressions of 'I-IT' and 'I-THOU' in how we relate to others:
   (a) Tom Chappel
   (b) Rumi
   (c) Martin Buber
   (d) Khalil Gibran
   (e) Moses

10. The founder of which company has said: "*The ultimate goal of business is not profit. Profit is merely a means toward the ultimate aim of affirming the health and dignity of human beings and their families, affirming aspirations of the community and affirming the health of the environment -- the common good.*"
    (a) Toms of Maine
    (b) Better World Books
    (c) Sounds True
    (d) Hantex
    (e) Honda

11. Which movement was associated with "the 99% that will no longer tolerate the greed and corruption of the 1%"?
    (a) Occupy Wall Street
    (b) Arab Spring
    (c) Dilli Chalo
    (d) Quit India
    (e) Quit China

12. Which of the following companies produced biscuits that did not have *maida* (refined flour), and noodles with less of *maida* and more of *atta* ('whole wheat flour')?
    (a) Patanjali
    (b) Nestle
    (c) Godrej
    (d) Unilever
    (e) Mars

13. Which is the first airport in the world to be full powered by solar energy?

(a) Cochin International Airport, Kochi.
(b) Chatrapati Shivaji International Airport, Mumbai.
(c) Rajiv Gandhi International Airport, Hyderabad.
(d) Kempegowda International Airport, Bangalore.
(e) San Diego International Airport, San Diego.

14. Name the Coimbatore based organisation that prepares Mysorepak from plant-based ingredients:
    (a) Ajay Sweets
    (b) Parajay Sweets
    (c) Sujay Sweets
    (d) Vijay Sweets
    (e) Jayjay Sweets

SHORT ANSWER QUESTIONS

1. Write a note on 'Limits to Growth'?
2. Why has Akshayapatra been inducted into the 'Hall of Fame' of Institute of Chartered Accountants of India (ICAI)?
3. With the help of an example, mention the 'triple bottom-line' framework of assessing an organisation's performance.

LONG ANSWER QUESTIONS

1. What are some of the issues and concerns related to the focus on the "business case" on CSR practices?
2. What are some of the ways through which philanthropy is practiced?

REFLECTIVE QUESTIONS

1. List some examples of companies creating 'competitive advantage' through CSR? Did the companies use CSR practices to create 'competitive advantage', OR, did 'competitive advantage' emerge naturally for these companies as a result of CSR?
2. You may be a student, employee, shareholder etc. of an organisation. What if your organisation redraws the organisational hierarchy chart with an 'Inverted Pyramid' model? Draw such a chart. Redefine the job descriptions and role allocations. What would be the impact of the 'Servant Leadership' model on the responsibility practices in the organisation?

About the chapter:

1. Learning from the chapter, if any:

2. Topics, concepts, themes, etc. that you may be interested to research/ refer/ study/ ponder upon:

3. Applications in daily life, if any:

Notes:

Chapter 2 completed... You may take a break...

'Channapatna' in Karnataka, India, has been known for its toy making tradition, focusing on wood-based lacware toys. Pictured above are wood-based toys from Maya Organic[140]. These wood-based toys are non-toxic and uses natural dyes.

140 www.mayaorganic.com

Chapter 3

MANAGING AND REPORTING CSR

"One of our activities is publishing spiritual, cultural, and educational books. We look upon this activity as a possibility of helping to make a better world. We are working to include the principles of human values, which are so central in our spiritual paths, in the books we are publishing for primary and secondary schools - not only into books about societal affairs, but also in books about mathematics, biology or history."[1]

—Francisco Roberto Canada,
One of the directors and partner at Errepar S.A., an Argentine publishing company

On completion of reading the chapter, the reader may:

1. understand the methodologies of reporting non-financial responsibility parameters that influence the operations of a company.

2. know the multiple number of sustainability reporting frameworks and methods

3. recognise the benefits of sustainability reporting

4. attempt to read and write a CSR report effectively

5. develop a CSR plan for a company

On hearing that his obituary had been published in the *New York Journal*, Mark Twain is widely attributed with declaring, *"The reports of my death are greatly exaggerated."*. There is a perception that for-profit organisations engaging in 'Corporate Social Responsibility' (CSR) practices, and reports about CSR practices are also *greatly exaggerated*. Many believe that CSR practices are only for generating and attracting public goodwill, while evading citizen scrutiny of misguided practices in business. Personal experiences, while interacting with for-profit organisations, may support such a belief. However, Warren Buffet, while pledging more than 99% of his wealth to philanthropy, mentions about the millions of individuals who give to others, through foregone movies, dinners and other personal pleasures[2].

1 http://www.globaldharma.org/Files%20-%20Adobe%20Acrobat/SBW/Practice%202.27%20A%20Transforming%20Attitude.pdf

2 https://givingpledge.org/Pledger.aspx?id=177, Accessed on July 23, 2017.

Scriptures from India invite attention to *Dharma* (Righteousness), *Artha* (Wealth), *Kama* (Desire) and *Moksha* (Spiritual Fulfilment), as that which give meaning and purpose to human existence. *Artha* has to be generated and sustained within the context of righteousness and supreme fulfilment. The society has thus entrusted businesses with the holy responsibility of providing the society with the basic material needs. Swami Chandrasekharendra Saraswati (1894-1994) of Kanchi Pitha says, *"With education we purify our intelligence, with meditation we cleanse our mind, with sloka or poetry we clarify our speech. How do we purify our body? By exerting ourselves in the service of others"*.[3]

Corporate Social Responsibility involves asking three questions during business decision making.

(a) Is it ideal?
(b) Is it ethical?
(c) Is it legal?

These three questions help a company in building a stable foundation in sustainability practices. If the answer is a 'Yes' to these three questions, it could imply that an organization would be a leader in responsibility practices. While these questions give a directional guidance, there is also a necessity for clarity on operational aspects. Asking 'Why?', 'When?', 'Where?', 'What?', 'Who?' (5W) and 'How?' (1H) related to CSR initiatives can provide this clarity. This could be referred as the '5W1H Method' for managing CSR.

5W1H METHOD

Table 3.1 indicates some pointers related to the 5W1H method.

Table 3.1

WHY?	WHEN?	WHERE?
1. Purpose and meaning for the existence of the company, regulatory necessities etc. 2. Nature of CSR initiative – Is it to benefit the society, regardless of any direct/ indirect benefit to the business?	Project Duration – is it going to be (a) short-term (b) medium-term or (c) long-term?	1. Geographical reach and spread of the project. 2. Is there a need for physical proximity between the CSR project area and the organisation's operational location?

3 *Hindu Dharma: The Universal Way of Life*, Bharathiya Vidya Bhavan, 1996.

WHO?	WHAT?	HOW?
1. Beneficiaries of the project 2. Will the project be directly implemented by the company?/ Partners to implement the project (not-for-profit organisations, leaders from the community, governmental bodies) 3. Human resource allocation to design, manage and operationalise the initiatives	Functional areas of projects	1. Allocation of monetary resources 2. Plans, Impact assessment, reporting and feedback

THE CSR PROCESS

Many organisations started their CSR practices as a spontaneous expression of some of the internal stakeholders (employees, members of the senior management etc.). As the CSR practices evolve, it involves planning and engagement with various stakeholders. For some organisations, CSR may be ingrained into their organisational ethos, while for some, it may not be. The chairman of a consulting company says, "*...the challenge is that companies are treating social development/ community work as a separate department. They are not galvanizing the entire organization to think about society... What they need to do is to make social responsibility part of the company's DNA.*"[4]

In addition to grass-root level projects and initiatives, the following are some of the practices undertaken by an organisation as part of the CSR process. Some of these may be done simultaneously or may be done sequentially. All organisations need not adopt all these practices.

(1) Impact Diagnosis

(2) Business Opportunity Identification

(3) Aligning CSR with organizational DNA

(4) Integrating PMS and Responsibility Metrics

4 http://www.livemint.com/Companies/roQ76qkNPcSKdiLV0nkpII/CSR-expenditure-should-be-a-percentage-of-revenue-not-profi.html, Accessed on May 9, 2016.

(5) Vendor Management

(6) Stakeholder Communication and Engagement

1) Impact Diagnosis

Through impact diagnosis, an organisation tries to find the impacts created on the societal stakeholders, on a short-term, medium-term and long-term basis. These impacts may be positive, negative or neutral. For example, a carbonated-drink manufacturer may ascertain the health and lifestyle impact that its products have on people through various time periods.

2) Business Opportunity Identification

Identifying opportunities that will contribute to the well-being of the organization and all its stakeholders. For example, a "soda and snacks company"[5] such as PepsiCo understands the customer requirement of products that quenches thirst and hunger. Knowing that carbonated-drinks and potato-chips cause adverse health impacts[6], the company diversified into products such as fruit based juices and healthier snacks (Tropicana juices, Quaker Oats etc.). This shift is beneficial to the health of the people, while also bringing revenue to the organisation.

3) Aligning CSR with the organizational DNA

There have been perspectives that CSR activities need to be embedded in the strategy and culture of the company, rather than remaining in the peripherals of organizational initiatives. Discovery of the organisation's purpose, mission and vision, and evoking human values at the workplace can contribute to aligning CSR with the organisational DNA.

4) Integrating PMS and Responsibility Metrics

Many successful sustainability programmes involve the integration of metrics related to social responsibility in Performance Management Systems (PMS) of employees. Annual appraisals and reward systems can influence employee behaviour in an organization. By including social responsibility metrics in employee appraisals and reward systems, the employees are incentivised to work towards sustainability goals and CSR practices.

5 http://fortune.com/2015/04/23/pepsico-ceo-weve-never-seen-consumers-so-confused/, Accessed on August 4, 2016.

6 http://www.newyorker.com/magazine/2011/05/16/snacks-for-a-fat-planet, Accessed on August 4, 2016.

Walmart, started a sustainability agenda in mid 2000s. Speaking about WalMart's progress in sustainability practices, Frank Dixon, a consultant focusing on sustainability practices from a system perspective, says, "*Its rapid progress is due largely to excellence in strategy execution and the strong commitment of senior management. Lee Scott[7] has made it clear that working on sustainability projects can accelerate careers within Wal-Mart. Compensation schemes are being adjusted to provide substantial incentives for improving sustainability performance.*"[8]

Integrating responsibility metrics in performance assessment can be illustrated with the example of DSM, a Netherlands based company engaged in life sciences and material sciences. The Managing Board of DSM has a remuneration package that incentivises the creation of sustainable value for all the stakeholders of the company[9]. DSM has integrated sustainability targets into their remuneration structure. This package balances short-term operational performance with long-term value additions (**Refer table 3.2**).

The table 3.2 indicates that for DSM's board members, 50% of the long-term incentive and almost 25% of the short-term incentive is related to initiatives related to sustainability, safety, employee engagement etc.

5) Vendor Management

Vendor Management involves integrating metrics related to social responsibility practices in vendor and supplier agreements. For many industries, the prime area of improvement on social and environmental metrics emerges from suppliers. For a company to achieve its CSR goals, support from the suppliers are necessary[10]. So, a fashion retailer may institute a code of conduct for suppliers to ensure that the supplier meets with social and environmental responsibility standards. This code of conduct can cover areas that include respecting worker's rights, humane working conditions, remuneration that meets or exceeds the pay that is stipulated by regulatory norms etc.

Fairphone is an example of an organisation that worked with its vendors to produce a better smartphone. Electronic gadgets may contain minerals that are sourced from conflict prone areas, such as Democratic Republic of

---

7 Lee Scott was the former CEO of WalMart.

8 http://globalsystemchange.com/sustainability-and-system-change-wal-marts-pioneering-strategy/, Accessed on June 4, 2016.

9 http://www.dsm.com/content/dam/dsm/cworld/en_US/documents/factbook-2015.pdf, Accessed on September 24, 2015.

10 Refer the section related to Puma's environmental profit and loss accounting.

Table 3.2

	Mode of incentive		**Performance Targets and Measure**		
Fixed	100% base salary	Cash			100.00%
Variable	50% short-term incentive (STI)	Cash	Financial	1. EBITA (before exceptional items) 2. Gross free cash flow 3. Organic net sales growth	(1). 10% (2). 7.5% (3). 7.5%
			Sustainability & Individual	1. ECO+ products 2. Safety 3. Employee Engagement Index 4. Individual	(1). 5% (2). 5% (3). 5% (4). 10%
			Threshold	Minimum performance threshold for STI payout set by Supervisory Board	
	100% Long Term Incentive	Performance Shares	Financial	1. Total Shareholder Return (relative) 2. Return On Capital Employed	(1). 25% (2). 25%
			Sustainability	1. Greenhouse gas emissions reduction 2. Energy efficiency improvement	(1). 25% (2). 25%

Congo (DRC)[11]. The mining and sales of these minerals may be controlled by armed groups. Business in these minerals goes to finance such conflicts. Fairphone, "the smart-phone with social values"[12] used conflict-free minerals[13]. A communications manager at Fairphone says, *"With the Fairphone 1, we sourced conflict-free tin and tantalum from the DRC, established worker representation at our top-tier manufacturer and a worker-controlled welfare fund, and collected literally tons of scrap phones in Ghana for safe recycling. With the Fairphone 2, we've continued with these projects, plus achieved the first Fairtrade gold supply chain in the electronics industry, released an open source version of our software and we're nearly ready to integrate conflict-free tungsten into our supply chain."*[14]

6) Stakeholder Communication and Engagement

Health of an organization is dependent on how the stakeholders perceive the organization. It is important for an organization to understand the needs of its stakeholders, viz., shareholders, employees, customers, suppliers, community, governmental authorities etc. Stakeholder needs may vary. To understand stakeholder needs, an organization has to seek their perspectives and feedback. Stakeholder engagement can contribute to successful CSR practices. Meaningful engagement from all stakeholders can also contribute to deepening and broadening of CSR initiatives.

> ***To read, which may not provide you with joy, yet, is of service to others, is also about strengthening your moral fibre...***
>
> ***You may take a break...***

AREAS OF CSR PRACTICES

A kindness is never wasted.
—Aesop's Fables[15]

Agriculture has been a reason for destruction of native forests, especially mono-culture plantations. Growing demand for chocolate increased

11 A country in the African continent.

12 https://www.fairphone.com/, Accessed on June 5, 2016.

13 Popularly referred to as 3TGs - cassiterite (for tin), wolframite (for tungsten), coltan (for tantalum), and gold ore.

14 https://www.fairphone.com/2016/05/26/100000-fairphone-owners/, Accessed on May 6, 2016.

15 http://www.read.gov/aesop/007.html, Accessed on August 16, 2015.

the demand for cocoa, resulting in 'land-use changes'[16][17][18]. Involvement of chocolate industry in 'child labour' have been a discussion-topic on necessitating changes in business operating practices. A few businesses have been attempting betterments. 'Mason' and 'Earth Loaf' are producers of chocolates. Their chocolates are priced much higher than some of the popular chocolates available in India. However, these organisations produce dark chocolates. Dark chocolates avoid milk or milk products, thereby making these chocolates 100% plant-based. Refined sugar is not used in these chocolates (**Refer table 3.3**). Being hand-crafted and produced in small batches, they are referred to as 'artisanal chocolates'. Based at Auroville and Mysuru respectively, 'Mason' (masonchocolate.com) and 'Earth Loaf' (earthloaf.co.in) makes their chocolates from ingredients that are organic. Pascati, another dark-chocolate brand that uses organic ingredients, is fair-trade certified (pascati.com).

Table 3.3

Types of Sugars	Description	Health Impact/ Quality Aspects
Artificial sweeteners (Sugar alcohol, sweeteners)		Can be harmful.
Refined sugar	Also known as "white sugar" or "table sugar". This is the final product after the sugar-producing raw ingredient (sugar-cane juice, etc.) is processed, resulting in de-mineralisation, de-colourisation, and crystal form of the raw ingredient. The process involves heating, clarifying, dehydration. Molasses** is separated.	Various chemicals are used during the process of "refining".

16 https://www.greenamerica.org/end-child-labor-cocoa/chocolate-scorecard, Accessed on November 25, 2019.

17 https://e360.yale.edu/features/the-real-price-of-a-chocolate-bar-west-africas-rainforests, Accessed on November 25, 2019.

18 https://blog.resourcewatch.org/2019/02/14/map-where-the-world-gets-its-chocolate/, Accessed on November 25, 2019.

** Sugarcane juice is extracted by the crushing of sugarcane. Depending on the range of boiling of sugarcane juice, products such as 'cane syrup', 'molasses' and 'blackstrap molasses' are obtained. Every additional boiling results in a product that has a lower amount of sugar content. Molasses is also known as 'treacle'.

Minimally refined sugars	There are sugars, with 'molasses' added to it, in varying quantities, after the sugar is refined. Demerara sugar, turbinado, muscovado, etc. are examples. However, these sugars may also be produced through only a partial refining, thereby retaining some of its original nature and ingredients. In such instances, they may be referred to as 'minimally refined sugars'.	Contains minerals, depending on the extent of retention of original raw ingredient, addition of molasses to the refined sugar etc.
Unrefined sugars	Rapadura ('Panela, Piloncillo, Chancaca), Sucanat and Jaggery are examples. These sugars are not separated from molasses,	Contains more nutrients as compared to 'refined sugars' and 'minimally refined sugars'.
Natural Sweeteners	Examples include sugar-cane juice, pastes of various fruits (banana, jack-fruit, mango) etc.	

Many chocolatiers are known for practices that adopt and communicate sustainability. In 2012, the 'Grenada chocolate company' of the Carribean region sought the services of 'Tres Hombres' to deliver chocolates to Europe. The 'Tres Hombres' is a sail-boat, fully powered by wind – no engines, though there is a solar-powered cooling system. This organic chocolate company already had the habit of delivering chocolates to the nearby islands in wind-powered boats. Organizations engage in CSR practices in a number of ways. Some of them are listed below (**Refer table 3.4**):

Table 3.4

Disaster Relief Projects	Care for the elderly	Adopting a village	Employee volunteering
Promoting organic farming	Providing skill training to youth	Adopting renewable energy	Public service advertising
Wildlife and bio-diversity conservation	Environmental education	Improving access to quality medical care	Supporting vulnerable communities
Shelters for animals and birds	Offering pro-bono services	Supply-chain transparency	Scholarships to students
Creating urban forests, maintaining public parks and playgrounds	Constructing toilets in schools and colleges	Awareness on hygiene and sanitation	Promotion of sustainable and low-impact technologies
Practice of 6R – Refuse, Reduce, Reuse, Repurpose, Recycle, Recover	Water harvesting, replenishment and rejuvenation of water bodies	Providing funds for research into issues of common cause	Funding not-for-profit organizations and humanitarian causes
Corporate reporting that go beyond compliance	Providing jobs to physically and mentally challenged people	Protection and maintenance of heritage sites	Providing nutritious and healthy food to the hungry

Criterion for determining the social responsibility areas of businesses

A global survey found that donating money to community causes or charities was the most prevalent CSR activity amongst various companies[19]. Determining the CSR areas of businesses may depend on various parameters, such as those listed below:

19 http://www.grantthornton.at/files/GTI%20IBR/corporate-social-responsibility-beyond-financials.pdf, Accessed on May 20, 2015.

(a) CSR areas where the organization is able to make the most effective impact.
(b) Resources that the organisation is willing to give for CSR activities. This could involve human resources, time, money that the organization is willing to spend, etc.
(c) Preferences of the influential people in the organization
(d) Historical CSR practices of the organization

An organization can engage in "materiality analysis"[20] to understand areas of CSR that can be adopted by the organization.

CSR Filter and its application

CSR Filtering is a process that helps to identify the impact of a business strategy (and its application, such as, day-to-day operational decisions) on its stakeholders. CSR filtering helps in avoiding business decisions that are not aligned to stakeholder interests, or, may have a negative impact on stakeholders.

Explaining the importance of CSR filter, Chandler and Werther says that *"a tactical or strategic decision that runs counter to stakeholder interests can undermine the firm's sustainable competitive advantage"*[21]. An example of application of a CSR filter can be the discovery by a power generation and distribution company that their decision to build a mega hydro-power plant in a rainforest region is not in alignment with stakeholder interests. This recognition may lead the company to opt, support and promote alternatives such as grid-connected or grid-free roof-top solar power projects for domestic households.

In contrast to the approach of finding areas where there is an alignment between stakeholder well-being and business interests, CSR filter is used to identify any misalignment between an organization's strategy and stakeholder interests.

CSR Threshold

The Japanese narrates the existence of a dragon lying underneath, with its head in the Indian sub-continent and the tail in Japan. During the times of Marco Polo, even "Japan" was "India". If the dragon shake its tail, earthquakes happen in Japan. Earthquakes are indeed terrible, be it

20 Explained in another section of the chapter.

21 David Chandler, William B. Werther, Jr., Strategic Corporate Social Responsibility: Stakeholders, Globalization, and Sustainable Value Creation, Sage Publications, 2013.

in Japan or India. So a bridge was constructed in Vietnam. The belief was that underneath Vietnam lay the dragon's chest region. Even centuries ago, people knew that Vietnam was almost mid-way between the extremes of India and Japan. The Hoi An bridge was thus a bridge – a trading town connecting people from the regions of South Asia, South East Asia and the Far East.

The people of this city has unique rituals. On the 14th day of every lunar cycle, they make offerings to the forefathers and the celestial beings. Lanterns are floated on the Bon river[22]. Members of the family play traditional folk games and merry-make watching and participating in street opera. The elderly men play fiddle[23], read poetry to children, and play Chinese checkers. Electric lights are a taboo on this day, as is the use of motorised vehicles. Among these who are healthy, a few skipped a meal or two, or some even fasted for the day. Some covertly avoided eating those items that are connected with violence, so that its avoidance may not offend those who consume these items out of ignorance.

Figure 3.1

The "Maharajah" motif of Air-India has become an icon through its multi-decade existence. Pictured above is the "Maharajah" at one of the South-east Asian cities. [24]

22 The Bon River that flows through central Vietnam merges with the South China Sea at Hoi An.

23 A musical instrument, a violin.

24 In 1954, Air India started flying to Bangkok, Singapore, Tokyo and Hong Kong. The 'Maharajah' mascot first made its appearance in 1946. The image included above is for educational/ informational purposes.

The "bridge" was an expression of the dragon's heart, connecting communities, and elevating habits to culture. Countries such as Vietnam, Cambodia, Burma, Laos, Thailand, etc. has benefited from the ascetic spirit of India, especially that of Buddhism and Hinduism (**Refer Figure 3.1**). Many people of these regions not only inherited the spirit, they also shared it with other parts of the world. More importantly, whenever the spirit of asceticism, *dharma* and compassion waned or weakened in the mother-source of India, these regions strengthened that spirit, returning the capital with so much interest.

'Threshold' refers to the point of beginning of some event, action, response etc. Threshold is also the level beyond which an existing process or status quo cannot be continued or sustained, and will necessarily undergo a change or transformation. CSR Threshold is the level/ point at which an organisation can no longer continue to be irresponsible or remain unbothered about its responsibility practices, and has to necessarily and sufficiently consider responsibility practices for its operational success.

The CSR threshold level varies. The threshold level for a business to engage in CSR may be lower in a society that imbue and embody human values (Case - I). For example, when consumers make conscious purchasing choices, they will consider the responsibility practices of the producers/ manufacturers. Or, when an owner of a factory believes that the neighbourhood should not harmed due to discharge from factory, the factory will necessarily take the necessary precautions, even if the law do not make it compulsory. Thus, the organization gives high priority to CSR, or does it pro-actively and have less room for inertia in this area. The maximum threshold level for a business to continue with its irresponsible practices is thus low/ minimal.

The threshold level for maintaining irresponsibility may be higher when people are ignorant (Case - II). For example, when consumers remain unsympathetic about the negative impact of needless packaging, businesses will remain inattentive to make any modifications, and continue with its wasteful practices. They have a larger operating space to be in inertia, and such societies provide businesses with a higher threshold level for continuing with their state of irresponsibility.

Case – I : Low threshold level for being irresponsible, usually seen in communities that imbue and live values that makes a homo-sapien a human-being

Irresponsible	**Threshold**	*Responsible*

Case – II : High threshold level for being irresponsible, usually seen in communities that are ignorant and devoid of values that makes a homo-sapien a human-being

Irresponsible	**Threshold**	*Responsible*

'CSR Threshold' is based on the premise that companies – inherently, usually and generally - are irresponsible or not fully responsible to its stakeholders. Some of the factors that may influence CSR Threshold are as below:

(a) The extent to which a society imbues human values, higher purpose etc.

(b) Consumer Awareness

(c) Governmental regulations and its enforcement

(d) Existing responsibility practices

(e) CSR Practices of peer group (other companies)

(f) Influence of industry associations

(g) Relationship between the company and its stakeholders

(i) Purpose of existence, for the business organisation and its stakeholders

Channels for CSR Engagement

Leningrad, during World War II, was an epitome of the Soviet character. The troubles and travails faced by its people were innumerable. The city was besieged. All the woes related to a war – bombings, injuries, starvation - and diseases to aggravate the sufferings – deaths from the city were more than a million. Prior to being called as Leningrad, the city was known as Petrograd. Following World War II, the city of Leningrad went through phases quientessential to any city of USSR.

Yet, imprints and memories of sacrifices may also be forgotten. Following the collapse of the USSR in the early 1990s, the city (now named as St. Petersberg) witnessed a boom in high-rises, and along came the wipe-off of dwellings and structures that carried the hues and smells of centuries. Its citizens lamented that more number of buildings were demolished due to this real-estate boom (**Refer Figure 3.2**) than due to the heavy damage inflicted on the city during the Second World War. Alarmed and alert, some of the residents started to work towards conserving its architectural heritage.

Figure 3.2[25]

Gagnam style buildings and towers are popular in many countries. Some of them received/ purchased green-certifications.

The rooftop of such high-rise buildings makes it easier to send hot-air-balloons for weather monitoring, installation of telescopes and other view-finders to monitor the directional path of the birds in these cities, recreational avenues such as fine-dine restaurants, installation of communication towers, star-gazing and city-gazing, etc.

Pictured above is the "Lakhta Center" in St Petersburg, Russia. An 87 storeyed building, it is also known as the "Gazprom Tower", being the headquarters of Gazprom, a Russian oil company.

In the context of architecture, "*Gagnam style*" is a 20-21st century building design style. Imagine the energy (and infrastructure) required to pump a litre of water to the top of these buildings.

---

25 Image Source: Monoklon, CC0, via Wikimedia Commons, https://commons.wikimedia.org/wiki/File:%D0%9B%D0%B0%D1%85%D1%82%D0%B0_%D0%BD%D0%B5%D0%B1%D0%BE%D1%81%D0%BA%D1%80%D1%91%D0%B1.jpg, Accessed on January 12. 2021.

'The Green Hotel' in Mysuru, India, channelises all its profits to environmental and social projects. This hotel is a result of a restoration of the Chittaranjan Palace, which was built by the Maharaja of Mysore, for his sister, in 1916. Before being a hotel, it was the headquarters of a film company. Charities Advisory Trust, a UK based charity has been pivotal in this restoration project that also supported traditional crafts. The hotel practices healthy environmental practices and maintains an award-winning garden on its premises (www.greenhotelindia.com). Two other accommodation properties in India that contributed to the conservation and restoration of culture and tradition include the *Chittur Kottaram* at Kochi and *Kalari Kovilakom*, at Kollengode, both in the southern state of Kerala.

Kalari Kovilakom and *Chittur Kottaram* are properties managed by 'CGH Earth' (earlier, Casino Group of Hotels), a hotel management company, which, through the past few decades, earned accolades for maintaining higher standards of sustainability, in the way their hotel properties in India are managed. Many decades ago, or, a century earlier, these two properties were neither hotels nor properties that were accessible to outsiders. The 1990s, and the decades that followed, was also the time when many palaces and dwellings of archaeological, historical and nostalgic values were deconstructed and sold-off, piece-by-piece. Fearing such a sell-off of *Kalari Kovilakom*, at Kollengode, in the district of Palakkad, there were protests from the citizens, and they requested the government to protect and preserve these palaces for posterity. While the stay at these palaces may be princely, it is also pricey, almost comparable with the five-star hotels of the cities of the state. However, these are palaces, and not a hotel, and these palaces arrive with their unique practices and peculiarities – both serve only vegetarian food and are non-alcoholic. At *Chittur Kottaram*, you can choose any room for your sleep. Both palaces discourage the use of footwear within their premises. *Kalari Kovilakom* is now an Ayurvedic wellness centre.

A company may deliver its CSR initiatives in multiple ways:

(a) directly by the company

(b) through a not-for-profit organisation, which is started by the company

(c) through an external implementation agency/ service provider

Examples of not-for-profit organisations started by companies to manage their CSR programmes include Infosys Foundation, Wipro Foundation, GVK Foundation, Piramal Foundation, Srinivasan Services Trust,

Kamalnayan Jamnalal Bajaj Foundation, Bharti Foundation etc. A company can also associate with an implementation agency or a service provider. This may include entering into a partnership with a not-for-profit organisation and providing them with funds and other resource requirements. For example, Chennai based Vernalis Systems provided its employees with social-investment vouchers from RangDe, an organisation, which, during its initial years of operations, provided affordable micro-credit services[26] to borrowers, and a choice for investors to invest only in socially responsible investments (avoiding investments resulting in violence or pain on animals, investments related to recycling and repurposing, cleaner energy production, etc.). Vernalis also made a social-investment in RangDe. There are also companies that have full-fledged CSR departments and they manage their CSR initiatives directly through these departments. There are companies that use all the above approaches in their CSR endeavours.

You may take a break...

SUSTAINABILITY REPORTING

"Well it has seemed to me for a long time that we are living off the Earth's natural capital rather than the income derived from that capital, and that if this continues it will have the direst possible consequences for us all... ...those who find ways to use natural resources in a sustainable, "circular" way, with nothing going to waste, will find themselves uncovering new sources of innovation, reducing their risks and increasing their competitive advantage."[27]

—Prince Charles of Wales

'Sustainability Reporting' is the process of communicating a comprehensive and wholistic perspective about the organization to its stakeholders, and the organization's relationship with its stakeholders and contextual environment. This process involves detailing an organization's economic, environmental and social performance. Writing a sustainability report is one of the aspects related to sustainability reporting.

---

26 https://www.rangde.org/corporate-partners, http://vernal.is/social-responsibility.html, Accessed on June 1, 2016.

27 http://www.princeofwales.gov.uk/media/speeches/speech-hrh-the-prince-of-wales-the-princes-accounting-sustainability-projects-annua-0, Accessed on January 3, 2016.

Companies are discovering that reporting their social responsibility and environmental sustainability practices to the stakeholders goes beyond writing a 'Corporate Social Responsibility Report' (also referred to as 'CSR report', 'corporate responsibility report', 'accountability report', 'sustainable development report', 'citizen report', 'sustainability report', etc.).

'Sustainability Reporting' is also known as 'social accounting', 'corporate social responsibility reporting', 'social and environmental accounting', 'non-financial reporting' etc. Sustainability Reporting is applicable for all organizations - for-profit and non-profit (governmental organizations, charitable institutions, educational institutions).

Reporting Process

A comprehensive CSR report can be generated only if the company has:

(a) contemplated on the purpose of its existence, and the values that guide its culture

(b) ascertained the sustainability parameters relevant for its stakeholders

(c) meaningful CSR projects and involvement of stakeholders in these projects

(d) chosen the relevant sustainability metrics, and,

(e) collected and analysed data pertaining to the sustainability metrics

An effective CSR report depends on the extent of clarity on the below:

(a) *Audience*

Who will read the report? Does the report meet the requirements of its stakeholders?

(b) *Frequency*

Is the report going to be published regularly (for example, annually or once in few years)/ a one-time event? Will there be comparison amongst the data of various years?

(c) *Adherence to regulatory requirements*

Does the report only meet regulatory requirements, or will it go beyond compliance?

(d) *Reporting format*

Is the organization adhering to any reporting standards/ frameworks, while writing the report?

(e) *Outputs and Outcomes*

What will be the outputs that will be communicated to the stakeholders? What may be the outcomes on communicating the report to the stakeholders?

(f) *Contacts for Clarification*

Does the report provide contact details for stakeholder communication?

(g) *Content Generation*

Does the organisation generate the necessary data for the report?

(h) *Integrity of the content*

Can the organization vouch for truthfulness in the report content? Will the organization be confident to do an audit of their report with an independent audit agency?

(i) *Presentation*

Does the report communicate objective data that can substantiate and support CSR claims, while also providing subjective narrations that connects with the audience?

'Materiality Analysis'

'Materiality Analysis' is the process used to identify those sustainability (CSR) related aspects that an organization choose to address in its communication to stakeholders. These aspects may be chosen from an elaborate list. This is based on a process that involves identifying those sustainability issues that are relevant for stakeholders and those sustainability issues that has an impact on business performance. Feedback is collected from stakeholders through surveys, meetings, interviews etc. The company may also review industry reports, peer practices, ratings and rankings surveys etc.

The table below (**Refer table 3.5**) indicates some of the sustainability related aspects considered by organisations as part of their materiality analysis. Many of these parameters can be categorised within one of the 'triple bottom-line' aspects (financial performance and governance of a company, relationship with the society, relationship with the planet).

Table 3.5

Customer experience	Energy consumption	Management of waste
Bio-diversity preservation	Procurement and supply chain	Disclosure and Transparency
Health and well-being of employees	Usage of hazardous materials and chemicals	Working conditions of employees
Business ethics	Engagement with society	Rural development
Product quality and quality of services	Voluntary standards and certifications	Standards in product labelling
Anti-corruption	Sustainable agriculture	Food safety
Healthy products	Optimization in packaging	Product innovation
Data privacy	Fuel efficiency	Brand perception
Road safety awareness	Dealer relationship	End-of-life recycling
Products and non-product solutions for low-income families	Employee learning and development	Percentage of revenue shared for a societal cause
Community development	Ecosystems management	Quarry rehabilitation
Corporate governance	Diversity	Human rights
Usage of renewable energy	CO2 emissions management	Greenhouse gas emissions
Business integrity	Customer service	Heritage management
Community investments	Political stability	Financial performance
Geopolitical tension	Cyber-risk	Terrorism
Social acceptability of projects	Chronic and pandemic diseases	Management of contaminated land
Water stewardship	Natural capital	Food security
Animal welfare	Employee relations	Responsible marketing
Food waste	Vehicle safety	Occupational Hazards
Impact of technology in human behaviour	Maternal, infant and young child nutrition	Over-nutrition and under-nutrition

Child labour	Light pollution	Noise management
Anti-competitive Behaviour	Forced and compulsory labour	Research and development
Conservation of resources	Climate change	Demographic change
Trust and reputation	Population growth	Urbanization
Malnutrition	Sustainability valuation	Land-use change
Access to financial solutions	Life cycle thinking in value chain	Socially responsible investment
Poverty	Impact investments	Being a thought leader
Relation with governmental authorities	Relation with aboriginal communities	Relation with employee unions
Spills and Leakages	Arctic drilling	Road safety awareness

A 'materiality matrix' is mapped as a two-dimensional X-Y axis plot where one of the axis reflects the importance of an issue to the stakeholder or an impact on the stakeholder, while the other axis reflects the importance of the issue to the organization or a concern to the organization.

The materiality matrix of BBVA, a Spanish banking group,[28] is shown in **Figure 3.3**.

The below list mentions the parameters associated with the numbers mentioned in matrix:

- Products with good value for money (without abusive clauses).
- Communication and commercialization practices: foster informed decisions.
- Quality of customer care and service.
- Response to the demand for credit in society.
- Customer security, privacy and protection (including 'big data').
- A solution for customers in a difficult situation.

28 Image included with permission from BBVA. Available https://accionistaseinversores.bbva.com/TLBB/micros/bbvain2015/en/performance-in-2015/primary-stakeholders/materiality-and-dialog-with-stakeholders/, Accessed on September 23, 2017.

Figure 3.3

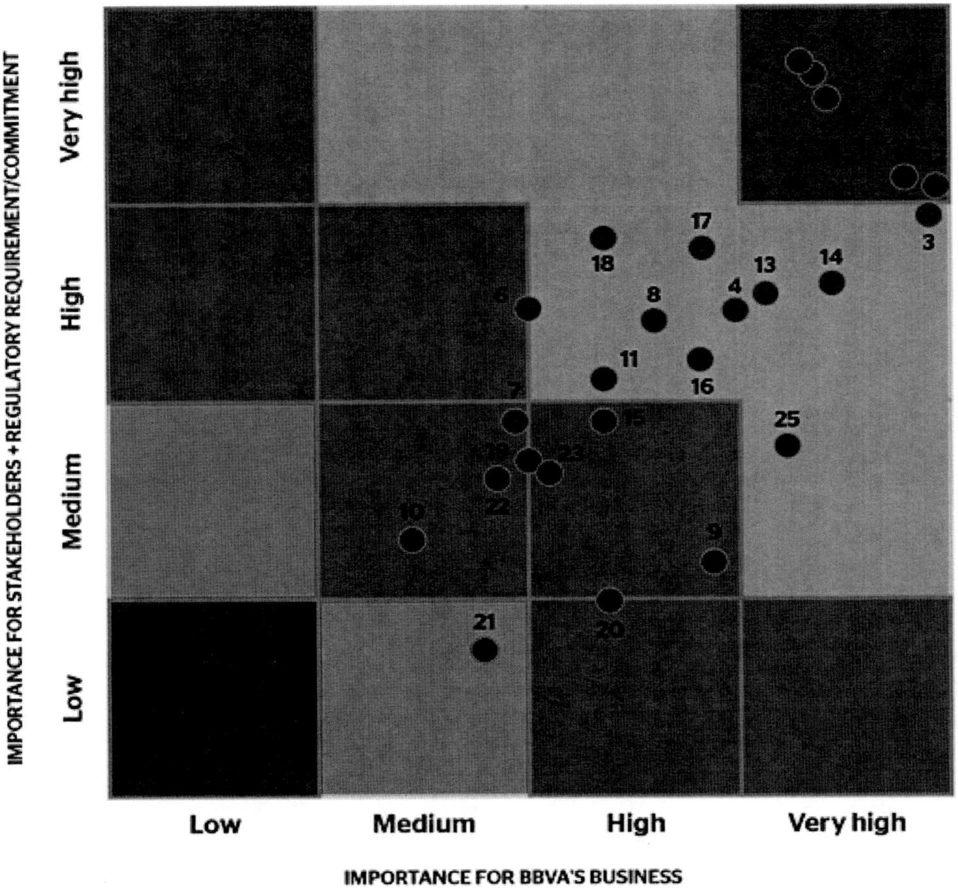

- Quality of employment (temporary, outsourcing, relocation, etc.).
- Respect for employee rights.
- Talent attraction, development and retention.
- Remuneration policy for senior management and the Board of Directors.
- Social and environmentally responsible finance.
- Prevention of money laundering and terrorist financing.
- Compliance with the tax code.
- Ethical behavior.
- Responsible procurement and outsourcing.
- Good corporate governance.

- Financial solvency and management.
- Respect for human rights.
- Contribution to the development of local communities (job creation, support for SMEs, etc.).
- Financial inclusion.
- Community involvement not linked to the business.
- Diversity and work/life balance.
- Eco-efficiency and the environment.
- Digitalization: providing customers with the benefits of digitalization.
- Financial literacy.

Based on the standing of the various issues, organisations may classify the issues under different levels of priority. BBVA has classified them as 'Low', 'Medium', 'High' and 'Very High'. Organisations give priority to those issues that are of important concern to both the stakeholders and the organization. For BBVA, the top priority will be given for those issues that falls under the top right hand corner square (1, 2, 5, 24, 12).

Ford Motor Company has mapped its matrix under nine sections, and they are as below[29] (**Refer table 3.6**):

Table 3.6

Low Impact, High Concern	Medium Impact, High Concern	High Impact, High Concern
Low Impact, Medium Concern	Medium Impact, Medium Concern	High Impact, Medium Concern
Low Impact, Low Concern	Medium Impact, Low Concern	High Impact, Low Concern

The issues that falls under "high impact, high concern" classification will be given the highest priority by Ford. The next priority will be given for the two classifications of "medium impact, high concern" and "high impact, medium concern". This may be followed by the three classifications of "medium impact, medium concern", "low impact, high concern" and "high impact, low concern". The lowest priority may be given to the classification of "low impact, low concern".

29 http://corporate.ford.com/microsites/sustainability-report-2013-14/blueprint-materiality-matrix.html, Accessed on June 10, 2016.

Figures 3.4 and 3.5 provide more examples of materiality matrices, from (a) Kesko, a retailing conglomerate headquartered at Helsinki, Finland and (b) MTR, a public transport network in HongKong.

Figure 3.4[30]

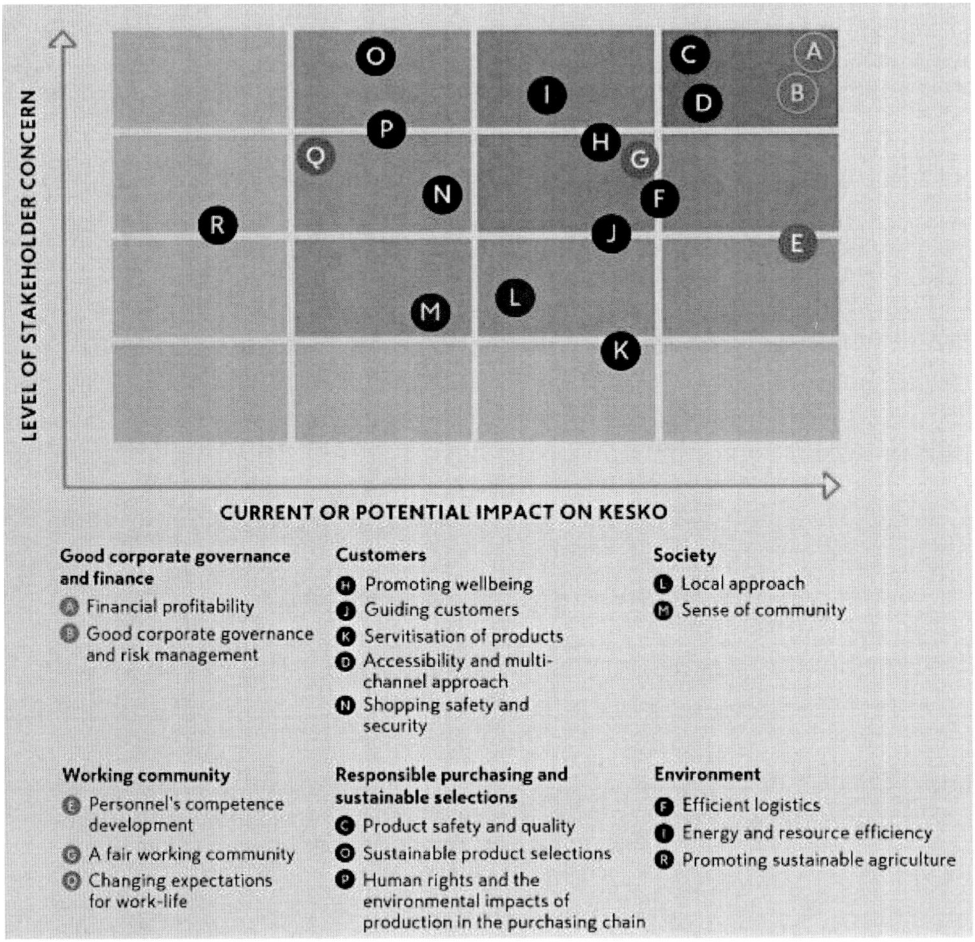

30 Image included with permission from Kesko. Available at http://www.kesko.fi/en/company/responsibility/how-do-we-manage-responsibility/materiality-assessment-of-keskos-corporate-responsibility/, Accessed on September 23, 2017.

Figure 3.5[31]

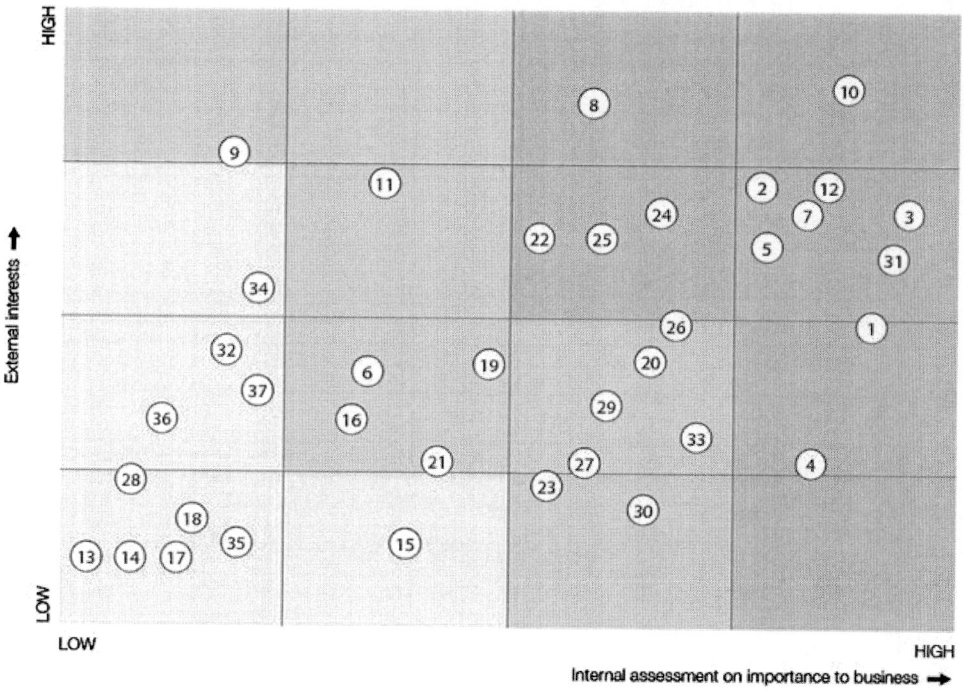

	FAIR OPERATING PRACTICES
1	Organisational governance structure & process
2	Fair operating practices (including ethical dealings with other organisations)
3	Anti-corruption
4	Responsible political involvement
5	Fair competition
	CONSUMER ISSUES
6	Fair marketing (including factual and unbiased information)
7	Customer education
8	Customers' health & safety

31 Image included with permission from MTR. Available at http://www.mtr.com.hk/en/corporate/sustainability/2014rpt/corp-report.php, Accessed on September 29, 2017.

9	Sustainable products & services
10	Customer service, support, & complaint handling
11	Customer data protection & privacy
12	Access to essential services (including avoidance of service disruption)
	HUMAN RIGHTS AND LABOUR PRACTICES
13	Human rights risks assessment
14	Human rights risk issues
15	Human rights grievances mechanism
16	Diversity and Equal Opportunity
17	Fundamental principles & rights at work (based on Internal Labour Organisation standards)
18	Protection of civil & political rights of staff
19	Employment practices
20	Conditions of work & social protection
21	Staff consultation & engagement (including freedom of association & collective bargaining)
22	Employee and contractor health & safety
23	Employee development & training
	THE ENVIRONMENT
24	Prevention of pollution (including air, water & waste)
25	Sustainable resource use (including resource efficiency & water use)
26	Climate change
27	Biodiversity
	SUPPLY CHAIN
28	Supply chain human rights risk
29	Promoting social responsibility in the value chain
	COMMUNITY INVOLVEMENT AND DEVELOPMENT
30	Payment from government / tax payment

31	Community involvement & development (including stakeholder engagement)
32	Education and culture
33	Employment creation & skills development
34	Technology development & access
35	Wealth & income creation
36	Community health
37	Community investment (including staff volunteering)

A disadvantage of the existing practice is that companies may ignore issues that are of high concern to stakeholders, yet, of low importance to business.

External Assurance

Some of the sustainability reports provide additional credibility through external assurance. An independent third party verifies whether the report is prepared in accordance with the standards of a reporting framework, which the organisation has claimed that the report adheres to (for example, GRI reporting standards). In an assurance report to BMW Group's Sustainable Value Report 2014, PricewaterhouseCoopers mentions that the management responsibility also includes *"the selection and application of appropriate methods to prepare the Report and the use of assumptions and estimates for individual sustainability disclosures which are reasonable in the circumstances. Furthermore, the responsibility includes designing, implementing and maintaining systems and processes relevant for the preparation of the Report."*[32]

Sustainability Reporting Frameworks

Some of the reporting frameworks emerge from the following:

1. ***Global Reporting Initiative (GRI)***
2. ***Sustainability Accounting Standards Board (SASB)***
3. ***EU Directive on Non-financial Reporting***
4. ***The Prince's Accounting for Sustainability Project* and *International Integrated Reporting C'uncil (IIRC)***

32 http://www.bmwgroup.com/com/en/_common/_pdf/Independent_Assurance_Report_EN_SVR2014_BMW_Group.pdf, Accessed on May 24, 2015.

Global Reporting Initiative (GRI)

Generating a responsibility report based on GRI principles is based on two aspects – (a) Principles for Defining Report Content (b) Principles for Defining Report Quality. These are detailed as follows (**Refer tables 3.7 and 3.8**):

Table 3.7

GRI Principles for Defining Report Content

Stakeholder Inclusiveness	The organization should identify its stakeholders, and explain how it has responded to their reasonable expectations and interests.
Sustainability Context	The report should present the organization's performance in the wider context of sustainability.
Materiality	The report should cover aspects that (a) reflect the organization's significant economic, environmental and social impacts; or (b) substantively influence the assessments and decisions of stakeholders.
Completeness	The report should include coverage of material aspects and their boundaries, sufficient to reflect significant economic, environmental and social impacts, and to enable stakeholders to assess the organization's performance in the reporting period.

Table 3.8

GRI Principles for Defining Report Quality

Balance	The report should reflect positive and negative aspects of the organization's performance to enable a reasoned assessment of overall performance.
Comparability	The organization should select, compile and report information consistently. The reported information should be presented in a manner that enables stakeholders to analyze changes in the organization's performance over time, and that could support analysis relative to other organizations.

Accuracy	The reported information should be sufficiently accurate and detailed for stakeholders to assess the organization's performance.
Timeliness	The organization should report on a regular schedule so that information is available in time for stakeholders to make informed decisions.
Clarity	The organization should make information available in a manner that is understandable and accessible to stakeholders using the report.

Sustainability Accounting Standards Board (SASB)

SASB has attempted developing accounting standards that considers material sustainability factors. SASB, through 2019, has developed accounting standards for approximately 80 industries across 10 sectors. SASB standards comprise of (a) disclosure guidance (b) standardised sustainability metrics.

EU Directive on Non-financial Reporting[33]

European Union (EU) has mandated certain disclosures *"on policies, risks and outcomes as regards environmental matters, social and employee-related aspects, respect for human rights, anti-corruption and bribery issues"*[34] for approximately 6000 large companies and groups across the EU. These requirements will apply to financial years beginning January 1, 2017.

The Prince's Accounting for Sustainability Project and **International Integrated Reporting Council (IIRC)**

This project was launched by Prince Charles of Wales in 2004. He mentioned that the objective of the Accounting for Sustainability (A4S) project was to *"help ensure that sustainability - considering what we do not only in terms of ourselves and today, but also of others and tomorrow - is not just talked and worried about, but becomes embedded in organizations' 'DNA'."*[35] This project resulted in the creation of International Integrated Reporting Council.

33 http://eur-lex.europa.eu/legal-content/EN/TXT/?uri=CELEX:32014L0095, Accessed on June 26, 2015.

34 https://www.frc.org.uk/Our-Work/Codes-Standards/Accounting-and-Reporting-Policy/Clear-and-Concise-Reporting/Narrative-Reporting/EU-Directive-on-non-financial-reporting.aspx, Accessed on June 26, 2015.

35 https://www.accountingforsustainability.org/about-us, Accessed on January 2, 2016.

IIRC lists the 'summary of requirements' for designing an Integrated Report as below (**Refer table 3.9**):

Table 3.9[36]

USING THE FRAMEWORK
Form of report and relationship with other information
An integrated report should be a designated, identifiable communication.
Application of the Framework
Any communication claiming to be an integrated report and referencing the Framework should apply all the requirements identified in bold italic type unless: (a) The unavailability of reliable information or specific legal prohibitions results in an inability to disclose material information (b) Disclosure of material information would cause significant competitive harm.
In the case of the unavailability of reliable information or specific legal prohibitions, an integrated report should: (a) Indicate the nature of the information that has been omitted (b) Explain the reason why it has been omitted (c) In the case of the unavailability of data, identify the steps being taken to obtain the information and the expected time frame for doing so
Responsibility for an Integrated Report
An integrated report should include a statement from those charged with governance that includes: (a) An acknowledgement of their responsibility to ensure the integrity of the integrated report (b) An acknowledgement that they have applied their collective mind to the preparation and presentation of the integrated report (c) Their opinion or conclusion about whether the integrated report is presented in accordance with this Framework or, if it does not include such a statement, it should explain: (a) What role those charged with governance played in its preparation and presentation (b) What steps are being taken to include such a statement in future reports (c) The time frame for doing so, which should be no later than the organization's third integrated report that references this Framework.

36 Copyright © December 2013 by the International Integrated Reporting Council ('the IIRC'). All rights reserved. Used with permission of the IIRC. Contact the IIRC (info@theiirc.org) for permission to reproduce, store, transmit or make other uses of this document. For details, https://integratedreporting.org/wp-content/uploads/2013/12/13-12-08-THE-INTERNATIONAL-IR-FRAMEWORK-2-1.pdf

GUIDING PRINCIPLES
Strategic focus and future orientation
An integrated report should provide insight into the organization's strategy, and how that relates to its ability to create value in the short, medium and long term and to its use of and effects on the capitals.
Connectivity of information
An integrated report should show a holistic picture of the combination, interrelatedness and dependencies between the factors that affect the organization's ability to create value over time.
Stakeholder relationships
An integrated report should provide insight into the nature and quality of the organization's relationships with its key stakeholders, including how and to what extent the organization understands, takes into account and responds to their legitimate needs and interests.
Materiality
An integrated report should disclose information about matters that substantively affect the organization's ability to create value over the short, medium and long term.
Conciseness
An integrated report should be concise.
Reliability and completeness
An integrated report should include all material matters, both positive and negative, in a balanced way and without material error.
Consistency and comparability
The information in an integrated report should be presented: (a) On a basis that is consistent over time (b) In a way that enables comparison with other organizations to the extent it is material to the organization's own ability to create value over time.
CONTENT ELEMENTS
Organizational overview and external environment
An integrated report should answer the question: What does the organization do and what are the circumstances under which it operates?

Governance
An integrated report should answer the question: How does the organization's governance structure support its ability to create value in the short, medium and long term?
Business model
An integrated report should answer the question: What is the organization's business model?
Risks and opportunities
An integrated report should answer the question: What are the specific risks and opportunities that affect the organization's ability to create value over the short, medium and long term, and how is the organization dealing with them?
Strategy and resource allocation
An integrated report should answer the question: Where does the organization want to go and how does it intend to get there?
Performance
An integrated report should answer the question: To what extent has the organization achieved its strategic objectives for the period and what are its outcomes in terms of effects on the capitals?
Outlook
An integrated report should answer the question: What challenges and uncertainties is the organization likely to encounter in pursuing its strategy, and what are the potential implications for its business model and future performance?
Basis of preparation and presentation
An integrated report should answer the question: How does the organization determine what matters to include in the integrated report and how are such matters quantified or evaluated

Benefits of Sustainability Reporting

A sustainability report can/ may reveal:

(a) the Key Result Areas (KRAs) of an organisation regarding sustainability endeavours

(b) the measurements used by the organisation to ascertain its progress in sustainability endeavours

(c) a contextual analysis of the organisation's business environment

(d) the achievements made by the organisation in meeting its sustainability goals

(e) areas that provide opportunities for improvement in sustainability related endeavors

These can happen only through setting up of systems and processes for data collection, measurement and assessment of data. An organization also needs to evolve various policies and processes.

Sustainability reporting can thus:

(a) provide authentic communication to its stakeholders

(b) generate respect for the company from its stakeholders

(c) result in policies and processes that improves business performance

(d) increase clarity in role allocation, decision-making, implementation of vision and mission of the company

(e) fine-tune strategies for implementing the aspects mentioned in (d)

(f) be a source of competitive advantage, and

(g) provide an organisation with an influential, if not leadership role amongst its peers.

Increasingly, organizations are providing information in metrics that are internationally comparable. This helps stakeholders of businesses to make informed decisions.

While reporting responsibility practices to stakeholders are helpful, attention has been drawn to the necessity to remain focused on the practice of responsibility ideals. During a conference on spirituality and leadership[37], SK Chakraborty, Founder - 'Centre for Human Values', IIM Kolkatta, and author of many books relating to values and management, shared the perspective that discussions related to 'ontology' and 'epistemology' related to research on spirituality in management, business and leadership, etc., need to emerge from a living guided by spiritual values.

Financial Metrics related to Sustainability

a. *Increase in revenues because of customer appreciation*

Sensitivity towards societal and planetary well-being and humanitarian commitment makes people purchase products from companies that are

37 February 1-5, 2011.

socially and environmentally responsible. In addition to recommending such companies amongst their networks, people tend to avoid companies that cause harm to the society.

b. *Cost savings and monetary gains from increased employee commitment due to socially responsible practices.*

Employees tend to contribute in organizations that contribute to the well-being of all. Employee commitment can result in increased productivity and reduced employee turnover. This can also result in monetary savings on recruitment and training.

c. *Savings in operational cost*

Sustainability practices can result in cost savings. A habit of reducing the font-size while taking print-outs, and using both sides of the paper can save paper and money.

d. *Growth rate in revenues for products that set higher standards in sustainability practices viz-a-viz the usual products*

There are examples, where products and product categories that set higher standards in social responsibility and environmental sustainability usually have a higher growth rate as compared to conventional products and conventional product categories. GE launched its 'Ecomagination' range of products in 2005. It has been reported that the company has aimed for double the revenue growth rate for the 'Ecomagination' range of products, in comparison to the total growth rate of the company, and it has been able to achieve this objective[38]. As part of 'Ecomagination', the company has been able to reduce its greenhouse gas (GHG) emissions, energy intensity, and the usage of freshwater.[39][40]

e. *Environmental impact values*

Companies such as Puma have started Environmental Profit and Loss (E P&L) accounting. E P&L involves ascertaining the monetary values of environmental impact through the value chain, which may also include the company's suppliers.

---

38 http://www.businesswire.com/news/home/20120628006287/en/GE%E2%80%99s-ecomagination-Reaches-105-Billion-Revenue#.VTQjB61Vikp, Accessed on July 25, 2017.

39 http://www.ge.com/about-us/ecomagination/strategy, Accessed on October 4, 2015.

40 http://www.gesustainability.com/performance-data/building-things-that-matter-goals-metrics/, Accessed on July 25, 2017.

f. *Pricing of carbon emissions within an organisation*

Companies such as Microsoft have launched carbon-trading within the organization. "*The price on carbon is determined by the total cost of the carbon fee fund investment strategy, which is set to meet the organizational carbon reduction policy objectives,*" says a note from Microsoft that details its carbon fee practice.[41]

You may take a break...

NATURAL AND SOCIAL CAPITAL ACCOUNTING

Responsibility does not only lie with the leaders of our countries or with those who have been appointed or elected to do a particular job. It lies with each one of us individually.[42]

—Tenzin Gyatso, the 14th Dalai Lama

Accounting was about financial information. It indicated the financial health of a company. However, there was recognition that business decisions driven solely on the basis of monetary aspects, ignoring aspects related to nature and society is not just comprehensive, but also cause negative impacts on the society and the planet. Huge financial growth of firms was almost always driven by exploitation of the planet or its inhabitants. A need was thus felt to account for the non-monetary aspects that are critical to businesses. These non-monetary aspects were not accounted in conventional accounting systems, primarily due to the difficulty in giving a monetary value to the natural and social entities.

'Natural capital' entities include resources such as water, air, minerals, timber, natural phenomena that has significant value for human sustenance (such as pollination, breeze, recreational enjoyment, climate regulation, rainfall) etc. The economic value of 'Columbia River Basin' is estimated at $199 billion[43] considering the various services it provides, including

41 http://download.microsoft.com/download/2/3/C/23C9C89B-664B-4D1D-BD7B-C0724E52A568/Microsoft%20Carbon%20Fee%20Guide.pdf, Accessed on October 4, 2015.

42 http://www.nobelprize.org/nobel_prizes/peace/laureates/1989/lama-lecture.html, Accessed on March 10, 2016.

43 https://www.columbiana.org/PDFs/CRBV-FINAL-DIGITAL.pdf, Accessed on January 13, 2018.

recreational value, irrigation services, ecosystem services etc. Of this, almost $190 billion is accounted for ecosystem services. It is estimated that the public parks in London helped the people to avoid £950 million per year on health related expenses[44]. Protected areas (tiger reserves, national parks, etc.) have been providing benefits worth millions (**Refer table 3.10 and figure 3.6**). 'Social capital' includes volunteering work done by people, network of relationships amongst people within and outside the organization, capabilities and potential of individuals to contribute to the greater common good, etc. Business organizations rely on natural capital and social capital. Natural capital and social capital are necessary for the prosperity of a company and its stakeholders. Natural and social capital accounting involves considering factors related to environment and society in business decisions, reporting and assessments.

Table 3.10[45]

Economic value of ecosystem-services at three tiger reserves in India

Economic Value (million rupee/ year)	**Pakke**	**Nagarjunasagar – Srisailam**	**Valmiki**
Provisioning Services (Employment Generation, Fishing, Fodder, Fuel wood, Bamboo, Non-timber Forest Produces, etc.)	86.13	766.99	332.38
Regulating Services (Carbon Sequestration, Water Provisioning, Water Purification, Sediment Retention, Soil Conservation, Nutrient Retention, Biological Control, Pollination, Gas Regulation, Waste Assimilation, Climate Regulation, Gene pool Protection, etc,)	86754.3	160,411.54	68,460.55

44 https://www.london.gov.uk/sites/default/files/11015viv_natural_capital_account_for_london_v7_full_vis.pdf, Accessed on January 13, 2017.

45 Data included is from a study commissioned by National Tiger Conservation Authority (NTCA), India. The study provides economic valuation of ecosystem services in ten tiger reserves of India, of the more than forty protected areas in India that are designated as tiger reserves. Study report available at http://www.indiaenvironmentportal.org.in/content/465276/economic-valuation-of-tiger-reserves-in-india-a-value-approach/, Accessed on February 16, 2020.

Cultural Services (Cultural Heritage, Recreation, Religious and spiritual visits, Research, education and nature interpretation, etc.)		17.40	
Supporting Services (Habitat for Species, etc.)	381.70	818.11	210.02

Note: In this study, while assigning a monetary value for water-provisioning services, researchers applied a monetary value of approximately 18 rupees per cubic metre of water. Application of monetary values, and the methods adopted towards such application, have limitations. A person wearing a diamond-studded gold ring (or, a chain, or, a bracelet, etc.), stranded in a desert, and craving for a gulp of water, may assign a different monetary value for water, at that instance. However, economic valuation studies attempt to communicate the importance of ecosystem services.

Figure 3.6[46]

Water Buffaloes at Lunugamvehera National Park, Sri Lanka.

46 Image Source: https://commons.wikimedia.org/wiki/File:Wild_water_buffaloest_Lunugamvehera_National_Park.JPG, Accessed on February 23, 2020.

Vallathol Narayana Menon, a poet from Kerala, writes,
"The universe is my home,
With its greens, grass and worms also being my family,
Sacrifice, is, the gain; while the rise, being, Humility..." [47]

Benefits and Advantages

An organization benefits in a number of ways by engaging in Natural and Social Capital Accounting. Some of them are as follows:

(1) Process Improvement – When an organization understands that its operations are resulting in erosion of societal and planetary wealth, it can choose to improvise on its processes. This may also contribute to increased efficiency and cost-savings.

(2) Management of Risk - Availability of data and information related to 'natural capital' and 'social capital' helps an organization to foresee and manage risks. For example, as raw material extraction from the planet increases, it may contribute to resource scarcity, increased pollution etc. This results in stricter regulations and difficulty in business operations. With natural and social capital accounting, an organization will able to understand and foresee the role and impact of natural resources in its operations, and vice-versa. This helps it to evolve solutions that can contribute to sustainable development.

(3) Venture into new businesses – As an organisation ascertain its relationship with society and planet, they may find areas where they can add value through new businesses.

Metrics and methodologies

Some of the prominent and popular metrics and methodologies used in accounting for 'Natural Capital' and 'Social Capital' are as follows (**Refer table 3.11**):

---

47 The translation is from Vallathol Narayana Menon's *'Lokame Tharavdu'*, a poem in Malayalam language. Vallathol Narayana Menon lived in Kerala between 1878 and 1958. The poet uses the word *'tharavadu'* (for 'home' in the translation mentioned above), which refers to an ancestral home. In Kerala, a state in southern India, multiple families (relatives, etc.) used to stay together, as a joint or extended family, in a *'tharavadu'*. Vallathol Narayana Menon has been influenced by the ideals as practised by Mahatma Gandhi.

Table 3.11

Cost Benefit Analysis (CBA)	CBA is to identify, enumerate and evaluate all measurable benefits and costs associated with a project.
Ecosystem Service Valuation (ESV)	Ecosystem services provided by nature sustain life on earth. "Ecosystem service valuation assigns monetary value to ecosystem services"**.
Environmental Profit and Loss Account (E P&L A)	In E P&L A, a monetary value is provided to the natural-resources and ecosystem-services impacted due to a company's operations or from which the company has derived benefits. This approach helps the stakeholders to have a broader perspective about the company. It is presented in a way similar to a financial profit and loss account.
Social Return on Investment (SROI)	While similar to CBA, SROI is focused on activities that will have a social impact. SROI relates inputs and impact on monetary terms and can be used to identify those activities that are most effective in terms of social returns.
Life Cycle Assessment (LCA)	LCA does a comprehensive environmental impact assessment through the entire life cycle of a product – from the extraction of raw material for manufacturing a product, to the recycling of product after its use.

In addition to the above, concepts such as Triple-bottom-line, which have been detailed elsewhere in this book[48], are also used in Natural and Social Capital Accounting.

Environmental Profit and Loss Accounting

An environmental profit and loss account (E P&L) attempts to ascertain the impact caused by an organization's operations on the natural environment - in monetary value. Questions has been raised on the appropriateness of assigning a monetary value to a service offered by nature and assigning a monetary cost to harm inflicted on them. The E P&L document of Novo Nordisk, a Danish pharmaceutical company, states, "*It can certainly*

48 Chapter 1, Chapter 2, Caselets, etc.

** Ajith Sankar, Environmental Management, Oxford University Press, 2015.

be discussed whether or not money is the best unit with which to measure environmental impacts, since it is difficult to place universal monetary values on fundamental services such as fresh water, clean air, biodiversity and land. Nevertheless, a monetary value allows for direct comparison between the E P&L and the regular Profit and Loss Account, which shows company's net earnings."[49]

Puma's Environmental Profit and Loss Account

In 2011, Puma, a German company that designs and sells footwear and clothing designed the world's first environmental profit and loss account. Through this process, Puma aimed at measuring the financial value of services given by nature (such as fresh water, clean air, healthy biodiversity and productive land) to the business operations. Puma aimed at finding the true costs of its operations from this process.

A press release from its parent company, PPR Home, mentioned that *"Ecosystem services are not infinitely available and many are in a growing state of decline with resulting negative impacts on businesses and the global economy. At present this crucial link is not explicitly addressed in corporate sustainability strategies because businesses have traditionally taken ecosystem services for granted and treated them as 'free' services which go unaccounted for in their traditional profit and loss accounting and the delivery of their bottom lines."*[50]

Puma considered greenhouse gas emissions (GHGs), water use, land use, air pollution and waste as areas where it is having significant environmental impacts, and included these in its E P&L. All environmental impacts from raw material production till the point of sale were considered. Majority of the company's manufacturing processes were outsourced. Thus, in addition to considering the environmental impacts made directly by Puma ("Puma Operations"), the company also considered the environmental impact caused by its suppliers while contributing to the work of Puma. The suppliers were classified into four tiers (**Refer table 3.12**).

---

49 http://www2.mst.dk/Udgiv/publications/2014/02/978-87-93178-02-1.pdf, Accessed on June 12, 2016.

50 http://pwc.blogs.com/files/about-ppr-home-e-p-and-l.pdf, Accessed on June 11, 2016.

Table 3.12

Area	Activities
Puma Operations	Offices, Shops, IT, Warehousing, Business related travel, Logistics.
Tier I Suppliers	Manufacturing of shoes, apparels and accessories.
Tier II Suppliers	Outsole production, Insole production, Textile embroidery and cutting, Adhesive and paint production.
Tier III Suppliers	Leather tanning, Petroleum refining, Cotton weaving and dyeing.
Tier IV Suppliers	Cattle rearing, Rubber plantations, Cotton farming, Petroleum production, Other material production.

The assessment considered the data for 2010. Puma concluded that its environmental impacts amounted to almost 145 million[51] Euro (**Refer table 3.13**). In the same year, the company had a net-profit of 202.2 Euro million. This indicated that almost three-fourth of the company's profits would have got removed if the company considered its environmental costs. This exercise also made the company realise (and communicate to its stakeholders) that a large portion of its environmental costs are at the supplier level (137 Euro million).

Benefits of Environmental Profit and Loss Accounting

1. Identifying economic risks due to environmental impacts.
2. Increased transparency in stakeholder communication.
3. Improvement in efficiency and effectiveness of sustainability initiatives.
4. Meaningful engagement with the suppliers.
5. Better understanding about the operations of the company.

The Process of Environmental Profit and Loss Accounting

1. Deciding the scope of the project – what to measure, which segments of the business to be included etc.
2. Mapping the value chain: To identify and detail the production

51 http://about.puma.com/damfiles/default/sustainability/environment/e-p-l/EPL080212final-3cdfc1bdca0821c6ec1cf4b89935bb5f.pdf, Accessed on June 12, 2016.

Table 3.13

Euro Million	Water Use	GHGs (Green House Gas)	Land Use	Other air pollution	Waste	Total	% of Total
	33.00%	33.00%	25.00%	7.00%	2.00%	100.00%	
TOTAL	**47**	**47**	**37**	**11**	**3**	**145**	100.00%
Puma Operations	<1	7	<1	1	<1	8	6.00%
Tier I Suppliers	1	9	<1	1	2	13	9.00%
Tier II Suppliers	4	7	<1	2	1	14	9.00%
Tier III Suppliers	17	7	<1	3	<1	27	19.00%
Tier IV Suppliers	25	17	37	4	<1	83	57.00%

process through the entire life cycle - from production of raw material, through manufacturing of the product, to the point of sales or beyond.

3. Identification and Collection of Data.

4. Calculation and Analysis.

THE WBCSD SELF-ASSESSMENT QUESTIONNAIRE[52]

This questionnaire designed by World Business Council for Sustainable Development (WBCSD) will help *"to gauge how well your company is engaging CSR."*

VISION

A statement of a company's long-term goals and aspirations.

The company has a written vision?

- ❑ Yes, we have a vision approved by the board
- ❑ It is promulgated throughout the company
- ❑ It is available to the public
- ❑ The vision was prepared in consultation with stakeholders
- ❑ There is a process for reviewing the vision

COMMITMENT

A formal expression of a company's intentions in the area of CSR.

- ❑ There is a board minute recording the company's commitment to Corporate Social Responsibility (CSR)
- ❑ There is a board member with specific responsibility for CSR policy

Name:..

Title:...

52 Included with permission. From the document *"Corporate Social Responsibility: Making good business sense"*, available at http://old.wbcsd.org/pages/edocument/edocumentdetails.aspx?id=83&nosearchcontextkey=true, accessed on July 15, 2017.

- ❑ Each director has responsibilities for implementing the CSR policy
- ❑ CSR performance is included on the Board/Committee agenda
- ❑ There is a strategy for implementing CSR

VALUES

The fundamental principles to which a company declares adherence.

- ❑ Corporate values have been approved by the Board
- ❑ The values are defined and explained
- ❑ The values were formulated in consultation with stakeholders
- ❑ The values have been communicated to employees
- ❑ The values have been communicated to the public

VALUES IMPLEMENTATION

The processes for ensuring adherence to corporate values.

- ❑ There is a code of conduct
- ❑ The values are included as part of employee training
- ❑ The values are included in the reward process
- ❑ The business objectives and processes are checked for alignment with values

STAKEHOLDER ISSUES

Those matters which stakeholders believe a company influences.

- ❑ The company has identified its stakeholder groups
- ❑ The company has determined the nature of it's relationship with the stakeholder groups
- ❑ The issues relevant to the company and it's stakeholder groups have been identified
- ❑ The issues have been modified/ confirmed through dialogue with it's stakeholder groups

IMPACT ASSESSMENT

Assessment of the direct and indirect consequences of a company's activities.

The company has assessed the social and ethical impacts of it's:

Products/Services

- ❑ past
- ❑ present
- ❑ planned

Business operations

- ❑ past
- ❑ present
- ❑ planned

FORMULATE POLICY

CSR policy is the set of principles which inform and guide the implementation of a corporate social responsibility strategy in a company.

The company has formulated a CSR policy?

- ❑ Yes
- ❑ The policy was formulated in consultation with stakeholder groups
- ❑ The policy has been communicated to employees
- ❑ The policy is published and available to the public

PROGRAMMES/ TARGETS

The CSR program is the plan for implementing CSR policy, and will where applicable, include targets to achieve performance improvement.

- ❑ A program for monitoring CSR policy has been established
- ❑ Targets and time scales for CSR improvement have been identified and set
- ❑ The program and targets cover all of the issues identified through stakeholder dialogue

MONITOR/ MEASURE PERFORMANCE

The processes and measures by which performance is assessed (against targets as applicable).

- ❑ Indicators have been identified which measure performance against targets

- ❑ Indicators have been defined in consultation with stakeholder groups
- ❑ The indicators have been checked to ensure that these are appropriate to the issues
- ❑ CSR performance is monitored by management and the Board

REPORT AND COMMUNICATE

The various means by which a company's approach to CSR and it's performance are conveyed to stakeholders.

Progress in implementing CSR programs and achievement of targets is communicated to:

- ❑ Employees
- ❑ The public
- ❑ Other stakeholder groups
- ❑ The reports fully address all of the issues identified in dialogue with stakeholders

The company's performance with respect to it's values, issues and targets is published:

- ❑ As a hard copy report
- ❑ On the Internet

INDEPENDENT VERIFICATION

The process of independent review to provide assurance that company reporting fairly represents corporate activity.

- ❑ Published reports are subject to external, independent verification

The verification assures:

- ❑ Completeness of published reports
- ❑ Accuracy
- ❑ The rigor of support systems

REASSESSMENT

The process by which a company continuously reviews and updates CSR strategy and actions taking account of stakeholders' changing expectations.

The company reviews and re-assesses:

- ❑ Vision, values, issues, programs and targets in the light of performance

- ❑ This review is undertaken with stakeholders
- ❑ The programs and targets are modified as a result of this process

SUPPORT SYSTEMS

The part of the overall management system which includes the organisational structure and processes for supporting the management, measurement and auditing of CSR performance.

There is a system for:

- ❑ Collecting stakeholder input
- ❑ Analysing
- ❑ There is a system for collecting and analysing data relevant to CSR programs and targets

There is an internal audit program which covers:

- ❑ Values support systems
- ❑ CSR support systems
- ❑ CSR performance
- ❑ The findings of the audits are reported to the Board/ Committee

Swami Chandrasekharendra Saraswati also mentions, "*Annadaana or the gift of food is one kind of service or paropakara... (Service) includes digging wells and ponds for the public, feeding the poor, building temples for the spiritual well-being of people, laying out gardens. Excavating wells and ponds has been mentioned first. The importance of this work may be gauged from such remarks in ordinary conversation, "What's he doing? Digging a well or something?" It is extremely meritorious to excavate a pond outside the village to slake the thirst of cattle. All people in a village or locality must join toget[53]her in such work...*".

CHAPTER SUMMARY

- An organisation pondering on questions related to aspects that are ideal, ethical and legal, at all stages of business decision making, can help an organisation to bring clarity in its responsibility practices.
- A formal CSR process may involve steps such as (a) Impact Diagnosis (b) Business Opportunity Identification (c) Aligning CSR with organisational DNA (d) Integrating PMS and Responsibility Metrics

53 Hindu Dharma: The Universal Way of Life, Bharathiya Vidya Bhavan, 1996.

(e) Vendor Management and (f) Stakeholder Communication and Engagement.

- 'Materiality Analysis' is the process used to identify those sustainability (CSR) related aspects that an organization choose to address in its communication to stakeholders.
- There are various frameworks for reporting CSR practices.
- There are multiple advantages to sustainability reporting.
- An environmental profit and loss account (E P&L) attempts to ascertain and assign, in monetary value, the impact caused by an organization on the natural environment.
- Puma pioneered 'environmental profit and loss accounting'.

KEYWORDS

Dharma, Artha, Kama, Moksha, Sustainability Reporting, Corporate Social Responsibility Report, Materiality Analysis, Materiality Matrix, Sustainability Reporting Frameworks, International Integrated Reporting Council (IIRC), Sustainability Accounting Standards Board (SASB), External Assurance, Natural Capital, Social Capital, Natural Capital Accounting, Social Capital Accounting, Cost Benefit Analysis (CBA), Ecosystem Service Valuation (ESV), Environmental Profit and Loss Account (E P&L A), Social Return on Investment (SROI), Life Cycle Assessment (LCA), Risk Management, Process Improvement, Materiality Analysis, 5W1H Method, CSR Process, Performance Management System, Vendor Management, CSR Threshold.

MULTIPLE CHOICE QUESTIONS

1. Which of the below may also used to indicate, or, used as a synonym to 'Sustainability Reporting'?
   (a) Social Accounting
   (b) Corporate Social Responsibility Reporting
   (c) Social and environmental accounting
   (d) Accountability Reporting
   (e) All the above options
2. Which of the following are 'Sustainability Reporting Frameworks'?
   (a) Global Reporting Initiative
   (b) ISO 9000

(c) Carbon Cool
(d) Bharat Jaivik
(e) 'Energy Star' from 'Bureau of Energy Efficiency'

3. Which brand/ company pioneered 'Environmental Profit and Loss Accounting'?
(a) Kochi Metro
(b) Wipro
(c) Ecosia
(d) Delhi Metro
(e) Puma

4. What is the 6R Principle?
(a) Refuse, Reduce, Reuse, Repurpose, Recycle, Recover
(b) A management framework jointly developed by Tom Peters, Peter Drucker and CK Prahalad
(c) A Japanese management concept - Remember, Rethink, Recharge, Revolve, Reengineer, Reposition
(d) An acronym for scoring six runs in a cricket match
(e) None Of The Above

5. Which amongst the following is a hotel that gives all its profits to philanthropic, social and environmental causes:
(a) Green Hotel, Mysuru
(b) White Hotel, Mysuru
(c) Yellow Hotel, Mysuru
(d) Violet Hotel, Mysuru
(e) Blue Hotel, Mysuru

6. Which of the following are examples of 'Natural Capital Valuation':
(a) The economic value of the ecosystem services of 'Columbia River Basin' is estimated at $190 billion
(b) Public parks in London helped the people to avoid £950 million per year on health related expenses
(c) Economic value of ecosystem-services at the Nagarjunasagar - Srisailam tiger reserve in India is esimated at more than 150,000 million rupees per year

(d) Economic value of ecosystem-services at the Pakke tiger reserve in India is esimated at more than 85,000 million rupees per year

(e) All of the above

SHORT ANSWER QUESTIONS

1. Which are the three questions that can help a company to build a stable foundation in sustainability practices?
2. What is 'Sustainability Reporting'?
3. What is 'External Assurance' in the context of 'Sustainability Reporting'?
4. Mention any two 'Sustainability Reporting' frameworks?
5. List any three benefits of 'Sustainability Reporting'?
6. What is natural and social capital accounting?
7. What is the expansion of 'SROI' and 'ESV'?
8. What are the four steps in Environmental Profit and Loss Accounting?

LONG ANSWER QUESTIONS

1. Provide examples for each of the six steps in the 'CSR Process'?
2. In the context of a GRI reporting framework, explain any two principles related to 'report content' and any two principles related to 'report quality'?
3. Mention any ten parameters/ aspects that can be included in 'Materiality Analysis'.

REFLECTIVE QUESTIONS

1. Study the CSR initiatives of any three companies operating in India. If you were given an opportunity to improvise on these initiatives, how would you do the same?
2. Read through the sustainability reports of any five companies. Which one did you like the most? State the reasons for your likeness for that report.
3. *"By including social responsibility metrics in employee appraisals and reward systems, the employees are incentivised to work towards sustainability goals and CSR practices."* Examine the advantages and disadvantages of this practice.

About the chapter

1. Learning from the chapter, if any:

2. Topics, concepts, themes, etc. that you may be interested to research/ refer/ study/ ponder upon:

3. Applications in daily life, if any:

Notes:

Chapter 3 completed... You may take a break...

Towers, exclusively made for staircases, features in many of the architectural marvels in Europe. The photograph above depict a church at Puy-l'Évêque, Lot, in the Occitanie region of France, and the staircase tower is visible to the right-side of the entrance[54].

"Incorporating physical activity into daily routines is the best way to get the many health benefits of exercise," said Dr. Thomas Farley, Health Commissioner, New York City, during an event to promote the usage of staircases[55]. This event was supported by Michael Bloomberg, who was the mayor of city, and also the CEO and founder of Bloomberg L.P. The headquarters' building of Bloomberg L.P. has been designed as to encourage its employees to use stairs (instead of elevators).

54 https://commons.wikimedia.org/wiki/File:Puy-l'%C3%89v%C3%AAque_%C3%89glise_Saint-Sauveur5.JPG, Accessed on November 17, 2018.

55 https://www1.nyc.gov/office-of-the-mayor/news/250-13/mayor-bloomberg-first-ever-center-active-design-promote-physical-activity-and, Accessed on November 17, 2018.

Chapter 4

GUIDELINES, REGULATIONS AND LEGISLATIONS

"A little rearrangement of words in the phrase CSR produces another — SRC or 'Socially Responsible Corporation'. Now that would be something to strive for, to be proud of! To be meaningful, the word 'responsibility' needs to be incorporated in the way corporate affairs are carried out.... Responsibility is much more than merely abiding by the 'letter of the law'... Responsibility stems from a view one has about oneself, an enlightened sensitivity of the context one is a part of."[1]

—Deep Joshi,
Executive Director, PRADAN

On completion of reading the chapter, the reader may:

know the important guidelines and regulations related to the practice of social responsibility by business organisations

The frailty of humans, their dilemmas, wants and needs, and the infinite powers that holds influence on them, has been a theme of writings and discussions through the centuries. Paakkanaar[2] is a known character amongst many in Kerala, a state in Southern India. His stories, as well as those of his ten brothers and a sister, are legendary, orally communicated by parents and grandparents to children. Paakkanaar used to work with bamboo for making products that help in agriculture and household. This thus involved visits to nearby forests, for collecting raw material. One of the legends mentions about Paakkanaar and his wife, Kaanthi[3], chancing upon a treasure (gold coins) in the forests, and the events that followed.

1 http://articles.economictimes.indiatimes.com/2010-04-11/news/27627125_1_corporate-philanthropy-csr-social-responsibility, Accessed on August 9, 2015.

2 It is believed that Paakkanaar is one of the twelve children of Vararuchi and Panchami. The children were Mezhathol Agnihotri, Rajakan, Uliyannoor Perunthachan, Vsllon, Vayillakkunnilappan, Vaduthala Nair, Karackalamma, Uppukuttan, Pananaar, Naranathu Braanthan, Akavoor Chaathan, and Paakkanaar.

3 Legends are there about Paakkanaar's wife (Kaanthi) too. Once Paakkanaar called for his wife when she was drawing water from a well. Immediately, she moved towards him, leaving the rope and the water-filled vessel mid-way. The legend is that the rope and the vessel stood as it is.

Bhartrihari went to the forest too. He was a king[4] and had the urge to undergo practices of penance. He left the kingdom. The forests facilitated him. One day, he saw something glittering lying on the ground - an unnatural animation on the forest floor – similar to that of light reflecting on gems or precious stones. Bhartrihari ran towards it, only to find that the glitter was a reflection of the world in a spit of saliva. Bhartihari pondered on all that glitters. *"I've spent much time here in the forests, and underwent various practices of penance. Yet, i was easily lured"*. He returned to the kingdom and ruled for many years[5].

The forests provides opportunities for learning. It also holds riches of various forms. *The Ramayana* of Valmiki mentions about the existence of more than 50 varieties of trees near a lake, 'Pampa Sarovar'. One of the narratives about Manikanda (the one adorning a bell in the neck), the prince of Panthala (a region in Southern India), is that he conveyed his father about his wishes to be in the forests. His father was affectionate. Manikanda evoked respect from many - humans and non-humans. It is not of common reference where-when a population of leopards and tigers visit human habitation in a spirit of non-animosity, with the lead-leopard carrying this prince. Those who devote to him also refers to him as *Kaananavaasan* (the one living in the forests) and "*Bhoomiprapanchan*" (the one in whom the Earth and Universe manifests).

Responding to a Public Interest Litigation (PIL), the Uttarakhand High Court at Nainital, in 2017, observed that the Rivers Ganga and Yamuna are losing their very existence and measures need to be taken to preserve these rivers. The court observed that "*Rivers Ganga and Yamuna are central to the existence of half of Indian population and their health and well being. The rivers have provided both physical and spiritual sustenance to all of us from time immemorial...*". The court further stated that "*the Rivers Ganga and Yamuna, all their tributaries, streams, every natural water flowing with flow continuously or intermittently of these rivers, are declared as juristic/ legal persons/ living entities having the status of a legal person with all corresponding rights, duties*

4 Bhartrihari was the son of King Gandhavasen of Malwa.

5 In *Vairagya Shataka*, Bhartrihari mentions (as translated by JM Kennedy (*The Satakas or Wise Sayings of Bhartrihari*, T Werner Laurie Ltd., 1913), "*In our periods of health, we are alarmed by the fear of disease; in the pride we take in our family, by the fear of a sudden fall; in wealth, by the fear of a grasping ruler; in honour, by the fear of degradation; in power, by the fear of enemies; in beauty, by the fear of old age; in our knowledge of the Scriptures, by the fear of controversy; in virtue, by the fear of evil; and in our body, by the fear of death.*" Bhartrihari also observes: "*"Are you a chandal? Are you a Brahmin? Are you a Sudra or an ascetic? Or a lord of devotion whose mind has been developed by meditating on the truth?" Ascetics, when loud-voiced men ask them questions like these, experience neither pleasure nor irritation, but quietly pursue their way.*"

and liabilities of a living person in order to preserve and conserve river Ganga and Yamuna."[6]

The Uttarakhand High Court also accorded the status of a living entity to *"the Glaciers including Gangotri & Yamunotri, rivers, streams, rivulets, lakes, air, meadows, dales, jungles, forests wetlands, grasslands, springs and waterfalls"*[7]. Similar announcements have been made in other parts of the world too. Bolivia, through 2010-12, accorded nature with similar rights as for humans, through the 'Law of the Rights of Mother Earth'. In 2008, Ecuador included a chapter related to 'Rights of Nature' in its constitution. New Zealand has accorded the status of a living entity to Whanganui river[8] and 'Te Urewera'[9]. These exemplify legal acknowledgements to the inherent worth of all entities of this planet.

Figure 4.1[10]

6 http://lobis.nic.in/ddir/uhc/RS/orders/22-03-2017/RS20032017WPPIL1262014.pdf, Accessed on June 15, 2017.

7 http://lobis.nic.in/ddir/uhc/RS/orders/31-03-2017/RS30032017WPPIL1402015.pdf, Accessed on June 15, 2017.

8 https://www.parliament.nz/en/get-involved/features/innovative-bill-protects-whanganui-river-with-legal-personhood/, Accessed on June 15, 2017.

9 A national park, de-established in 2014, with the implementation of the Urewera Act 2014. The Act provided "a legal identity and protected status for Te Urewera for its intrinsic worth, its distinctive natural and cultural values, the integrity of those values, and for its national importance".

10 Credits: Ralph Underhill/ Cartoonralph; Source: http://www.cartoonralph.co.uk, Image included with permission.

While this may be an awakening amongst the humanity, it can also be due to the recognition about the erosion of the quality of life, despite economic growth, and the decreasing human connect with nature (**Refer Figure 4.1**). A similar recognition is emerging about the role of businesses in society, and this recognition is reflected in various guidelines, regulations and legislations related to the business operations.

GUIDELINES IN INDIA

"Political rhetoric alone do not build a nation unless it is backed by the power of sacrifice, toil and virtue. That is true nation-building."[11]

—APJ Abdul Kalam

The annual revenue of some of the largest companies of the world, is higher than or comparable with the GDP of many nations. Indian Oil Corporation and Reliance Industries Limited had an annual revenue of approximately USD 70,000 million[12] and USD 65,000 million[13] in 2017-18, while the GDP of Tuvalu, an island nation located in the Pacific, was approximately USD 48,000 million[14] in 2017. The combined revenue of the top ten global companies would be higher than or comparable to (individual GDP) of approximately 40 countries or independent territories of the world, including countries such as Maldives, Bhutan, Somalia and Seychelles (**Refer Figure 4.2**).

Businesses exert considerable influence on people's living. Businesses provide some of the necessary goods and services to people. It also provides employment and contributes to economic development. It is thus important that businesses are guided by values and principles that contribute to the well-being of all. These values and principles may be coded in the form of guidelines, laws and regulations that governs the various aspects of conducting a business.

Mirakle Couriers is a Mumbai based courier company that primarily employs low-income deaf adults. Most of its staff, including the delivery personnel and the back-office staff engaged in work such as data entry,

---

11 APJ Abdul Kalam, My Journey: Transforming Dreams into Actions, Rupa Publications, 2014.

12 https://www.iocl.com/download/AnnualReport2017-18.pdf, Accessed on September 25, 2018.

13 http://www.ril.com/getattachment/e5d8ddac-3899-4a0f-beb5-aa7f8100010c/AnnualReport_2017-18.aspx, Accessed on September 25, 2018.

14 https://data.worldbank.org/indicator/NY.GDP.MKTP.CD?year_high_desc=true, Accessed on September 25, 2018.

Figure 4.2

Spot the difference!

The two images below are the posters of the football (soccer) World Cup help in Brazil - in 1950 and in 2014. Spo(r)t the difference between the two images:

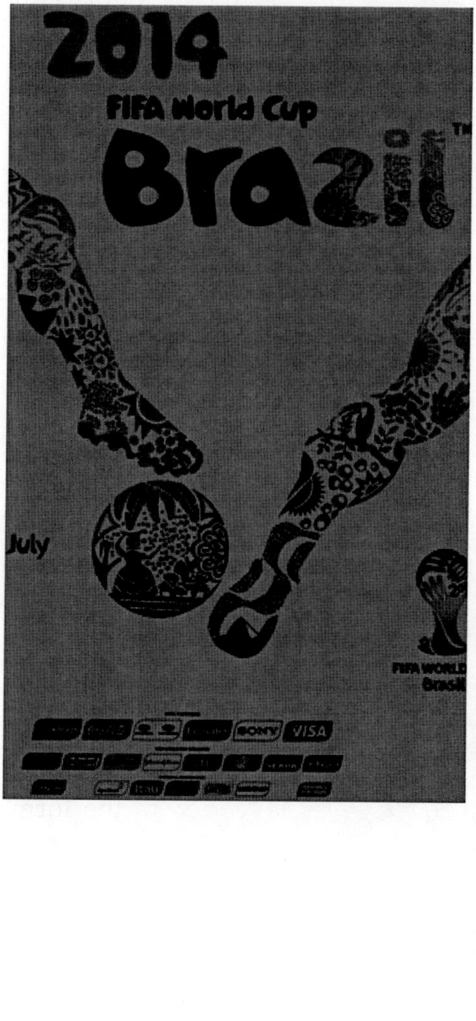

This image included here is a low-resolution version of the original 2014 world-cup poster. Also, the border section of the original image has been removed. The image has been included here for educational and informational purposes.

scanning, sorting, tracking and delivery-reporting, are deaf people. The organisation which started functioning in January 2009, was based on the idea that courier delivery does not require verbal communication. In addition to document deliveries, the organisation also makes deliveries emerging from e-commerce transactions. All the members of Mirakle Couriers are fluent in 'Indian Sign Language', which is the primary mode of communication at the office of Mirakle Couriers. The organisation also use technological help such as mobile based SMS and smartphone applications.

The Rights of Persons with Disabilities Act, 2006, from Government of India, encourages for-profit organisations to provide employment to those with disabilities. One of the clauses of this legislation states that, "*The appropriate Government and the local authorities shall, within the limit of their economic capacity and development, provide incentives to employer in private sector to ensure that at least five per cent of their work force is composed of persons with benchmark disability*"[15]. Such legislations draw attention to and acknowledge the opportunities available with governmental agencies and private sector enterprises towards making business a transformative experience. These legislations may also help organisations similar to Mirakle Couriers to gain recognition and maintain their financially sustainability.

In 2013, India became the first country to mandate CSR spending. Many legislations in India consider the responsibility aspects related to private enterprises. A few of these acts (with amendments, as applicable) include the Consumer Protection Act 1986, Environment Protection Act 1986, Prevention of Corruption Act 1988, Public Liability Insurance Act 1991, etc."[16] In the context of CSR practices in India, three important guidelines include:

1. Section 135 of Companies Act 2013
2. SEBI Notification on Business Responsibility Reporting
3. National Voluntary Guidelines on Social, Environmental and Economic Responsibilities of Business

15 http://disabilityaffairs.gov.in/upload/uploadfiles/files/RPWD%20ACT%202016.pdf, Accessed on December 21, 2018.

16 For a detailed listing of various legislations related to responsibility practices in business, one may refer to Annexure C ("Indicative List of Relevant Laws & Acts Mapped Against Principles") of a document related to 'National Voluntary Guidelines on Social, Environmental and Economic Responsibilities of Business', available at http://www.mca.gov.in/Ministry/latestnews/National_Voluntary_Guidelines_2011_12jul2011.pdf, Accessed on December 21, 2018.

Section 135 of Companies Act 2013

The Companies Act 2013, passed by the Parliament of India, deals with the governance of companies - listed and unlisted. Section 135 of the Companies Act 2013, which deals with 'Corporate Social Responsibility' parameters, came into effect from April 1, 2014. "*The Companies Act, 2013 has introduced the idea of CSR to the forefront and through its disclose-or-explain mandate, is promoting greater transparency and disclosure,*" says a report[17]. Some of the salient features of Section 135 are listed below. These are applicable for "*Every company having net worth of rupees five hundred crore or more, or turnover of rupees one thousand crore or more or a net profit of rupees five crore or more during any financial year*".[18]

1. Such companies "*shall constitute a Corporate Social Responsibility Committee of the Board consisting of three or more directors, out of which at least one director shall be an independent director.*"
2. This CSR committee is to formulate and recommend a 'Corporate Social Responsibility Policy' to the Board. This committee will recommend the amount to be incurred for the various CSR related activities to be undertaken by the company. This committee also has the responsibility to monitor the CSR policy of the company on a regular basis.
3. The Board of the company, "*after taking into account the recommendations made by the Corporate Social Responsibility Committee, approve the Corporate Social Responsibility Policy for the company and disclose contents of such Policy in its report and also place it on the company's website*".
4. The Board of the company has to "*ensure that the activities as are included in Corporate Social Responsibility Policy of the company are undertaken by the company*".
5. The Board "*shall ensure that the company spends, in every financial year, at least two per cent of the average net profits of the company made during the three immediately preceding financial years*".

In a clarification dated June 18, 2014, Ministry of Corporate Affairs (MCA) has mentioned that CSR spending should be done on a project basis, and not as "*one-off events such as marathons/ awards/ charitable contribution/*

17 http://www.pwc.in/assets/pdfs/publications/2013/handbook-on-corporate-social-responsibility-in-india.pdf, Accessed on May 24, 2015.

18 http://www.mca.gov.in/Ministry/pdf/CompaniesAct2013.pdf, Accessed on April 6, 2015.

advertisement/ sponsorships of TV programmes etc".[19] The notification also mentioned that the salaries paid by the companies to the regular CSR staff of the company can be factored into CSR project cost.

SEBI Notification on Business Responsibility Reporting

Securities and Exchange Board of India (SEBI) is the regulator for the securities market in India. In a notification[20] dated August 13, 2012, SEBI stated that for-profit enterprises are *"accountable not merely to their shareholders from a revenue and profitability perspective but also to the larger society which is also its stakeholder"*. SEBI mandated that the top 100 listed entities, based on market capitalisation at BSE and NSE, need to include a 'business responsibility report' in their annual report. The 'business responsibility reports' were made voluntary for other listed companies. On November 30, 2015, SEBI extended this mandate to top 500 listed entities. *"As a green initiative, the business responsibility reports can be given on the websites of the companies providing website link for the same in their annual reports,"* says the SEBI press release.[21] In 2019, SEBI extended the mandate to the top 1000 listed entities[22]. SEBI also suggested a format that can be used while providing these reports.

National Voluntary Guidelines on Social, Environmental and Economic Responsibilities of Business

There are tendencies, also reflected in literatures of the world, which communicate the path of "an eye for an eye". This iron-fist rule is also reflected in popular culture - such as the "angry young man" image of Amitabh Bachhan in his movies of 1970s. Yet, spiritual and religious traditions across the world invite a relook at this perspective. Amongst the offerings that can be made at Sabarimala, one of the temples in South India, are *'Sathrupushpanjali'* (Sathru-pushpam-anjali) and *'Sathrusookthaanjali'* (Sathru-sooktham-anjali). *'Sathru'* means 'enemy'. However, as can be noted for these offerings, the word *'Sathru'* is followed by the usage of the word *'anjali'*, which means, an offering. *'Pushpam'* refers to flower/s and *'sooktham'* refers to prayers or communications with a noble intent. The *Adi*

19 http://www.mca.gov.in/Ministry/pdf/General_Circular_21_2014.pdf, Accessed on April 6, 2015.

20 Notification Number CIR/CFD/DIL/8/2012

21 http://www.sebi.gov.in/media/press-releases/nov-2015/sebi-board-meeting_31145.html, Accessed on November 6, 2017.

22 https://www.sebi.gov.in/sebi_data/meetingfiles/dec-2019/1576469077048_1pdf, Accessed on February 17, 2020.

Granth[23] says, "*By thinking, He cannot be reduced to thought, even by thinking hundreds of thousands of times. By remaining silent, inner silence is not obtained, even by remaining lovingly absorbed deep within. The hunger of the hungry is not appeased, even by piling up loads of worldly goods. Hundreds of thousands of clever tricks, but not even one of them will go along with you in the end.*"

The Tibetan perspective on health and healing holds that the root cause of diseases are ignorance, desire or hatred. Living in a world of phenomenon, it may be difficult to fully rid oneself of these, while, it may be possible to discover their existence in oneself, leading to acknowledgement and acceptance. Further, dissolution of these causes, and their channelisation and transformation may also help in moving the physical and mental bodies towards a state of equilibrium.

In 2011, the Ministry of Corporate Affairs, Government of India, released the 'National Voluntary Guidelines on Social, Environmental and Economic responsibilities of Business'[24] (**Refer Table 4.1**).

Table 4.1

Principle 1: Businesses should conduct and govern themselves with Ethics, Transparency and Accountability
1. Businesses should develop governance structures, procedures and practices that ensure ethical conduct at all levels; and promote the adoption of this principle across its value chain 2. Businesses should communicate transparently and assure access to information about their decisions that impact relevant stakeholders 3. Businesses should not engage in practices that are abusive, corrupt, or anti-competition 4. Businesses should truthfully discharge their responsibility on financial and other mandatory disclosures 5. Businesses should report on the status of their adoption of these Guidelines as suggested in the reporting framework in this document 6. Businesses should avoid complicity with the actions of any third party that violates any of the principles contained in these Guidelines

23 The quote is from the first page of 'Sri Guru Granth Sahib', as translated to English by Dr Sant Singh Khalsa from Gurmukhi. 'Sri Guru Granth Sahib' is a text of the Sikh religion. This text had its beginnings as 'Adi Granth'. The Sikhs also refers to the original text, the "Adi Granth", as the "Kartaarpur Vaali Bir".

24 http://pib.nic.in/newsite/PrintRelease.aspx?relid=73107, Accessed on August 18, 2017.

Principle 2: Businesses should provide goods and services that are safe and contribute to sustainability throughout their life cycle 1. Businesses should assure safety and optimal resource use over the life-cycle of the product – from design to disposal – and ensure that everyone connected with it - designers, producers, value chain members, customers and recyclersare aware of their responsibilities. 2. Businesses should raise the consumer's awareness of their rights through education, product labelling, appropriate and helpful marketing communication, full details of contents and composition and promotion of safe usage and disposal of their products and services. 3. In designing the product, businesses should ensure that the manufacturing processes and technologies required to produce it are resource efficient and sustainable. 4. Businesses should regularly review and improve upon the process of new technology development, deployment and commercialization, incorporating social, ethical, and environmental considerations. 5. Businesses should recognize and respect the rights of people who may be owners of traditional knowledge, and other forms of intellectual property. 6. Businesses should recognize that over-consumption results in unsustainable exploitation of our planet's resoseurces, and should therefore promote sustainable consumption, including recycling of resources.
Principle 3: Businesses should promote the well-being of all employees 1. Businesses should respect the right to freedom of association, participation, collective bargaining, and provide access to appropriate grievance redressal mechanisms. 2. Businesses should provide and maintain equal opportunities at the time of recruitment as well as during the course of employment irrespective of caste, creed, gender, race, religion, disability or sexual orientation. 3. Businesses should not use child labour, forced labour or any form of involuntary labour, paid or unpaid. 4. Businesses should take cognizance of the work-life balance of its employees, especially that of women. 5. Businesses should provide facilities for the wellbeing of its employees including those with special needs. They should ensure timely payment of fair living wages to meet basic needs and economic security of the employees.

6. Businesses should provide a workplace environment that is safe, hygienic humane, and which upholds the dignity of the employees. Business should communicate this provision to their employees and train them on a regular basis.
7. Businesses should ensure continuous skill and competence upgrading of all employees by providing access to necessary learning opportunities, on an equal and non discriminatory basis. They should promote employee morale and career development through enlightened human resource interventions.
8. Businesses should create systems and practices to ensure a harassment free workplace where employees feel safe and secure in discharging their responsibilities.

Principle 4: Businesses should respect the interests of, and be responsive towards all stakeholders, especially those who are disadvantaged, vulnerable and marginalised

1. Businesses should systematically identify their stakeholders, understand their concerns, define purpose and scope of engagement, and commit to engaging with them
2. Businesses should acknowledge, assume responsibility and be transparent about the impact of their policies, decisions, product & services and associated operations on the stakeholders
3. Businesses should give special attention to stakeholders in areas that are underdeveloped.
4. Businesses should resolve differences with stakeholders in a just, fair and equitable manner.

Principle 5: Businesses should respect and promote human rights

1. Businesses should understand the human rights content of the Constitution of India, national laws and policies and the content of International Bill of Human Rights. Businesses should appreciate that human rights are inherent, universal, indivisible and interdependent in nature.
2. Businesses should integrate respect for human rights in management systems, in particular through assessing and managing human rights impacts of operations, and ensuring all individuals impacted by the business have access to grievance mechanisms.
3. Businesses should recognize and respect the human rights of all relevant stakeholders and groups within and beyond the workplace, including that of communities, consumers and vulnerable and marginalized groups.

4. Businesses should, within their sphere of influence, promote the awareness and realization of human rights across their value chain. 5. Businesses should not be complicit with human rights abuses by a third party.
Principle 6: Business should respect, protect, and make efforts to restore the environment 1. Businesses should utilize natural and manmade resources in an optimal and responsible manner and ensure the sustainability of resources by reducing, reusing, recycling and managing waste. 2. Businesses should take measures to check and prevent pollution. They should assess the environmental damage and bear the cost of pollution abatement with due regard to public interest. 3. Businesses should ensure that benefits arising out of access and commercialization of biological and other natural resources and associated traditional knowledge are shared equitably. 4. Businesses should continuously seek to improve their environmental performance by adopting cleaner production methods, promoting use of energy efficient and environment friendly technologies and use of renewable energy 5. Businesses should develop Environment Management Systems (EMS) and contingency plans and processes that help them in preventing, mitigating and controlling environmental damages and disasters, which may be caused due to their operations or that of a member of its value chain 6. Businesses should report their environmental performance, including the assessment of potential environmental risks associated with their operations, to the stakeholders in a fair and transparent manner. 7. Businesses should proactively persuade and support its value chain to adopt this principle
Principle 7: Businesses, when engaged in influencing public and regulatory policy, should do so in a responsible manner 1. Businesses, while pursuing policy advocacy, must ensure that their advocacy positions are consistent with the Principles and Core Elements contained in these Guidelines. 2. To the extent possible, businesses should utilize the trade and industry chambers and associations and other such collective platforms to undertake such policy advocacy.

Principle 8: Businesses should support inclusive growth and equitable development

1. Businesses should understand their impact on social and economic development, and respond through appropriate action to minimise the negative impacts.
2. Businesses should innovate and invest in products, technologies and processes that promote the wellbeing of society.
3. Businesses should make efforts to complement and support the development priorities at local and national levels, and assure appropriate resettlement and rehabilitation of communities who have been displaced owing to their business operations.
4. Businesses operating in regions that are underdeveloped should be especially sensitive to local concerns.

Principle 9: Businesses should engage with and provide value to their customers and consumers in a responsible manner

1. Businesses, while serving the needs of their customers, should take into account the overall well-being of the customers and that of society.
2. Businesses should ensure that they do not restrict the freedom of choice and free competition in any manner while designing, promoting and selling their products.
3. Businesses should disclose all information truthfully and factually, through labelling and other means, including the risks to the individual, to society and to the planet from the use of the products, so that the customers can exercise their freedom to consume in a responsible manner. Where required, businesses should also educate their customers on the safe and responsible usage of their products and services.
4. Businesses should promote and advertise their products in ways that do not mislead or confuse the consumers or violate any of the principles in these Guidelines.
5. Businesses should exercise due care and caution while providing goods and services that result in over exploitation of natural resources or lead to excessive conspicuous consumption.
6. Businesses should provide adequate grievance handling mechanisms to address customer concerns and feedback.

To read, which strengthens your will to serve humanity, is also about strengthening your spiritual muscles...

You may take a break...

INTERNATIONAL GUIDELINES RELATED TO CSR

Kind, is a New York based snack food company, whose products have been considered healthier amongst its peers. Its founder, Daniel Lubetzky, who also founded organisations such as Peaceworks, Maiyet and 'Feed the Truth' says, *"Social contributions should have a soul, a sentiment, and a sincerity of purpose. Corporations are driven by human beings, so hopefully they will be driven to make our world better because this too is their world... But the trouble is that sometimes some corporate business models or junctures present people with concentrated profit-maximizing opportunities that cause harm to society overall"*. The observation - that an attitude of 'concentrated profit-maximixing' cause harm - is also reflected in the below excerpt, from the sustainability report of AP Moller – Maersk Group, for 2013[25].

Combating corruption and facilitation payments in the maritime industry depends on the skills and mindset of the captain and crew. A report from a Maersk Tankers captain serves as an illustration:

"Today we transited a narrow waterway. Only one of the three necessary pilots sent by the port authority signed the required documents. The second one threatened to leave the vessel if I did not give him cigarettes. He stayed and did his job, though, after we refused his demand. The third pilot refused to do his job. First, he brought the ship out of steering by giving orders to steer hard back and forth between starboard and port to 'prove' that the vessel was not trimmed correctly. He then told me 'No Marlboro, no pilot!'," the captain reports.

The pilot lived up to this promise and for half the passage the captain had to pilot the ship himself. Meanwhile, the pilot was busy outside the bridge talking on the phone, reading newspapers and taking pictures with his tablet despite the crew's request to not go outside with electronic equipment.

"Before he left the vessel, he asked us to increase the speed up to 10 knots and as soon as this happened, he wanted us to immediately slow down so he could disembark to the pilot vessel. I told to him that this was not safe but he didn't listen. Slowing down the ship caused us to lose steering and approach shallow waters. When he left the bridge I immediately increased the speed and steering was gained back. All of this happened because I refused to give him cigarettes," the captain adds.

Our captains should always seek to combat facilitation payments. If a situation escalates, the captain faces a dilemma but he should always

25 http://www.maersk.com/en/the-maersk-group/sustainability/~/media/97169B32CA46458897FAE47C780CF69F.ashx, Accessed on May 23, 2015. Included with permission.

prioritise the safety of the crew and vessel. The pilot is considered an advisor to the captain in ports and canals, and safe navigation is the responsibility of the captain. It is therefore his duty to override the pilot's instructions if there is danger to the vessel. In this case, the captain did take over when needed, and at no time was the vessel in any immediate navigational danger.

Ernesto 'Che' Guevara, who played a prominent part in the Cuban revolution of 1959, mentions about how corruption permeated many of the "allies" that were part of the Cuban revolutionary movement. Che refers to instances of luxury - "*...the first bill arrived from the Hotel... it was for $15,000 in food and drink for a small number of beneficiaries...*", and of desire towards "*comfortable state jobs*", that "*were not particularly well-paying positions, but they had one characteristic; they had all been sources of graft during the pre-revolutionary regime... all the places where money changed hands...*"[26]

By 2020, all megalopolises have become identically similar – they all have stock-exchanges, dizzying lights, traffic woes, non-sleepy nights, multi-storied buildings, water problems, imports almost all necessities, has many shopping malls, some museums, and a few green patches – that an advertiser may replace a photo of an urbanscape with that of another – and the difference may not be easily spotted.

Not even a "forbidden city" - Lhasa – has been able to conserve and protect its unique feel and rhythm. Prior to the existing geo-political demarcations, travels to Tibetan regions, was a spiritual and religious journey to many Indians – usually by foot. Even the infamous robbers and marauders who roamed the regions of Kailas and Manas were kind, by providing food to the wanderers and the pilgrims, while looting those who travel with comforts and conveniences.

Cuba, it may be claimed, has withstood the onslaught of global homogenisation and misplaced uniformity, being amongst the few geographies of the world that is determined – a traveler may find it difficult to find a commercial-billboard or an advertisement-flex in a Cuban city. If that may be considered as a "wonder of the world", to travel after...

UN Global Compact

"*Corporate sustainability starts with a company's value system and a principled approach to doing business,*" says UN Global Compact (UNGC)[27]. The UNGC

26 Ernesto 'Che' Guevara, *Reminiscences of the Cuban Revolutionary War*, Ocean Press, 2006.

27 https://www.unglobalcompact.org/what-is-gc/mission/principles, Accessed on June 15, 2016.

is an initiative by United Nations with a participation of more than 9000 organizations[28]. UNGC principles come under the categories of Human Rights, Labour, Environment and Anti-corruption (**Refer table 4.3**).

Table 4.2

Human Rights	Principle 1: Businesses should support and respect the protection of internationally proclaimed human rights; and Principle 2: make sure that they are not complicit in human rights abuses.
Labour	Principle 3: Businesses should uphold the freedom of association and the effective recognition of the right to collective bargaining; Principle 4: the elimination of all forms of forced and compulsory labour; Principle 5: the effective abolition of child labour; and Principle 6: the elimination of discrimination in respect of employment and occupation.
Environment	Principle 7: Businesses should support a precautionary approach to environmental challenges; Principle 8: undertake initiatives to promote greater environmental responsibility; and Principle 9: encourage the development and diffusion of environmentally friendly technologies.
Anti-Corruption	Principle 10: Businesses should work against corruption in all its forms, including extortion and bribery.

28 https://www.unglobalcompact.org/what-is-gc/participants/search?utf8=%E2%9C%93&search%5Bkeywords%5D=&search%5Breporting_status%5D%5B%5D=active&search%5Bper_page%5D=10&search%5Bsort_field%5D=&search%5Bsort_direction%5D=asc, Accessed on June 15, 2016.

UN Guiding Principles on Business and Human Rights

These principles[29] are grounded in the recognition of:

(a) States' existing obligations to respect, protect and fulfil human rights and fundamental freedoms.

(b) The role of business enterprises as specialized organs of society performing specialized functions, required to comply with all applicable laws and to respect human rights.

(c) The need for rights and obligations to be matched to appropriate and effective remedies when breached.

United Nations Convention against Corruption

The United Nations Convention against Corruption (UNCAC) is a legally binding agreement signed by more than 170 countries. UNCAC covers areas including preventive measures, enforcement of law, information exchange etc. Specific references are made to private sector, through Articles 12, 21, 22 and 39[30]:

Article 12. Private sector

1. Each State Party shall take measures, in accordance with the fundamental principles of its domestic law, to prevent corruption involving the private sector, enhance accounting and auditing standards in the private sector and, where appropriate, provide effective, proportionate and dissuasive civil, administrative or criminal penalties for failure to comply with such measures.

2. Measures to achieve these ends may include, inter alia:

   (a) Promoting cooperation between law enforcement agencies and relevant private entities;

   (b) Promoting the development of standards and procedures designed to safeguard the integrity of relevant private entities, including codes of conduct for the correct, honourable and proper performance of the activities of business and all relevant professions and the prevention of conflicts of interest, and for the promotion of the use of good commercial practices among businesses and in the contractual relations of businesses with the State;

---

29 http://www.ohchr.org/Documents/Publications/GuidingPrinciplesBusinessHR_EN.pdf, Accessed on June 15, 2016.

30 http://www.unodc.org/documents/treaties/UNCAC/Publications/Convention/08-50026_E.pdf, Accessed on August 28, 2016. Included with permission.

(c) Promoting transparency among private entities, including, where appropriate, measures regarding the identity of legal and natural persons involved in the establishment and management of corporate entities;

(d) Preventing the misuse of procedures regulating private entities, including procedures regarding subsidies and licences granted by public authorities for commercial activities;

(e) Preventing conflicts of interest by imposing restrictions, as appropriate and for a reasonable period of time, on the professional activities of former public officials or on the employment of public officials by the private sector after their resignation or retirement, where such activities or employment relate directly to the functions held or supervised by those public officials during their tenure;

(f) Ensuring that private enterprises, taking into account their structure and size, have sufficient internal auditing controls to assist in preventing and detecting acts of corruption and that the accounts and required financial statements of such private enterprises are subject to appropriate auditing and certification procedures.

3. In order to prevent corruption, each State Party shall take such measures as may be necessary, in accordance with its domestic laws and regulations regarding the maintenance of books and records, financial statement disclosures and accounting and auditing standards, to prohibit the following acts carried out for the purpose of committing any of the offences established in accordance with this Convention:

   (a) The establishment of off-the-books accounts;

   (b) The making of off-the-books or inadequately identified transactions;

   (c) The recording of non-existent expenditure;

   (d) The entry of liabilities with incorrect identification of their objects;

   (e) The use of false documents; and

   (f) The intentional destruction of bookkeeping documents earlier than foreseen by the law.

4. Each State Party shall disallow the tax deductibility of expenses that constitute bribes, the latter being one of the constituent elements of the offences established in accordance with articles 15 and 16 of this Convention and, where appropriate, other expenses incurred in furtherance of corrupt conduct.

Article 21. Bribery in the private sector

Each State Party shall consider adopting such legislative and other measures as may be necessary to establish as criminal offences, when committed intentionally in the course of economic, financial or commercial activities:

(a) The promise, offering or giving, directly or indirectly, of an undue advantage to any person who directs or works, in any capacity, for a private sector entity, for the person himself or herself or for another person, in order that he or she, in breach of his or her duties, act or refrain from acting;

(b) The solicitation or acceptance, directly or indirectly, of an undue advantage by any person who directs or works, in any capacity, for a private sector entity, for the person himself or herself or for another person, in order that he or she, in breach of his or her duties, act or refrain from acting.

Article 22. Embezzlement of property in the private sector

Each State Party shall consider adopting such legislative and other measures as may be necessary to establish as a criminal offence, when committed intentionally in the course of economic, financial or commercial activities, embezzlement by a person who directs or works, in any capacity, in a private sector entity of any property, private funds or securities or any other thing of value entrusted to him or her by virtue of his or her position.

Article 39. Cooperation between national authorities and the private sector

1. Each State Party shall take such measures as may be necessary to encourage, in accordance with its domestic law, cooperation between national investigating and prosecuting authorities and entities of the private sector, in particular financial institutions, relating to matters involving the commission of offences established in accordance with this Convention.
2. Each State Party shall consider encouraging its nationals and other persons with a habitual residence in its territory to report to the national investigating and prosecuting authorities the commission of an offence established in accordance with this Convention.

United Nations Principles on Responsible Investment

In 2018, Ireland decided not to make any investments in companies engaged in fossil fuel businesses (coal, oil, gas and peat), and also to sell its existing investments in the sector[31]. Ireland's national investment fund (Ireland Strategic Investment Fund) manages more than 8 billion euro, and has more than 300 million euro in fossil fuel related investments in approximately 150 companies.

There has been a global trend to divest from fossil-fuel related companies due to their role in climate change (**Refer Figure 4.3**). Examples of organisations and governments that have decided to divest from fossil-fuel investments include the Church of England, University of Glasgow and Rockefeller Brothers Fund.

Figure 4.3[32]

The photograph indicates the probable sea level in the future years. 'Climate Change' increases environment risk.

United Nations Principles on Responsible Investment (UN PRI) is an initiative that brought together investors to include Environmental, Social

31 https://www.oireachtas.ie/en/bills/bill/2016/103/, Accessed on September 25, 2018.

32 Photo: Julie G. Source: https://www.flickr.com/photos/go_greener_oz/3046225225/, Accessed on July 3, 2016. Made available under a Creative Commons Attribution-NoDerivs 2.0 Generic Licence (https://creativecommons.org/licenses/by-nd/2.0/).

and Governance (ESG) perspectives into investment practices. Almost 1500 organizations representing more than 50 countries have signed on UN PRI. The six principles of UN PRI are as follows[33]:

1. *We will incorporate ESG issues into investment analysis and decision-making processes.*

   Possible Actions:

   - Address ESG issues in investment policy statements.
   - Support development of ESG-related tools, metrics, and analyses.
   - Assess the capabilities of internal investment managers to incorporate ESG issues.
   - Assess the capabilities of external investment managers to incorporate ESG issues.
   - Ask investment service providers (such as financial analysts, consultants, brokers, research firms, or rating companies) to integrate ESG factors into evolving research and analysis.
   - Encourage academic and other research on this theme.
   - Advocate ESG training for investment professionals.

2. *We will be active owners and incorporate ESG issues into our ownership policies and practices.*

   Possible Actions:

   - Develop and disclose an active ownership policy consistent with the Principles.
   - Exercise voting rights or monitor compliance with voting policy (if outsourced).
   - Develop an engagement capability (either directly or through outsourcing).
   - Participate in the development of policy, regulation, and standard setting (such as promoting and protecting shareholder rights).
   - File shareholder resolutions consistent with long-term ESG considerations.
   - Engage with companies on ESG issues.
   - Participate in collaborative engagement initiatives.

---

33 https://www.unpri.org/about/the-six-principles, Accessed on August 30, 2016. Included with permission.

- Ask investment managers to undertake and report on ESG-related engagement.

3. *We will seek appropriate disclosure on ESG issues by the entities in which we invest.*

   Possible Actions:

   - Ask for standardised reporting on ESG issues (using tools such as the Global Reporting Initiative).
   - Ask for ESG issues to be integrated within annual financial reports.
   - Ask for information from companies regarding adoption of/ adherence to relevant norms, standards, codes of conduct or international initiatives (such as the UN Global Compact).
   - Support shareholder initiatives and resolutions promoting ESG disclosure.

4. *We will promote acceptance and implementation of the Principles within the investment industry.*

   Possible Actions:

   - Include Principles-related requirements in requests for proposals (RFPs).
   - Align investment mandates, monitoring procedures, performance indicators and incentive structures accordingly (for example, ensure investment management processes reflect long-term time horizons when appropriate).
   - Communicate ESG expectations to investment service providers.
   - Revisit relationships with service providers that fail to meet ESG expectations.
   - Support the development of tools for benchmarking ESG integration.
   - Support regulatory or policy developments that enable implementation of the Principles.

5. *We will work together to enhance our effectiveness in implementing the Principles.*

   Possible Actions:

   - Support/ participate in networks and information platforms to share tools, pool resources, and make use of investor reporting as a source of learning.

- Collectively address relevant emerging issues.
- Develop or support appropriate collaborative initiatives.

6. *We will each report on our activities and progress towards implementing the Principles.*

   Possible Actions:

   - Disclose how ESG issues are integrated within investment practices.
   - Disclose active ownership activities (voting, engagement, and/or policy dialogue).
   - Disclose what is required from service providers in relation to the Principles.
   - Communicate with beneficiaries about ESG issues and the Principles.
   - Report on progress and/ or achievements relating to the Principles using a comply-or-explain approach.
   - Seek to determine the impact of the Principles.
   - Make use of reporting to raise awareness among a broader group of stakeholders.

Transparency International Business Principles for countering Bribery

Transparency International (TI) is a Berlin based transnational not-for-profit organization working towards a non-corrupt society. TIs 'Business Principles For Countering Bribery' is considered as a framework for for-profit organisations to develop anti-bribery programmes. The principles are as follows:[34]

1. The enterprise shall prohibit bribery in any form whether direct or indirect.
2. The enterprise shall commit to implementing a programme to counter bribery. The programme shall represent the enterprise's anti-bribery efforts including values, code of conduct, detailed policies and procedures, risk management, internal and external communication, training and guidance, internal controls, oversight, monitoring and assurance.

---

34 http://www.transparency.org/whatwedo/tools/business_principles_for_countering_bribery/1, Accessed on August 30, 2016.

On July 4, 2018, the Uttarakhand High Court at Nainital, India, declared[35] that, *"to protect and promote greater welfare of animals including avian and aquatic, animals are required to be conferred with the status of legal entity/ legal person... ...The entire animal kingdom including avian and aquatic are declared as legal entities having a distinct persona with corresponding rights, duties and liabilities of a living person. All the citizens throughout the State of Uttarakhand are hereby declared persons in loco parentis as the human face for the welfare/ protection of animals."* (**Refer Figure 4.4**).

Figure 4.4[36]

A street view from Mussorie, Uttarakhand, India.

In Japan, 'the land of rising sun', exists the *'Todai-ji'*, also known as the Eastern Great Temple, with origins in the seventh century. It is common to see the sika deer roaming in the temple premises and areas nearby. Located in the region of Nara, it houses the *Vairochana Buddha* (*"Daibutsu"*). On the midnight of December 31, the bell-sound from this temple reverberates,

35 http://lobis.nic.in/ddir/uhc/RS/judgement/07-07-2018/RS04072018WPPIL432014.pdf, Accessed on September 25, 2018.

36 https://commons.wikimedia.org/wiki/File:Mussoorie_India_Uttarakhand_%28183710205%29.jpeg, Accessed on December 16, 2018.

with the bell being rung 108 times – a prayer to dispel human frailities. The *Panchatantra*[37] informs and alerts,

> *As muddied garments dirty*
> *All that you sit upon,*
> *So, when one virtue tumbles.*
> The rest are quickly gone.

Swami Vivekananda says, "*Never mind failures; they are quite natural, they are the beauty of life, these failures. What would life be without them? It would not be worth having if it were not for struggles. Where would be the poetry of life? Never mind the struggles, the mistakes. I never heard a cow tell a lie, but it is only a cow - never a man. So never mind these failures, these little backslidings; hold the ideal a thousand times, and if you fail a thousand times, make the attempt once more.*"[38].

CHAPTER SUMMARY

- There is legal acknowledgment to the inherent worth of all entities of this planet. Examples include according the status of a legal entity to rivers Ganga and Yamuna in India, and Whanganui river in New Zealand.
- A number of national and international guidelines exist that can facilitate and guide for-profit organisations to practice responsibility.
- Securities and Exchange Board of India (SEBI) has mandated business responsibility reports for the leading listed companies, based on market capitalisation, while the reports are voluntary for other listed companies.
- The 'National Voluntary Guidelines on Social, Environmental and Economic responsibilities of Business' communicated that the role of businesses is not just making profits, but also includes the (a) well-being of all employees (b) restoring the natural environment (c) provides goods and services that are safe and sustainable (d) operating with ethics, transparency and accountability etc.
- As per Section 135 of Companies Act, 2013, a company that meets certain riteria has to necessarily engage in CSR activities.

---

37 The Panchatantra, translated from the Sanskrit by Arthur W Ryder, Phoenix Books (University of Chicago Press), 1956.

38 The Complete Works of Swami Vivekananda, Volume 2, Jnana-Yoga, Chapter VII God In Everything (Delivered in London, 27th October 1896). Available at https://en.wikisource.org/wiki/The_Complete_Works_of_Swami_Vivekananda/Volume_2/Jnana-Yoga/God_in_Everything, Accessed on February 17, 2020.

KEYWORDS MENTIONED

Socially Responsible Corporation (SRC), Section 135 of the Companies Act 2013, Business Responsibility Reporting, Principles on Responsible Investment

MULTIPLE CHOICE QUESTIONS

1. The high court in which state of India accorded the status of a living entity to the rivers Ganga and Yamuna.
   (a) Kashmir
   (b) Kerala
   (c) Karnataka
   (d) Uttar Pradesh
   (e) Uttarakhand
2. As per Section 135 of the Companies Act 2013, which of the following criteria for a company mandates a CSR spend of at least two percentage of the average net profit?
   (a) Net worth of rupees five hundred crore or more
   (b) Turnover of rupees one thousand crore or more
   (c) Net profit of rupees five crore or more
   (d) Any of the above options
3. Which of the following parameter is used by Securities and Exchange Board of India (SEBI) to decide on the inclusion of a Business Responsibility Reports in the company's annual report?
   (a) Market capitalisation
   (b) Revenue
   (c) CSR spend
   (d) Number of employees
   (e) All of the above
4. Expand UNCAC:
   (a) Union of New Companies Against Corruption
   (b) United Nations Convention Against Corruption
   (c) United Nations Conference Against Crime
   (d) United Nations Conference Against Corruption
   (e) United Nations Convention Against Crime

5. Which of the following is a Berlin based not-for-profit organisation working towards a non-corrupt society.
   (a) United Nations
   (b) Transparency International
   (c) World Bank
   (d) Medecins Sans Frontieres
   (e) Mozilla Foundation

SHORT ANSWER QUESTIONS

1. What are the two principles of the Transparency International's Business Principles for countering Bribery?

LONG ANSWER QUESTIONS

1. Of the nine principles under 'National Voluntary Guidelines on Social, Environmental and Economic Responsibilities of Business', list any one principle, and detail the sub-principles.
2. List any two principles of UN PRI along with the sub-principles.

REFLECTIVE QUESTIONS

1. Principle 1 of the 'National Voluntary Guidelines on Social, Environmental and Economic Responsibilities of Business' states that businesses should conduct and govern themselves with Ethics, Transparency and Accountability.
   - Cite personal examples/ incidents where you faced dilemma in conducting and governing yourself with ethics, transparency and accountability?
     — Remembering those incidents, do you see possibilities for improvement on how you could have improved your personal conduct then?
   - State examples where you believe that businesses can improvise on their existing practices to be more ethical, transparent and accountable.
     — Are there ways through which you can support/ help/ facilitate businesses to be more ethical, transparent and accountable?

2. During the training period of a recruit to the 'Border Security Force' (BSF), one of the para-military forces in India, the below pledge is made:

   "I will not disgrace the borderman's arms, nor abandon the comrade, who stands at my side.
   Whether alone or with many, i will defend everything that my country holds sacred."

   As a student or practitioner of responsibility practices, what may be a new practice that you may imbibe, to ensure that whatever you hold in your life, is sacred or increasingly becomes sacred?

WEB READING

Global Compact Self-Assessment Tool:
http://www.globalcompactselfassessment.org

ABOUT THE CHAPTER:

1. Learning from the chapter, if any:

2. Topics, concepts, themes, etc. that you may be interested to research/ refer/ study/ ponder upon:

3. Applications in daily life, if any:

Notes:

Chapter 4 completed... You may take a break...

SAI (Save Animals Initiative) Sanctuary is a private sanctuary located in Kodagu, Karnataka. It began as an initiative of two individuals, by purchasing some acres of land and maintaining its pristinity. The sanctuary (www.saisanctuary.com) has few cottages that facilitate an eco-friendly stay. Electricity used within the sanctuary is powered by solar and wind. Food is organic, and cooking is through bio-gas. Revenue from the cottages helps towards bio-diversity conservation and related aspects.

Shankara, when he was a boy, started walking from Kaladi, in Southern India, a journey that moved him amongst the loftiest, as also the deplorable. He pushed away the stones and altars, where violence was inflicted in the guise of pleasing deities and celestials. Consecrating, energising and rejuvenating innumerable places of worship, be it at Kashmir or Kathmandu, Shankara flowed forth. Rivers and Shankara were neither distinct nor discrete. It is not common for a river to change its course, Yet, a child's selfless prayer, the river in his village decides otherwise. An earnest prayer from a boy, and lo and behold, another river self-subdued its overflowing might. *Narmada,* for Shankara, was worshipped by the living, the non-living, the demonic and the non-demonic. *Yamuna,* for Shankara, was able to remove the sorrows of the three worlds. At the presence of *Ganges,* Shankara seeks refuge, and says:

> *"...Your qualities, unknown to me,*
> *protect me, the bestower of grace, from my ignorance..."*

Chapter 5

ETHOS, VALUES AND CORPORATE GOVERNANCE

"Do not sacrifice your freedom for the sake of pomp and show."[1]

—Aesop's Fables

On completion of reading the chapter, the reader may:

1. Understand the linkage between Ethos and Values, Ethics, and responsibility practices in business.

2. Recognise the major codes and/or norms related to business ethics and corporate governance.

3. Know the importance and influence of personal character and responsibility in influencing organisational character and responsibility.

Bridgeway Capital Management, an investment management company based in Houston, USA, has unwritten rules. No full-time employee at Bridgeway can make total compensation greater than seven times the total compensation of the lowest paid employee. The company also avoids transactions that may possibly create conflict-of-interest. For example, the company do not accept any perks from stock-broking firms (A stock broking firm can be assigned the responsibility to execute the trading and investment decisions made by an investment management company) to ensure that the interest of the shareholder, for whom Bridgeway makes the investment decision, is not diluted by any influence from a broking firm[2].

ETHOS AND VALUES – THE FOUNDATION OF CORPORATE GOVERNANCE

Ethics refer to moral principles. Business ethics involves application of ethical principles in the practice of business. The quote "*...in the ultimate analysis, we are all mere temporary custodians of the wealth we generate, whether it be financial, intellectual, or emotional. The best use of all your wealth is to share it with those less fortunate*",[3] by NR Narayana Murthy, Co-founder,

1 http://www.read.gov/aesop/068.html, Accessed on August 16, 2015.

2 https://www.bloomberg.com/amp/news/articles/2003-06-15/who-says-nice-guys-finish-last, Accessed on June 16, 2017.

3 http://www.rediff.com/money/2007/may/28bspec.htm, Accessed on July 3, 2016.

Infosys, indicates an application of moral principle. The word 'Ethics' draws from *Ethicus* and *Ethikos*, with roots in the Greek word *'Ethos'*, referring to character. 'Ethos' is derived from the Sanskrit word *'Ithiha'* that can have meanings such as "thus indeed"[4], the nature of things, 'as it is' etc. Generations in India grew up listening to *'Ithihaas'*[5]. It may also be concluded that the codes of conduct, including that in business, can be found in ethos and values (**Refer figure 5.1**).

Figure 5.1

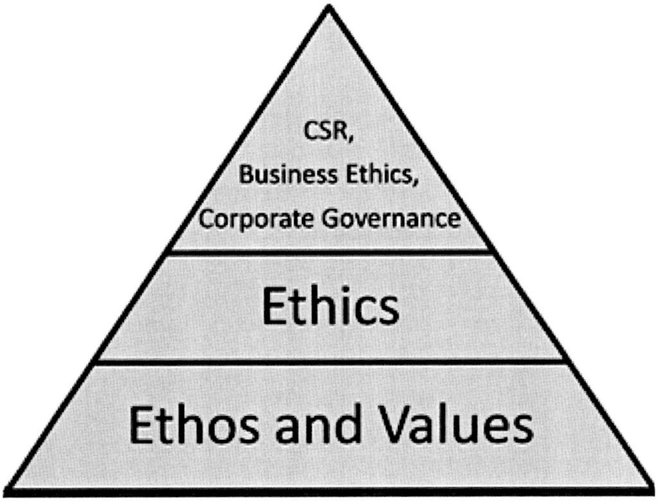

Stephen Covey, author of *'The 7 Habits of Highly Effective People'*, says,

"There are two kinds of success. Primary success has to do with strength of character and contribution to others. Secondary success has to do with formal authority and with being rich, famous, popular, and positioned. So moral authority, which is the only real basis on which formal authority can ever work over time and be sustainable, is primary success.

Such moral authority is gained via serving and contributing... Those with high moral authority, people who have character, organizational competence, initiative, positive energy, and respect, have been given formal authority as a result of their living their principles and serving others. The leader's strength of character leads those he or she serves, both within and external to the organisation, to create emotional identification with the leader, as well as with the principles and values the leader embraces.

4 http://sanskritdictionary.com/itiha/33136/1, Accessed on July 3, 2016.

5 *Ramayan(am)* and *Mahabharat(am)* are considered as *Ithihaas(am)*.

...example, though one I have not personally witnessed, is provided by Mahatma Gandhi.... The whole world is different because of him.... His gradual development of humility, integrity, courage, discipline and vision, were all governed by his conscience, by his inner awareness. He demonstrated that leadership can be an enabling art that empowers individuals, organisations and societies to serve others.."[6]

ETHICAL BEHAVIOUR AND ETHICAL DECISION-MAKING

When you offer milk to a hungry child, or a blanket to a shivering brother on payment, you are but placing a gift of god into the hands of god...

—Sathya Sai Baba[7]

The Ramayanam narrates how Ram (Rama/ Raman), the heir prince to the kingdom of Ayodhya, was asked to let go of his claim to the throne, moments before his coronation as the king. Ram also had to live in the forests for 14 years, devoid of material comforts. These were towards the fulfilment of certain promises given by his father. The epic conveys that Ram approaches these sudden turn of events with serene-calmness. In the absence of Ram, his brother Bharath (Bharatha/ Bharathan) was to be the king. However, on knowing that Ram was moving to the forests, Bharath refuses to adorn the throne, and pleads Ram to return. Yet, Ram insists that Bharath be responsible for the well-being of the subjects of the kingdom. Bharath's yearning for Ram was such that he carried Rama's sandals and kept them on the throne, and ruled the kingdom on behalf of Ram, till his return[8].

This relationship between Ram and Bharath has been a subject for contemplation on relationships. In a movie song, the lyricist refers to Rama

6 Quotations extracted from the public knowledge base of the "Spiritual Based Leadership Research Programme" are © 2006 by the Global Dharma Center (GDC). GDC retains the copyright to all excerpts from this knowledge base.

7 The Will to Will Not, *Sri Sathya Sai Speaks*, Sri Sathya Sai Sadhana Trust, Volume 9, 1969.

8 On returning to Ayodhya, Bharatha meets many - ministers and other administrators, scholars and preceptors, citizens and their leaders, etc., and entrusts them with duties and responsibilities. In '*Rama Katha Rasavahini*', Sathya Sai Baba writes, "*...That day, he prostrated before the mothers, Kausalya, Sumitra and Kaikeyi and then proceeded to the throne with the sandals borne on his head. Praying for the blessings of Vasishta and permission from him and all those assembled, he placed them on the throne, offering them reverential loyalty. He placed all his responsibilities safely in their custody. Later that steadfast adherant of Dharma, that incomparable hero, Bharatha walked towards the village of Nandigrama... His food and dress were the same as those of the ascetics of the forest; his acts, thoughts, and words too were austere and spiritually oriented.*".

as the "*the fullness of gentleness*" and says that "a glance from you, And *Nila* flows as the *Sarayu*..." [9]. Scriptures from India has proven to be treasure-houses to debate, discuss and dialogue on ideals, ethics and legality. Micheal Nagler[10] says, "*Indian aesthetics holds that the essence of every moment in an artistic performance is its rasa, which corresponds to one of nine moods or dispositions... If the Upanishads are an archetypal art form in that sense, what is their rasa? That question occupied Indian aestheticians a great deal, and their answer was skillful: the Upanishads come from the disposition of shanta, 'peace', which is not really a disposition or mood but what happens when all mental dispositions are brought to rest...*"[11]

What constitutes an Ethical Decision?

To ascertain what constitute an ethical decision and behaviour, it may be worthwhile to ponder on some business practices.

Marketers have been targeting children to sell their products. A senior lecturer at University of Sheffield says, "*Advertisers aim for children because they want to establish tastes and preferences that will last a lifetime.*"[12] Sweden and Norway have made it illegal to advertise to children under the age of twelve. Quebec, in Canada, made a similar decision. "*Because younger children do not understand persuasive intent in advertising, they are easy targets for commercial persuasion.... This is a critical concern because the most common products marketed to children are sugared cereals, candies, sweets, sodas and snack foods. Such advertising of unhealthy food products to young children contributes to poor nutritional habits that may last a lifetime and be a variable in the current epidemic of obesity among kids,*" says a professor of psychology at the University of Nebraska.[13]

Concerns have also been raised about how advertisements that are meant

9 Lyrics by Gireesh Putencherry, from a song in the Malayalam movie '*Arayannangalude Veedu*'. The lyricist words the qualities of Rama, as held to heart, in the spirit of India. 'Nila' and 'Sarayu' are rivers in India. 'Nila', also known as Bharathapuzha, flows through the state of Kerala, in Southern India. Similar to many rivers of the world, Nila has given rise to, and is associated with the evolution and development of culture and cultural expressions through the centuries. 'Sarayu' is revered also for its association with Sri Ramachandra (Rama). Ayodhya, is located in the banks of this river.

10 Professor Emeritus, University of California, Berkeley.

11 Eknath Easwaran, The Upanishads, Nilgiri Press, 2008.

12 http://legacy.fordham.edu/campus_resources/enewsroom/inside_fordham/inside_fordham_archi/20092010/may_17_2010/news/researcher_shows_neg_75386.asp, Accessed on March 12, 2016.

13 http://www.apa.org/news/press/releases/2004/02/children-ads.aspx, Accessed on March 12, 2016.

for adults can influence children. Commenting about a situation in USA, a professor of communication at the University of California at Santa Barbara says, "*For example, beer ads are commonly shown during sports events and seen by millions of children, creating both brand familiarity and more positive attitudes toward drinking in children as young as 9-10 years of age. Another area of sensitive advertising content involves commercials for violent media products such as motion pictures and video games. Such ads contribute to a violent media culture which increases the likelihood of youngsters' aggressive behavior and desensitizes children to real-world violence.*"

Brands use and misuse cultural and religious ceremonies for selling their products. The frequency of advertisements mentioning product discounts tend to increase during festival seasons. Days that commemorate certain themes and national ethos, have taken commercial tones. Commenting about Valentines Day, a columnist mentioned, "*We would hold protests outside flower shops, ...chocolate factories and ...stores. The protests would continue until these businesses stop bombarding us with commercials or until Valentine's Day is moved -- from February 14 to February 29 so that we are only compelled to observe it once every four years.*". Fortunately, in Japan and South Korea, only men receive gifts on that day. Women have to wait for March 14, known as 'White day'. 'Akshaya Tritiya', a holy day for Hindus and Jains, emerged as a popular occasion for gold marketing since the mid-2000s. This is the day when devout Jains, undergoing fasting every alternate day, makes a climb of 4000 steps to the Shatrunjaya temple in Gujarat, with the climb considered as the final expression of their penance and austerity.

There have been calls to ban advertisements - for misleading citizens, providing incorrect information or being distractions. An advertisement of a business school referring to its accreditation credentials while collection a fee that is higher than what is mentioned in the prospectus is not practicing legal and ethical norms. A company using a green colour in its advertisement to project environment-friendliness, while not improving the environment-friendliness of its products and processes, indicates a lack of sincerity. The press releases from The Advertising Standards Council of India (ASCI) indicate the innumerable instances where advertisements have been misleading consumers[14]. Globally, many advertisements have been banned, and companies have been asked to pay fines for misleading people through advertisements.

Pondering on the above provide clues about what could be ethical decisions and behaviours in business practices. Marketing becomes ethical

14 http://ascionline.org/index.php/press-releases.html, Accessed on August 15, 2016.

when stakeholders associated with the marketing process lives the highest levels of ethical values (**Refer Figure 5.2**). Milton Hershey, who founded the Hershey Chocolate Company, mentioned, *"Give them quality. Thats the best kind of advertising in the world"* [15].

Figure 5.2[16]

Don't Let Your Ethics Slip

A campaign by 'Neo', inviting attention to the importance of ethics. This image was created to celebrate the anniversary of Fairtrade.

For Milton Hershey, respect for quality constitutes the most effective advertising. A reading from an interview give by S K Welling, Former Executive Director of HMT International, Ltd. (Hindustan Machine Tools) can contribute to our perspective on what an ethical behaviour and decision could be. S K Welling says,

15 Interview with Abe Heilman, 1953. Paul Wallace Research Collection, Accession 97004, Box 2, Folder 24; Hershey Community Archives, Hershey, PA, USA.

16 Source: http://www.weareneo.com/our-thoughts/dont-let-your-ethics-slip/; Also available at https://www.flickr.com/photos/neocommunications/12947713033/, Included with permission.

"I don't own a car. I have a company car with a driver; I can use it wherever I want to go. Normally Saturdays and Sundays are the driver's day off. Other company officers use their driver even then. But in our house there is always concern for people - that driver also has a family. My son once asked, 'Why do you disturb him on a holiday and call him up to serve you? Just because you want him to drive all of us somewhere, why would you spoil his family life? If you're a principled man then don't drive the company car; take a 3-wheeler. The three of us can sit in it, give the fellow 15 rupees, no parking, no headache, nothing. He'll drop us where we want. Take another 3-wheeler, come back home.' This is the concern for people that I also try to have.

Now there are many times when we will bump into a friend or an employee who will see us getting out of the 3-wheeler. Back comes the question, 'Sir, you are Executive Director, why are you not in your car? Why are you coming in this manner?' I respond, 'When I retire, I will have to go by public transport. Why not take it now?'"[17]

> ***Reading can also be an expression of compassionate understanding – of the writer, their contextual environment, life experiences, etc.***
>
> ***You may take a break...***

Individual and Organizational Factors Contributing to Ethical Behavior and Decision Making

Mathew B Ridgway, a former General of the US Army, Commander of the UN forces in Korea in the 1950s, and a veteran of World War II, mentions, *"During a critical phase of the Battle of Bulge in World War II, the Germans launched a counter-offensive and nearly broke through the Allied lines in France. When i commanded the 18th Airborne Corps, another Corps commander just entering the fight next to me remarked, "I am glad to have you on my flank...". I had long known him and knew what he meant. I replied, "that goes for me too". There was no amplification; none was necessary. Each knew the other would stick, however great the pressure; would extend help before it was asked, if he could; and would tell the truth; seek no self-glory, and everlastingly keep his word"*[18].

---

17 Quotations extracted from the public knowledge base of the "Spiritual Based Leadership Research Programme" are © 2006 by the Global Dharma Center (GDC). GDC retains the copyright to all excerpts from this knowledge base.

18 .John Adair, *Effective Leadership: A Self-development manual*, Gower, 1983.

Speak to war veterans, and you may hear experiences of camaraderie, sacrifice, valor and leadership. Yet wars have proven to be costly, dreadful and traumatic. The 'Battle of Bulge' was one of the fiercest battles fought in the Second World War. This battle (Dec 1044 – Jan 1945), fought primarily in the in the Ardennes region of Belgium, caused havoc in the region, which was known for its forests, and was later compared to places that meet the onslaught of a tornado. Thousands of soldiers died in this battle. Millions of people lost their lives in the second world war, mostly that of soldiers. "Soldiers", many of them, were youngsters. For novices, a war may be exciting. Referring to the warring factions of the Peloponnesian War (that happened four centuries prior to Jesus), Thucydides, a Greek historian, mentions that, *"...they were both full of enthusiasm and no wonder, for all men are energetic when they are making a beginning. At that time the youth of Peloponnesus and the youth of Athens were numerous; they had never seen war, and were therefore very willing to take up arms. All Hellas was excited by the coming conflict between her two chief cities...."*.

United States, Britian, Japan, France, Italy, Germany and Soviet Union were some of the countries that made military enlistment mandatory for the youth. The fiercest battle fought by the British forces was not the battle at Normandy or the battle at Waterloo. No, it was not even fought anywhere in continental Europe. It was fought miles away, in North Eastern India, against the Japanese forces. NE India is almost 5000 miles (8000 kms) away from Britian and 2500 miles (4000 kms) away from Japan, straight route. And the casualties – many were "privates", a name given to unranked "soldiers", youngsters in their late teens and early twenties. Indians fought on both sides, either directly or indirectly.

Wars also exemplified resilience and endurance. Leningrad, during World War II, was an epitome of the Soviet character. The troubles and travails faced by its people were innumerable. The city was besieged. All the woes related to a war – bombings, injuries, starvation - and diseases to aggravate the sufferings – deaths from the city were more than a million. The siege of the city lasted for almost two years, and yet, the city did not fall.

Imprints of a war travel through. 'Shakespeare and Company'[19] is a book-store in Paris. Between the book-shelves, in that store, one can find beds. The bookstore offers this as free boarding for aspiring writers. This bookstore inherited this tradition from another bookstore, of similar name, which existed in Paris, during the Second World War, and had a practice of offering a sleeping bed to writers, during times of need and emergencies.

19 Www.shakespeareandcompany.com

One of the fundamental tenets of living, as per the culture of India, is related to *Trikaranasuddhi*. 'Trikaranasuddhi' is a Sanskrit word that indicates the purity and unity of thought, word and deed (**Refer Figure 5.3**). It can also be referred to as the congruence or harmony amongst thought, word and deed. Trikaranasuddhi can be considered as both the path and goal for ethical behaviour and ethical decision-making.

Figure 5.3

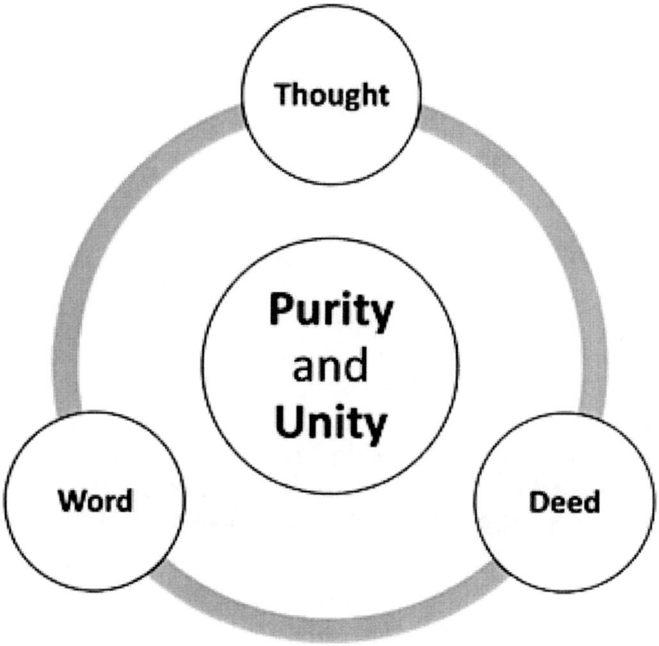

Some of the factors contributing to ethical behaviour and decision making involve:

a. Purity of Intent
b. Strength of Character
c. Congruence of thought, word and deed
d. Meaningfulness and purposefulness in daily living
e. An attitude to serve
f. Existence of visionaries, leaders and facilitators who live by noble ideals
g. A supportive environment

Codes of Ethics

Organisations develop written and unwritten norms of behavior. While these may be for their long-term sustenance, these codes may also progressively enter the realm of caring, respect and reverence[20]. Many cultures of the world evolved ways that provided opportunities for people to ponder on 'right', 'wrong' and the 'shades of grey'. The tales of 'Vikrama and Vetal' had been in narration in India for hundreds of years, being adapted as television series and movies. Nature, with its dynamics, creates roller-coaster rides for people, and makes them ponder on meaning and purpose.

'Statement of Ethics' from 'American Marketing Association'

American Marketing Association is a Chicago based non-governmental association whose code of ethics is referred below (**Refer table 5.1**)

Table 5.1[21]

Preamble
The American Marketing Association commits itself to promoting the highest standard of professional ethical norms and values for its members (practitioners, academics and students). Norms are established standards of conduct that are expected and maintained by society and/ or professional organizations. Values represent the collective conception of what communities find desirable, important and morally proper. Values also serve as the criteria for evaluating our own personal actions and the actions of others. As marketers, we recognize that we not only serve our organizations but also act as stewards of society in creating, facilitating and executing the transactions that are part of the greater economy. In this role, marketers are expected to embrace the highest professional ethical norms and the ethical values implied by our responsibility toward multiple stakeholders (e.g., customers, employees, investors, peers, channel members, regulators and the host community).

20 Jack Hawley, *Reawakening the Spirit in Work: The Power of Dharmic Management*, Berrett-Koehler Publishers, 1995.

21 https://www.ama.org/AboutAMA/Pages/Statement-of-Ethics.aspx, Accessed on August 15, 2016. Included with permission.

Ethical Norms

As Marketers, we must:

- Do no harm. This means consciously avoiding harmful actions or omissions by embodying high ethical standards and adhering to all applicable laws and regulations in the choices we make.
- Foster trust in the marketing system. This means striving for good faith and fair dealing so as to contribute toward the efficacy of the exchange process as well as avoiding deception in product design, pricing, communication, and delivery of distribution.
- Embrace ethical values. This means building relationships and enhancing consumer confidence in the integrity of marketing by affirming these core values: honesty, responsibility, fairness, respect, transparency and citizenship.

Ethical Values

Honesty – to be forthright in dealings with customers and stakeholders. To this end, we will:

- Strive to be truthful in all situations and at all times.
- Offer products of value that do what we claim in our communications.
- Stand behind our products if they fail to deliver their claimed benefits.
- Honor our explicit and implicit commitments and promises.

Responsibility – to accept the consequences of our marketing decisions and strategies. To this end, we will:

- Strive to serve the needs of customers.
- Avoid using coercion with all stakeholders.
- Acknowledge the social obligations to stakeholders that come with increased marketing and economic power.
- Recognize our special commitments to vulnerable market segments such as children, seniors, the economically impoverished, market illiterates and others who may be substantially disadvantaged.
- Consider environmental stewardship in our decision-making.

Fairness – to balance justly the needs of the buyer with the interests of the seller. To this end, we will:

- Represent products in a clear way in selling, advertising and other forms of communication; this includes the avoidance of false, misleading and deceptive promotion.
- Reject manipulations and sales tactics that harm customer trust.
- Refuse to engage in price fixing, predatory pricing, price gouging or "bait-and-switch" tactics.
- Avoid knowing participation in conflicts of interest.
- Seek to protect the private information of customers, employees and partners.

Respect – to acknowledge the basic human dignity of all stakeholders. To this end, we will:

- Value individual differences and avoid stereotyping customers or depicting demographic groups (e.g., gender, race, sexual orientation) in a negative or dehumanizing way.
- Listen to the needs of customers and make all reasonable efforts to monitor and improve their satisfaction on an ongoing basis.
- Make every effort to understand and respectfully treat buyers, suppliers, intermediaries and distributors from all cultures.
- Acknowledge the contributions of others, such as consultants, employees and coworkers, to marketing endeavors.
- Treat everyone, including our competitors, as we would wish to be treated.

Transparency – to create a spirit of openness in marketing operations. To this end, we will:

- Strive to communicate clearly with all constituencies.
- Accept constructive criticism from customers and other stakeholders.
- Explain and take appropriate action regarding significant product or service risks, component substitutions or other foreseeable eventualities that could affect customers or their perception of the purchase decision.

- Disclose list prices and terms of financing as well as available price deals and adjustments.

Citizenship – to fulfil the economic, legal, philanthropic and societal responsibilities that serve stakeholders. To this end, we will:

1. Strive to protect the ecological environment in the execution of marketing campaigns.
2. Give back to the community through volunteerism and charitable donations.
3. Contribute to the overall betterment of marketing and its reputation.
4. Urge supply chain members to ensure that trade is fair for all participants, including producers in developing countries.

Implementation

We expect AMA members to be courageous and proactive in leading and/ or aiding their organizations in the fulfilment of the explicit and implicit promises made to those stakeholders. We recognize that every industry sector and marketing sub-discipline (e.g., marketing research, e-commerce, Internet selling, direct marketing, and advertising) has its own specific ethical issues that require policies and commentary. An array of such codes can be accessed through links on the AMA Web site. Consistent with the principle of subsidiarity (solving issues at the level where the expertise resides), we encourage all such groups to develop and/or refine their industry and discipline-specific codes of ethics to supplement these guiding ethical norms and values.

The Advertising Standards Council of India (ASCI) Code for Self-Regulation in Advertising

ASCI is a non-governmental organisation pertaining to the advertising industry in India. The organisation has a self-regulating code for advertising content (Refer table 5.2).

Table 5.2[22]

Truthful and Honest Representation
To ensure the Truthfulness and Honesty of Representations and Claims made by Advertisements and to Safeguard against misleading Advertisements.
1.1. Advertisements must be truthful. All descriptions, claims and comparisons which relate to matters of objectively ascertainable fact should be capable of substantiation. Advertisers and advertising agencies are required to produce such substantiation as and when called upon to do so by The Advertising Standards Council of India.
1.2. Where advertising claims are expressly stated to be based on or supported by independent research or assessment, the source and date of this should be indicated in the advertisement.
1.3. Advertisements shall not, without permission from the person, firm or institution under reference, contain any reference to such person, firm or institution which confers an unjustified advantage on the product advertised or tends to bring the person, firm or institution into ridicule or disrepute. If and when required to do so by The Advertising Standards Council of India, the advertiser and the advertising agency shall produce explicit permission from the person, firm or institution to which reference is made in the advertisement.
1.4. Advertisements shall neither distort facts nor mislead the consumer by means of implications or omissions. Advertisements shall not contain statements or visual presentation which directly or by implication or by omission or by ambiguity or by exaggeration are likely to mislead the consumer about the product advertised or the advertiser or about any other product or advertiser.
1.5. Advertisements shall not be so framed as to abuse the trust of consumers or exploit their lack of experience or knowledge. No advertisement shall be permitted to contain any claim so exaggerated as to lead to grave or widespread disappointment in the minds of consumers.
For example:
(a) Products shall not be described as 'free' where there is any direct cost to the consumer other than the actual cost of any delivery, freight, or postage. Where such costs are payable by the consumer, a clear statement that this is the case shall be made in the advertisement.

22 http://ascionline.org/images/pdf/asci_code_new.pdf, Accessed on August 17, 2016. Included with permission.

(b) Where a claim is made that if one product is purchased, another product will be provided 'free', the advertiser is required to show, as and when called upon by The Advertising Standards Council of India, that the price paid by the consumer for the product which is offered for purchase with the advertised incentive is no more than the prevailing price of the product without the advertised incentive.

(c) Claims which use expressions such as "Upto five years' guarantee" or "Prices from as low as Rs. Y" are not acceptable if there is a likelihood of the consumer being misled either as to the extent of the availability or as to the applicability of the benefits offered.

(d) Special care and restraint has to be exercised in advertisements addressed to those suffering from weakness, any real or perceived inadequacy of any physical attributes such as height or bust development, obesity, illness, impotence, infertility, baldness and the like, to ensure that claims or representations directly or by implication, do not exceed what is considered prudent by generally accepted standards of medical practice and the actual efficacy of the product.

(e) Advertisements inviting the public to invest money shall not contain statements which may mislead the consumer in respect of the security offered, rates of return or terms of amortisation; where any of the foregoing elements are contingent upon the continuance of or change in existing conditions, or any other assumptions, such conditions or assumptions must be clearly indicated in the advertisement.

(f) Advertisements inviting the public to take part in lotteries or prize competitions permitted under law or which hold out the prospect of gifts shall take clearly all material conditions as to enable the consumer to obtain a true and fair view of their prospects in such activities. Further, such advertisers shall make adequate provisions for the judging of such competitions, announcement of the results and the fair distribution of prizes or gifts according to the advertised terms and conditions within a reasonable period of time. With regard to the announcement of results, it is clarified that the advertiser's responsibility under this section of the Code is discharged adequately if the advertiser publicizes the main results in the media used to announce the competition as far as is practicable and advises the individual winners by post.

1.6. Obvious untruths or exaggerations intended to amuse or to catch the eye of the consumer are permissible provided that they are clearly to be seen as humorous or hyperbolic and not likely to be understood as making literal or misleading claims for the advertised product.

1.7. In mass manufacturing and distribution of goods and services it is possible that there may be an occasional, unintentional lapse in the fulfilment of an advertised promise or claim. Such occasional, unintentional lapses may not invalidate the advertisement in terms of this Code. In judging such issues, due regard shall be given to the following: (a) Whether the claim or promise is capable of fulfillment by a typical specimen of the product advertised. (b) Whether the proportion of product failures is within generally acceptable limits. (c) Whether the advertiser has taken prompt action to make good the deficiency to the consumer.
Non-Offensive to Public To ensure that advertisements are not offensive to generally accepted standards of public decency. Advertisements should contain nothing indecent, vulgar, especially in the depiction of women, or nothing repulsive which is likely, in the light of generally prevailing standards of decency and propriety, to cause grave and widespread offence.
Against Harmful Products/ Situations To safeguard against the indiscriminate use of advertising in situations or of the promotion of products which are regarded as hazardous or harmful to society or to individuals, particularly minors, to a degree or of a type which is unacceptable to society at large. 3.1. No advertisement shall be permitted which: (a) Tends to incite people to crime or to promote disorder and violence or intolerance. (b) Derides any race, caste, colour, creed, gender or nationality. (c) Presents criminality as desirable or directly or indirectly encourages people - particularly minors - to emulate it or conveys the modus operandi of any crime. (d) Adversely affects friendly relations with a foreign State. 3.2. Advertisements addressed to minors shall not contain anything, whether in illustration or otherwise, which might result in their physical, mental or moral harm or which exploits their vulnerability.

For example, Advertisements:

(a) Should not encourage minors to enter strange places or to converse with strangers in an effort to collect coupons, wrappers, labels or the like.

(b) Should not feature dangerous or hazardous acts which are likely to encourage minors to emulate such acts in a manner which could cause harm or injury.

(c) Should not show minors using or playing with matches or any inflammable or explosive substance; or playing with or using sharp knives, guns or mechanical or electrical appliances, the careless use of which could lead to their suffering cuts, burns, shocks or other injury.

(d) Should not feature minors for tobacco or alcohol-based products.

(e) Should not feature personalities from the field of sports and entertainment for products which, by law, require a health warning such as "............. is injurious to health" in their advertising or packaging.

3.3. Advertisements shall not, without justifiable reason, show or refer to dangerous practices or manifest a disregard for safety or encourage negligence.

3.4. Advertisements should contain nothing which is in breach of the law, nor omit anything which the law requires.

3.5. Advertisements shall not propagate products, the use of which is banned under the law.

3.6. Advertisements for products whose advertising is prohibited or restricted by law or by this Code must not circumvent such restrictions by purporting to be advertisements for other products the advertising of which is not prohibited

or restricted by law or by this Code. In judging whether or not any particular advertisement is an indirect advertisement for a product whose Advertising is restricted or prohibited, due attention shall be paid to the following:

(a) Whether the unrestricted product which is purportedly sought to be promoted through the advertisement under the complaint is produced and distributed in reasonable quantities, having regard to the scale of the advertising in question, the media used and the markets targeted.

(b) Whether there exist in the advertisement under complaint any direct or indirect clues or cues which could suggest to consumers that it is a direct or indirect advertisement for the product whose Advertising is restricted or prohibited by law or by this Code.

(c) Where Advertising is necessary, the mere use of a brand name or company name that may also be applied to a product whose Advertising is restricted or prohibited, is not a reason to find the advertisement objectionable provided the advertisement is not objectionable in terms of (a) and (b) above.

Fair in Competition

To ensure that advertisements observe fairness in competition such that the consumer's need to be informed on choice in the marketplace and the canons of generally accepted competitive behaviour in business are both served.

4.1. Advertisements containing comparisons with other manufacturers or suppliers or with other products including those where a competitor is named, are permissible in the interests of vigorous competition and public enlightenment, provided:

(a) It is clear what aspects of the advertiser's product are being compared with what aspects of the competitor's product.

(b) The subject matter of comparison is not chosen in such a way as to confer an artificial advantage upon the advertiser or so as to suggest that a better bargain is offered than is truly the case.

(c) The comparisons are factual, accurate and capable of substantiation.

(d) There is no likelihood of the consumer being misled as a result of the comparison, whether about the product advertised or that with which it is compared.

(e) The advertisement does not unfairly denigrate, attack or discredit other products, advertisers or advertisements directly or by implication.

4.2. Advertisements shall not make unjustifiable use of the name or initials of any other firm, company or institution, nor take unfair advantage of the goodwill attached to the trademark or symbol of another firm or its product or the goodwill acquired by its advertising campaign.

4.3. Advertisements shall not be similar to any other advertiser's earlier run advertisements in general layout, copy, slogans, visual presentations, music or sound effects, so as to suggest plagiarism.

4.4. As regards matters covered by sections 2 and 3 above, complaints of plagiarism of advertisements released earlier abroad will lie outside the scope of this Code except in the under-mentioned circumstances:

(a) The complaint is lodged within 12 months of the first general circulation of the advertisements/campaign complained against.

(b) The complainant provides substantiation regarding the claim of prior invention/usage abroad.

Swami Prabhupaada says. "Maya-sukhaya. *Actually this is a fact. We have a humbug civilisation. So many cars are being manufactured every year, and for that purpose so many roads have to be excavated and prepared. This creates problem after problem. Therefore it is maya-sukhaya, illusory happiness, and yet we are trying to be happy in this way. We are trying to manufacture some way to be happy, but this only creates other problems... When my disciple Dayananda wants me to take to a doctor in Los Angeles, i had to take the trouble to travel thirty miles before i could even consult the doctor. Once you create cars, then you must travel thirty or forty miles to meet your friends. You can fly from New York to Boston in one hour, but it takes even longer than that just to get to the airport. This situation is called* Maya-sukhaya. Maya *means "false", "illusory". We are trying to create some very comfortable situation, but we have created another uncomfortable situation."*[23]

Genuineness in Marketing and Advertising, Greenwashing and Cause Marketing

Creating advertisements that evokes a sentiment of environment-friendliness works when audience recognise the authenticity of the advertiser. A case in example is the advertisement from SunPower, a US based solar energy company (**Refer Figure 5.4**). The upper portion of this print advertisement depicts the flying of Solar Impulse[24], a solar-powered aircraft that used Sun Power's solar technology. The advertisement communicates that the expertise of the company in providing advanced solar-based innovations can benefit the domestic households also.

Extraction of minerals that are used in solar panels, the usage and adaptation of these minerals, storage of electricity generated from solar power, etc., causes pollution. However, overall, solar power is less polluting, in comparison with electricity produced from other generation sources such as thermal power plants. Some of the companies also set higher standards in the industry. As per the criteria of Solar ScoreCard (http://www.solarscorecard.com) (**Refer Table 5.3**), a project of the Silicon Valley Toxics Coalition, SunPower has been ranked amongst the

23 Swami Prabhupada, *The Science of Self-Realization*, The Bhaktivedanta Book Trust, 1968.

24 http://www.solarimpulse.com/

leading solar-power producing companies. Considering that the company practices higher standards[25][26] in managing its materials sustainably, non-creation of waste and reduction in usage of water during its manufacturing process, the audience, including those who have an inclination towards environmentally-friendly living, may tend favourably towards the advertisement.

Figure 5.4

25 https://us.sunpower.com/company/corporate-social-responsibility/, Accessed on June 13, 2016.

26 As per the Solar ScoreCard (http://www.solarscorecard.com), a project of the Silicon Valley Toxics Coalition, SunPower has been ranked amongst the leading solar power producing companies. The ranking for 2018-19 can be accessed at: http://www.solarscorecard.com/2018-19/scorecard-2018-19.php

Table 5.3

Criteria of Solar ScoreCard

'Extended Producer Responsibility'	Participation/ commitment of a solar company, to a fully-funded collection and recycling of its end-of-life PV modules
'Reporting on emissions and waste'	Reporting on chemical and hazardous waste, air-pollutants, ozone-depleting substances, landfill-disposal, GHG, energy usage, etc.
'Worker Rights, Health and Safety'	Protection of worker rights, health, and safety that goes beyond compliance with local laws and regulations
'Supply Chains'	Suppliers to protect workers and the environment across all tiers of the supply chain
'Module Toxicity and Minerals'	PV modules that set higher standards in avoidance of toxic heavy metals
'Water'	Reduction of impact on water, reporting on water usage, waste-water generation, etc.
'Conflict Minerals'	Non-usage of conflict minerals

However, when the consumers feel a misalignment between the sustainability parameters professed in an advertisement and the intention of the company, the advertisement may be referred to as 'green-washing'. Greenwashing occurs when an organisation misguides customers by communicating environmental-friendly aspects in the organisation's products or practices, while in actuality, not be giving respect for the natural environment. 'Cause-Marketing' is the process by which an organization markets their products by associating themselves with a good cause. Examples of cause-marketing include Baba Ramdev making the statement that all profits from the sale of 'Patanjali Ayurvedic'[27] products will go to charitable causes[28], and 'Better World Books' donating one book for every book purchased from them[29]. It may also include companies advertising in 'click-to-donate' websites.

27 Refer the section in this textbook related to case-studies/ caselets, to access more details about 'Patanjali Ayurved'.

28 http://www.business-standard.com/article/companies/ramdev-to-launch-swadeshi-baby-care-beauty-products-115111600927_1.html, Accessed on June 13, 2016.

29 http://www.betterworldbooks.com/go/book-for-book, Accessed on June 14, 2016.

For cause marketing to be successful, the audience has to authenticate, acknowledge and appreciate the genuineness of the company's intentions. Patagonia[30], a US based company that manufactures adventure sports clothing and accessories, has been known for its cause-marketing practices and also for environmental-friendly practices worthy of emulation. The below is an excerpt from an interview conducted by TreeHugger website[31] with Yvon Chouinard, founder of Patagonia[32]. The interview communicates what Patagonia stands for, and the alignment between the values lived by the company's founder, and the sustainability practices of Patagonia.

TreeHugger Magazine:

You gave the keynote address at this year's conference of Net Impact in Nashville, and at the end of your talk — the Net Impact coordinator came up and handed you the obligatory swag bag, the corporate goodie bag, which you very politely declined to take. You said something like, "Thank you, but I have everything I need." And that might have been an off-hand remark for you, but it was a striking thing to see. And it certainly made an impression on the audience.

Yvon Chouinard:

It sure did. I've gotten more of a response from that than anything else I said!

TreeHugger Magazine:

But it's a commentary on your attitude toward material possessions. But then again, selling things is your business. So is that a conflict?

Yvon Chouinard:

Yeah, it is. Absolutely. We did an ad one time that said instead of owning a pair of volleyball shorts, a pair of running shorts, a pair of tennis shorts, a pair of walking shorts (we listed all these different uses for shorts), buy one pair of Baggies, and they'll do it all. And it's the truth...

You may take a break...

30 Refer the section in this textbook related to case-studies/ caselets, to access more details about Patagonia.

31 An online media, also referred to as Treehugger magazine.

32 http://www.treehugger.com/treehugger-radio/the-th-interview-yvon-chouinard-founder-of-patagonia-part-two.html, Accessed on April 20, 2016, Included with permission.

SOCIAL RESPONSIBILITY OF STAKEHOLDERS IN BUSINESS

Deeds count, not boasting words.
—Aesop's Fables[33]

"Politicians" are blamed for many of the ills prevalent in the society. It is said that they are not giving necessary attention to governance, not being accountable to people, and not considering the well-being of all inhabitants of this planet. However, it is also said that "Every nation gets the government it deserves"[34], as, in a democracy, it is the citizens who elect the government. Similarly, if an attribution is made to corporate goodness and ill-wills, the other stakeholders - consumers, regulatory bodies, business partners, shareholders, NGOs, peer group – may also have a role to play in this.

Simon Robinson, Founder, Holonomics Education, says, "*...There is a big difference between social networks, communities and cultures. Communities may have the appearance and structure of social networks, but the outcome when networks are inauthentic is the continuation of fragmentation in society. Social networks by themselves do not lead us to authentic sharing and collaboration. You need to analyse a human network in terms of its values. It is not just about having shared values, but universal human values: peace, truth, love, right-action and non-violence. ...when these values are present, and absolutely lived by each and every member, then communities develop culture and therefore you raise culture to its highest potential...*"[35]

Ippimail could be an example of how a lack of support from the business environment, including that of the consumers, resulted in the closing down of a business venture that could have benefited the society. Ippimail.com (In Japanese language, 'Ippi' refers to a helping hand) was a UK based email service provider that was built on an operating model of donating a significant amount of their profits to a charitable cause. Despite the company offering email services free of cost, not many people registered for their email service. It did not have enough advertisement revenues to sustain its operations, and finally, discontinued its business. As this venture was planning to give a significant share of their profits to noble causes (almost 50% of their profits to charities and open-source software

33 http://www.read.gov/aesop/057.html, Accessed on August 16, 2015.

34 https://en.wikiquote.org/wiki/Joseph_de_Maistre, Accessed on March 23, 2016.

35 http://www.sustainablebrands.com/news_and_views/leadership/simon_robinson/what_can_systems_view_life%E2%80%99_teach_us_about_sustainable_lead, Accessed on May 19, 2015.

development)[36][37], and if the venture was able to sustain through the years, it could have created positive impacts through the donations it promised to make.

Consumers

On a positive note, we have examples of consumers asking for practices of social and environmental responsibility from businesses, and rewarding such organizations by purchasing their products. Consumers are recognising that they are citizens of this world, and not just consumers of what is marketed to them. 'Vote with your wallet' is a practice that many socially responsible consumers have adopted. A report by 'Global Sustainable Investment Alliance' indicates that between 2012 and 2014, there has been a 61% growth in financial assets that are managed through Socially Responsible Investment (SRI) principles.[38] As per 'The forum for sustainable and responsible investment', there has been a 33% increase in SRI investments in US between 2014 and 2016.[39]

Conscious Consuming

The practice of a consumer being attentive to one's purchase decisions and incorporating human values in purchase decisions is referred to as 'Conscious Consuming'. Consumers include responsibility parameters during shopping in a number of ways.

Some do this by purchasing those products that:

- supports local economy (Example: purchasing groceries and vegetables from a weekly market)
- maintain higher standards in quality, including reduced negative impacts on health
- reduce packaging wastage
- can be reused (for example, purchasing reusable glasses for drinking water rather than using disposable glasses)
- provides an option to repair and replace the parts

36 http://www.belfasttelegraph.co.uk/life/charity-begins-online-28793310.html, Accessed on March 23, 2016.

37 http://www.freesoftwaremagazine.com/articles/welcome_ippimail, Accessed on March 23, 2016.

38 http://www.gsi-alliance.org/wp-content/uploads/2015/02/GSIA_Review_download.pdf, Accessed on July 2, 2016.

39 http://www.ussif.org/files/SIF_Trends_16_Executive_Summary(1).pdf, Accessed on November 12, 2017.

- provides fair wages to those who manufacture the products
- cause lesser harm to the natural environment as compared to the existing products
- are manufactured by companies that share a significant percentage of their profit for humanitarian causes and enhances the well-being of the inhabitants of the planet
- provides meaningful jobs to people

"*...Consumers can also play a role, starting by reconsidering their own purchasing decisions. They should aim for truly sustainable products – but the golden rule of sustainable consumption is to only buy things that are really needed, and to make sure existing products can be reused, exchanged and repaired.*", says a report 'The false promise of certification'[40].

EMPLOYEES

Employees are one of the prime contributors to promoting sustainability practices within an organization. As employees have inside information, they also have the opportunity to influence decision making. Many CSR activities that has won acknowledgement, recognition and respect has emerged from the practice of 'caring, sharing and giving' from a few employees.

'Citizen First, Employee Next' and Whistle-blowing

Historical examples indicate that employees have brought public attention to the corrupt and societally harmful practices perpetrated by organizations. Those who bring attention to the illegal and unethical activities within an organization are referred to as whistle-blowers. There is an awakening among many that while they may be employees, they are also citizens of this world (**Refer figure 5.5**). Being a good citizen is an important social responsibility parameter for all employees in an organization.

It is easy for a worker to fall a prey to the daily routine and usual reactionary tendencies. Federico Cuneo, Senior Partner with Ernst & Young in Peru, Chair of Peru 2021 (an NGO comprised of business executives working on sustainable development and corporate social responsibility) narrates an example of how people in an organisation were able to move beyond their reactionary tendencies and respond to the situation with solutions.

---

40 http://changingmarkets.org/wp-content/uploads/2018/05/False-promise_full-report-ENG.pdf, Accessed on May 16, 2018.

Figure 5.5

"Every time something happens, whether a material fails or does not perform up to standard, people tend to look to the external environment for the cause. Marketing tries to put the blame on production, production tries to put the blame on R&D and it is a vicious cycle. Whereas if all of us were to look within ourselves we would more likely find the answer about what went wrong.

We used to emit a lot of dust from our chimneys at the plant. Then the pollution control board came to us and told us that this was very bad, and that if we didn't do something about it they would shut down our plant. We found that if we put up an electrostatic filter it would be a large expenditure. The immediate reaction by many people was that we could not spend that much money. But then we did more research and had the dust chemically analysed. We found that the dust could be collected and put back into the operation. So we re-looked at the costs in light of this and showed everyone that within one and a half years we could recover the initial costs.

You see the initial reaction that people had come from was their outward reaction to spending the money. But when we went inside and looked for solutions that would not cause harm, we came out with this idea to analyse the material and see if there was something we could do with it."[41]

41 Quotations extracted from the public knowledge base of the "Spiritual Based Leadership Research Programme" are © 2006 by the Global Dharma Center (GDC). GDC retains the copyright to all excerpts from this knowledge base.

Insider Trading

'Insider Trading' involves employees or directors engaging in legal and illegal buying or selling in securities (stocks) in their own companies. The term 'Insider Trading' is usually used to refer to illegal transactions. An insider trading becomes illegal when employees or directors engage in trading of securities while possessing important information which are not available to the public. Some of the examples provided below relates to illegal insider trading, as per the 'US Securities and Exchange Commission (US SEC)'[42].

a. Trading in securities (stocks) of a company, after learning about significant and confidential matters (about the company), which can have an impact on the stock price of the company

b. Providing information to people external to the organisation, about significant and confidential matters, which can have an impact on the stock price of the company.

Shareholders

Shareholders invest in the company. While shareholders are considered investors, some are speculators. Speculators are interested in immediate returns. They hold the shares of the company for the short-term, and is generally non-interested about the long-term well-being of the company. There has been a consensus - that a short-term investment behaviour has a negative impact on the way companies make decisions[43]. Pressure from short-term investors may force the company management to focus on short-term returns, ignoring the long-term risks. On the contrary, long-term investors urge the company to study, disclose and act on long-term risks. Peabody Energy, which was the world's largest coal producer, has been criticised for non-disclosure and misrepresentation of long-term risks related to climate change[44]. In 2016, for various reasons that also included the company not charting a path towards clean energy, the company filed for bankruptcy, thereby eroding shareholder value[45].

---

42 https://www.sec.gov/fast-answers/answersinsiderhtm.html, Accessed on June 19, 2017.

43 http://www.uk.mercer.com/newsroom/mercer-loyalty-shares-research-indicates-consensus-negative-impact-short-termism.html, Accessed on July 3, 2016.

44 https://ag.ny.gov/press-release/ag-schneiderman-secures-unprecedented-agreement-peabody-energy-end-misleading, Accessed on June 18, 2017

45 https://www.wsj.com/articles/peabody-energy-files-for-chapter-11-protection-from-creditors-1460533760, Accessed on June 18, 2017.

Rewarding long-term shareholders

Suggestions to facilitate long-term investment behaviour include providing long-term investors with loyalty dividends, loyalty shares and additional voting rights. There are a number of companies that reward long-term shareholders. For example, Lafarge, a cement company from France, has been paying additional dividend to those shareholders who hold its shares for at least two years[46].

Shareholders, being owners of the company, are uniquely positioned to chart a sustainability path in the company they have invested. Many shareholders ask their companies to engage in sustainability practices.

Suppliers

Suppliers have a prominent role in the success of a company's sustainability objectives. Retailers are known for outsourcing their manufacturing processes to various companies located in different parts of the globe, and in turn these companies may be outsourcing their needs for packaging solutions etc. to other companies. A large number of organizations have indicated that the largest opportunity for sustainability improvement exists at the supplier level.

Industry Associations and Peer Groups

Some of the ways through which industry association and peer groups can help in promoting responsibility practices are through:

- Knowledge sharing
- Recognition of best practices
- Advocacy on common issues that will benefit the society
- Rewarding and supporting businesses and organisations that are known for designing and instituting higher standards of ethical practices in business
- Creating a business ecosystem that supports values such as honesty and integrity
- Providing guidance to citizens and regulatory authorities on creating forward-looking legal and governance framework
- Promoting self-regulation amongst the members of the peer group

46 http://www.lafarge.com/en/dividend, Accessed on July 3, 2016.

In 2016, *Outlook Traveller* magazine instituted the "Responsible Tourism" awards in India. Tourism related to business travel, religion, wildlife, adventure, driving holidays, romantic holidays, etc. have resulted in pollution of pristine spaces, while also providing some economic benefits. Accumulation of waste is easily visible, whereas exploitation of rivers and other water bodies may not be. Such awards and events may help in information dissemination of good practices in areas related to corporate social responsibility (**Refer figure 5.6**), long-term sustenance of businesses, networking, new market development, etc.

Figure 5.6 (a)

Tropical bathrooms', usually, semi-enclosed, is a design feature in some resorts, eco-villas, forest-cottages, beach-stays, etc. A guest in a tropical bathroom may find a palm-tree, coconut tree or any other tropical tree, growing nearby. This idea is drawn from the traditional practice, found in many regions, of people (bucket) bathing near the trees. Pictured above is a brick placed between a coconut-tree and a jack-fruit-tree. Application of (only) natural oils (such as coconut oil), powdered green-gram, paste of neem leaves, etc. are non-toxic on the body, and, the soil. However, bathing directly underneath a coco'nut' tree is hazardous, unless the coco'nut' tree is slanted, or there are branches of other trees that can deflect the 'nut's and 'leaf' that can fall down. It is also common in many tropical regions to bind thatched coconut leaves, with bamboo, to form a fully-enclosed bathing space, without a roof. Pictured below is another brick, in the vicinity of herbs and shrubs – hibiscus and other flowering plants, curry leaves, etc. A bucket holds approximately ten litres of water whereas a bath-tub requires 10-20 times as much water.

Figure 5.6 (b)

In India, awards on CSR, sustainable development and leadership are given by industry associations such as CII, FICCI, ASSOCHAM and regional business associations. Similar awards are also instituted by media organizations, academic institutions, and not-for-profit organizations. Through workshops, training programmes, expert lectures, discussion forums and other knowledge sharing sessions, industry associations can support the emergence of best practices in this area.

Estimates are that the 35 five-star hotels in Delhi consumes approximately 14 million litres of water daily and generate nearly 10 million litres of sewage everyday[47]. Malta in Europe is a region that faces water-scarcity. Business organisations has been one of the major consumers of water. The five-star hotels in Malta used 462 litres per guest night, four-star hotels used 292 litres and three-star hotels used 199 litres of water per guest night. Offices consumed 25 litres of water per employee per day whereas manufacturing enterprises consumed 24 litres of water per employee per day (without shower facilities)[48]. The Malta Business Bureau (MBB) is a conglomeration of associations related to businesses. MBB started a project aimed at water conservation. This project of MBB contributed to conservation awareness

47 https://www.news18.com/news/india/delhi-five-star-hotels-asked-to-cut-down-water-consumption-603025.html, Accessed on October 11, 2020.

48 https://timesofmalta.com/articles/view/water-consumption-in-hotels-industry.421162, Accessed on October 11, 2020.

among businesses, leading to better availability of water resources. MBB supported institution of water-harvesting designs, recycling of water, and application of designs that reduces the consumption of water at usage-sources such as showers, hand-wash taps, etc[49].

Community

In 1965, yet another attempt was made towards stealing the statue of Mannekin Pis, in Brussels. The original was, thus, shifted to Brussels city museum, while a copy ("replica") was kept at the fountain. Historians say that, in the 15th century, this fountain was a way of providing drinking water. The bronze sculpture was made in late 1610s, which replacing another statue of this boy whose legends has been in existence, for least a few centuries before. Legendary, because, this boy saved his native-city from enemies. How? While spying on the enemies, he saw that enemies are putting explosives on the castle walls. As they lit fire to the explosives, and ran away, the boy dashed near, and urinated on the fire-line. Legendary, also because, this boy, saved the lives of many, by standing on top of a castle and pee'ing on all those who were fighting a war. These are just two legends associated with this boy.

Role of NGOs in sustainable development

In 2005, the parliament of India passed the Right to Information (RTI) Act, 2005. This law has resulted in easier access for citizens to governmental information. RTI empowered a citizen to ask queries to most governmental establishments, and to receive reply from them, contributing to increased transparency and accountability. Many non-governmental organisations such as Mazdoor Kisan Shakti Sangathan (MKSS), National Campaign for People's Right to Information (NCPRI), Parivartan, The Association for Democratic Reforms, Public Affairs Centre etc. has significantly contributed to the enactment of this law by Government of India.

"NGO" is an acronym for a Non-Governmental Organization. Many NGOs are engaged with causes that enhance the well-being of the society. This may span a number of areas – care for children and elderly, research on bio-diversity, protection of wetlands, advocacy issues related to strengthening democracy, civic engagement and more. An article from 'Harvard Business School' states that environmental organizations such as Greenpeace or 'World Wide Fund for Nature' create value for the society by "increasing the world's willingness-to-pay on environmental issues"[50]. Many NGOs

49 https://mbb.org.mt/projects/archive/investinginwater/industry-saving-118000000-litres-of-water/, Accessed on October 11, 2020.

50 http://hbswk.hbs.edu/item/5797.html, Accessed on June 8, 2015.

have played a prominent role in drawing the attention of civil society to developmental issues.

Roles played by NGOs:

- Serving the society
- Drawing attention of the government and citizens to governance deficits that exist in the society
- Influencing the opinion of government, for-profit organizations and citizens on causes of greater common good
- Providing specialist and expert opinion on developmental issues
- To facilitate discussions and dialogues amongst various sections of the society

Regulators

Regulatory bodies play a significant role in creating an environment where businesses can operate in a socially and environmentally responsible manner. Some of the ways through which this could be done is:

a) Tax shifts:

This is done by increasing taxes on behaviours that negatively impact the planet and people, decreasing taxes (or not taxing) on those aspects that are necessary for a living, and providing tax incentives for projects that contribute to the greater common good (For examples, **refer table 5.4**).

Table 5.4

Taxing the "bad"	Not taxing the "good"
Pollution and degradation of the natural environment	Savings and income made by individuals that contributes to the necessities of living (while not to desirables and luxuries).
Inefficiency in resource utilisation	
Resource extraction	
Luxury	
Harmful and dysfunctional spending (For example, spending on tobacco, alcohol, etc.)	
Conspicuous consumption	

This practice also involves removing subsidies associated with practices that are socially and environmentally harmful. For example, it may not be necessary to subsidise or provide funds to transportation and related infrastructure that primarily benefit individual or private transportation, which is more resource-intensive, instead of public transportation or mass transportation.

b) Product Labelling:

Regulatory bodies can help the consumer make informed decisions through the launch of product labelling practices. The energy labelling program started by Bureau of Energy Efficiency (BEE), or the Food Safety and Standards Authority of India (FSSAI)'s norm of green and brown dot-marking for indicating vegetarian and non-vegetarian ingredients or foods are two examples.

c) Progressive strengthening of standards:

Regulatory agencies are expected to progressively set higher standards, wherever necessary. For example, the Euro standards for emission from automobiles and Bharat Emission standards got progressively stringent through the years.

d) Setting leadership examples and standards:

Governmental organizations can be examples of practising the ideal. Their practice may influence or inspire others. When Ministry of Environment, Forests and Climate Change (MoEFCC), Government of India, started construction of a new office building, they've designed it with green features. The building, named as 'Indira Paryavaran Bhawan', has been designed as a greener building. Through the usage of green materials, energy and water saving systems, generation of solar energy, design that is friendly to differently-abled people, usage of natural daylighting etc., this building has set exemplary environmental standards in design and construction of a building.[51]

Ministry of Drinking Water and Sanitation, Government of India, has requested various governmental departments to avoid usage of plastic bottles to provide drinking water during governmental meetings, conferences, workshops etc., and instead provide water in a manner that do not result in the creation of plastic waste. Prior to making this request to other departments, the ministry initiated the practice of not using plastic bottles in their official functions.[52]

---

51 http://pib.nic.in/newsite/PrintRelease.aspx?relid=104214, Accessed on September 23, 2016.

52 http://himachal.nic.in/WriteReadData/l892s/17_l892s/Circular_WATER%20 BOTTLED-21798821.pdf, Accessed on September 23, 2016.

The Indian Railways' base-kitchen at Mumbai-Central provide catering to super-fast and express trains, such as, the Rajdhani. With the objective of maintaining cleanliness and hygiene, and to avoid cross-contamination, the kitchen has separate cooking areas for vegetarian and non-vegetarian. This was also in compliance with FSSAI's hygiene rules that mentions about (a) cleanliness of the cooking premises (b) usage of multiple and covered waste-bins for various types of wastes generated in the kitchen (c) usage of separate utensils, equipments, knives, chopping boards, dusters, etc. for vegetarian and non-vegetarian, (d) separate areas for cooking vegetarian and non-vegetarian, and, separate storage areas (e) usage of clean dusters (f) personal hygiene of personnel involved in food preparation (such as wearing clean clothes, washing hands before cooking, etc.) (g) keeping hot food above 60 degree C and cold food below 5 degree C (h) respect for the guest/ customer/ consumer/ visitor[53] (for example, using only potable or drinkable water during cooking), etc.

e) Penalties and Cancellations of Licences to operate:

Regulatory organisations has been empowered to revoke operating licences of businesses or to impose penalties on business organisations, depending on the extent to which a business organisations has been engaged in irresponsible practices.

f) Information and Education:

Regulatory agencies empower citizens with information and advisories. For example, there has been discussions about efficient air-conditioning systems[54]. 'Bureau of Energy Efficiency' (BEE), under 'Ministry of Power', India, stated that "*In summers, it is estimated that in a typical building, air-conditioning consumes maximum amount of electricity. Air conditioning consumes more than 50% of total electricity in commercial or residential buildings*"[55][56]

53 One of the quotes included in many informatory boards mention that a customer is the most important visitor on the premises of an organisation. This quote is attributed to Mahatma Gandhi. However, this is a mis-attribution.

54 http://www.newsonair.com/Main-News-Details.aspx?id=355270, Accessed on May 14, 2019.

55 http://www.mca.gov.in/Ministry/pdf/AcTempNotice_21082018.pdf, Accessed on May 14, 2019.

56 Research studies have indicated that human responses to artificial cooling are influenced by non-thermal factors and need to consider cultural, social and contextual dimensions. For example, a person acclimatised to a tropical environment may find it uncomfortable to be in a room where air-conditioning is set at 26 degree Celsius and may find setting at a higher temperature to be more comfortable. Even the most efficient air-conditioning consumes power, discharges heat to the external environment and is made from minerals mined from the earth.

(Refer figure 5.7). National Oceanic and Atmospheric Administration (NOAA), under 'US Department of Commerce', has been providing weather forecasts, storm warnings, climate monitoring services, etc. (**Refer figure 5.8**).

Figure 5.7

Heat-disposal ventilators of air-conditioning units.

Figure 5.8[57]

Variation from average temperature, at Utqiagvik (Barrow), Alaska, USA.

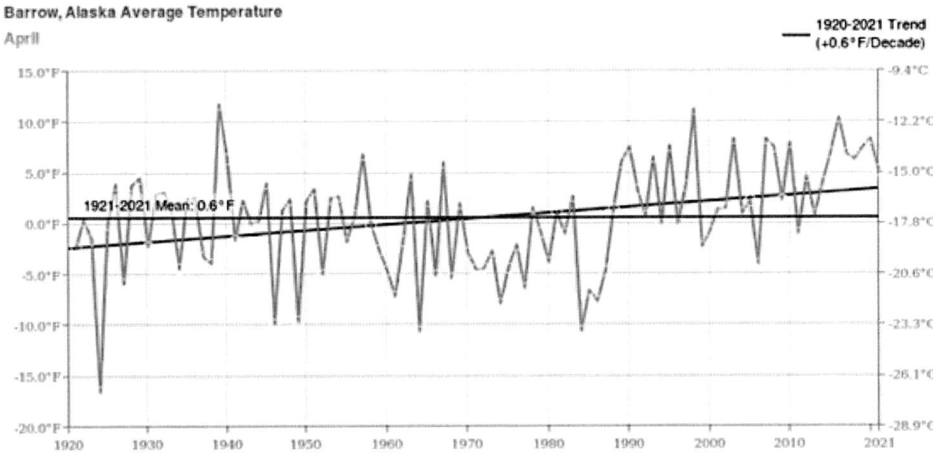

The above graph indicates the average temperature for the month of April, between 1920 and 2020, for Utqiagvik (Barrow), Alaska. Utqiagvik is one of the northernmost cities of the world and is located more than 300 miles north of the Arctic-circle.

You may take a break...

INDIVIDUAL SOCIAL RESPONSIBILITY

"My school was a happy place. All of us who started our schooling there completed our studies till the eighth standard. I don't remember even a single person dropping out. These days, when i visit schools, both big and small, all across the country, i tell them that true quality does not come from a great building or great facilities or great advertisements. It happens when education is imparted with love by great teachers."[58]

—APJ Abdul Kalam

57 NOAA National Centers for Environmental information, Climate at a Glance: City Time Series, published May 2021, retrieved on May 10, 2021 from https://www.ncdc.noaa.gov/cag/

58 APJ Abdul Kalam, My Journey: Transforming Dreams into Actions, Rupa Publications, 2014.

CSR will become meaningful and fruitful if there is awareness and practice of 'Individual Social Responsibility' (ISR). Speaking about the importance of being responsible in all phases of life, Mahatma Gandhi says, "*For one man cannot do right in one department of life whilst he is occupied in doing wrong in any other department. Life is one indivisible whole.*"[59] For a person to whom 'caring for the planet and people' is a guiding value, expressions of this value will manifest in their personal and professional life. Such a person will bring sincerity, purposefulness and efficiency to the CSR practices in an organisation. The words 'corporate' and 'corporeal', from their Latin roots, refer to 'senses' and 'body'. An implication may thus be made that 'Corporate Social Responsibility' may also refer to the responsibility of the individual at the level of the senses and the body.

ISR involves the ethos and practice of discovering[60], invoking[61], infusing[62], evoking[63] and radiating[64] the human values of righteousness (*Dharma*) and love (*Prema*) by an individual, in one's own life, be it at home or in the workplace or in the society. Mahatma Gandhi, on the eve of Dandi March (1930), invites attention to the importance of adhering to the human values of truth and non-violence. "*...I wish that there should be no suspension or abandonment of the war that commences tomorrow morning or earlier, if I am arrested before that time. I shall eagerly await the news that ten batches are ready as soon as my batch is arrested. I believe there are men in India to complete the work begun by me. I have faith in the righteousness of our cause and the purity of our weapons. And where the means are clean, there God is undoubtedly present with His blessings. And where these three combine, there defeat is an impossibility. A Satyagrahi, whether free or incarcerated, is ever victorious. He is vanquished only, when he forsakes truth and non-violence and turns a deaf ear to the inner voice. If, therefore, there is such a thing as defeat for even a Satyagrahi, he alone is the cause of it. God bless you all and keep off all obstacles from the path in the struggle that begins tomorrow.*"[65]

ISR can start with simple practices of kindness. The book author's third

---

59 https://en.wikiquote.org/wiki/Mahatma_Gandhi, Accessed on March 23, 2016.

60 dis-cover.

61 to call (as in, "invoking the presence of a spiritual master, deity, higher power, a human value etc. during a prayer").

62 to inspire, instil, impart, etc.

63 to elicit, to draw (as in, "evoking the memories and emotions of goodness, helpfulness, charity and virtuosity").

64 to shine, illuminate, emit, spread, etc.

65 http://wikilivres.ca/wiki/On_The_Eve_of_Dandi_March, Accessed on September 22, 2016.

standard class-teacher used to tell students about engaging in 21 acts of kindness on a daily basis. *"A corporate is responsible only when individuals within that corporate are responsible,"* says the chairman of a consulting company[66].

Work Values from Indian Ethos

Stephen Covey, author of the book, *The 7 Habits of Highly Effective People*, says, *"I had an interesting experience recently in India. I had just read the book, 'The Argumentative Indian'. Essentially it's a very well written cultural history of India and how the argumentative tendency is part of their cultural DNA. When I got into that, I could see how under developed their country was with respect to teamwork and how over developed their democracy was. They have so many parties and so much fighting and contention. I spoke to an audience of a thousand people about the spiritual principle of seeking first to understand before seeking to be understood. I then opened things up to the audience and said, "Let us see if we right now can listen to each other and re-make the other person's point before we make our own." They were unable to do it. So I said, "Let me see if you could ask a question on what we have covered to this point without making an oratorical statement." They were unable to do it. So I had one half of the audience just observe to see if the other half could practice this principle. They could not do it. And they could see that they could not do it. Then I said, "Look at what has happened to your infrastructure here in India, look at the bureaucracy, the extent of rules and regulations that have taken the place of human creativity – which is really interesting when you consider that you have more knowledge workers in this country than any other country in the world." I said, "Just look at this! You are capable of transcending your cultural DNA, because deeper than that is your spiritual DNA, it is deep in your natures, you really are capable of doing it." They were so intrigued with this approach, and I became intrigued with their awareness. Awareness, the space between stimulus and response, is a huge thing to me. They were aware of their cultural DNA. Rather than looking at life through it, they now chose to look at it. They could then see that true leaders don't work through systems rather that they work on the systems, and they do this through a principle-centred approach that rests on universal spiritual principles. This was a fascinating learning experience for all of us. The more I get to know the Indian culture, the more I use this approach, and my audiences and the leaders I speak to know that it is authentic. That it is real. They know I am not some American over there trying to Americanise them. They know that I respect the development over more than 5,000 years of their magnificent spiritual and cultural tradition. I ask*

66 http://www.livemint.com/Companies/roQ76qkNPcSKdiLV0nkpII/CSR-expenditure-should-be-a-percentage-of-revenue-not-profi.html, Accessed on May 9, 2016.

them to look at what has happened to this cultural DNA, and I ask them if they can practice a couple of principles. They become amazed and then they become very humble and open to learn empathetic listening – and how to re-make the other person's point before making your own point, which is a spiritual principle."[67]

Indian Ethos recommends many 'normative values' that has the potential to support an individual in transcending the cultural DNA that Stephen Covey refers to. These values are applicable to all phases of one's life, including work, and can enrich social responsibility practices (**Refer table 5.5**). A few of them are as below:

1. *Paropakaaraartham Idam Shareeram*

This is one of the foundational ethos of Indian work values. A translation could be 'This body is for helping others'. It could also be interpreted as 'This body is for serving nobler ideals'.

Implication in Responsibility Practices: To consider 'service' as one of the guiding values

2. *Sathyam Naasthi Paro Dharmah*

'Truth is the supreme ideal'. Thus, to serve Truth is the supreme work. This work value also helps an individual to understand the nature of many of the transient aspects witnessed on a daily basis. MS Swaminathan, the agricultural scientist, whose intention and work to provide food to many, has been respected by all, says, *"The following message of Swami Vivekananda always inspires me. 'This life is short. Its varities are transient. He alone lives who lives for others'."*[68] The value of considering 'Truth' as the supreme ideal helps one to witness the vagaries of media-driven-ethics and situational ethics. 'Indian values' are based on universal principles that transcend the boundaries of time and space, as exemplified in Katha Upanishad, which communicates a conversation between Nachiketas and Yama, the Lord of Death (**Refer table 5.4**[69]). Nachiketas visits the Lord of Death, and has been waiting to meet him, for three days and nights, while being without food and water, and devoid of sleep. Lord of Death, on his arrival, grants this boy with three boons.

---

67 Quotations extracted from the public knowledge base of the "Spiritual Based Leadership Research Programme" are © 2006 by the Global Dharma Center (GDC). GDC retains the copyright to all excerpts from this knowledge base.

68 In a message sent to the author.

69 This excerpt is an English translation of 'Katha Upanishad' by Eknath Easwaran. From The Upanishads, translated by Eknath Easwaran, founder of the Blue Mountain Center of Meditation, copyright 1987, 2007; reprinted by permission of Nilgiri Press, P. O. Box 256, Tomales, Ca 94971, www.bmcm.org.

Implications in Responsibility Practices: To be truthful and transparent in one's dealings.

Table 5.4

Yama:	...Thus have I granted you the second boon, Nachiketa, the secret of the fire That leads to heaven. It will have your name. Ask now, Nachiketa, for the third boon.
Nachiketa:	When a person dies, there arises this doubt: "He still exists," say some; "he does not," Say others. I want you to teach me the truth. This is my third boon.
Yama:	This doubt haunted even the gods of old, For the secret of death is hard to know. Nachiketa, ask for some other boon And release me from my promise.
Nachiketa:	This doubt haunted even the gods of old; For it is hard to know, O Death, as you say. I can have no greater teacher than you, And there is no boon equal to this.
Yama:	Ask for sons and grandsons who will live A hundred years. Ask for herds of cattle, Elephants and horses, gold and vast land, And ask to live as long as you desire. Or, if you can think of anything more Desirable, ask for that, with wealth and Long life as well. Nachiketa, be the ruler Of a great kingdom, and I will give you The utmost capacity to enjoy The pleasures of life. Ask for beautiful Women of loveliness rarely seen on earth, Riding in chariots, skilled in music, To attend on you. But Nachiketa, Don't ask me about the secret of death

Nachiketa:	These pleasures last but until tomorrow, And they wear out the vital powers of life. How fleeting is all life on earth! Therefore Keep your horses and chariots, dancing And music, for yourself. Never can mortals Be made happy by wealth. How can we be Desirous of wealth when we see your face And know we cannot live while you are here? This is the boon I choose and ask you for. Having approached an immortal like you, How can I, subject to old age and death, Ever try to rejoice in a long life For the sake of the senses' fleeting pleasures? Dispel this doubt of mine, O king of death: Does a person live after death or does he not? Nachiketa asks for no other boon Than the secret of this great mystery...

3. *Sathyam Vada, Dharmam Chara*

'Speak the Truth, Live Righteousness'. 'Speak the Truth' expresses the idea of not only being honest, but also to spread that knowledge, which is eternal. This is also related to "*Sathyam Brooyat, Priyam Brooyat, Na Brooyat Sathyamapriyam*", which means "Speak the truth, speak in a pleasant manner, do not speak truth in an unpleasant manner". This statement does not indicate a non-speaking of truth. It draws our attention to the importance of ensuring that our intentions and expressions are dharmic, while not having the intention to hurt or harm. "*There is no such thing as a 'brutal truth',*" says a teacher. *Dharma* is considered the foundation of all human endeavours.

Implications in Responsibility Practices: To be righteous, fair, truthful and humane in communications to stakeholders and also in business practices

4. *Atmano Mokshartham, Jagat Hitayacha*

'Towards one's liberation, and the well-being of the world'. This statement communicates the necessity that the choices that we make to support our personal well-being, need to be in congruence with the well-being of the world. One may also infer that we should not make choices that harms the world.

Implications in Responsibility Practices: To ascertain the impact of business decisions on the well-being of all creations of the planet

5. *Vasudaiva Kutumbakam*

'The world is a divine family'. While there may be diversity, we are all connected.

Implications in Responsibility Practices: To ensure that businesses enhance the well-being of all and to consider this as a guiding principle in business practice.

6. *Ahinsa Paramodharma*

'Non-violence is the supreme ideal'. A scriptural text that have influenced and inspired many is *The Bhagavad Gita*. The Bhagavad Gita, set in the context of a war, speaks about the necessity to consider every work, including that of fighting a war, as a holy endeavor. Even a war needs to be fought in a righteous manner, and should not be fought for power or material gains. It has to be fought without the mental volition to hurt or harm. This scriptural text also communicates that an individual need to overcome their weaknesses. *The Mahabharatha* provides multiple examples of the effects of wars, fought due to reasons that are non-dharmic.

Implications in Responsibility Practices: To ensure that business decisions do not cause harm.

7. *Yagnayacharatah karma*

Yagna refers to 'Sacrifice'. The word 'Sacrifice' from its Latin roots, stands for, 'Sacred'. Work is thus considered a sacred endeavour. Referring to this spirit of '*Yagna*', Michael Nagler[70] mentions, "*It was Gandhi who really brought this abstruse doctrine back to vibrant life: act, by all means, but make your act, in the modern sense of the word, a sacrifice. That is, he explained, choose selfless goal, use right means (non-violence), and never be pushed into action for your own benefit - a tall order. Gandhi was not waxing metaphorical when he called his programs for the deliverance of India - and of the individual activist - yajna. By drawing upon the not-to-be-denied need in all of us to work for a selfless goal he elevated even his political campaigns to the level of models for every action we might want to take today.*"[71]

70 Professor Emeritus, University of California, Berkeley.

71 Eknath Easwaran, The Upanishads, Nilgiri Press, 2008.

Implications in Responsibility Practices: To evoke a feeling of divinity and sacredness in all endeavors.

8. *Loka Samastha Sukhino Bhavantu*

'Let all, in all worlds, be happy'.

Implications in Responsibility Practices: To ensure that the endeavours undertaken by an organization is towards the happiness of all beings in all worlds.

Table 5.5

Statements related to Indian Work Ethos	Human Values* related to CSR practices
"Paropakaaraartham Idam Shareeram"	Service, Dedication, Duty
"Sathyam Naasthi Paro Dharmah", "Sathyam Vada Dharmam Chara"	Truth, Curiosity, Focus, Holistic Thinking, Honesty, Integrity, Inquiry, Intuition, Objectivity, Reasoning, Righteousness, Simplicity, Proper usage of (i) time (ii) money (iii) energy and (iv) resources, Character, Conscience, Determination
"Atmano Mokshartham Jagat Hitayacha"	Concern for the well-being of all, Responsibility, Morality
"Vasudaiva Kutumbakam", "Samastha Loka Sukhino Bhavantu"	Universal well-being, Balance, Good citizenship, Global Awareness, Charity, Empathy, Helpfulness
"Ahinsa Paramodharma"	Non-violence, Gentleness, Harmony, Fearlessness, Ethics, Courage, Forgiveness
"Yagnayacharatah karma"	Holiness, Awareness, Enthusiasm, Initiative

As part of an interview during the publication of his earlier book "Environmental Management",[72] the book author was asked, "*What special care did you take in writing this book?*" The reply was, "*Reminds me about*

72 Oxford University Press, 2015.

* The list of human values accessed from "Cross-cultural expressions of the Human Values", made available by Global Dharma Center at www.globaldharma.org

the lyrics from a Malayalam song 'Rajahamsame...'. The lyrics plays this way, 'Nimisha Meghamaay Njaan, Peythu Thornnidaam, Nooraayiram Ithalaayi Nee Vidaruvaan....'. This is the culture of India, a land that create individuals who dedicate their life for the well-being of all - Paropakaaraartham Idam Shareeram, while living in the knowledge that a blossomed flower is also a dissipated cloud. This exemplifies the concept of Yagna, which can be translated as 'Sacrifice', a word, which from its Latin roots, means to make things holy.

The shift from 'Bhoga' to 'Thyaga'

It has been noted that inequality in wealth generation and distribution is on an increase[73]. One of the ways through which attempts has been made to reduce this inequality is through philanthropy. One realizes experientially that once the basic needs for living are met, increased accumulation of monetary wealth do not contribute to increased happiness. Empirical research also supports this realization[74]. People are also realising that consumption, referred to as "*Bhoga*" in Sanskrit, is negatively impacting planetary relations, as is visible in pollution and other societal and environmental concerns, and a diseased existence. Many people are bringing about a shift in their lifestyle, from being a 'consumer', to a living focused on contribution, which results in giving and volunteerism. The attitude towards life thus shifts from '*Bhoga*' to '*Thyaga*'. From an attitude of 'taking', the shift is to "giving".

You may take a break...

CONCEPTS AND ROLE OF CORPORATE GOVERNANCE

"In the Kingdom of Fools, both the king and the minister were idiots. They didn't want to run things like other kings, so they decided to change night into day and day into night. They ordered that everyone should be awake at night, till their fields and run their businesses only after dark, and go to bed as soon as the sun came up. Anyone who disobeyed would be punished with death. The people did as they were told for fear of death. The king and the minister were delighted at the success of their project."[75]

73 http://equitablegrowth.org/research-analysis/u-s-top-one-percent-of-income-earners-hit-new-high-in-2015-amid-strong-economic-growth/, Accessed on September 23, 2016.

74 http://www.pnas.org/content/107/52/22463, Accessed on September 23, 2016.

75 AK Ramanujan, Folk Tales from India: A Selection of Oral Tales from Twenty-two Languages, Pantheon Books, 1991 (The story may also be accessed at http://www.ncert.nic.in/ncerts/l/iemo104.pdf).

An OECD report states that the purpose of corporate governance is *"to help build an environment of trust, transparency and accountability necessary for fostering long-term investment, financial stability and business integrity, thereby supporting stronger growth and more inclusive societies."*[76] Board of Directors (BoDs) are responsible for the corporate governance practices of a company, and explores the relationships through which a company manages the long-term interests of its various stakeholders. The Infosys web-link[77] detailing its corporate governance practice states, *"We believe that an active, well-informed and independent board is necessary to ensure the highest standards of corporate governance."*

Guidelines for Corporate Governance Practices

Policies and practices related to corporate governance practices of a region is influenced by the norms and behaviour of that region. A CEO of an organisation that helps people to excel says, *"The Chinese thinking paradigm is the opposite of the American. When we write an address on an envelope, we write the country first, then the city, the street third, then the apartment number and finally your name. This is very illustrative of our thinking orientation. The same goes for our way of thinking about business."*[78]

> *The words 'corporate' and 'corporeal', from their Latin roots, refer to 'senses' and 'body'. An implication may thus be made that 'Corporate Social Responsibility' may also refer to responsibility at the level of the senses and the body.*

Companies Act 2013

Companies Act 2013[79] has provided significant amount of inputs into governance aspects related to a company. A few of them are as below:

1. Section 181 of Companies Act 2013 acknowledges the possibility of the Board of Directors of a company contributing to bonafide charitable funds. The Act states that, if such contribution exceeds five percent of the company's average net profits for the three immediately preceding

76 http://www.oecd-ilibrary.org/governance/g20-oecd-principles-of-corporate-governance-2015_9789264236882-en, Accessed on April 6, 2016.

77 https://www.infosys.com/investors/corporate-governance/, Accessed on April 6, 2016.

78 Quotations extracted from the public knowledge base of the "Spiritual Based Leadership Research Programme" are © 2006 by the Global Dharma Center (GDC). GDC retains the copyright to all excerpts from this knowledge base.

79 http://www.mca.gov.in/MCASearch/search_table.html, Accessed on September 25, 2016.

financial years, then prior permission has to be obtained in the annual general meeting.

2. Section 149 of Companies Act 2013 necessitate a company to have board of directors with a minimum of three people for a public company, two for a private company and one person for a 'One Person Company'. Listed public companies should have at least one-third of the total number of directors as independent directors, whose detailed definition has been included in the Act. At least one of the directors of the board has to be a woman.
3. Section 165 of Companies Act 2013 mentions that a person can be appointed as a director to a maximum of twenty companies. The maximum number of public companies in which a person can be appointed as a director is ten.
4. Section 166 lists out the 'Duties of the Directors' which are as follows: (a) ... a director of a company shall act in accordance with the articles of the company. (b) ...act in good faith in order to promote the objects of the company for the benefit of its members as a whole, and in the best interests of the company, its employees, the shareholders, the community and for the protection of environment. (c) ...exercise his duties with due and reasonable care, skill and diligence and shall exercise independent judgment. (d) ...not involve in a situation in which he may have a direct or indirect interest that conflicts, or possibly may conflict, with the interest of the company. (e) ...shall not achieve or attempt to achieve any undue gain or advantage either to himself or to his relatives, partners, or associates and if such director is found guilty of making any undue gain, he shall be liable to pay an amount equal to that gain to the company. (f) ...shall not assign his office and any assignment so made shall be void. (g) If a director of the company contravenes the provisions of this section such director shall be punishable with fine which shall not be less than one lakh rupees but which may extend to five lakh rupees.
5. Section 195 communicates that directors and key managerial personnel of a company shall not enter into insider trading.
6. Section 197 states that the total remuneration payable by a public company to its directors shall not exceed eleven per cent of the net profits of that company. The remuneration payable to any one managing director or whole-time director or manager shall not exceed five per cent of the net profits and if there is more than one such director remuneration shall not exceed ten per cent of the net profits to all such directors. The remuneration payable to directors who are

neither managing directors nor whole-time directors shall exceed one per cent of the net profits of the company, if there is a managing or whole-time director, and three per cent of the net profits in any other case. However, exceptions to these can be made through the annual general meeting.

SEBI Clause 49

Some of the important aspects related to Clause 49 of the Equity Listing Agreement include[80]:

1. Shareholders:
    a. Shareholders should have the right to participate in, and to be sufficiently informed on, decisions concerning fundamental corporate changes.
    b. Shareholders should have the opportunity to participate effectively and vote in general shareholder meetings.
    c. Shareholders should have the opportunity to ask questions to the board, to place items on the agenda of general meetings, and to propose resolutions, subject to reasonable limitations.
    d. The company should ensure equitable treatment of all shareholders, including minority and foreign shareholders.
2. The company should devise a framework to avoid 'insider trading' and abusive self-dealing.
3. The company should recognise the rights of stakeholders and encourage co-operation between company and the stakeholders.
4. The company should ensure timely and accurate disclosure on all material matters including the financial situation, performance, ownership, and governance of the company.
5. The company should implement the prescribed accounting standards in letter and spirit in the preparation of financial statements taking into consideration the interest of all stakeholders and should also ensure that the annual audit is conducted by an independent, competent and qualified auditor.
6. Members of the Board should fulfil certain key functions, including: (a) Reviewing and guiding corporate strategy, major plans of action,

---

80 http://www.sebi.gov.in/cms/sebi_data/attachdocs/1397734478112.pdf and http://www.sebi.gov.in/cms/sebi_data/attachdocs/1410777212906.pdf, Accessed on September 28, 2016.

risk policy, annual budgets and business plans; setting performance objectives; monitoring implementation and corporate performance; and overseeing major capital expenditures, acquisitions and divestments. (b) Monitoring the effectiveness of the company's governance practices and making changes as needed. (c) Selecting, compensating, monitoring and, when necessary, replacing key executives and overseeing succession planning. (d) Aligning key executive and board remuneration with the longer term interests of the company and its shareholders. (e) Ensuring a transparent board nomination process with the diversity of thought, experience, knowledge, perspective and gender in the Board. (f) Monitoring and managing potential conflicts of interest of management, board members and shareholders, including misuse of corporate assets and abuse in related party transactions. (g) Ensuring the integrity of the company's accounting and financial reporting systems, including the independent audit, and that appropriate systems of control are in place, in particular, systems for risk management, financial and operational control, and compliance with the law and relevant standards. (h) Overseeing the process of disclosure and communications.

7. The Board should apply high ethical standards. It should take into account the interests of stakeholders.
8. The Board of Directors of the company shall have an optimum combination of executive and non-executive directors with at least one woman director and not less than fifty percent of the Board of Directors comprising non-executive directors.
9. Independent Directors:
    a. Where the Chairman of the Board is a non-executive director, at least one-third of the Board should comprise independent directors and in case the company does not have a regular non-executive Chairman, at least half of the Board should comprise independent directors.
    b. Provided that where the regular non-executive Chairman is a promoter of the company or is related to any promoter or person occupying management positions at the Board level or at one level below the Board, at least one-half of the Board of the company shall consist of independent directors.
    c. A person shall not serve as an independent director in more than seven listed companies.
    d. A person who is serving as a whole time director in any listed

company shall serve as an independent director in not more than three listed companies.

e. The company shall familiarise the independent directors with the company, their roles, rights, responsibilities in the company, nature of the industry in which the company operates, business model of the company, etc., through various programmes.

f. Independent directors shall not be entitled to any stock option.

10. All fees/compensation, if any paid to non-executive directors, including independent directors, shall be fixed by the Board of Directors and shall require previous approval of shareholders in general meeting. The shareholders' resolution shall specify the limits for the maximum number of stock options that can be granted to non-executive directors, in any financial year and in aggregate.

11. The Board shall meet at least four times a year, with a maximum time gap of one hundred and twenty days between any two meetings.

12. A director shall not be a member in more than ten committees or act as Chairman of more than five committees across all companies in which he is a director. Furthermore, every director shall inform the company about the committee positions he occupies in other companies and notify changes as and when they take place.

13. The company shall establish a vigil mechanism for directors and employees to report concerns about unethical behaviour, actual or suspected fraud or violation of the company's code of conduct or ethics policy.

14. Audit Committee:

    a. A qualified and independent audit committee shall be set up.

    b. The audit committee shall have minimum three directors as members.

    c. Two-thirds of the members of audit committee shall be independent directors.

    d. All members of audit committee shall be financially literate and at least one member shall have accounting or related financial management expertise.

    e. The Chairman of the Audit Committee shall be an independent director.

    f. The Chairman of the Audit Committee shall be present at Annual General Meeting to answer shareholder queries.

g. The Audit Committee may invite such of the executives, as it considers appropriate (and particularly the head of the finance function) to be present at the meetings of the committee, but on occasions it may also meet without the presence of any executives of the company. The finance director, head of internal audit and a representative of the statutory auditor may be present as invitees for the meetings of the audit committee.

h. The Company Secretary shall act as the secretary to the committee.

i. The Audit Committee should meet at least four times in a year and not more than four months shall elapse between two meetings. The quorum shall be either two members or one third of the members of the audit committee whichever is greater, but there should be a minimum of two independent members present.

j. The role of the Audit Committee shall include (a) Oversight of the company's financial reporting process and the disclosure of its financial information to ensure that the financial statement is correct, sufficient and credible; (b) Recommendation for appointment, remuneration and terms of appointment of auditors of the company; (c) Approval of payment to statutory auditors for any other services rendered by the statutory auditors (d) Reviewing, with the management, the annual and quarterly financial statements and auditor's report thereon before submission to the board for approval (e) Reviewing, with the management, the statement of uses/application of funds raised through an issue (public issue, rights issue, preferential issue, etc.), the statement of funds utilized for purposes other than those stated in the offer document/ prospectus/ notice and the report submitted by the monitoring agency monitoring the utilisation of proceeds of a public or rights issue, and making appropriate recommendations to the Board to take up steps in this matter; (f) Review and monitor the auditor's independence and performance, and effectiveness of audit process (g) Scrutiny of inter-corporate loans and investments (h) Valuation of undertakings or assets of the company, wherever it is necessary (i) Evaluation of internal financial controls and risk management systems (j) Reviewing, with the management, performance of statutory and internal auditors, adequacy of the internal control systems

15. The company, through its Board of Directors, shall set up a nomination and remuneration committee which shall comprise at least three

directors, all of whom shall be non-executive directors and at least half shall be independent. Chairman of the committee shall be an independent director.

16. The company through its Board of Directors shall constitute a Risk Management Committee. There will be procedures to inform Board members about the risk assessment and minimization procedures. The Board shall be responsible for framing, implementing and monitoring the risk management plan for the company.

OECD Principles of Corporate Governance[81]

Principle 1: *The corporate governance framework should promote transparent and fair markets, and the efficient allocation of resources. It should be consistent with the rule of law and support effective supervision and enforcement.*

1. The corporate governance framework should be developed with a view to its impact on overall economic performance, market integrity and the incentives it creates for market participants and the promotion of transparent and well-functioning markets.
2. The legal and regulatory requirements that affect corporate governance practices should be consistent with the rule of law, transparent and enforceable.
3. The division of responsibilities among different authorities should be clearly articulated and designed to serve the public interest.
4. Stock market regulation should support effective corporate governance.
5. Supervisory, regulatory and enforcement authorities should have the authority, integrity and resources to fulfil their duties in a professional and objective manner. Moreover, their rulings should be timely, transparent and fully explained.
6. Cross-border co-operation should be enhanced, including through bilateral and multilateral arrangements for exchange of information.

Principle 2: *The corporate governance framework should protect and facilitate the exercise of shareholders' rights and ensure the equitable treatment of all shareholders, including minority and foreign shareholders. All shareholders should have the opportunity to obtain effective redress for violation of their rights.*

1. Basic shareholder rights should include the right to: a) secure methods of ownership registration; b) convey or transfer shares; c) obtain

81 OECD (2015), G20/OECD Principles of Corporate Governance, OECD Publishing, Paris. http://dx.doi.org/10.1787/9789264236882-en. Included with permission.

relevant and material information on the corporation on a timely and regular basis; d) participate and vote in general shareholder meetings; e) elect and remove members of the board; and f) share in the profits of the corporation.

2. Shareholders should be sufficiently informed about, and have the right to approve or participate in, decisions concerning fundamental corporate changes such as: a) amendments to the statutes, or articles of incorporation or similar governing documents of the company; b) the authorisation of additional shares; and c) extraordinary transactions, including the transfer of all or substantially all assets, that in effect result in the sale of the company.

3. Shareholders should have the opportunity to participate effectively and vote in general shareholder meetings and should be informed of the rules, including voting procedures, that govern general shareholder meetings:

   a. Shareholders should be furnished with sufficient and timely information concerning the date, location and agenda of general meetings, as well as full and timely information regarding the issues to be decided at the meeting.

   b. Processes and procedures for general shareholder meetings should allow for equitable treatment of all shareholders. Company procedures should not make it unduly difficult or expensive to cast votes.

   c. Shareholders should have the opportunity to ask questions to the board, including questions relating to the annual external audit, to place items on the agenda of general meetings, and to propose resolutions, subject to reasonable limitations.

   d. Effective shareholder participation in key corporate governance decisions, such as the nomination and election of board members, should be facilitated. Shareholders should be able to make their views known, including through votes at shareholder meetings, on the remuneration of board members and/or key executives, as applicable. The equity component of compensation schemes for board members and employees should be subject to shareholder approval.

   e. Shareholders should be able to vote in person or in absentia, and equal effect should be given to votes whether cast in person or in absentia.

   f. Impediments to cross border voting should be eliminated.

4. Shareholders, including institutional shareholders, should be allowed to consult with each other on issues concerning their basic shareholder rights as defined in the Principles, subject to exceptions to prevent abuse.
5. All shareholders of the same series of a class should be treated equally. Capital structures and arrangements that enable certain shareholders to obtain a degree of influence or control disproportionate to their equity ownership should be disclosed.
   a. Within any series of a class, all shares should carry the same rights. All investors should be able to obtain information about the rights attached to all series and classes of shares before they purchase. Any changes in economic or voting rights should be subject to approval by those classes of shares which are negatively affected.
   b. The disclosure of capital structures and control arrangements should be required.
6. Related-party transactions should be approved and conducted in a manner that ensures proper management of conflict of interest and protects the interest of the company and its shareholders.
   a. Conflicts of interest inherent in related-party transactions should be addressed.
   b. Members of the board and key executives should be required to disclose to the board whether they, directly, indirectly or on behalf of third parties, have a material interest in any transaction or matter directly affecting the corporation.
7. Minority shareholders should be protected from abusive actions by, or in the interest of, controlling shareholders acting either directly or indirectly, and should have effective means of redress. Abusive self-dealing should be prohibited.
8. Markets for corporate control should be allowed to function in an efficient and transparent manner.
   a. The rules and procedures governing the acquisition of corporate control in the capital markets, and extraordinary transactions such as mergers, and sales of substantial portions of corporate assets, should be clearly articulated and disclosed so that investors understand their rights and recourse. Transactions should occur at transparent prices and under fair conditions that protect the rights of all shareholders according to their class.

b. Anti-take-over devices should not be used to shield management and the board from accountability.

Principle 3: *The corporate governance framework should provide sound incentives throughout the investment chain and provide for stock markets to function in a way that contributes to good corporate governance.*

1. Institutional investors acting in a fiduciary capacity should disclose their corporate governance and voting policies with respect to their investments, including the procedures that they have in place for deciding on the use of their voting rights.
2. Votes should be cast by custodians or nominees in line with the directions of the beneficial owner of the shares.
3. Institutional investors acting in a fiduciary capacity should disclose how they manage material conflicts of interest that may affect the exercise of key ownership rights regarding their investments.
4. The corporate governance framework should require that proxy advisors, analysts, brokers, rating agencies and others that provide analysis or advice relevant to decisions by investors, disclose and minimise conflicts of interest that might compromise the integrity of their analysis or advice.
5. Insider trading and market manipulation should be prohibited and the applicable rules enforced.
6. For companies who are listed in a jurisdiction other than their jurisdiction of incorporation, the applicable corporate governance laws and regulations should be clearly disclosed. In the case of cross listings, the criteria and procedure for recognising the listing requirements of the primary listing should be transparent and documented.
7. Stock markets should provide fair and efficient price discovery as a means to help promote effective corporate governance.

Principle 4: *The corporate governance framework should recognise the rights of stakeholders established by law or through mutual agreements and encourage active co-operation between corporations and stakeholders in creating wealth, jobs, and the sustainability of financially sound enterprises.*

1. The rights of stakeholders that are established by law or through mutual agreements are to be respected.
2. Where stakeholder interests are protected by law, stakeholders should have the opportunity to obtain effective redress for violation of their rights.

3. Mechanisms for employee participation should be permitted to develop.
4. Where stakeholders participate in the corporate governance process, they should have access to relevant, sufficient and reliable information on a timely and regular basis.
5. Stakeholders, including individual employees and their representative bodies, should be able to freely communicate their concerns about illegal or unethical practices to the board and to the competent public authorities and their rights should not be compromised for doing this.
6. The corporate governance framework should be complemented by an effective, efficient insolvency framework and by effective enforcement of creditor rights.

Principle 5: *The corporate governance framework should ensure that timely and accurate disclosure is made on all material matters regarding the corporation, including the financial situation, performance, ownership, and governance of the company.*

1. Disclosure should include, but not be limited to, material information on:
    a. The financial and operating results of the company.
    b. Company objectives and non-financial information.
    c. Major share ownership, including beneficial owners, and voting rights.
    d. Remuneration of members of the board and key executives.
    e. Information about board members, including their qualifications, the selection process, other company directorships and whether they are regarded as independent by the board.
    f. Related party transactions.
    g. Foreseeable risk factors.
    h. Issues regarding employees and other stakeholders.
    i. Governance structures and policies, including the content of any corporate governance code or policy and the process by which it is implemented.
2. Information should be prepared and disclosed in accordance with high quality standards of accounting and financial and non-financial reporting.
3. An annual audit should be conducted by an independent, competent

and qualified, auditor in accordance with high-quality auditing standards in order to provide an external and objective assurance to the board and shareholders that the financial statements fairly represent the financial position and performance of the company in all material respects.

4. External auditors should be accountable to the shareholders and owe a duty to the company to exercise due professional care in the conduct of the audit.
5. Channels for disseminating information should provide for equal, timely and cost-efficient access to relevant information by users.

Principle 6: *The corporate governance framework should ensure the strategic guidance of the company, the effective monitoring of management by the board, and the board's accountability to the company and the shareholders.*

1. Board members should act on a fully informed basis, in good faith, with due diligence and care, and in the best interest of the company and the shareholders.
2. Where board decisions may affect different shareholder groups differently, the board should treat all shareholders fairly.
3. The board should apply high ethical standards. It should take into account the interests of stakeholders.
4. The board should fulfil certain key functions, including:
   a. Reviewing and guiding corporate strategy, major plans of action, risk management policies and procedures, annual budgets and business plans; setting performance objectives; monitoring implementation and corporate performance; and overseeing major capital expenditures, acquisitions and divestitures.
   b. Monitoring the effectiveness of the company's governance practices and making changes as needed.
   c. Selecting, compensating, monitoring and, when necessary, replacing key executives and overseeing succession planning.
   d. Aligning key executive and board remuneration with the longer term interests of the company and its shareholders.
   e. Ensuring a formal and transparent board nomination and election process.
   f. Monitoring and managing potential conflicts of interest of management, board members and shareholders, including misuse of corporate assets and abuse in related party transactions.

   g. Ensuring the integrity of the corporation's accounting and financial reporting systems, including the independent audit, and that appropriate systems of control are in place, in particular, systems for risk management, financial and operational control, and compliance with the law and relevant standards.
   h. Overseeing the process of disclosure and communications.
5. The board should be able to exercise objective independent judgement on corporate affairs.
   a. Boards should consider assigning a sufficient number of non-executive board members capable of exercising independent judgement to tasks where there is a potential for conflict of interest. Examples of such key responsibilities are ensuring the integrity of financial and non-financial reporting, the review of related party transactions, nomination of board members and key executives, and board remuneration.
   b. Boards should consider setting up specialised committees to support the full board in performing its functions, particularly in respect to audit, and, depending upon the company's size and risk profile, also in respect to risk management and remuneration. When committees of the board are established, their mandate, composition and working procedures should be well-defined and disclosed by the board.
   c. Board members should be able to commit themselves effectively to their responsibilities.
   d. Boards should regularly carry out evaluations to appraise their performance and assess whether they possess the right mix of background and competencies.
6. In order to fulfil their responsibilities, board members should have access to accurate, relevant and timely information.
7. When employee representation on the board is mandated, mechanisms should be developed to facilitate access to information and training for employee representatives, so that this representation is exercised effectively and best contributes to the enhancement of board skills, information and independence.

Corporate Governance and Reputation Risk

A company may categorise risks that impact the functioning of the company. Various risks include Operational risks, Strategic risks, Financial risks, Regulatory risks, etc. Risks related to technology, supply-chain, project-management, legal and policy, environment, labour, etc., may be included within another risk or considered as independent category.

Reputation risk involves the risk of company facing losses, or the probability to meet with disadvantages, due to an erosion in its reputation.

This loss may arise because of various reasons such as:

(a) the company being refused permission to sell a product in the market
(b) being asked by the regulatory authorities to pay a fine
(c) the consumers deciding not to purchase the products and services of the company
(d) a collaborator refusing to transfer technology
(e) an investor withdrawing capital and
(f) employees refusing to work.

Numerous examples in corporate history indicate how companies incurred heavy losses due to their reputational damage, while some organizations discontinued their operations.

Some of the ways through which governance practices can manage reputation risk of a company can be through:

a) ensuring alignment in the organisation's vision and mission, culture, strategy, and routine operating practices,
b) bridging any existing gap between the company's character (what a company is) and its external projection (how others think a company is),
c) continuously strengthening human-values and nobility in organizational character,
d) considering the needs of stakeholders.

Organisations may adopt certain principles that guide their corporate governance practices. Some of them may be:

— **Beyond legal compliance.** By practicing this principle, the organisation satisfy the minimum standards of legal compliance, meets both the "letter of the law" and the "spirit of the law", and also sets higher operational standards.

— **Honest Disclosures. And, when in doubt, disclose.** This results in a higher degree of transparency and disclosure that keeps the many stakeholders informed (thereby helping the stakeholders in informed decision-making), This principle also includes maintaining integrity and honesty in external communications, and also in external communications to stakeholders about the internal practices of the company.

— **The management is the trustee of the various stakeholders.** The "stakeholders" here refers to both internal stakeholders and external stakeholders, as well as the human and non-human.

— **To perceive, differentiate and mark the distinction between the resources of the company and personal conveniences, and apply wise judgment.**

— **Accessibility across the hierarchy**.

Corporate Governance Rating

Corporate Governance Rating is considered an indicator of an organization's adherence to the norms and guidelines related to corporate governance, and excellence in setting higher standards in these practices. A rating may be helpful for stakeholders to understand the extent to which an organization may be following corporate governance norms and guidelines. These ratings may be provided by an independent agency who usually charges a fee for assessing the company about their governance practices. While some organizations disclose their ratings in public, some organizations keep their ratings confidential.

RESPONSIBILITY OF THE BOARD OF DIRECTORS

"In great attempts it is glorious even to fail."

—Bruce Lee[82]

Some of the responsibilities of the Board of Directors (BoDs) include:

- **Being role models:** The Board of Directors (BoDs) needs to be role models in practicing human-values such as integrity, honesty, caring, service, etc. so that the senior management and staff of the organization look forward to emulate and radiate these values in themselves, and thus, in the culture of the organization. In many companies, the BoDs institute a 'Code of Ethics' or a 'Code of Conduct', and adopt it for themselves and the senior management. Such codes may also detail into insider-trading, fair trade practices, and aspects related to ethics,

82 'Striking Thoughts', Tuttle Publishing, 2002.

integrity, transparency, accountability and vigil ("whistle-blower-policies"). Such practices and policies also helps the BoDs to comply with the legal guidelines, which is one of the responsibilities of the Board of Directors (BoDs).

- **To constitute Board-Committees or Committees of the Board (CoB):** Towards effective functioning of these committees, the BoDs also decides on the terms of references for these committees, considering legal guidelines, if any (For example, the laws of India mandates the BoDs to form a CSR committee, towards designing, implementing, monitoring and reporting the CSR policy of the company.). This "terms if reference", or, the charter, mentions about the roles and responsibilities of the committee, its composition, power and the resources that it can draw upon. Some of the committees instituted by the Board-of-Directors, depending on compliance to the legal laws of the region and the needs of the company's stakeholders, may include:

  (a) Audit Committee

  (b) Corporate Social Responsibility Committee

  (c) Stakeholder Relationship Committee

  (d) Nomination and Remuneration Committee

  (e) Securities Issue Committee

  (f) Environmental Management Committee

  (g) ESOP Committee

  (h) Risk Management Committee

  (i) Investors' Grievance Committee

  (j) Management Committee, etc.

  Some of the committees listed above may be given responsibilities that also include the responsibilities of another committee that is listed above. For example, the BoDs may authorise the remuneration-committee, rather than constituting a separate ESOP committee, to provide the guidelines for implementing an employee stock option plan (ESOP), in addition to the usual role of remuneration-committee, which is, being the recommender of compensation and benefits for senior management (Directors, etc.), and assessment of HR practices in the company.

  Also, the title/ nomenclature/ names provided for the committees may vary with companies, though their functions may be identical or similar. For example, a "corporate governance commitee" may be assigned with the sole responsibility of a "nomination and

Note: The data in the above table is as per the data provided by the company in their sustainability reports. In FY 2019-20, SBI was a public-sector-enterprise with majority of its shares held by Govt, of India/ governmental organisations.

The indicators of the above table, provide a perspective about the economic responsibilities of business organisations, and may, to an extent, be a justification for why a business organisation may exist in the society. As can be found, significant amount of sums are being distributed to various sections of the society.

However, the parameters of this table is primarily human-centric, if not, entirely.

'*Parambikulam Tiger Reserve*' is a protected area in southern India, A 2014 doctoral research study[84] on Parambikulam Tiger Reserve recorded "*479 species of flowering plants, of which, 214 were tree species, 78 belonged to shrubs, 116 Herbs and 71 Climbers*". The tiger reserve is also the home for many spiders, a range of avifauna, a variety of fishes, and also the tiger, the elephant, the deer, the crocodile and other wild animals. The total species population of this tiger reserve, including the human species, will be higher.

Estimates vary about the total number of species of this planet. More than a million species has been recorded, and estimates of the total number may range to millions[85]. Assume that each species of Planet Earth is being plotted or represented as a dotted mark or an asterisk (*) in an A4 size paper (the size of paper that is normally used for photocopying, printing, etc.), with each dot or an asterisk representing each species. The space on this sheet of paper is distributed to one million (ten lakh) species, a number lower than what has been the actual recording. Fold that paper into half – and the space will have half a million species (five lakh), or, fold into quarter, and that space will be for quarter a million (2.5 lakh) species. In this way, thence, the representation of human species (i.e. one amongst the million species that has been considered here, or, 1/ 10,00,000)) will not even have the size of an asterisk (*) or a dot on the paper.

Neither EVG, nor EVD, and not even 'natural capital accounting', with practices such as 'Environmental Profit and Loss Accounting', is able to incorporate this infinitesimal minuteness of the human species amongst the vastness of inter-relational planetary web. Yet, the gross impact of this human species on the planet is easily visible all around.

---

84 Magesh G, *Ecological studies of the Parambikulam Tiger Reserve in the Western Ghats of India, using Remote Sensing and GIS*, 2014.

85 https://www.nature.com/news/2011/110823/full/news.2011.498.html, Accessed on March 23, 2021.

Amongst the thousands of companies in India, a few publishes sustainability reports, and fewer publishes sustainability reports that are externally assured. As part of the external assurance of the 2020 sustainability report of the Mumbai International Airport Ltd., (MIAL), the external assurance agency (Bureau Veritas) states that "*MIAL has a process in place for engaging with a range of key stakeholders including passengers, employees, airlines, the Airports Authority of India, vendors, concessionaires, ground handlers, cargo logistics companies, fuel supplying companies as well as other Government and local and municipal bodies.*" Travel thousand kilometres down-south from Mumbai airport, and one reaches the international airport at Kochi. This airport, managed by Cochin International Airport Limited (CIAL), is the first of its kind in the world, that, it is fully-powered by solar energy – an achievement, probably, worthy of emulation in a world powered by more-polluting and less-safe forms of energy sources (such as coal, diesel, nuclear).

Yet, it is known that the airport was constructed in a land that also consisted of paddy-fields and wetlands, and is located in a region that receives higher amount of rainfall, in comparison with other regions of the state, the country and the world. Who will be the "*key stakeholoders*" here?

CHAPTER SUMMARY

- 'Ethos' refers to character, while 'Ethics' refers to moral principles. 'Business Ethics' involves application of ethical principles in the practice of business.
- Stephen Covey mentions about the importance of moral authority in leadership.
- Advertisements are influencing children, and, many a times, in a negative manner.
- Milton Hershey mentions that quality is the best form of advertisement.
- *Trikaransuddhi* refers to the purity and unity of thought, word and deed.
- Various stakeholders of a business enterprise - consumers, employees, shareholders, suppliers, peer groups, civil society, governmental authorities - have a role to play in contributing to responsibility practices in business.
- Individual Social Responsibility (ISR) involves the infusion and evoking of human values such as *Dharma* (Righteousness) and *Prema*

(Love) by an individual, in one's own life, be it at home or in the workplace or in the society.

- Companies Act 2013 and SEBI Clause 49 of the equity listing agreement offers guidelines on corporate governance practices in India.

KEYWORDS MENTIONED

Individual Social Responsibility, Dandi March, Indian Ethos, *'Paropakaaraartham Idam Shareeram'*, *'Sathyam Naasthi Paro Dharmah'*, *'Sathyam Vada Dharmam Chara'*, *'Atmano Mokshartham Jagat Hitayacha'*, *'Vasudaiva Kutumbakam'*, *'Ahinsa Paramodharm'*, *'Yagnayacharatah karma'*, *Yagna*, Sacrifice, *'Loka Samastha Sukhino Bhavantu'*, *Bhoga*, *Thyaga*, Socially Responsible Investment (SRI), Conscious Consuming, Responsible Tourism, Right to Information Act, NGO, Product Labeling, GRIHA, Corporate Governance, Board of Directors, OECD Principles, *Trikaranasuddhi*, Companies Act 2013, Corporate Governance Rating, Reputation Risk, AMA Statement of Ethics, ASCI Code, Cause Marketing, Green-washing.

MULTIPLE CHOICE QUESTIONS

1. What does the word 'Ethos' mean?
   (a) Character
   (b) Pathos
   (c) *Ithihaas*
   (d) Lemon juice
   (e) Pineapple juice

2. In which time period did Akshaya-Tritiya started becoming popular for gold marketing?
   (a) Late 1950s
   (b) Early 1990s
   (c) Late 1980s
   (d) Mid 2000s
   (e) Early 1950s

3. To which business leader is this quote attributed to: *"Give them quality. Thats the best kind of advertising in the world."*
   (a) Lee Iacocca
   (b) Milton Hershey

(c) Akiro Morita
(d) Dhruv Lakra
(e) N S Raghavan

4. Expand ASCI
(a) Another Scam Creator of India
(b) Appraisal of Social and Communicative Intelligence
(c) Army School for Communication and Instrumentation
(d) Academic Standards for Cognitive Intelligence
(e) Advertising Standards Council of India

5. Which of the following cannot be considered as an example of 'Conscious Consuming'?
(a) Purchasing a soap because of a 'buy one, get one free' offer
(b) Purchasing a soap because the soap company donates resources towards constructing toilets in schools where there are no toilets
(c) Purchasing a soap because the ingredients are not harmful to health
(d) Purchasing a soap because the packaging material is made from bio-degradable material
(e) Purchasing a soap because the soap company recycles the waste produced during manufacturing

6. ISR is an acronym for:
(a) Individual Social Responsibility
(b) International Society for Responsibility
(c) Individual Societal Responsibility
(d) Iridium Society of Researchers
(e) Irish Society for Research

SHORT ANSWER QUESTIONS

1. Write a note on *Trikaranasuddhi*.

2. List some of the ways through which long-term investors can be rewarded.

3. Mention any two of the six principles in the OECD Principles of Corporate Governance.

4. Write a note about the provisions made in Section 197 of Companies Act 2013 regarding remuneration payable to directors.

5. What is a reputation risk and what could be the result of a company facing reputation risk?

LONG ANSWER QUESTIONS

1. Discuss about the effectiveness of ASCI Code for Self-Regulation in Advertising.

2. Detail about the application of the six ethical values in the 'Statement of Ethics' from 'American Marketing Association'?

3. Mention any five work values from Indian ethos.

4. Mention any five functions of the Members of the Board, as per the SEBI Equity Listing Agreement.

REFLECTIVE QUESTION

1. The text mentions that companies have incurred losses due to reputational damage. Give an example. Would the company have avoided this damage if it practiced moral leadership and values that Stephen Covey was referring to?

ABOUT THE CHAPTER:

1. Learning from the chapter, if any:

2. Topics, concepts, themes, etc. that you may be interested to research/ refer/ study/ ponder upon:

3. Applications in daily life, if any:

Notes:

Chapter 5 completed... You may take a break...

Non-motorised water transportation in the state of Kerala, India. The boat is made from wood, using simple tools, and manual labour, thereby providing employment. These boats do not discharge waste to water, or pollute the air. Bicycling is another human powered transportation option. Approximately 60% of people living in the city of Copenhagen, Denmark, travel to workplaces and study, using bicycles.

Non-motorised boats for hire, at Antigua Boat Shed, on the banks of the Avon River. This boat shed, which started as a commercial boat shed in 1882 and is a heritage destination now, is located in Christchurch, Canterbury Region, New Zealand.[86]

Thor Heyerdahl, a member of the *Kon-Tiki* voyage, known for using a raft to travel almost across the Pacific ocean (Peru to Polynesian islands in three months) says, *"The sea contains many surprises for him who has his floor on a level with the surface and drifts along slowly and noiselessly. A sportsman who breaks his way through the woods may come back and say that no wild life is to be seen. Another may sit down on a stump and wait, and often rustlings and cracklings will begin and curious eyes peer out. So it is on the sea too. We usually plow across it with roaring engines and piston strokes, with the water foaming round our bow, Then we come back and say that there is nothing to see far out on the ocean."*

86 https://commons.wikimedia.org/wiki/File:Antigua_Boatsheds_Canoe_Hire._Christchurch.jpg, Accessed on November 26, 2018.

Chapter 6

BUSINESS PRACTICES FOR SUSTAINABILITY AND INCLUSION

"The true leader proves himself by his qualities."
—Aesop's[1] Fables

Who wouldn't be impressed by the revelry and ribaldry surrounding a 'Mexican wave'? Energy, excitement and exhilaration, they bring to a football match. Not so, however, in the Salt Lake Stadium at Kolkatta, the arena for the clash between two football-clubs of Bengal – East Bengal FC and Mohun Began FC. Mexican waves are a damp squib here, like *sambar* gone sour, because, if Mohan Began fans start a wave, it will not be supported by East Bengal fans. If East Bengal fans start a wave, it will not be followed up by Mohan Began fans. Fanatic loyalty are sometimes fierce. The fans of one club will not wear dresses with colors that even remotely resembles the color of the rival team's jersey. Stories abound that the cold-war-ish fans of one club wouldn't mind standing for hours together, rather then sitting on a sofa with a color belonging to the rival team. In Bengali, the language spoken in Bengal, the 'Salt Lake Stadium' is referred to as *Yuvabhaarathi kreedarangan* - 'the playground for India's youth'. 'Spelling mistakes' are quite normal in India. After all, in an episode of a multi-decade old 'TV serial', *Bhagwan* Krishna himself says, "*Mein unpadh hi acha hoon*" - "I am better uneducated". His playfulness may be influential - '*kreedarangan*' rhymes and resembles with '*keedarangan*' – the playground for pest-ivities.

On completion of reading the chapter, the reader may:

1. appreciate the mainstreaming of 'social entrepreneurship'

2. recognise labels that indicate responsibility practices associated with a company or products

3. recognise business practices that attempts to address humanitarian and environmental issues

---

Eyebrows raise when people are insisted to wear attire, which is neither

1 http://www.read.gov/aesop/126.html, Accessed on August 16, 2015.

aligned with the traditions and culture, nor aligned to functionality and needs[2] - an example of this non-alignment can be seen in instances of wearing a suit and a tie in India. In a tropical country, wearing a tie and a blazer add to the discomfort. Ironically, to reduce this discomfort, people engage in temperature-control mechanisms. Usage of an air-conditioner not only results in energy consumption, but also heat discharge to the external environment. As the temperature outside increases, there is increased demand for air-conditioning, which causes a further increase in temperature, thus contributing to a vicious cycle. A report stated, "*Cooling by means of an AC, which simply moves heat around, requires the evacuation of hot air to the outside of buildings... Higher outdoor temperatures in the summer increase the overall need for cooling, leading to more hot air, higher temperatures and increased use of cooling in a classic feedback loop... higher outdoor temperatures will result in reduced efficiency of cooling equipment.*"[3]

Discussions on 'balance' between business and environment are misguided. If the planet is in peril, there is no scope for any business enterprise. Ecology in balance is about relationships in balance – inter-species and intra-species. Interdependent relationships that are in balance gives opportunity for imagination, creativity and innovation in business.

BUSINESS MODELS

A business venture is sustainable when it is in harmony with the natural environment and its inhabitants. State governments in India have been requesting citizens to wear clothing made by traditional weavers. Examples of such clothing include *khaadi* (**Refer Figure 6.1**), which is hand-spun and hand-woven. Usage of *khaadi* generates employment for many. *Khaadi* has been preferred by many authentic leaders[4] due to its association with sustainability and simplicity. While various fashion trends appeared and disappeared, *khaadi* continues to 'remain in fashion'. Many entrepreneurs have been promoting ventures associated with *khaadi* as a way of contributing to economic, social and environmental well-being. They have adopted practices that are usually seen in businesses – marketing, retailing

---

2 *In 'Return to Nature!'* (1899, fourth edition), Adolf Just, a practitioner of natural healing, mentions that (as translated by Benedict Lust) "*......In Jesus' time there was a small sect, called the Essenes... These Essenes lived strictly natural lives, partly as hermits in the desert and on the mountains. In this manner they hoped to live a joyous, happy life on earth, free from sickness and want, and thus to prepare themselves for heaven... ...the Essenes avoided every superfluity and always possessed only one white cloak, their sole bodily attire...*

3 https://www.iea.org/publications/freepublications/publication/The_Future_of_Cooling.pdf, Accessed on September 25, 2018.

4 Authentic Leadership focuses on honesty and integrity in leadership practices.

etc. - to contribute to societal well-being. When individuals engage in enterprising ways to address humanitarian or environmental concerns, while adopting practices usually seen in business ventures, they are referred to as social entrepreneurs, and their practice is referred to as "social entrepreneurship".

Figure 6.1

An awareness initiative in the state of Kerala, India, inviting citizen's attention towards wearing khadi/ handloom products at least a few days every week.

Social Entrepreneurship

More than 30,000 'Mitticool's has been sold in India. Mitticool (https://mitticool.com/) is a 'refrigerator' made from clay, and do not require electricity[5]. It also provides cool drinking water. Mitticool can extend the shelf-life of vegetables and fruits by some days. It works on the principle of evaporation. Water from the top chamber, which is used to hold drinking water, slowly percolates down, through the sides and evaporates outside,

5 http://www.business-standard.com/article/beyond-business/what-s-cooking-in-his-lab-114112801252_1.html, Accessed on June 30, 2017.

thereby, cooling the interior. 'Mitti' means 'mud'/ 'soil' / 'clay' in Hindi. This product was designed by Mansukh Bhai Prajapati, an example of a social entrepreneur. The following are examples of organisations incorporating the principles of social entrepreneurship (**Refer table 6.1**). As the table indicates, some of them are not-for-profit organizations, while some are for-profit organizations.

Table 6.1

Name of the organization	Description
Millets of Mewar	A restaurant in Udaipur that serves organic food, with a focus on traditional grains such as millets
Back2basics	A fruits and vegetable supplying organisation in Bangalore that supplies organic fruits and vegetables on the same day it is harvested
Aatike	Wood-based hand-made toys

Walking can contribute to health. Yet, for various reasons, people are increasingly, many a times unnecessarily, relying on motor transport. *Avoid stating the obvious*[6]. Yet, in 2017, the author of this textbook did two random surveys to ascertain the occupancy levels of passenger cars. The first survey was done at a rural location and ascertained the occupancy levels of vehicles with a seating capacity upto five people. Vehicles moving on the national highway were observed. It was found that less than 5% of the cars were operating with full occupancy. 16% of the cars had only one person, while a little more than 40% of the cars carried two people. 23% had occupancy of three people and 11% of the cars had an occupancy of four people. The second survey (**Refer figure 6.2**) was done at a metro location with a 50+ lakh population. 170 four-wheeled passenger vehicles with a seating capacity of 5-8 were observed. The observation revealed that 97 cars (57%) were carrying only one person. 57 cars (33.5%) had only two people, while ten cars (5.9%) had three people. The cars that carried four people numbered six (2.4%). None of the cars had an occupancy more than four people.

6 As mentioned by LA Hill as one of the "*Principles of Good Writing*".

Figure 6.2

Occupancy level for cars in a megacity

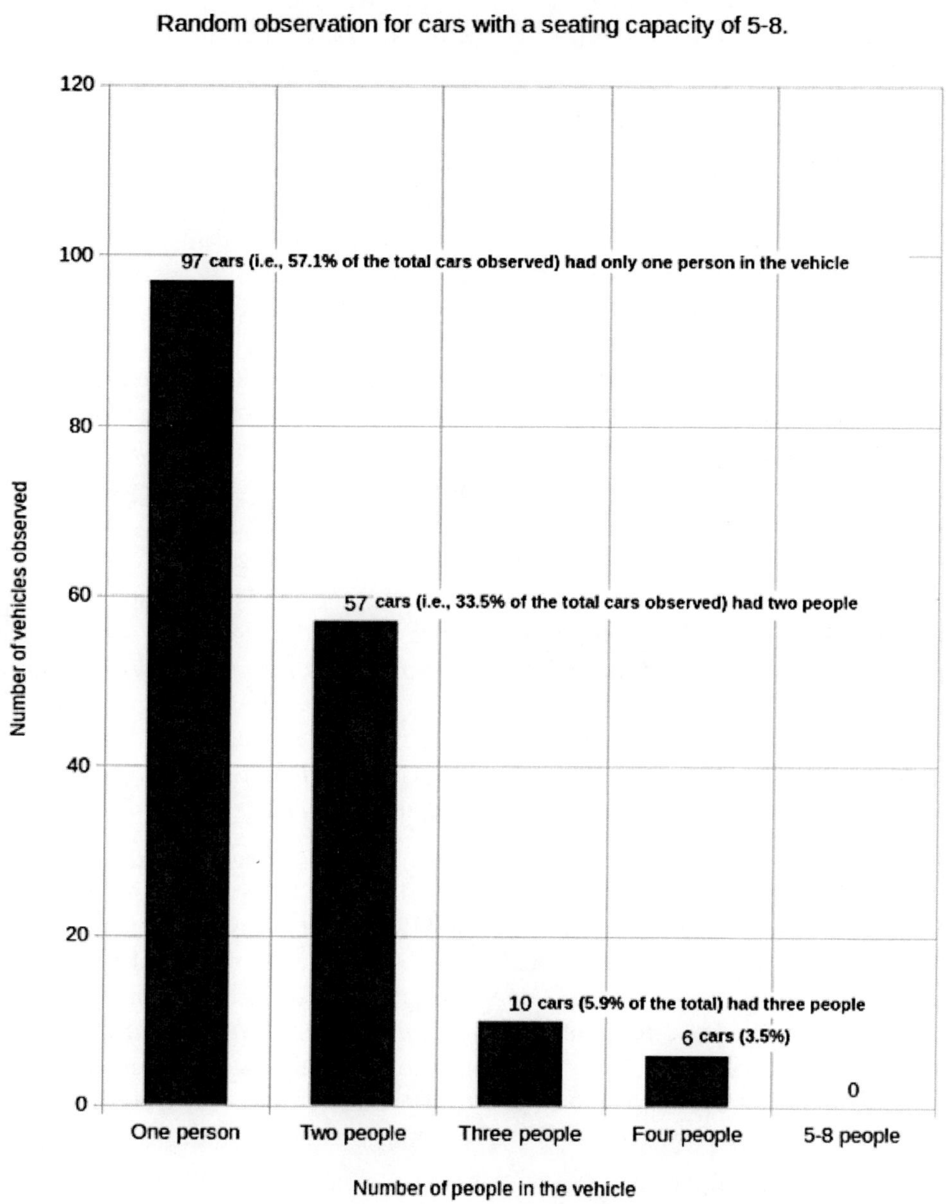

The survey was done in 2017.

In 2016, the Government of Delhi, in 2016, aimed to reduce vehicular pollution through a road-space-rationing practice, popularly referred to as the 'Odd-Even' scheme, whereby vehicles were to be on the roads, only on alternate days, depending on the last digit of the vehicle registration number. Discussing this scheme with students, the chief minister of Delhi, said, "*Convince your parents, relatives and friends to follow the odd-even scheme. We are to do this not out of any imposition, but because it is important for our health and life.*"[7] If there is an addition to the occupancy levels in passenger vehicles, it can contribute to a reduction in travelling expense, reduction in pollution and efficient usage of energy and materials. QuickRide.in attempts to address this through a mobile application that promotes car pooling. This company, while aiming to generate profits, also addresses societal issues. "*...If we take our car out only 4 days in a week, and join others' shared vehicles on the fifth day, 20% traffic reduction can easily happen. 40% traffic reduction is possible – if we just do the same for 2 days in a week!,*" says a blog article from the company[8]. QuickRide.in is a social enterprise. Social enterprises provide solutions that address societal issues through imbibing practices adopted by business organisations.

Co-operatives

The International Co-operative Alliance (ICA) defines a co-operative as "*an autonomous association of persons united voluntarily to meet their common economic, social, and cultural needs and aspirations through a jointly owned and democratically-controlled enterprise*"[9]. ICA states that "*Co-operatives are based on the values of self-help, self-responsibility, democracy, equality, equity and solidarity. In the tradition of their founders, co-operative members believe in the ethical values of honesty, openness, social responsibility and caring for others.*"[10]

Co-operatives attempts to share benefits amongst a large group of people. An example could be an assessment of the Key Performance Indicators (KPIs) of Co-operative Group Ltd., a UK based consumer cooperative that has diverse business in retail, finance etc. One of the KPIs for this organization was membership engagement. The company's annual report for 2014 indicates that "*the more engaged our members are, the more successful our business is*". The organization assessed membership engagement through the parameters such as (a) the total number of members (b) dividend paid to members (c) members qualifying to vote.

7 http://www.thehindu.com/news/cities/Delhi/oddeven-scheme-arvind-kejriwal-administer-pledge-to-students/article8045018.ece, Accessed on March 23, 2018.

8 https://quickride.in/blog/ridesharing-tech-matures/, Accessed on March 17, 2018.

9 http://ica.coop/en/what-co-operative, Accessed on March 20, 2016.

10 http://ica.coop/en/what-co-operative, Accssed on March 20, 2016.

The COO of Planters Development Bank in The Philippines, says,

"We have set up a cooperative for the economically depressed area around our parish. Today, the cooperative has grown and flourished, providing loans for working capital for very small entrepreneurs. The cooperative also set up to inculcate good values for its members such as financial discipline, honesty and integrity, responsible parenthood. The cooperative has grown to 3,000 members from our original 15, and resources have ballooned from the original 30,000 to 20 million pesos (US$400,000.). It is a God-given privilege that has enriched our lives as much as we've enriched theirs.

There are still struggles along the way. One time a co-worker in the parish asked, "How come we always end up doing all of these things and yet there are many others who say they want to help, but when I call them to let them know how they can help, they are always busy?" It's easy to get frustrated but we try to remember that God calls people in His own time. We cannot judge those who may not be prepared – we were once like that too.

This work I do for other people has helped me to grow spiritually. I feel that since I have more material resources I can help and I am glad for the opportunity. I believe we should go out and share whatever talents we have with our community, our workplace, our parish, and even our country and the world at large."[11]

Differential Pricing Model

Differential Pricing is about charging different prices from different categories of consumers, for the same quality and quantity of a product. While differential pricing can be considered as a pricing method with the objective of maximising profits, it can also be done to make a product affordable to a larger group of customers. Differential pricing operates on the idea that some customers attribute a higher value to a product, can afford to do the same, and are willing to pay a higher price as compared to others. Indian Railways gives price discounts to physically and mentally challenged passengers, patients, senior citizens, students, medical professionals, etc[12]. However, when there is increased demand for train tickets, Indian Railways engages in "dynamic pricing" where a passenger has to make a higher payment for train travel[13]. Similarly, airlines such as

11 Quotations extracted from the public knowledge base of the "Spiritual Based Leadership Research Programme" are © 2006 by the Global Dharma Center (GDC). GDC retains the copyright to all excerpts from this knowledge base.

12 http://www.indianrailways.gov.in/railwayboard/uploads/directorate/traffic_comm/Concession_list_different_persons.pdf, Accessed on September 20, 2016.

13 https://www.services.irctc.co.in/betadoc/salient%20features%20of%20premium%20special%20train%20on%20dynamic%20pricing.pdf, Accessed on September 20, 2016.

Air India offers a number of discounts to personnel from armed forces, visually challenged, students, youth etc.[14], while also charging different prices for travelling on the airline.

Base of Pyramid Model

Base of Pyramid is an economic model that indicates that the economically underprivileged of the society can also contribute to the growth of the economy. 'Base of Pyramid' model is also referred to as 'Bottom of Pyramid' model. The term "Bottom of Pyramid" was popularised by professors CK Prahalad[15] and Stuart L Hart in the initial decade of 2000s.

Studies have indicated the contribution of people from 'Bottom of Pyramid' to economic growth. It is also a common knowledge that they provide some of the relevant and important services to the society, including work involving manual labour. Examples include waste collection and disposal, construction activities, agriculture, etc. Some of the companies have innovated their product availability to meet the needs of people in this category. Making consumer products available in smaller quantities (for example, sachets) and thus at a lower price, has been one of the strategies adopted by companies to cater to the needs of people in this economic strata. The companies also profited from such strategies. However, the convenience provided by the 'sachet revolution' also resulted in accumulation of non-bio-degradable waste. This has caused health hazards, blockage of drainages, erosion of the purity of water bodies, pollution of natural environment, etc.

Micro-credit and Micro-Finance

Micro-credit, also referred to as a micro-loan, is about extending small loans to economically poor people without any collateral. Though some organisations operated with a profiteering attitude, the micro-credit practice enabled many people to access capital, which they were not able to access earlier due to the necessity of providing collateral. The borrower is to return the borrowed money through payments extending through a fixed time period. Considering that loans are provided without any collateral, a higher interest is charged from the borrower. While this interest rate is higher than the interest rate charged by a bank, it is considerably lower in comparison to the interest rate charged by "loan sharks", from whom poor people may avail loans for emergency situations.

14 http://www.airindia.in/concessionary-fare.htm, Accessed on September 20, 2016.

15 CK Prahalad was also associated with the development of the management concept of 'core competency' that later became a business jargon.

Examples of other financial services offered to the economically marginalised communities could include (a) a bank account with zero-balance or very minimal balance (b) insurance services that require the payment of low premium etc. When such varied financial services, which also include micro-credit, are offered, it is referred to as micro-finance or micro-banking. Grameen Bank, a Bangladesh based micro-finance organization, has been considered a pioneer in providing micro-credits. It was founded by Muhammad Yunus, who, along with Grameen Bank, was awarded the Nobel Peace Prize for 2006, for their efforts to create economic and social development.

BUSINESS PRACTICES

Writing about his experiences in "Seeking touch with Indians" in Pretoria (South Africa), Gandhi mentions in his autobiography, "*...my first step was to call a meeting of all the Indians... my speech at this meeting may be said to have been the first public speech in my life. I went fairly prepared with my subject, which was about observing truthfulness in business....*".

Labels/ certifications indicating social responsibility

The European labeling norms indicate that food and feed containing genetically modified ingredients need to be labelled. However, "*if food or feed contains less than 0.9 % GMOs, it does not need to be labelled – as long as the GMO content is technically unavoidable*".[16] However, considering the hazards and uncertainties related to genetic manipulation or modification, many countries, including those in the Europe, has chosen not to grow or sell genetically-modified crops or research on them.

In the mid 2010s, the author of this book was gifted with chocolates. These chocolates were purchased from USA and brought to India. The author had concerns about the ingredients. In India, genetically modified ingredients ("GMO") are not used in food, while in USA, genetically modified ingredients are used. It was also not easy for the author to find out whether these chocolates were made from ingredients that had animal products. Seeking clarity, the author emailed the chocolate companies, receiving replies that the chocolates may have ingredients derived from animals, and may also contain ingredients that are genetically modified. Existence of food labels (similar to the green-brown dot vegetarian non-vegetarian marks in India) would have made it easier for the author to easily identify the quality and nature of ingredients used in the chocolate.

16 https://eur-lex.europa.eu/legal-content/EN/TXT/?uri=LEGISSUM:l21154, Accessed on September 17, 2019.

The following are the advantages of labelling practices:

- Helps a consumer to make informed decisions.
- A consumer can ascertain the quality standard associated with a product.
- Helps a consumer to channelize money to those businesses/ products that meet higher standards in business responsibility practices.
- Organizations can communicate their uniqueness to its stakeholders, especially consumers.
- Learning opportunity for organisations to improve their social and environmental standards.
- Enhancing the responsibility standards in the sector/ industry.
- Reasons hindering organisations to adopt socially-responsible labels and certifications are:
- Certifications may be expensive, especially, the international certifications.
- The certification process may be time-consuming and prone to corruption.
- Lack of consumer awareness about the existence of such labels/ certifications.
- Lack of honesty and integrity in the certification standards and processes, leading to a fall in stakeholder respect about the worthiness of a label or certification.

Constituents of an effective certification/ label

Many labels and certifications exist in the market. It is important to consider the quality of certifications. The parameters that can be considered include:

a. Higher Standards – It may be ascertained, whether the certification/ label is given to those organizations or products that set higher operational standards amongst the peers.

b. Defined Standards – It may be ascertained, whether there is the existence of criteria or parameters that states and identifies the sustainability practices or guidelines that are adhered to by the product or organisation.

c. Transparency - It may be ascertained, whether the certification/ labelling process is transparent, is open to audit, and is open to improvement based on feedback.

d. Continuous Improvement - It may be ascertained, whether the certifier and the certified engages in a process of continuous improvement.

e. Principles Driven - It may be ascertained, whether the certification/ labelling process incorporates the application of universal principles/ human values.

Various Labels/ Certifications

The below are some of the seals/ labels[17] indicating the practice of social and environmental responsibility.

Green Seal

Green Seal (http://www.greenseal.org/AboutGreenSeal.aspx) has been a pioneer in non-profit environmental certification. This has also helped Green Seal to develop standards for a wide range of product categories (**Refer figure 6.3**).

Figure 6.3

The Benefit Corporation and the Certified B Corporation Label

In USA, it was felt that there was a requirement for a new form of legislation for for-profit companies that has social benefit as a central purpose of their existence. Unlike "C Corporations", which focus on providing monetary returns to shareholders, "B Corporations" or "Benefit Corporations" considers the creation of positive impact on stakeholders. A white paper on 'The Benefit Corporation' indicates that "*The major characteristics of the benefit corporation form are: 1) a requirement that a benefit corporation must have a corporate purpose to create a material positive impact on society and the environment; 2) an expansion of the duties of directors to require consideration*

17 Logos/ seals are included with permission, or, are available in the public domain.

of non-financial stakeholders as well as the financial interests of shareholders; and 3) an obligation to report on its overall social and environmental performance using a comprehensive, credible, independent and transparent third-party standard."[18] It is voluntary to register a company as a Benefit Corporation. In 2010, Maryland became the first state in USA to pass benefit corporation legislation.

Figure 6.4

Certified

B

Corporation

bcorporation.net

The 'Certified B Corporation' label is awarded by 'B Labs', a not-for-profit organisation (**Refer figure 6.4**). The 'Certified B Corporation' certification is not mandatory to be registered as a 'Benefit Organisation', also referred to as "B Corps". "B Corps"[19] adheres to higher performance standards in parameters such as social and environmental performance and employee well-being, in comparison with the usual industry standards. This certification is awarded to for-profit organizations that receives at least a minimum score related to standards during the company's interactions with stakeholders[20].

GoodWeave

Through the GoodWeave label[21], an assurance is given to purchasers of

18 http://benefitcorp.net/storage/documents/Benecit_Corporation_White_Paper_1_18_2013.pdf, Accessed on June 4, 2015.

19 Refer the section in this textbook related to case-studies/ caselets, to access more details about 'Certified B Corps'.

20 https://www.bcorporation.net/become-a-b-corp/how-to-become-a-b-corp, Accessed on November 11, 2017.

21 http://goodweave.org/proven-approach/standard/, Accessed on November 11, 2017.

rugs, carpets and home textiles that no exploitative child labour was used in the making of the product. To earn the GoodWeave label, exporters in producing countries, and importers in consumer countries must be licensed under the GoodWeave certification program and sign a legally-binding contract to adhere to GoodWeave's no-child-labour standard, and allow unannounced random inspections by independent GoodWeave inspectors. GoodWeave's certification process encompasses (a) mandatory requirements covering child labor, forced and bonded labor (b) a broader set of progress principles that considers related labor rights and environmental impacts (**Refer figure 6.5**).

Figure 6.5

CO_2 Neutral Website Mark

The 'CO_2 neutral website' label (**Refer figure 6.6**) is given to websites that neutralizes the carbon footprint of the website. The service provider does this by investing in renewable energy projects such as windmills, and providing energy efficient stoves that saves on carbon emissions. For more details, https://www.co2neutralwebsite.com.

Figure 6.6

EPA WaterSense

The WaterSense label by US Environmental Protection Agency (US EPA) are given to products and programs that meets EPA's criteria for water efficiency. The label encourages consumers to purchase water-efficient products. Some of the product categories certified by WaterSense includes showerheads, urinals, toilets etc. (**Refer figure 6.7**).

Figure 6.7

LEED

Leadership in Energy and Environmental Design (LEED) is associated with buildings that incorporate green features. The rating encompasses parameters such as water and energy efficiency, design innovation, usage of environmentally-friendlier materials, indoor environmental quality etc. There are four levels of certification with the highest certification being given the 'Platinum' rating (**Refer figure 6.8**). Web-link: https://igbc.in/ and http://in.usgbc.org/leed

Figure 6.8

USDA Organic

USDA Organic food label (**Refer Figure 6.9**) is issued by the United States Department of Agriculture (USDA)[22]. USDA Organic label is one of the popular organic labels in the world. Organic products that have USA as one of their major markets usually carry this label.

Figure 6.9[23]

Vegetarian/Non-vegetarian Mark

This indicator, used in packaged food products in India, indicates whether the product is vegetarian or non-vegetarian. This is a mandatory mark as per the norms prescribed by the Food Safety and Standards Authority of India (FSSAI, Food Safety and Standards (packaging and labeling) Regulation, 2011)[24]. A green colour dot surrounded by a green colour square indicates that the product is vegetarian. A brown colour dot surrounded by a brown coloured square indicates that the product is non-vegetarian (**Refer figure 6.10**).

---

22 https://www.ams.usda.gov/rules-regulations/organic, Accessed on September 15, 2017.

23 https://commons.wikimedia.org/wiki/File:USDA_organic_seal.svg, Accessed on July 7, 2016.

24 http://www.fssai.gov.in/Portals/0/Pdf/Food%20Safety%20and%20standards%20(Packaging%20and%20Labelling)%20regulation,%202011.pdf, Accessed on June 20, 2017.

Figure 6.10 (a)

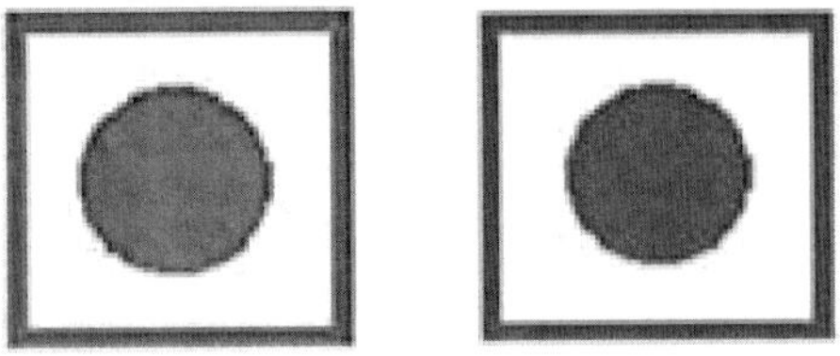

Figure 6.10 (b)

A refill pack of a food-drink repurposed as a pen-pencil-holder stand. One can find the "green dot" in the refill pack (right-hand-side), providing an indication of the nature of ingredients.

As per the FSSAI regulations (Food Safety and Standards (Labelling and Display) Regulations, 2020), the logo pertaining to vegetarian and non-vegetarian, has to be included in menu-cards and boards at food-service-establishments, at 'point-of-sale', in websites facilitating online food purchase, packaged food products, etc.

EPEAT

Electronic Product Environmental Assessment Tool (EPEAT) (http://www.epeat.net/) is a rating system for electronic products that considers the environmental impact of a product through its life-cycle. Depending on a product's ability to necessarily meet the 'required criteria', and the ability to meet the 'optional criteria', a product is rated as Bronze, Silver or Gold, with each rating referring to an increasingly higher environmental standard for the product (**Refer figure 6.11**).

Figure 6.11

Ecotel

In a tourism survey done near a protected area in India (*"hotels, lodges, resorts, camps and guest houses in and around Corbett National Park, Uttarakhand"*), it was found that, of the *"77 existing resorts/ hotels"*, more than two-thirds of the rooms were air-conditioned, less than one-fifth generate some solar energy, and 10% have eco-friendly buildings. The report considered *"Concrete buildings, heavy vehicular traffic, no proper waste segregation & disposal, loud music/ DJ"* as some of the areas that were of concern. A few of these establishments also provided facilities for consumption of alcoholic-drinks, while the survey report[25] did not mention how many of these establishments were vegetarian and non-vegetarian. Corbett National Park is easily accessible to some of the larger towns and cities of India.

Ecotel (http://www.ecotelhotels.com/) is a sustainability certification provided to hotels. This certification was managed by HVS Sustainability, with HVS being a consulting company. The certification considers parameters such as a commitment to sustainability, involvement of employees and community, and management of energy, water and waste **(Refer figure 6.12)**

25 This survey was done by IHMCTAN, Delhi, in the late 2000s or early 2010s, and before the instructions issued by the Supreme Court of India, temporarily banning any tourism activity within a "tiger reserve". Later, the Supreme Court of India also issued guidelines, evolved by multi-stakeholder-groups, that entrusted the forest departments for the demarcation of a core-zone and buffer-zone within the tiger reserves. A "national park" has more progressive guidelines, in comparison with a "tiger reserve", aimed towards protection and conservation of the natural environment.

Figure 6.12

While discoursing on the *Bhagavad Gita*, Swami Sandeepananda Giri, Founder-Acharya, '*School of Bhagavad Gita*' mentions that, we need to leave a toilet or a wash-room, a little more cleaner than what it was, prior to our use. Concern for others is an essence of living, as per the '*The Song Divine*'.

Green Globe

Green Globe (http://greenglobe.com/green-globe-certification/) is a certification given to organizations engaged in travel and tourism businesses, such as tour operators, tourism related travel organisers, meeting venues, hospitality organisations, cruise liners etc. Assessment standards are based on parameters that encompass environmental management, community development and protection of heritage and culture **(Refer figure 6.13)**. Some of the principles considered by Green Globe includes:

Figure 6.13

SCS Biodegradable

Usage of soap and detergents pollutes the water-bodies and land. The environmental impacts caused by packaging of the containers that carry these, and the pollution caused during their manufacture and transportation is additional. SCS Biodegradable (https://www.scsglobalservices.com/biodegradable) is a certification given to various cleaning and sanitation products such as soaps, solvents and degreasers that are bio-degradable.

This certification is given to products that verify that these products degrade safely and efficiently in an aerobic environment (**Refer figure 6.14**).

Figure 6.14

Bharat Jaivik

Bharat Jaivik is a certification given for food produces from India that is organically cultivated (**Refer figure 6.15**). The organic certification is given only to food produces that are traceable to the producer. The insecticide/ pesticide residue found in the food produce has to be lesser than the 'maximum residual limits' that is permitted.

Figure 6.15

A "*Jaivik Bharat*" badge, distributed by FSSAI (Food Safety and Standards Authority of India), in the 19th Organic World Congress, hosted in India, in 2017.

In many countries, including in India and USA, it is not necessary for an organic farmers' co-operative (a collective, an association, etc.) to go through an official organic certification process, if these farmers' collectives are pooling/ bringing together their produces and selling these produces directly to the consumers through a retail store, shop etc.

This enables the farmers to:

(a) save on expenses related to an organic certification process,

(b) to retain independence (i.e, non-dependency on any third-party to verify and certify the integrity of the organic farming practices),

(c) to trade (including, barter) the produces within the farming community, supportive networks, nearby regions, etc. For example, one farmer may be producing fruits, while another farmer may be producing nuts and vegetables, and collectively, these producers may be sharing their produces amongst themselves.

However, the success and integrity of such a self-certification of being organic is dependent on the maturity of the human values as practised within the collective. The image below (**Figure 6.16**) indicates the packaging of red rice produced in the district of Palakkad ("*Palakkadan Matta Ari*") in the state of Kerala, India. This packaging was used in a 5kg sack of organic red rice, produced by an organic farmers' collective – *Vadakkencherry Jaiva Padasekhara Nellulppaadana Samithi.*

Product Environmental Footprint

During the mid of the decade of 2010s, various organisations and individuals, under the auspices of the European Commission, engaged in discussions, researches and consultations, towards evolving a '"Product Environmental Footprint" (PEF) of various products and product categories. The PEF of a product or a product category is calculated through a "Life-Cycle-Assessment" of how a product is made and sold. The manufacture and sale of a product involves resource-consumption, climatic-impact, impact on water, etc. A PEF educate the consumer about how much a product is environmentally-friendly (in comparison with other products in that category). The finding of the PEF assessment is communicated as a ranking or it may be communicated in the form of a label.

Reading, is also a peep into the "collective unconscious" as well as the collective-conscious. Hasten slowly, says those who've ventured into the terrain.

You may take a break...

Figure 6.16

Palakkad and Kuttanad, which are regions in the state of Kerala, are referred to as rice bowls. The *Palakkadan Matta Ari* (or, red rice from the paddy fields of Palakkad) has been accorded geographical identification. Red rice (unlike refined/ white/ polished rice) retains more nutrients, has higher amount of fibre, etc.

Socially Responsible Investing

Socially Responsible Investing or SRI, is an investment philosophy of investing only in opportunities that maintains higher standards of environmental and social responsibility. SRI, while attempting to maximise financial returns, considers environmental and social good too. SRI is also referred to as Ethical Investing. The Forum for Sustainable and Responsible Investment states that varied terminologies such as 'community investing,' 'green investing,' 'impact investing,' 'mission-related investing,' 'responsible investing,' 'sustainable investing' and 'values-based investing' are also used.[26]

SRI has various components associated with it:

a) Divestment – Divestment involves withdrawing investments that are harmful to the planet and society. For example, in 2015, Norway decided to divest fossil fuel based investments from its wealth fund, which is the world's largest.

b) Negative Screening – Negative Screening involves choosing to avoid investment in companies that belongs to certain categories that are harmful to the planet and society, and/ or hurt sentiments of people. This may include investments in production, promotion and sales of intoxicants, weapons and gambling, etc.

c) Shareholder Activism – Many investors who practice an SRI philosophy uses shareholder advocacy to bring about management attention towards sustainability practices. For example, 'As You Sow', an Oakland based not-for-profit organisation working towards enhancing responsible business practices, filed for 23 resolutions in 2014[27] and 52 resolutions in 2017[28], in areas related to labelling of GMOs in food products, carbon asset risk, minimising environmental and community risk from hydraulic fracturing, environmental impact of consumer packaging, health concerns about nano-materials, usage of antibiotics for growth promotion in poultry and meat industry, continued use of foam based packing materials and reduction of greenhouse gas emissions.

d) Positive Investing – Investments that has the capability to create and

---

26 http://www.ussif.org/sribasics, Accessed on November 11, 2017.

27 http://www.asyousow.org/our-work/current-resolutions/?program=&ays_year=2014&initiative=&company=&keyword=, Accessed on October 24, 2015.

28 https://www.asyousow.org/our-work/current-resolutions/?program=&ays_year=2017&initiative=&company=&keyword=, Accessed on November 11, 2017.

enhance social and environmental well-being. This is also referred to as Impact Investing. Examples of positive investing, in the contemporary context, includes support towards individuals, organisations and communities involved in recycling, natural and organic farming, repurposing and upcycling of used materials, bicycle sharing, etc. The investments may also be on individual entrepreneurs or on companies that maintain best-in-class standards or elevate the existing industry standards in social and environmental practices.

e) Community Investment – Community investments involves channelizing investments towards those communities that are unserved or underserved by mainstream financial institutions.

An example of SRI Investing through a mutual fund in India is the Tata Ethical Fund. The mutual fund scheme document stated, *"Tata Ethical Fund prohibits from investing in companies categorized as morally deficient, such as those related to tobacco, alcohol, gambling, lottery, banking & finance services and other prohibited companies"*[29].

Extended Producer Responsibility

Manufacturers have difficulty in procuring raw-materials without planetary impacts. Extraction and procurement of raw-materials may involve destruction of forests, water-bodies and wetlands, relocation of people, pollution of land, air and water, etc. In this scenario, businesses finds that recycling waste materials can be a source of raw-materials. Consumers also have difficulty in discarding non-usable or non functional goods that they have purchased. Dumping of waste cause health hazards. While an individual consumer may not have the skill, scale and infrastructure for efficient waste management, it would be easier for an organisation or a multi-stakeholder-group to develop the required skill, scale and infrastructure towards efficient and effective utilisation of resources.

'Extended Producer Responsibility' (EPR) extends the boundary of responsibility of the producer. EPR has the objective of decreasing the total environmental impact of a product. It may include making the producer or manufacturer of a product responsible for post-usage take-back, recycling, and disposal. However, EPR may also involve multi-stakeholder organisations.

An EPR resolve by the state of Maine, in USA, for consumer goods

29 http://www.tatamutualfund.com/docs/scheme-documents/tef_1pager.pdf?sfvrsn=52, Accessed on October 24, 2015.

packaging and containers ("*materials used to wrap or protect consumer goods, including food and personal care products, and containers and packaging used in the shipping, storage, protection and marketing of consumer products*"[30]) had the following features:

1. packaging manufacturers to provide funds for (a) recycling at least 80% of the cost of recycling packaging material sold in Maine, (b) investments in education and awareness programmes related to waste reduction and recycling,
2. improvement in packaging design, through: (a) discouraging the creation of materials needing disposal, or, are not readily recyclable, or, are made of multiple materials - through charging a higher fee on such packaging material, (b) encouraging the creation of packaging materials that have a higher value of reusable components and contain higher percentage of recycled content - through charging a lower fee on such packaging material,
3. online retailers to make payments if the products they sell are from producers who are not part of the program,
4. the establishment of a non-profit organization that will work towards the above objectives, etc.

Globally, EPR has been in implementation for various products/ sectors, and some of them are as below:

Plastics and Tetrapaks	Used oil (lubricating and industrial oil)	Consumer appliances	Paper and printing products
Tires	Non-bio-degradable carpets, mattresses and textiles	Pharmaceuticals	Debris related to buildings and constructions
Paint	Lighting (including those containing mercury)	Smoke alarms	Automotive products
Batteries	Agricultural plastics and pesticides	Furniture	Electronics and electrical products

30 https://legislature.maine.gov/legis/bills/bills_129th/billtexts/HP104101.asp, Accessed on December 12, 2019.

Deposit Return Scheme

The packaging and containers carrying a merchandise or a product may be non-bio-degradable. Such packaging and containers may be collected back, after purchase or use, so that these packaging or containers may be re-used, re-purposed. or re-cycled. There are various methods to collect the non-bio-degradable packaging and non-bio-degradable containers that carries the merchandise or product. A 'Deposit Return Scheme' (DRS) is one of these. In this practice, the buyer of a product is charged an amount ("deposit"), whenever the purchase involves a product or merchandise that has non-bio-degradable packaging or non-bio-degradable containers. A person returning the non-bio-degradable packaging or container will be refunded ("return") the deposit amount collected, fully or partially. A DRS may also be known as a 'Deposit Refund System'.

Advantages and Disadvantages

A DRS is expected to result in a quantitative improvement in collection of non-bio-degradable packaging and containers. However, a DRS will will not result in waste-minimisation, if it is not combined with practices aimed at non-creation of waste. In such instances, a DRS will only be a waste-collection practice.

Existing channels of waste collection may be operationally limited to certain regions and functionally limited to collecting specific types of non-bio-degradables (such as PET bottles, and may not involve the collection of plastic wrappers or plastic packaging covers). A DRS need not be operationally and functionally restricted. It can work along with the existing practices of waste-collection.

By reusing, repurposing and recycling the collected materials, a 'Deposit Return Scheme' can contribute towards reducing the need for additional extraction and usage of minerals and planetary resources. A 'Deposit Return Scheme' contribute towards a 'Circular Economy'.

Effectiveness and Efficiency

An effective and efficient 'Deposit Return Scheme' involves:

(a encouraging reuse, repurpose and recycling (of non-bio-degradable packaging and non-bio-degradable containers), This may involve both downcycling and upcycling[31],

(b) discouraging inefficient and harmful disposal practices (of non-bio-degradable packaging and non-bio-degradable containers) such as burning[32], or discard in landfills,

(c) participation and allocation of resource-management responsibility to multiple stakeholders – consumers, producers of the product (manufacturers), supply-chain intermediaries (retail, distribution, transportation), recycling organisations, etc., considering principles of 'Polluter Pays' and 'Extended Producer Responsibility',

(d) a deposit payment that has both a non-returnable tax component and a returnable component.

Calculation of Deposit Price

Some of the parameters that may be considered during the calculation of deposit price may be:

(a) the environmental and societal cost of the material through its life-cycle (extraction and mining of minerals, manufacturing and supply, usage and after-usage, etc.),

(b) the monetary value of the material,

(c) monetary incentive to be provided to the consumer or third parties for returning the material, and

(d) expenses that may be incurred for effective reuse, repurpose and recycling of the collected material.

A few of the reasons for instituting the non-returnable tax component includes:

(a) generation of funds for practices that involves a higher common purpose and multiple stakeholders (for example, creating a business

31 In downcycling, a product is recycled to make another product, of a quality that is lower in comparison with the original material. Upcycling involves the making of a product that provides a better quality, in comparison with the original. Most recycling processes are only downcycling. The term upcycling may also refer to a qualitative improvement in utility or usage purpose of the product, rather than an improvement in quality of the product material.

32 In certain instances, electricity is produced from 'incineration' through the utilisation of heat. However such "energy recovery" practices has not been considered effective, or has been considered to be least efficient, amongst the various waste-management practices.

unit that employs people working towards reuse, repurpose and recycling of the collected material), and

(b) a penalty for (i) pollution, and (ii) extraction, misutilisation and underutilisation of resources,

(c) encourage the consumer to choose/ prefer products that use bio-degradable material in packaging and containers, while also encouraging manufacturers/ producers to prefer such materials,

(d) discourage the consumer from choosing/ preferring products that use non-bio-degradable material in packaging and containers, while also discouraging manufacturers/ producers from providing such materials,

(e) encouraging consumers to bring refillable containers during purchases, while also encouraging manufacturers/ producers to provide such a facility to consumers.

The non-returnable tax, thus, is the responsibility of various stakeholders considering their roles and responsibilities in production of waste. In many regions, funding of starting and maintaining organisations and processes that facilitate reuse, repurpose and recycling was done by governmental bodies, which provided limited funds. EPR and DRS practices, through taxation and also extending the boundaries of responsibility, may result in better facilitation of such organisations and processes, and creation and sustenance of jobs in these sectors.

Reading can also be an expression of tolerance to the ignorance of the writer, and further, the sharing of goodwill and kindness with the writer.

You may take a break...

SHARING ECONOMY AND SHARED RESOURCES

"Every atom you possess has almost certainly passed through several stars and been part of millions of organisms on its way to becoming you. We are each so atomically numerous and so vigorously recycled at death that a significant number of our atoms—up to a billion for each of us, it has been suggested—probably once belonged to Shakespeare. A billion more each came from Buddha and Genghis Khan and Beethoven, and any other historical figure you care to name."

—Bill Bryson[33]

33 A Short History of Nearly Everything, Black Swan, 2003.

During a spiritual-devotional discourse in the 1990s, Swami Tejomayananda, Acharya, Chinmaya Mission, asked the question *"How to see Atman?"*, thereby making many in the the audience ponder on the same. And Swamiji answered it himself. *"Listen! Hear! Not with eyes – to see anything, you have to hear! To see a flower, you have to know what a flower is first! You see, but you don't know, and you cannot know without hearing!"*

Sharing Economy

'Sharing economy' involves transactions amongst individuals who primarily engage in sharing of products and services, rather than purchasing them. This could be done in various ways. People may directly share products with others. They may also share products anparty or an online mechanism, such as a website or a mobile application, through which this could be done. BlaBlaCar[34] is an example of an online facility to share vehicles. Most private vehicles travel with occupancy levels below their carrying capacity. BlaBlaCar connects people who are travelling on similar routes. Higher vehicle occupancy results in higher efficiency in the utilisation of resources (**Refer table 6.2**). The travel expenses are shared. A reduction in the number of vehicles reduces air pollution, noise pollution, light pollution and dust pollution. Such a practice also reduces extraction of resources from the planet.

Examples for a sharing economy may also include:

- A lending library. A customer pays a membership fee. As the lending library has multiple users, it generates higher monetary resources towards purchasing more books. A user can access more books, while not owning them, and the cost of reading a book is reduced.
- Sourcing of extra chairs and tables for family events from a service provider. On completion of the event, these chairs and tables are returned to the service provider, with a rental charge.
- 'Plate banks' are a category of organisations that provide food-service utensils on rent. Bengaluru based 'Rent-a-cutlery' is such an organisation.
- Cloud Computing is an example of a shared practice in the technology domain.

There have been recommendations that *"lowering demand for new products by making them longer lasting, and increasing reuse and sharing"*[35] can contribute

34 https://www.blablacar.in/

35 http://www.green-alliance.org.uk/resources/Less_in_more_out.pdf. Accessed on June 3, 2018.

to increased efficiency in usage of resources, reduction in green-house-gas emissions and pollutants, and will contribute to the well-being of the planet and its inhabitants.

Table 6.2

	Carrying Capacity (Number of passengers)	Fuel Efficiency (km per litre)	Consumption per vehicle (litres, diesel)	Vehicles required	Total fuel consumption (litres)	Fuel consumption per passenger (litres)
Bus	45 (Max.)	5	10.0	1.1	11.1	0.2
	60 (Actual)	5	10.0	0.8	8.3	0.1
	30 (Actual)	5	10.0	1.7	16.7	0.6
Car 1	5 (Max.)	20	2.5	10.0	25.0	5.0
	2 (Actual)	20	2.5	25.0	62.5	31.3
	1 (Actual)	20	2.5	50.0	125.0	125.0
Car 2	7 (Max.)	18	2.8	7.1	19.8	2.8
	2 (Actual)	18	2.8	25.0	69.4	34.7
	1 (Actual)	18	2.8	50.0	138.9	138.9
Car 3	5 (Max.)	17	2.9	10.0	29.4	5.9
	2 (Actual)	17	2.9	25.0	73.5	36.8
	1 (Actual)	17	2.9	50.0	147.1	147.1
Car 4	5 (Max.)	18	2.8	10.0	27.8	5.6
	2 (Actual)	18	2.8	25.0	69.4	34.7
	1 (Actual)	18	2.8	50.0	138.9	138.9
Car 5	8 (Max.)	12	4.2	6.3	26.0	3.3
	2 (Actual)	12	4.2	25.0	104.2	52.1
	1 (Actual)	12	4.2	50.0	208.3	208.3
Car 6	8 (Max.)	11	4.5	6.3	28.4	3.6
	2 (Actual)	11	4.5	25.0	113.6	56.8
	1 (Actual)	11	4.5	50.0	227.3	227.3
Car 7	5 (Max.)	15	3.3	10.0	33.3	6.7
	2 (Actual)	15	3.3	25.0	83.3	41.7
	1 (Actual)	15	3.3	50.0	166.7	166.7
Van 1	32	6	8.3	1.6	13.0	0.4
Van 2	18	8	6.3	2.8	17.4	1.0

Notes:

1. Table 6.2 indicates data for carrying 50 passengers through a distance of 50 kilometres.
2. Approximations are included.
3. 'Carrying capacity' and 'fuel efficiency' are, as prevalent in India, in 2019. These may be similarities with standards in other regions of the world. For example, average passenger occupancy in private cars has been found to be approximately two (or lesser) in many countries.
4. The table includes road vehicles that uses diesel. The table do not mention non-motorised and rail-based transportation options.
5. For buses, considering both seating and standing, a carrying capacity higher than seating capacity is also mentioned.

Giftivism and 'Pay as you wish'

Many contemporary transactions are driven and substantiated on a monetary basis, and are based on self-importance, self-prominence and survival. In 'giftivism', people offer whatever they can, as gifts. Unlike charity, where the giver may be considered to be in a state of superiority and the receiver may be in a state of deprivation, gifting is primarily an expression of friendship and caring. Giftivism could include gifting one's time, knowledge, money, resources and talent. These practices may contribute to a mind-shift from that of consumption to contribution, and from a state of being deprived to a state of being abundant.

'Pay as you wish' is an operating model that espouses the concept of Giftivism. In this practice, the receiver of the service can decide on the amount to be paid in return for receiving a service. 'Pay-as-you-wish' is also referred as 'Pay-what-you-want', 'Pay-what-you-like', 'Pay-as-your-heart-feels', etc., depending on the quality of the contextual environment, the transactions and relationships amongst the organisational stakeholders, and how the stakeholders perceive the organisation. 'Pay-as-you-wish' may operate in various ways. While some of them may be unconditional, some of the service providers mentions a 'recommended amount' or communicate their expenses, so that the customer or the receiver of the service can make an informed choice regarding the amount that needed to be paid. The below are examples of the 'Pay as you wish' model:

a. Udai Jadav drives an auto-rickshaw in the city of Ahmedabad. Since 2010, he has not been demanding any fixed charges from the passengers. The passengers can give whatever they feel to give. Inside the auto-rickshaw, there are inspirational quotes. One can also find drinking water and a container that has snacks. The auto-rickshaw also has a waste-bin inside it.

b. One of the earliest known instances of 'pay as you wish' is that of the Annalakshmi restaurant at Bangsar, Kuala Lumpur, Malaysia. This restaurant was associated with Swami Shantananda Saraswati (a disciple of Swami Sivananda) and his disciples. This concept was replicated to some Annalakshmi restaurants in other countries.

   Other examples of food service outlets that operate on this model and similar models, with varying levels of success, includes the 'Karma Kitchen' at Berkeley, 'Seva Cafe' at Ahmedabad, 'Lentil as Anything' restaurants in multiple locations of Australia etc.

c. Dasparkhotel in Austria provides lodging facilities at Bernepark and Ottensheim. This facility was created from concrete drainage pipes, thereby providing robustness and sturdiness to the exteriors. The facilities are minimal - *"full-headroom, double-bed, storage, light, power, wooly blanket and light cotton sleeping bag"*, says the website. Toilets, showers, cafe etc. are available outside, nearby. An article about this accommodation facility mentions, *"Payment is simple: before you go, leave an amount in your room that you think is fair for the length of your stay"* (dasparkhotel.net).

Crowd-sourcing and Crowd-funding

In business practices, crowd-sourcing refers to the practice of involving a large group of people, many of them unrelated to the business organisation, to contribute their ideas and services to improve upon a business process. This usually involves the usage of online technologies. Jeff Howe, who has authored an book on this subject, says, '...*crowdsourcing represents the act of a company or institution taking a function once performed by employees and outsourcing it to an undefined (and generally large) network of people in the form of an open call. This can take the form of peer-production (when the job is performed collaboratively), but is also often undertaken by sole individuals.*'[36] A synonym to crowd-sourcing is 'Peer Production'. Wikipedia is a successful example of crowd-sourcing or peer production. Crowd-sourcing, in non-business practices, may not involve monetary payments.

Crowd-funding involves raising capital for a venture from a large number of people. Earlier, capital for a new venture used to emerge from owner's

36 http://crowdsourcing.typepad.com/cs/2006/06/crowdsourcing_a.html, Accessed on December 19, 2015.

savings, relatives and friends, financial organisations and angel investors/ venture capitalists. Crowd-funding expands this boundary and many people are given an opportunity to invest in the new venture. The size of the investment is usually small. Investment of smaller denominations increases participation, and this may also help the owner to raise the required capital. Kairali TV, during its launch as a Malayalam TV channel in 2000, had more than two lakh shareholders. The channel was launched with the support of the communist parties in Kerala.

Free and Open Source Software (FOSS)

Most software available in the market has copyright restrictions and the source code is not shared. Most of these softwares are priced, while some of them may be provided for free. Software available free of cost are referred to as freeware. An 'open source software' is a software whose source code is made available to the public, and do not have any restrictions for modifications and duplications. An open source software may be available free of cost, while sometimes they may charge a nominal fee from the buyer.

This book was documented on the 'OpenOffice Writer' and 'LibreOffice Writer'. These are document applications included in 'OpenOffice' and 'LibreOffice'[37]. 'OpenOffice' and 'LibreOffice' are 'Free and Open Source Softwares'. A FOSS, or a 'Free and Open Source Software', is a software that is made available free[38] of cost - to download, use, duplicate, share and modify. FOSS combines the features of 'free software' and 'open source software'.

A few of the popular open-source softwares that are also available free of cost are:

a) Moodle – Used in educational institutions
b) Mozilla Thunderbird – Used for e-mail management
c) Drupal – Content Management Framework
d) Mozilla Firefox – Web Browser
e) VLC – Video Player

37 The web addresses for OpenOffice and LibreOffice are www.OpenOffice.org and www.LibreOffice.org, as accessed on December 13, 2019.

38 George Orwell, known for his '*Animal Farm*', mentions in one of his fictional works, *"The word 'free' still existed..., but it could only be used in such statements as "This dog is free from lice" or "This field is free from weeds". It could not be used in its old sense of "politically free" or "intellectually free", since political and intellectual freedom no longer existed even as concepts, and were therefore of necessity nameless".*

Usage of FOSS has resulted in reduced costs related to software spending, improved e-security, customisation etc. Many for-profit organizations support open source projects through monetary funding, talent sharing, etc. Examples include Google, Facebook, IBM and HP[39]. The reasons for such support may be philanthropic, to influence future product developments, access knowledge, networking with technology teams, etc.

'Closed Loop Design' and 'Circular Economy'

A product usually generates waste at various stages of its life-cycle. For example, the packaging for a popular snack – noodles, is made from plastic, which is not bio-degradable. To manufacture plastic, fossil fuels are used. After usage, the plastic packet may be deposited on the ground, causing harm to the soil or preventing the seepage of water. If the packaging reaches a water body, it can harm the aqua-beings. Burning of this waste plastic can result in emissions harmful to health.

In contrast to this, in nature, all processes are 'closed-loop' - what may be considered 'waste', is food for something else. 'Closed Loop Design' refers to a design process that does not result in the creation of waste. This design process could be for a product or a non-product.

There have been attempts to replicate closed-loop-design in manufacturing. A number of organizations in India make bio-degradable food plates from arecanut palm leaf. After usage, these plates can be washed and re-used at least a few times, or these plates can be disposed. There are also organisations that produce 'edible cutlery'[40], which can be eaten after usage. They are made from various grains. This is in contrast to the usage of disposables made from non-bio-degradable materials such as plastic, styrofoam or tetrapak materials.

'Closed Loop Design' has similarities with 'Circular Economy'. Circular economy refers to an economic system where any waste generated is a fully reusable raw material for another economic process. It promotes the '6R' principle of 'Refuse, Reduce, Reuse, Repurpose, Recycle and Recover'. A report on circular economy mentions that "*...reuse could lead to a further reduction of greenhouse gas emissions. Extending the lifespan of computers and tablets by one year reduces the greenhouse gas emissions of these products by around 20%. Reuse of products is not limited to reusing entire products; reuse of components also reduces the need to produce new components and thus reduces*

39 https://opensource.org/sponsors, Accessed on September 18, 2016.

40 Refer the section in this textbook related to case-studies/ caselets, to access more details about 'edible cutlery'.

carbon emissions."[41] The existing economic processes have resulted in non-bio-degradable waste and pollution. Circular economy focuses on well-being and sustainability.

Product as a Service

'Product as a Service' is a business model whereby a customer, instead of purchasing the product, pay for its usage. The customer will pay the manufacturer every time their service is used. This contract will be for a short period or a long period.

> ***Reading can also be an exercise in self-restraint – from the overload of information, sensory stimulii, distorting impressions, and conspicuous consumption.***
>
> ***You may take a break...***

EDUCATION IN RESPONSIBILITY PRACTICES

'There is no school equal to a decent home and no teachers equal to honest, virtuous parents.'

—Mahatma Gandhi[42]

The usual practice in India is to leave the footwear outside homes. There are also places where this habit is extended to workplaces (**Refer figure 6.17**). The inherent spiritual values makes many Indians live in harmony with the natural environment. Though a large percentage of Indian population lack the technical understanding of aspects related to environmental issues and its impacts, and there is also the impact of population, India's environmental footprint[43] and carbon footprint, on a per capita basis, is lower as compared to the nations that have achieved higher economic growth.

41 https://www.cedelft.eu/en/publications/1803/the-circular-economy-as-a-key-instrument-for-reducing-climate-change, Accessed on June 28, 2018.

42 Harijan, February 20, 1937.

43 Refer the first chapter in this textbook.

Figure 6.17

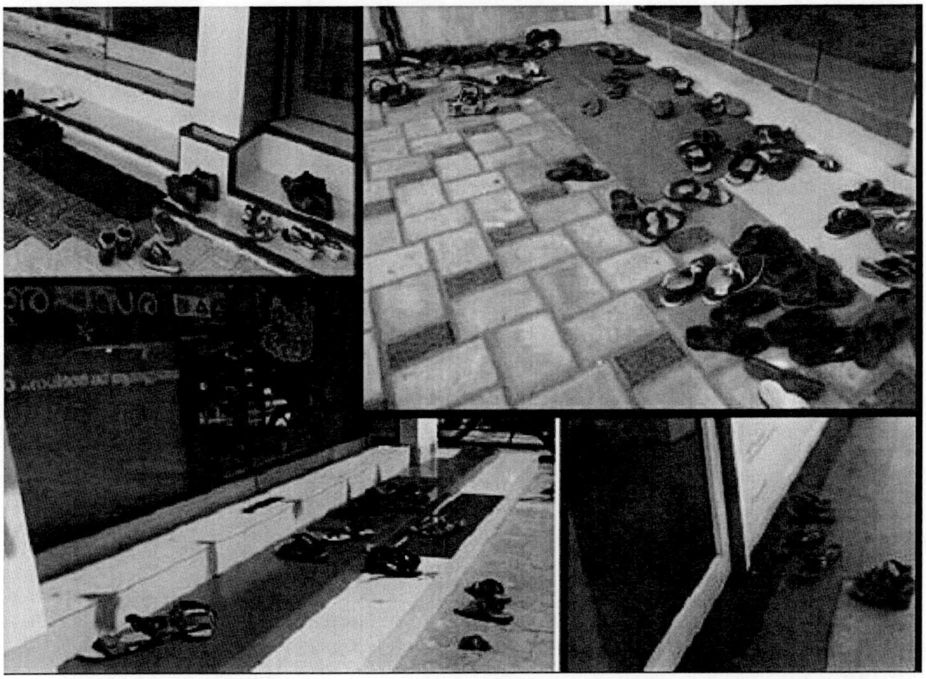

Customers leaving their footwear outside the entrance door of banks, shops etc. in Vadakkencherry, a town in the district of Palakkad, Kerala.

Referring to Einstein ("the man (who) doesn't wear socks"), it was mentioned, *"the deep feeling behind them was genuine enough... there was also an urgency which for Einstein had a particular poignancy. All those buttons; all those tails; all that putting on and taking off, wasting valuable minutes and hours... And so with shoes, which could be replaced by sandals, and socks that could be dispensed with altogether, How he would have sympathised with his near-contemporary J. B. S. Haldane, who rejoiced on his emigration to India that he would now be able to go foot-free, and added: "Sixty years in socks is enough".*[44][45]

Few in India know the parameters that constitute an ecological footprint, though many Indians experienced the medicinal value of *Amla*, *Neem* and *Tulsi.* Many temples in India are landmarked by trees such as banyan. The culture attempted to respect everything for its inherent nature, not just for

44 Ronald W Clark, Einstein: The Life and Times, Avon Books.

45 In '*Return to Nature!*', (1899, fourth edition), Adolf Just, a practitioner of natural healing, mentions that (as translated by Benedict Lust) "*...The order of barefoot monks, who always went barefooted, well knew that the blessings of Jesus' doctrine of salvation and happiness were not to be had without obeying the precepts with regard to a natural mode of life and the care of health...*".

its utility for humans. Worship of snakes emerged from the recognition of their role in sustaining the ecosystem, helping to protect that species from societal violence, while also caring for the safety of one's near and dear.

In India, sanctified water is referred to as *'Theertha'*, which also refers to locations that holds sanctified water or their sources. In places of worship, the children are told that they should partake *'Theertha'* with reverence. *'Theertha'* is the word that is also used while referring to the wise who've been gifting onself for others, while giving up anything they have for themselves[46].

Referring to an educational institution reflecting values-driven practices, Victor-Krishna Kanu, Former High Commissioner (Ambassador) for Sierra Leone to the UK, Norway and Sweden, and Director of The African Institute of Sathya Sai Education in Zambia, says, "*For instance, at Sathya Sai School in Ndola, teachers and students do not wear coats and ties... We were going to dress simply like our people. Well, that was a big challenge.*" He continues, "*The teachers didn't like it. There was going to be a rebellion. But we stood very, very firmly... Today the teachers are very happy... ...They are very simply dressed. Even when the president of the country comes to visit the school there are no coats and no ties. I said to them, 'See, you are not judged by the clothes you wear, but by the work you do'.*" The institute introduced songs and greetings in the local language. Victor-Krishna Kanu mentions, *'In Zambia, people don't want to sit on the floor; you must have chairs. We said, 'No.' We got mats, and everybody must sit on the floor - students and teachers as well as parents. At first, they didn't like it at all, but now they love it... In addition, shoes are taken off when entering the Auditorium for prayers...'*[47]

Values such as Non-violence (*Ahinsa*), Righteousness (*Dharma*) and Love (*Prema*) contributed to make India a country that preferred and enriched plant-based diet practices, which is a diet pattern with a lower carbon and ecological footprint. Values such as Truth (*Sathya*) and Peace (*Shanti*) contributed to creating a society that understand the transient nature of advertisement-driven-ethics and consumption, and also to make decisions

46 Adi Shankara established four "seats of learning" (or, *'mutt')* or monasteries in the four directional regions of India, towards debates and discussions, and conversations and contemplations on 'The perennial wisdom' (*Sanathana Dharma*). These *mutt*s are the Govardhan Mutt at Jagannath Puri (East), Dwaraka Mutt (West), Jyotir Mutt at Joshimath, Badrinath (North), and Sringeri Mutt (South). The *sannyasi*s of the western monastery are titled as *'Theertha'* and *'Ashrama'*. The *sannyasis* of other monasteries are titled as *Vana* and *Aaranya* (eastern monastery), *Giri* and *Parvata* (northern monastery), and *Saraswathi*, *Bharathi* and *Puri* (southern monastery).

47 Quotations extracted from the public knowledge base of the "Spiritual Based Leadership Research Programme" are © 2006 by the Global Dharma Center (GDC). GDC retains the copyright to all excerpts from this knowledge base.

with clarity, while leading a life focused on Caring, Sharing and Giving - thus, there is lesser exploitation and better utilisation of natural resources. The epic *Ramayana* narrates that the four sons of King Dasaratha were tutored on various aspects that befit princes. Referring to this, Sathya Sai Baba says, "*Rama and Lakshmana were revealing knowledge of strategems and skills which even expert instructors did not know about... But, the four princes never shot an arrow at an animal or bird. They never broke the vow taken solemnly by them that they will use arms only on occasions of great urgency, not for the pleasure of killing or wounding.*"[48]

On December 10, 1932, while addressing the first batch ("pioneers") of the cadets of the Indian Military Academy (IMA), Dehradun, Field Marshal Sir Philip W Chetwode, the Commander-in-Chief of British India, mentioned,

"*... I would ask you to remember that you have come here to have your first lessons in three principles which must guide an officer of a National Army, and they are:*

First, the safety, honour and welfare of your country come first, always and every time.

Second, the honour, welfare and comfort of the men you command come next.

Third, your own ease, comfort and safety come last, always and every time...

These, with minor modifications, has been accepted as the credo of IMA.

Sustainability MBA

Motithang Takin Preserve was originally a mini-zoo in the Motithang region of Thimpu, the capital city of Bhutan. This zoo caged Takin, a wild animal found near the Himalayan mountain regions. While it looks similar to a goat or a sheep, Takin is heavily built. However, the fourth king of Bhutan did not like cageing the animals. After all, a zoo enclose animals and birds within a narrow space. The king felt that a zoo is not in alignment with the environmental and religious beliefs of Bhutan[49]. The caged animals were freed. However, it was found that not all of these domesticated takins were returning to the wild. Some of them started roaming the streets. The Bhutanese soon designed a 'zoo without cages' – with the zoo being

48 Ramakatha Rasavahini, Part 1.

49 The constitution of Bhutan, which begins as,"*We, the people of Bhutan: Blessed by the Triple Gem...*", states that "*a minimum of sixty percent of Bhutan's total land shall be maintained under forest cover for all time*" and accords every Bhutanese citizen "*a trustee of the Kingdom's natural resources and environment for the benefit of the present and future generations*". Further, the constitution also mentions that "*A person shall not be subjected to torture or to cruel, inhuman or degrading treatment or punishment*" and "*A person shall not be subjected to capital punishment.*"

converted into 'Motithang Takin Preserve', a protected area of eight acres in the city. In 2005, Takin was also declared the national animal of Bhutan.

Till a few years ago, Aspen Institute did an assessment of MBA programs about their sensitivity to the needs of the society. This ranking was named as 'Beyond Grey Pinstripes'. The following were the parameters and weightage that were considered to ascertain the ranking[50]:

1. Relevant Coursework (20%) - Number of courses offered that contain social, environmental or ethical component.
2. Student Exposure (25%) - Teaching hours and full-time student enrolment in relevant courses.
3. Business Impact (30%) - Number of courses that specifically address the intersection of social impact management and mainstream for-profit business.
4. Faculty Research (25%) - Number of scholarly articles published in peer-reviewed business journals that contain some degree of social, environmental or ethical content.

A 'Sustainability MBA' program focus on facilitating a learning environment where the student can ponder on the linkages amongst business, purpose, universal principles, social responsibility and respect for the nature, in addition to the conventional areas of business strategies, methodologies and functional aspects. They may also be referred to as 'Green MBAs'.

MBA programmes that have the vision to create noble leaders usually have human values embedded in their curriculum. For example, the vision of Sri Sathya Sai Institute of Higher Learning (SSSIHL) is to '*To assist generations of students acquire Self-knowledge (Atma Vidya) and Self-confidence (Atma Vishwas), so as to cultivate Self-sacrifice and earn Self-realisation; thereby moulding them into leaders who will benefit society.*'[51] SSSIHL also offers an MBA programme and do not charge fee from the students[52]. The students engage in service programmes in the villages, termed as '*Grama Seva*'.

As part of the '*Grama Seva*', "*...nearly 150 villages with a population of around 2,00,000 are served...*" mentions a case-study about SSSIHL[53]. It is also

50 http://www.aspeninstitute.org/sites/default/files/content/docs/pubs/BGP%20 2011-2012%20Global%20Report-small.pdf, Accessed on March 20, 2016.

51 http://sssihl.edu.in/sssuniversity/AboutSSSIHL/VisionMissionPhilosophy.aspx, Accessed on March 20, 2016.

52 The institute charges a nominal fee for boarding and lodging.

53 As written by Shashank Shah and G Srinivas Srirangarajan in the case-study "*Sri Sathya Sai University: A Value-based System of Education*" and published in *Indian Ethos and Values in Management*, Tata McGrawHill, 2011.

mentioned, *"As the student's of the men's campuses take up the responsibility of serving the food and clothes, the student's of women's campuses undertake the task of assisting in food preparation and packing. Each day, the vehicle go in a convoy to pre-identified villages early in the morning. On reaching their destination, the students go around the village engaging in congregational singing of devotional songs and hymns. Subsequently, they distribute the food and clothes... stationery material is distributed to the school children in their respective schools"*

The students of SSSIHL are also responsible for the management of many of the day-to-day functions at the institute, and also many of the maintenance work at the institute. Sathya Sai Baba refers to an MBA as *"Mind, Body, Atma"*.

Institutions focused on sustainability education, in addition to offering values-based core courses (such as 'Indian Ethos and Values in Management', 'Spirituality in Management', 'Business Ethics', 'Human Values in Workplace', etc.) also offers courses on various sustainability based topics (such as 'Corporate Social Responsibility', 'Social Entrepreneurship', 'Environmental Management', 'Impact of business on the health of the inhabitants of the planet', etc.).

In 2010, 'Kerala Tourism' received the PATA (Pacific Asia Travel Association) award for 'Corporate Social Responsibility'. 'The Farm', in Philippines[54], is a hotel that provides only plant-based food, with the ingredients being mostly organic[55]. Of the 50 hectares of land owned by the hotel, only 10

54 'The Farm', is located in San Benitos, Batangas. Batangas is a province in Philippines. The capital of this province is known as the city of Batangas. The province is also referred to by its ancient name Kumintáng.

55 *In 'Return to Nature!'* (1899, fourth edition), Adolf Just, a practitioner of natural healing, mentions that (as translated by Benedict Lust) *"...Fruit culture affords an opportunity for the most agreeable and best physical work. With fruit culture we promote the cause upon which depend the rescue and redemption of mankind, and through which men will again be led to health and happiness. In future every one ought to raise his own fruit as much as possible; it must become less and less a matter of business. Whoever raises more fruit than he needs for himself can, if he is able, give it away, make presents of it to his friends, and thus cause much pleasure, while in making presents of other things (money, etc.) he frequently causes no pleasure, and does no real good, often even mischief. The labor involved in fruit culture is so fascinating, so agreeable, it gives so much pleasure and joy that it is for this reason very conducive to health. If we only begin to see things in their true light, and realize that the most natural is always the best and noblest, then the labor of fruit culture will soon be considered much more advantageous, and much finer than all gymnastics, cycling, and all other sport, and all our present so-called noble pastimes..."*. Perspectives of Adolf Just can also be found in another footnote of this chapter and also on a footnote of Chapter 2.

hectares are developed. The food ingredients, grown in the organic gardens, are cooked only 15%, so that there is no loss of nutrients, due to cooking (thefarmatsanbenito.com). The soaps used in the hotel are handmade. The hotel uses cold-pressed coconut oil. The hotel also conducts an 'Oil of Life' tour, introducing visitors to how the coconut is indeed a '*Kalpavriksha*'.

Amongst the states of India, Gujarat, in the western coast, has the longest shoreline – at more than 1200 kilometres. Yet, it is one of the states in India that has many vegetarians – almost two-thirds of its population being vegetarians, indicating that an access to a water-body (such as a sea. lake, lagoon, rivers or ponds) need not result in the infliction of violence on the water bodies, and the life there.

One of the rituals found in some of the Hindu temples in Kerala is to nurture the fishes in the temple-pond. Children finds this interesting, as it is they who feed the fishes, with plant-based food ("*meenoottu*", a ritualistic offering). Parents tell children – *feed the fishes, and your intelligence will increase*. For the adults, a visit to the Kutch region of Gujarat may be a learning experience. At the *Kala Dungar* (black hills) region is the practice where the hyenas are fed with a preparation made from rice and jaggery, with the quantity of rice being twice the weight of jaggery. This offering is made to honour the 'Pir of Pachchmai' (*Guru Dattatreya*) who, legends say, lived a life of harmony and friendship with the hyenas[56]. In one of his poems, Sri Narayana Guru writes,

> *Non-causal of harm, even to an ant;*
> *Oh Lord, you, kindness manifesting as a form,*
> *bestow me, always, this belongingness,*
> *as is the thought of non-leaving your presence...*[57]

---

56 KN Daruwalla mentions in "*Love Across the Salt Desert*":

A lamp was lighted in the Pir's honour every night on the hilltop and the flame could be seen all the way from Khavda. Over a hundred years earlier, the Panchmai Pir had trudged these salt wastes serving the people, accompanied, as legend had it, by a jackal. Reclusive by habit he used to retire to thorn jungles, where apart from his vulpine companions none else dared to disturb his nocturnal trysts. The custom of feeding the jackals lingered since then.

57 This translation is from '*Anukambadasakam*', written by Sri Narayana Guru, in Malayalam. '*Daivadasakam*' is another popular and respected work by Narayana Guru. The English translation included in this page may not be conveying the original meaning.

Open Courseware

To know, from the source. To live, at the source. This thirst led Huen-Tsang to embark on a journey to the land of Sramana Gotama. Historians, travelers, disciples, and his own writings say that he traveled through some of the most spectacular regions of he world, as also dangerous. The plains of the Silk Route, the plateaus of the Afghan, and the rugged ranges of the Karakoram and the Hindukush, and deserts of Turkestan – many, being regions where water is sparse. Deterrents and warnings rose about his destination – that this is a region that is very hot, and that the men there are *"without any sense of decorum, and not fit to look at!"*. Fa Hien's description of the desert of the northernly route between India and China was that *"In this desert are many evil demons and hot winds; when encountered, then all die without exception. There are no flying birds above, no roaming beasts below, but everywhere gazing as far as the eye can reach in search of the onward route, it would be impossible to know the way but for dead men's decaying bones, which show the direction."*[58] Yet manifestations and omens helped Huen-Tsang on his way, and strengthened his persistence and determination. The Bamiyan Buddha, for example, may have soothened his parched spirit, enthusing him to continue. Reaching Bactria[59], he may have took a southern turn. And soon, he enters India, with its springs and rivers, the soil fertile and the blooming orchards and fields – manifestations of the enterprise, simplicity and honesty of the people dwelling there. What can Nalanda, one of the seats of learning of that age, give to him who has walked almost 6000 kilometres through four years, almost circumambulating the majestic Himalayas!? Yet, this was the space whose air carried the memories, reasonings, impressions and perspirations of the legends, who were no less

58 SI–YU–KI. Buddhist Records of the Western World. (Translated from the Chinese of Hiuen Tsiang)

Samuel Beal, Trubner & Co., 1884.

59 Bactria was an ancient province of Persia, and now, in Afghanistan. The region has been revered by various communities. Zoraster lived here, and preached. The tomb of Hazrat Ali, and the Mosque of Nine Cupolas also contributes to the veneration of the region. Bactria was also the home of the temple of an Iranian goddess, Anahit or Anahita (Anahit in Pahlavi or Middle-Persian, Anahita in the hymns of Avesta). The Gandhara region, in proximity to the Bamiyan, has also been home to many scholars - *"...Narayanadeva, Asanga Boddhisattva, Vasubandhu Bodhisattva, Dharmatrata, Manorhita, Parsva the noble, and so on."*, writes Hieun Tsiang.

in stature with the visitor[60]. Following months of stay, and travel through India, he returns to his native land, carrying with him the priceless and the immensely priced. There were rare artefacts and manuscripts[61], and objects that were impressive. The wheels of time rolled. Translation of materials carried from India took many years. Determination evolves to dedication. In the remainder of his life, he was engaged in giving and gifting the knowledge he received and was gifted with.

Einstein says, "*Curiosity has its own reason for existence. One cannot help but be in awe when (one) contemplates the mysteries of eternity, of life, of the marvellous structure of reality. It is enough if one tries merely to comprehend a little of this mystery each day. Never lose a holy curiosity.*"[62]

Open Courseware are those courseware that are made available in the public domain. They are distributed free of cost, can be adapted and re-distributed. A learner can access varied learning resources through open courseware. Open courseware have enabled learners to access the most respected educational resources that are available anywhere in the world. A number of universities have been contributing to open courseware. Some organisations also conduct exams and provide the learner with certifications, though, for a fee.

And if the reader is keen and open to know on who an inquirer could be, E Mach is here to provide clues. Mach is not just a shaving instrument, or a unit associated with the breaking of a sound barrier. Dr Ernst Mach was the "Professor of the History and Theory of Inductive Science in the University of Vienna". At Prague, in May 1883, he wrote, "*...The quaint and naive traits of the great inquirers, which find in them their expression, have always*

---

60 Referring to Siladitya Harshavardhana, the renowned king of the time then, it is mentioned, "*...He gave himself up to religious duties; he prohibited the slaughter of any living creature. He himself set the example, and ordered all his people to abstain from flesh meat, and he founded Sangharamas wherever there were sacred traces of religion. Yearly during three or seven days (or, perhaps, during three seven-days, i.e. three weeks) he provided food for the whole body of priests. Every fifth year he convoked a grand assembly of deliverance (maha-moksha-parishad), and distributed the stores of his treasuries in charity.*" It is further stated, "*...The ground is perfectly level and straight. From ancient days till now, royal and noble personages endowed with virtue and love, in the distribution of their charitable offerings, have all resorted to this spot for the purpose; and hence the name of the 'Field of Great Beneficence' has been given to it. At the present time Siladitya raja, following this custom, has distributed here the accumulated wealth of five years, during a period of seventy-five days...*". ('*The Life of Hiuen-Tsiang*' (Samuel Beal, Trubner & Co., 1911)).

61 "*He returned to his own country with no less than 657 volumes of the sacred books, seventy-four of which he translated into Chinese, while 150 relics of the Buddha, borne by twenty horses...*", mentions written by L Cranmer Byng in the preface to '*The Life of Hiuen-Tsiang*' (Samuel Beal, Trubner & Co., 1911).

62 Ronald W Clark, Einstein: The Life and Times, Avon Books.

exerted upon me a refreshing influence in my studies, and I have desired that my readers should share this pleasure with me...", as a preface to one of his books, in which he dealt with questions that *"have occupied me since my earliest youth..."*[63].

In the *Chandogya Upanishad*[64], we find that Shwetaketu was asked by his father to go to a teacher[65] and learn all that is to be learned. And he went. *"Twelve years old was he when he went in; and when he was four-and-twenty years old he had read all the Vedas, and came home, swollen of soul, deeming himself learned and haughty."*[66] The proudness of learning that embodied Shwetaketu was visible to his father, Uddalaka Aruni. Once he asked his son about his learning - *"...hast thou sought the lore whereby that which is not heard is heard, that which is not thought is thought, that which is not understood is understood?"*[67] Shwetaketu said, *"Had they known it how should they not have spoken to me thereof?"*[68] And the father readied himself, and prepared his son and generations that followed, towards that knowledge...

CHAPTER SUMMARY

- Social entrepreneurship refers to the practice of applying business practices and models to bring about transformative and noble changes in living and society, through an enterprise, which is a for-profit or not-for-profit organisation.

---

63 Dr Ernst Mach, The Science of Mechanics: A Critical and Historical Account of its Development, The Open Court Publishing Company, 1893 (translated from the German *Die Mechanik in ihrer Entwickelung- historisch-kritisch dargestellt* by Thomas J McCormack).

64 The Upanishads are a collection of contemplations. It has drawn upon and contributed to the philosophical foundations of Dharmic religions, including Hinduism. '*Chandogya Upanishad*' is one among the classical Upanishads.

65 References are usually made to a '*Gurukula*'. In the tradition of 'Gurukulam', a student stays with a teacher, and participate in service to the teacher. It was during his childhood days as a gurukula student that Adi Sankara wrote the '*Kanakadhaara Strotram*'. The teacher may or may not have other students. The teacher may or may not have a family. Swami Chinmayananda, in his commentary on '*Taittiriya Upanishad*', writes, *"The student were not asked to pay any fees before they entered the gurukula institution... A student entering the portals of education was a pleasant challenge, as it were, to the teacher who took up the challenge and saw to it that he made out of that raw material an efficient and independent earning member of the society....The gurudaksina (the fee) was not even demanded of the boys when they were leaving the institution... ...early savings that he could make entirely go towards the gurudaksina. And who among them could forget their own days of gurukula activities and the fact how, during their days, the old students had maintained the rsi universities?"*

66 L D Barnett, Some sayings from the Upanishads, Luzac & Co., 1905.

67 L D Barnett, Some sayings from the Upanishads, Luzac & Co., 1905.

68 L D Barnett, Some sayings from the Upanishads, Luzac & Co., 1905.

- A co-operative is an autonomous organisation of people joining voluntarily to meet their common economic, social, and cultural needs and aspirations through a jointly-owned and democratically-controlled enterprise.
- Base of Pyramid ('Bottom of Pyramid') is an economic model that indicates that the economically underprivileged of the society can also contribute to the growth of the economy. The concept was popularised by CK Prahalad and Stuart L Hart.
- Micro-credit, also referred to as a micro-loan, is about extending small loans to poor people without any collateral. When varied financial services, which also include micro-credit, are offered, it is referred to as micro-finance or micro-banking.
- Labelling/certification that reflects corporate responsibility practice is beneficial in a number of ways. It helps the consumer to purchase products that meet the highest standard in social responsibility and environmental sustainability. Through such certifications, organizations can communicate their uniqueness to its stakeholders, especially consumers.
- Investors following the practice of 'Socially Responsible Investing' (SRI) look for investment opportunities that maintain higher standards of environmental and social responsibility. SRI, while attempting to maximise financial returns, considers environmental and social good too. Divestment, Negative Screening, Shareholder Activism, Positive Investing and Community Investment are some of the aspects of SRI. It is also referred to as ethical investing.
- Sharing economy involves individuals who primarily engage in sharing products and services rather than purchasing them.
- 'Pay as you wish' is an operating model that espouses the concept of Giftivism, where people offer whatever they can, including gifting one's time, knowledge, money, resources, talent etc. The operating model of 'Pay as you wish' is also referred to as 'Pay what you like', 'Pay as your heart feels' etc.
- Crowd-sourcing refers to the practice of involving a large group of people, many of them unrelated to the business organisation, to contribute their ideas and services to improve upon a business process. Crowd-sourcing may involve the usage of online technologies. Crowd-funding involves raising capital for a venture from a large number of people.

- Software available free of cost are referred to as freeware. An 'open source software' is a software whose 'source-code' is made available to the public, and do not have any restrictions for modifications. A FOSS is a software that is made available free of cost to download, use, duplicate, share and modify. FOSS combines the features of 'free software' and 'open source software'. An 'open source software' may be available free of cost, while sometimes they may charge a nominal fee from the buyer. All freewares do not provide the source code to the public domain.
- In nature, all processes are 'closed-loop' - what may be considered 'waste', is food for something else. 'Closed Loop Design' is an appealing term given to a design process that does not result in the creation of waste. This design process could be for a product or a non-product.

KEYWORDS MENTIONED

Social entrepreneurship, Social inclusion, Differential Pricing Model, Base of Pyramid, Bottom of Pyramid, Micro-credit, Micro-Finance, Sustainability Certification, Sustainability Labeling, Green Seal, Benefit Corporation, Certified B Corporation, GoodWeave, CO2 Neutral website, EPA WaterSense, LEED, USDA Organic, Vegetarian Mark, Electronic Product Environmental Assessment Tool (EPEAT), Ecotel, Green Globe, SCS Biodegradable, Socially Responsible Investing (SRI), Ethical Investing, Divestment, Negative Screening, Shareholder Activism, Positive Investing, Community Investment, Ethical Fund, Sharing Economy, Giftivism, Pay as your heart feels, Pay as you Wish, Pay what you like, Crowd-sourcing, Crowd-funding, Peer Production, Closed Loop Design, Product as a Service, *Khadi*, *Theertha*, Sustainability MBA, Green MBA, *Grama Seva,* Beyond Grey Pinstripes, Open Courseware.

MULTIPLE-CHOICE QUESTIONS

1. Which of the following is a rating system for electronic products that considers the environmental impact of a product through its life-cycle?
   (a) Fairtrade Certified
   (b) Leaping Bunny
   (c) EPA WaterSense
   (d) GoodWeave
   (e) Electronic Product Environmental Assessment Tool (EPEAT)

2. Which of the following is characteristic of an open-source software?
   (a) A software whose source code is made available in the public domain
   (b) It is always priced
   (c) It is always made available free of cost
   (d) Source code not available for modification
   (e) All open-source softwares are made by not-for-profit organisations

3. Which institution has its vision as '*To assist generations of students acquire Self-knowledge (Atma Vidya) and Self-confidence (Atma Vishwas), so as to cultivate Self-sacrifice and earn Self-realisation; thereby moulding them into leaders who will benefit society.*'?
   (a) Asian Institute of Management
   (b) Kaladi Sanskrit University
   (c) Vishwa Bharathi University
   (d) Sri Sathya Sai Institute of Higher Learning
   (e) London School of Economics
   (f) Kangri Vishwavidyalay

4. Which of the following business school rankings considered the parameters of social, environmental and ethical components in courses offered in an MBA program?
   (a) Beyond Green Berets
   (b) Best MBA School Survey
   (c) Best business schools of the world
   (d) Beyond Grey Pinstripes
   (e) Beyond Red Badges

5. In 1896, when Einstein was in his late teens, he joined the Swiss Federal Institute of Technology (ETH/ SFIT/ SPF/ EPF). Which among the following is a subject (or, were some of the subjects) studied/chosen for study by Einstein at this institute?
   (a) Banking and stock exchange business
   (b) The theory of scientific thought
   (c) The Geometry of Numbers
   (d) Kantian philosophy
   (e) Geology of Mountains

(f) Swiss politics
(g) Anthropology
(h) All of the above

SHORT-ANSWER QUESTIONS

1. What is differential pricing?
2. Differentiate between micro-credit and micro-finance.
3. Mention three attributes of an effective product certification/ label?
4. What are the advantages of a product labeling?
5. List five product certifications/ labels that are popularly recognised in your country.

LONG-ANSWER QUESTIONS

1. With an example, explain 'sharing economy'.
2. Explain 'Socially Responsible Investing'.
3. List the parameters/ criteria that are taken into consideration by different social responsibility labels.

REFLECTIVE QUESTIONS

1. Consider yourself as a fund manager managing a fund that invests on the basis of 'Socially Responsible Investing' principles. You have ten crore rupees with you, and you have decided to invest in fifteen companies. How would you decide the fifteen companies that you are going to invest in? List the principles based on which you will make the allocation? What are the sources of information that will help you to make the decision?
2. Select any product that you have purchased in the past one year. If you were given an opportunity to develop a product label for that product category, what would be the responsibility standards and parameters that you would associate with that label.

WEB-READING

1. List of free and open-source softwares

   https://en.wikipedia.org/wiki/List_of_free_and_open-source_software_packages

ABOUT THE CHAPTER:

1. Learning from the chapter, if any:

2. Topics, concepts, themes, etc. that you may be interested to research/ refer/ study/ ponder upon:

3. Applications in daily life, if any:

Notes:

Chapter 6 completed... You may take a break...

"Polar Pioneer"[69]. This drilling rig, owned by Transocean and manufactured by Hitachi, was built in 1985. Designed to operate in "harsh environment"s such as the Polar Regions, it had a maximum drilling depth of 25,000 feet. The rig was leased to the oil company, Royal Dutch Shell, and it was part of the company till 2015.

A photo of the Arctic region[70].

69 https://commons.wikimedia.org/wiki/File:BSEE_Approves_Limited_Drilling_Activities_in_Arctic_Waters_Under_Rigorous_Safety_Requirements_%2819302173133%29.jpg, Accessed on December 2,2018, Image available in the public domain.

70 https://commons.wikimedia.org/wiki/File:Arctic_Sky_%284371010590%29.jpg, Accessed on December 2,2018, Image available in the public domain.

CASELETS/CASE-STUDIES

WORLD COMMUNITY GRID: A DISTRIBUTED COMPUTING PROJECT BENEFITTING HUMANITY

The Science of Deduction and Analysis is one which can be acquired by long and patient study, nor is life long enough to allow any mortal to attain the highest possible perfection in it.

—Sherlock Holmes[1]

On November 16, 2004, IBM launched World Community Grid (WCG)[2], a public computing grid project that used the idle processing power of thousands of computers to engage in research projects that benefitted humanity, such as finding cures for diseases such as dengue, cancer and ebola, recognising compounds to make cheaper solar cells etc. While distributed computing projects were prevalent even before the launch of WCG, the support of IBM, and the innovations that IBM brought into this project, made WCG one of the most popular distributed computing projects available in the world.

Grid computing projects brought together a number of individuals from different parts of the world who shared the underutilized processing power of their computers for a common cause. The splitting up of work among many people ensured that the research time on these projects is reduced from years to months. For example, the clean energy project designed by Harvard University, and available at WCG, had been expected to shorten the research time to two years from 22 years if done in the conventional manner. A professor from The Scripps Research Institute, the designers of the FightAIDS@Home project available at WCG said, "*World Community Grid has enabled my lab at Scripps to engage in research projects that we would not have attempted in the absence of this powerful public computing grid. It has*

1 It may be noted that Sherlock Holmes is, of course, a fictional character. Arthur Conan Doyle's literary works introduced this character to the world. The above quote, as read by Dr Watson, is from an article titled "*The Book of Life*", written by Sherlock Holmes in a magazine.

2 https://secure.worldcommunitygrid.org/

allowed us to complete complex work in six months that would have taken five years"[3].

The success of WCG – with volunteer registration of approximately seven lakh and more than 30 lakh devices, and clocking a total research time of more than one million years had been significantly attributed to the support provided by IBM, which provided the hardware, software, technical services and expertise *"At IBM, we are committed to creating innovation that matters for our company and for the world. This is a value we live by"*, said a communique from the Corporate Community Relations of the company[4]. Referring to IBM's approach to corporate citizenship activities, its corporate responsibility report for 2013 states, *"Contributions are not connected to any sales transactions. Our contributions align to our business and use the best assets of our business, but are not made with intent to receive any direct benefit back from the recipient, its officers or directors, or to influence their purchasing decisions."*[5]

Presence of IBM brought in an aura of stability and confidence for supporters of WCG. Unlike the earlier public computing grids such as SETI@home[6] and Folding@home[7], WCG provided multiple humanitarian projects under a single umbrella. IBM also addressed security considerations. All files that were exchanged went encrypted. The individual computer, rather than the server, initiated contact. Firewalls and public-private key authentications were incorporated. *"We've had billions of calculations without a single virus to compromise privacy or interfere with the operation of volunteers' computers,"* said an IBM spokesperson[8]. The company also created an Advisory Board, which included experts from the field of health sciences and technology, belonging to research institutions and universities, as well as the U.S. federal government and WHO.

Supporting a massive project like this had helped IBM improve its competence in its grid computing business. This project had also been expected to communicate to customers of IBM, the capability of the company

3 http://www-03.ibm.com/ibm/history/ibm100/us/en/icons/worldgrid/words/, Accessed on June 27, 2015.

4 http://www.uschamber.com/bclc/media/newsletter/ibm_communitygrid.htm, Accessed on May 15, 2009.

5 http://www.ibm.com/ibm/responsibility/2013/at-a-glance/corporate-responsibility.html, Accessed on June 27, 2015.

6 A distributed computing project engaged in observational analysis to detect intelligent life outside Earth.

7 A distributed computing project designed to perform computationally intensive simulations of protein folding and other molecular dynamics.

8 http://www.independent.co.uk/life-style/health-and-families/features/in-10-years-crowdsourced-computing-has-changed-the-world-now-its-tackling-ebola-10311574.html, Accessed on June 27, 2015.

to deploy large-scale grid projects successfully. However, IBM ensured that its presence do not affect the WCG research objectives or results. Only public or not-for-profit organizations can use the platform provided by WCG to reach the volunteers worldwide. Also, all results from the project were published in the public domain. During its tenth anniversary, WCG launched a weblink with the theme "Decade of Discovery"[9], and this link listed the organisation's research accomplishments for a decade.

Questions:

1. Have you tried installing 'World Community Grid' in your computer/ smart-phone? What has been your experience?
2. Discuss examples of information technology companies using technology based CSR projects for public good? Would it be harsh and misinformed to state that CSR projects of these companies are an attempt to deflect citizen-focus on technology related ill-effects on the society?
3. Cite examples of how business organisations use 'big-data'. What are the benefits and advantages? Will the application of 'big-data' involve manipulation of stakeholders?

9 http://www.worldcommunitygrid.org/stat/tenthAnniversary.do, Accessed on June 27, 2015.

AKSHAYA PATRA: THE MID-MAY MEAL PROGRAMME FOR SCHOOL GOING CHILDREN

Akshaya Patra[10], the world's largest mid-day meal program run by a not-for-profit organization, was started in 2000 by serving approximately 1500 school going children in Bangalore, India. In 2009, the organization achieved a landmark of serving one million lunches to the school children. Currently, it feeds approximately 1.5 million children. *Akshaya Patra* also offered its services to people affected during natural calamities like floods and earthquakes. It is also the first NGO managed food programme in the world to receive the FSMS ISO 22000:2005 certification. The project has received an entry in the Limca Book of Records and India Book of Records[11]. The organisation was able to successfully create a partnership model that included governmental funding, contribution from individuals and support from for-profit companies.

Madhu Pandit Dasa, associated with International Society for Krishna Consciousness (ISKCON)[12], Bangalore, was one of the pioneers associated with the endeavour that was pioneered in mid 2000. Speaking about how the idea of scaling up the program came about, he mentioned, "*...we realized that this programme needs to expand to very large scale.... within a radius of 50 kilometers around this center here, there were 300,000 children, going to a school without a meal, in the afternoon.*"[13]

Scaling up the project required optimum usage of resources, both human and material. Akshaya Patra went in for mechanization in its kitchen. Cutting of vegetables were done with the help of machines. The kitchen consisted of a series of steam heated cauldrons. This mechanized and centralized kitchen was set up to prepare food for all the schools in Bangalore that were associated with *Akshaya Patra*. This hub and spoke model was replicated in other regions of India when *Akshaya Patra* started offering its services there. The kitchen at Hubli[14], considered to be one of the largest kitchens in India, cooked more than 180,000 meals daily, with

10 Means a 'Vessel of Abundance' in Sanskrit; from a legend in the Indian epic *Mahabharatha*

11 http://www.akshayapatra.org/news/enter-india-book-of-records, Accessed on June 29, 2015.

12 A faith based organisation, also referred to as the Hare Krishna movement.

13 http://www.bbc.co.uk/mediaselector/check/worldservice/programmes/outlook/meta/dps/2007/07/070718_dasaudio_india?size=au&bgc=003399&lang=en-ws&nbram=1&nbwm=1

14 A city in the state of Karnataka in India.

the total quantity of rice being used amounting to 15 tons (15,000 kgs) and 26,800 litres of *Sambar*[15].

However, when Akshaya Patra started serving rural schools, the centralized model turned out to be ineffective. This was due to the increased transportation costs, associated with dispersed location of schools and difficulty to reach these schools. The concept of decentralization was adopted whereby small individual kitchens were built in villages to serve the local schools. "*We ran a pilot to feed 600 tribal children in five villages of Baran district in April 2005 a self-help group of women was formed in each village and these women were trained in various aspects of cooking, hygiene and nutrition,*" said Madhu Pandit Dasa[16]. This provided employment to monetarily impoverished women from the villages. Sourcing of food materials from local areas also helped in improving the local economy.

Akshaya Patra planned to reach 5 million children by 2020, towards achieving its vision of an India where no child in India shall be deprived of education because of hunger. Media reports referred to the project as a good marriage of missionaries and business people. While the project had its root in faith based beliefs due to its association with ISKCON, the implementation had been secular – the distribution of food (referred to as '*Prasad*,' a sacred offering to the Divine and thus blessed) was done at government schools. An HBR blog cited, "*Akshaya Patra serves as a model for partnerships among public, private, and non-governmental organizations in India and elsewhere...*"[17] **(Refer Table 7.1)**

Table 7.1

List of some of the organisations that contributed to Akshayapatra

Organization	Mode of Contribution
Cisco	Employee volunteering, fund raising
Michael and Susan Dell Foundation	Health Screening and Health Education

15 A lentil based broth popular in southern part of India.

16 http://www.madhupanditdasa.info/akshaya-patras-success-story-in-soul-food-by-rashmi-bansal/, Accessed on October 19, 2016.

17 https://hbr.org/2010/07/breakthrough-innovation-school, Accessed on June 29, 2015.

Jamsetji Tata Trust, Infosys Foundation, Hans Foundation, Texas Instruments, Hyatt Palace Hampi, NMDC, VasudevAdiga's, Cisco, GE Healthcare, SAIL, NALCO, Odisha Mining Corporation, Kusuma Trust, RC Infinity Foundation, Bank of Tokyo-Mitsubishi UFJ, Ltd., GT Foundation, Diya Systems, Westbridge Capital, MTR Foods	Financial grant/ giving
Aris Global Software, BHEL,SAIL,HDFC Life, Texas Instruments, AUMA India, LIC, Syndicate Bank, Corporation Bank, Airbus India, Applied Materials Inc., Caterpillar Inc., IKOCL, State Bank of Travancore,Bosch, Union Bank of India, HPCL, SBI Mutual Fund, Vista Equity Partners, Laurus Labs, Vimta Labs	Vehicles for Food Distribution
SBI Foundation	Insulated vessels for storing food
MINT (SPMCIL) Hyderabad, Caterpillar Inc., SAIL, Alstom	Infrastructure Support (Reverse Osmosis Plant/ Steam Boiler, Waste to Energy Plant etc.)

Akshayapatra had been following the highest standards in financial transparency and complied with International Financial Reporting Standards (IFRS) requirement since 2008-09. The organization won ICAI Gold Shield Award for 'Excellence in Financial Reporting' for five consecutive years starting 2008-09[18] and was thus inducted into the 'Hall of Fame' of Institute of Chartered Accountants of India (ICAI).

The program resulted in increased enrolment and retention of children and enhanced classroom performance among the children, as the nutrition status had shown improvement. *Akshaya Patra* had been considered to be an effective "strategic intervention" that enhanced the value of all prevailing governmental spending on children's education. This was because *Akshaya Patra* catered to the basic need of alleviating hunger, which if not taken care of, will retard any effectiveness on the resources spending on textbooks, school building and other education related infrastructure. "*Akshaya Patra*

18 https://www.akshayapatra.org/five-time-winner-icai-award, Accessed on May 21, 2015.

is one of those organizations that has taken up the important work of handling the nutritional requirements of below-the-poverty-line children in schools because unless your stomach is full, it is very unlikely you will be in a position to concentrate on what is taught," said N R Narayana Murthy, Co-founder, Infosys Technologies Pvt. Ltd.[19]

Toms is a for-profit shoe company founded by Blake Mycoskie. Witnessing children in Argentina running on the streets without footwear, he created TOMS Shoes, a company that donate a pair of shoes for every purchase of shoes made from them. During 2013-2018, Toms Shoes gifted more than 15 lakh shoes to Akshaya Patra beneficiaries across India.

Questions:

1. Akshaya Patra had been known for following the highest standards in financial transparency and reporting. Discuss the benefits of (and, for) a not-for-profit organisation publishing its audited financial reports in the public domain?

2. Have you contributed (money, time, talent, knowledge, physical help etc.) to any not-for-profit organisations? What urged you to make that contribution?

19 http://www.mercurynews.com/2009/11/13/mercury-news-interview-narayana-murthy-of-infosys/, Accessed on July 11, 2017.

B-CORPORATIONS:
INCORPORATING TRIPLE BOTTOM-LINE IN THE LEGISLATIVE DNA

It was in 2007 that B Labs, a non-profit organization headquartered in Berwyn, Pennsylvania, USA launched its pet project - B Corporation (B Corp). B Corp was a certification given to any organization that worked with the objective of promoting the well-being of stakeholders, and not just the shareholders. *"B Corp provides 3 things: standards to define a sustainable company, a legal framework that allows companies to scale and raise capital, and a brand that makes it easy to support and patronize good businesses,"* said Bart Houlahan, co-founder, B Labs[20]. By mid 2018, there were more than 2600 companies certified as B Corp.

Earlier, Houlahan and the other two co-founders, Andrew Kassoy and Jay Coen Gilbert, wanted to start an investment fund that would support sustainable businesses. However, they discovered that the social investment community needed a system that helped people to decide whether a company was really sustainable. Gilbert mentioned, *"It's tough to put your values into action as an investor, as an entrepreneur, and as a consumer. Everybody is saying the same stuff. How am I supposed to know who's the real deal and who's just selling me a story?"* [21]. Thus was born B Ratings. B Ratings helped companies assess the impact of its operations on each of its stakeholders. *"Instead of everybody coming in and trying to reinvent the wheel, it makes sense for this data to be shared and benchmarked,"* said Kassoy[22]. B Ratings involved companies participating in a survey. Taking the survey was the first step for an organization to get certified as a B Corp. Companies that received a rating of more than 80 (the maximum being 200), were eligible to be a B Corp.

B Corp certification resulted in the insertion of sustainable values and practices in the legal framework of a company. The legal framework was modified by changing articles of incorporation and expanding the responsibilities of the company to include the interests of stakeholders like environment, community and employees. The B Corp framework enabled companies to maintain their social mission while deciding to go public, seek funds for expansion, or selling the company. *"Directors and executives*

20 http://insideclimatenews.org/news/20090713/b-corporation-new-way-doing-business, Accessed on June 30, 2015.

21 http://archive.onearth.org/article/the-buzz-about-a-b, Accessed on June 30, 2015.

22 http://www.businessweek.com/globalbiz/blog/globespotting/archives/2009/07/b_labs_and_the.html, Accessed on June 30, 2015.

have more options at the point of sale; they can consider the sales impact on other stakeholders, it isn't only about maximizing shareholder value," said Houlahan.[23]

Relevance[24], a company certified as B Corp, mentioned in a blog that they became B Corp as this certification represented the values held by the company[25]. *"B Corporations are an excellent synthesis of the best innovative thinking of how enterprises can be better organized for both financial return on investment and greater transparency and accountability for social and environmental outcomes,"* said the Managing Director, Rockefeller Foundation[26]. Such optimism had led Gilbert to comment that while the twentieth century belonged to the shareholder corporation, the twenty-first century will be the century of the stakeholder corporation[27].

Questions:

1. *"B Corp certification resulted in the insertion of sustainable values and practices in the legal framework of a company. The legal framework was modified by changing articles of incorporation and expanding the responsibilities of the company to include the interests of stakeholders like environment, community and employees."* Is this a unique practice? If so, how is this unique? State the benefits of this process.

2. Share incidents/ examples that can be considered as standards for a company considering the well-being of community and respect for the natural environment as their important responsibilities, on par with or higher than their responsibility to shareholders?

23 http://insideclimatenews.org/news/20090713/b-corporation-new-way-doing-business, Accessed on June 30, 2015.

24 A software company based in Durham, North Carolina, USA.

25 http://blog.thinkrelevance.com/2009/4/6/relevance-becomes-a-b-corporation, Accessed on June 30, 2015.

26 http://www.csrwire.com/press/press_release/14663-The-Rockefeller-Foundation-Awards-Grant-to-B-Lab, Accessed on June 30, 2015.

27 http://archive.onearth.org/article/the-buzz-about-a-b, Accessed on June 30, 2015.

PATAGONIA AND THE 'DON'T BUY THIS JACKET' CAMPAIGN

Patagonia, Inc. (Patagonia), an outdoor clothing company based in Ventura, California, USA had been in the forefront of incorporating socially and environmentally responsible practices since its founding by Yvon Chouinard in the early 1970s. Patagonia had been a certified B Corporation[28]. In 2011, the company launched the *'Don't Buy This Jacket'* campaign, with a full page advertisement in *The New York Times* and an online campaign, which detailed the negative environmental impacts caused by one of its products, the R2 jacket, and suggested the reader, *"Don't buy what you don't need. Think twice before you buy anything."*[29] The campaign was launched prior to Black Friday and Cyber Monday, the two days that report huge shopping spend in US, offline and online respectively.

Yvon had been known for his quotes like *"Since I'm trying to run this company like it's going to be around a hundred years from now, we have to limit our growth and keep it to what we call 'natural growth'."*[30] This not-so-common belief was visible in the responsibility initiatives prevalent at Patagonia. Since 1996, every cotton garment made in Patagonia was organic. The company has also been a founding member of '1% for the Planet', an alliance of businesses that contributed 1% of its sales to environmental causes.[31] In 2008, the company launched the Footprint Chronicles, an initiative that documented the ecological footprint of every link in the supply chain of a product. Patagonia also provided its employees with a paid two month 'Environmental Internship Program' through which some of the Patagonia employees chose to volunteer full-time with various not-for-profit organisations for a duration of two months. The company takes back its product for recycling, and is also engaged in philanthropic endeavors through grants, etc. The company had been contributing to the creation of a private national park in the Patagonian region, Chile.

Yvon had said, *"In my own personal life, I'm trying to simplify everything... it has to start with each and every one of us to make change in our lives. It's up to each*

---

28 Details about being certified as a B Corp can be found in a section on sustainability labeling, in an earlier chapter of the textbook.

29 http://www.patagonia.com/email/11/112811.html, Accessed on July 4, 2015.

30 http://www.treehugger.com/files/2008/02/the_th_interview_yvon_chouinard.php, Accessed on July 4, 2015.

31 Patagonia donates either 1% of sales revenue or 10% of its pre-tax profits, whichever is higher.

individual to lead an examined life."[32] This exploration to lead an examined life also led Patagonia to launch the "Don't Buy This Jacket" advertisement campaign. The advertisement had a picture of one of its jackets. Inviting attention to this picture, the advertisement mentioned, "...*Consider the R2 Jacket shown, one of our best sellers. To make it required 135 liters of water, enough to meet the daily needs (three glasses a day) of 45 people. Its journey from its origin as 60% recycled polyester to our Reno warehouse generated nearly 20 pounds of carbon dioxide, 24 times the weight of the finished product. This jacket left behind, on its way to Reno, two-thirds its weight in waste. And this is a 60% recycled polyester jacket...*". The advertisement also conveyed that while the jacket is durable and recyclable, it carried an environmental cost that is higher than its price.

An article in Adweek.com commented, "*As with almost any environmental appeal from a big corporation, the ad is, of course, hypocritical. Patagonia isn't totally altruistic. It's a company, it wants to grow, and it will continue to harm the environment in the process. Yet this isn't greenwashing. It comes off as a genuine attempt to get people to start thinking about sustainable consumption.*"[33] Criticisms ranged from reader comments such as "*If you (Patagonia) really believe in that ad, cap your annual sales at X and refuse to sell more once you reach that number. That would demonstrate your opposition to consumerism much more than feigning opposition in the New York Times.*" and "...*what a joke. How about shutting down your website on 'cyber Monday' – that'd send a real message*".[34]

In an equipment catalog, dated October 1974, Yvon Chouinard & Tom Frost[35] mentioned about the necessity to preserve the vertical wilderness and the adventure, to ensure the sustenance of climbing experiences. They said, "...*the only insurance to guarantee this adventure and the safest insurance to maintain it is exercise of moral restraint and individual responsibility. Thus, it is the style of the climb, not the attainment of the summit, which is the measure of personal success. Traditionally stated, each of us must consider whether the end is more important than the means. Given the vital importance of style, we suggest that the keynote is simplicity. The fewer gadgets between the climber and the climb, the greater the chance to attain the desired communication with oneself — and nature.*"[36]

---

32 http://www.grist.org/article/little-chouinard/, Accessed on July 4, 2015.

33 http://www.adweek.com/news/advertising-branding/ad-day-patagonia-136745, Accessed on July 4, 2015.

34 http://www.thecleanestline.com/2011/11/dont-buy-this-jacket-black-friday-and-the-new-york-times.html, Accessed on July 4, 2015.

35 A rock climber and photographer.

36 http://www.patagonia.com/us/patagonia.go?assetid=3316, Accessed on July 1, 2015.

Questions:

1. Yvon Chouinard speaks about 'natural growth' and limiting the growth of the company. What could be the 'natural growth' for Patagonia? What could be the optimum size for Patagonia?

2. Yvon speaks about the necessity to consider whether the 'end' is more important than the 'means'. Have you had any personal experience where you felt that 'means' is as important, or, more important than the 'end'? Reflect on the same.

ECOSIA – BEING A RESPONSIBLE BUSINESS

Ecosia, a CO_2 neutral web-search site, has planted almost one crore (10 million) tree saplings. Every search done on Ecosia contributes to the planting of tree saplings. These tree saplings were planted in the regions of Brazil, Burkino Faso, Ghana, Indonesia, Madagascar, Morocco, Nicaragua, Peru and Tanzania. Between December 2009 and March 2015, the website donated 2,482,669 Euro towards planting these saplings. The company, which started in 2009, planted the ten million tree saplings by 2017, and has announced that it will plant a billion tree saplings by 2020.

Figure 7.1

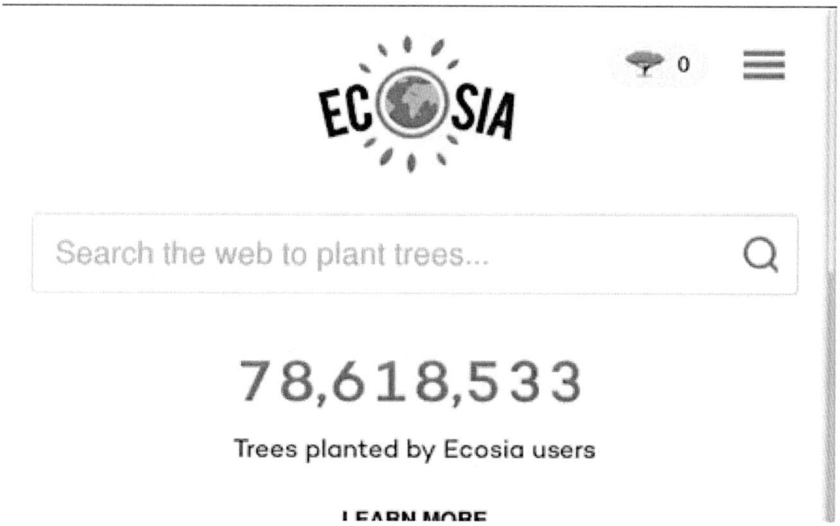

The homepage of the Ecosia search website.[37]

Founded by Christian Kroll, Ecosia generated money from advertisements displayed as part of the search results. In addition to the banner advertisements, it also generated revenue from 'ecolinks'. "*...These lead to retail websites. If we are the reason why a user accesses such sites and orders something from them, we receive a commission,*" said an Ecosia employee[38]. "*Thanks to sponsored links, search engines earn billions every year,*" said Christian. "*Ecosia believes that there is a more eco-friendly way of using these huge profits and that the money should better be used to fight global warming.*"[39]

37 Accessed on December 25, 2019.

38 https://www.goethe.de/en/kul/ges/20446262.html, Accessed on July 9, 2015.

39 http://www.theguardian.com/environment/2009/dec/03/ecosia-green-search-

This search site is owned by Ecosia GmbH, which is a social business company based at Berlin, Germany. During its initial phases, Ecosia used to donate 80% of its revenues, and this shifted to donating 80% of its surplus income. In 2016, Ecosia was donating approximately half of its cash inflow towards tree planting programs.[40] Renewable energy powered the website servers at Ecosia[41]. Ecosia kept aside approximately 10% of its inflows as reserves for developing new projects, and these were invested in GLS, a German co-operative bank.

The organization has associated with a number of not-for-profits since its inception. Some of them included 'The Nature Conservancy', World Wide Fund for Nature (WWF), 'The Friends of Usambara Society', 'The Eden Projects', 'Entrepreneurs Without Borders (OZG)', WeForest etc.

In 2014, the company became a 'Certified B Corporation', a certification that indicates an organisation's evidence-based-commitment to all its stakeholders including society, planet, and employees.[42] "*...the good thing about Ecosia is that we don't have investors or shareholders that would force us to go for revenue optimization... Our main mission is to help the environment, it's not just something to do on the side; it's the foundation that the whole company is built on,*" said Christian.[43]

Questions

1. "*Our main mission is to help the environment, it's not just something to do on the side; it's the foundation that the whole company is built on*". Do you feel that such a perspective is unique? How is it different from the existing notions and practices about corporate social responsibility?

2. Search sites such as Duckduckgo.com has referred to non-tracking the user of their website as their unique operating aspect. The Ecosia website says, "*We don't sell your data to advertisers, have no third party trackers and anonymize all searches within one week*". How do you consider aspects related to 'privacy' while browsing the internet?

---

engine, Accessed on March 13, 2015.

40 https://www.dropbox.com/sh/l45p3wry5u80z1i/AACxzlMBa5ZWK3MwYK9FHD4ha?dl=0, Accessed on October 17, 2016.

41 https://www.goethe.de/en/kul/ges/20446262.html, Accessed on March 13, 2015.

42 http://www.csrwire.com/press_releases/37004-Search-Engine-Ecosia-Awarded-B-Corp-Status, Accessed on October 16, 2016.

43 http://www.latinpost.com/articles/4164/20131129/green-google-alternative-ecosia-founder-christian-kroll-search-engine.htm, Accessed on March 13, 2015.

3. Examine the diverse businesses that a search-business company (and, their parental companies, if applicable) engage with. What implications will this have on your choices related to 'privacy', and sharing of personal data and information with these companies?

4. Ecosia has planted many tree saplings. If you are given an opportunity to plant tree saplings, how will you choose the tree saplings to be planted? List the parameters, and you may assign scores/ weightages, if you wish so.

5. Using the web-search sites and internet involves consumption of power (electricity). It was reported that a popular social-media company operates one of their data-stoage centres near the polar region. Generation and distribution of power involves various hazards, involving societal and environmental impacts. Discuss the advantages and disadvantages of web-usage from a societal and environmental perspective.

6. Every transaction online, for example, sending emails, is, or, can be, tracked by a a human, or, an application ("app"). In such a context, how relevant and valid is discussions and deliberations related to online privacy?

7. Discuss some of the examples of online privacy intrusions made by applications ("apps") and softwares. There was a discussion in the Indian Parliament about "foreign probing satellites" that were congesting the geostationary orbit. What are the roles of such foreign probing satellites?

8. *The Panchatantra*, a treatise on statecraft, says,

   "Until you have full information

   Of prowess, character, and station

   To no man let your trust be given –

   Such is the current saw in heaven"

   What are the implications of such statecraftly wisdom for a user of information–technology enabled businesses (ITEBs)?

DR V AND ARAVIND EYE CARE SYSTEM

Aravind Eye Care System (Aravind), based in Madurai, India, had been the most productive and largest eye care organization in the world, in terms of surgical volume and the number of patients treated. The initiatives of Dr Govindappa Venkataswamy (Dr V) made Aravind an organization that was referred as the "gem at the bottom of the pyramid" by C K Prahalad[44]. He said, *"I don't insist upon that the man (patient) must pay me before i do anything for him. I say, I'll give you the sight man. Let him give whatever he can give. If he cannot afford, doesn't matter, he can give later. So priority is for human welfare"*.[45]

After retirement, Dr V founded the Aravind Eye Care Hospital (the first initiative of Aravind) at Madurai, in 1976. The mission of Dr V was to eradicate needless blindness and he wanted to bring eye care facilities to the maximum number of people. The initial expenses towards his endeavor were met by mortgaging his house. It started as an eleven bedded hospital manned by four medical officers.

Considering the staggering numbers affected by blindness and their lack of access to financial resources, there was a need for Dr V to adopt an innovative approach. He dreamt of doing surgeries the way McDonald's sells hamburgers. *"See..., the McDonalds concept is simple. They feel they can train people all over the world... to produce a product in the same way and deliver it in the same manner in hundreds of places. Supposing I'm able to produce eye care techniques, methods, all those things in the same way and make it available in every corner of the world, the problem of blindness is gone,"* said Dr V.

Aravind followed the principle that large volume, with optimum service levels, resulted in low cost operations, yet sustainable. At Aravind, doctors were exclusively devoted to performing eye operations and taking medical decisions. All administrative work was carried out by others. Operation theatres were designed in a manner that facilitated the doctors to move easily between two tables – at Aravind, two or more patients were kept in the operating room at the same time. As soon as the doctor finished the first operation, the next patient was ready for the operation. This resulted in a system where the doctors at Aravind performed an average of approximately 2,200 surgeries annually compared with a national average of approximately 250 surgeries. The cost of a cataract surgery at Aravind

---

44 https://www.dnaindia.com/business/report-google-s-co-founder-larry-page-has-an-eye-on-madurai-1046349, Accessed on October 4, 2018.

45 https://www.youtube.com/watch?v=4Mg3-eOQYYQ, Accessed on August 14, 2015.

was approximately $10, the lowest in the world, while a comparable surgery could cost $1650 in United States.[46] The amount of wastage in the operating room of Aravind is approximately ten percent of what normally occurs in US.[47]

The hospitals were named after Sri Aurobindo[48], a spiritual leader. "*I remember my professor of anatomy in medical school. He used to push all his students to do better and better. From him I heard for the first time the word Yoga for perfection. Whether it was sharpening a scalpel, studying or dissection he said that one should always aspire to "do Yoga". These things helped me, these things became a part of me. Discipline became a part of me, hard work became a part of me and the aspiration for perfection too became a part of my nature,*" said Dr V[49]. This work ethos soon took Aravind to nobler heights.

Between April 2008 and March 2009, Aravind Eye Hospitals had a total of 2,748,216 outpatient visits. Out of the 309,015 surgical and laser procedures, 162,809 procedures were conducted for free (52.7%). The volume-driven paid services contributed towards the free medical services. Between April 2014 and May 2015, the number of free surgeries were 92,816 (23%), whereas subsidised surgeries were 110,290 (27.6%) and paid surgeries were 198,423 (49.4%). In this period, the total outpatient visits were 3,522,527, of which 45% were done free of cost. As of 2015, Aravind consisted of ten hospitals (at Madurai, Theni, Tirunelveli, Coimbatore, Pondicherry, Dindigul, Tirupur, Salem, Tuticorin and Udumalpet), a manufacturing centre for ophthalmic products (Aurolab)[50], a research foundation (AMRF) and a resource and training centre (LAICO). The model of Aravind had been replicated in more than 30 countries.

Dr V performed more than 100,000 successful eye surgeries. He also pioneered outreach programmes through eye camps. Dr V passed away in 2006. "*Our effort is to make Aravind an instrument of the Divine Will. We strive to forget our limitations and work with the direction of the Divine Will, not in a vain superficial way but with a deep commitment and faith that guidance comes from a higher level of consciousness. Then one is able to work with the great*

46 http://www.fastcompany.com/node/42111/print, Accessed on August 14, 2015.

47 http://www.aravind.org/content/downloads/aecsreport201415.pdf, Accessed on August 14, 2015.

48 http://www.sriaurobindoashram.org/ashram/sriauro/index.php, Accessed on August 14, 2015.

49 As mentioned in the activity report of Arvind Eye Care System for year 2008-09.

50 Aurolab's high quality ophthalmic consumables are primarily supplied to non-profit eye care programs. Aurolab produced intraocular lenses (IOLs) for approximately five dollars, when it costed USD 200 in developed countries.

confidence that comes only with that faith and realization that we are all part of a spiritual capacity or spiritual power. It is then that all of nature works with you. You don't feel that you are a superior being but you are an instrument in the hands of a higher force and it is in that spirit that we meet our day to day struggles and successes," said Dr V[51].

Questions

1. *"...priority is for human welfare"*, says Dr V. How was this expressed in the day-to-day operations of the Arvind Hospitals?
2. Refer the annual report of Aravind Eye Care System. Has the organisation been able to continue with the spiritual and human values that Dr V has been referring to?

51 http://www.aravind.org/aboutus/genesis.asp, Accessed on July 12, 2017.

PEACEWORKS – BUSINESS ACROSS BORDERS

PeaceWorks Holdings LLC (PeaceWorks), a 'not-only-for-profit' company was founded by Daniel Lubetzky (Lubetzky) in 1994. The company offered healthy food products while also creating co-operative businesses among the communities that are on the opposing sides of the conflict in the conflict-prone and distressed regions of the world. PeaceWorks had been doing business with communities in Egypt, Indonesia, Israel, Palestine, South Africa, Sri Lanka and Turkey. Lubetzky considers a 'not-only-for-profit' company as *"a business entity that explicitly and practically sets out to not just make money but also achieve some positive societal impact"*[52].

PeaceWorks promotes the Meditalia[53] range of tapenades[54] and pestos[55]. The products did not have preservatives and additives. The products were vegan or vegetarian, kosher[56], gluten-free and cholestrol-free. *"Meditalia spreads are produced in an Israeli factory south of Tel Aviv, using olives, basil and other fresh ingredients grown by Palestinian farmers in both Israel and the West Bank. The company also sources sun-dried tomatoes and glass jars from Turkey"*, says Leah Koenig, a culinary critic[57]. Leah notes that these business partnerships existed also because of the trading relationships that existed between Palestine and Israel for more than a generation.

One of the products of PeaceWorks was the healthy snack brand 'Kind', started by Lubetzky in 2004. Unhappy with the snacking options that were available, Lubetzky attempted to create 'Kind' bars "out of recognizable, unprocessed ingredients like real fruit and whole nuts".[58] *"I had been traveling a lot for PeaceWorks, my first company, and I was frustrated with the food choices on the road. I was always eating things that were either healthy and tasted like cardboard or were tasty and too indulgent."*[59] An article states that *"Lubetzky long ago nixed cutesy product names, instead opting for simple descriptions of what each bar contains"*. *"We don't come up with product names*

52 http://blog.peaceworks.net/2007/08/definition-not-only-for-profit/, Accessed on September 27, 2017.

53 http://meditaliafoods.com/

54 A popular dish from France, where it is eaten as a spread on bread.

55 A sauce from Italy.

56 Food that ascribe to Jewish dietary law.

57 http://forward.com/articles/154952/boycotting-israel-and-my-olive-tapenade/

58 ttps://www.fastcompany.com/3023368/kind-snacks-setting-a-high-bar, Accessed on September 24, 2017.

59 https://www.inc.com/magazine/20101201/the-way-i-work-daniel-lubetzky-of-kind.html, Accessed on September 27, 2017.

like 'Cookie Sugar à la Mode," says Lubetzky[60]. 'Kind' is now an independent venture. The website of Peaceworks states, 'Kind Healthy Snacks is no longer a part of PeaceWorks. We are very proud that Kind has gone on to become the fastest growing brand in the energy bar category!'[61].

PeaceWorks contracted out the production aspects related to their products to various organisations. "*We manage the relationships, start the ventures, own the brands and the formulas and work with local partners to produce a product - that is our model,*" said Lubetzky[62]. These factors helped the company to nurture and support organizations that were willing to work in concert with people from other countries that were in conflict with them. An organization seeking to work with PeaceWorks had to meet the social criteria of promoted co-operative relationships. "*We work with people who believe in what we do. We want to cement and strengthen and expand on good will and go to Israelis and Palestinians who are willing to begin exploring how they can collaborate,*" mentioned Lubetzky[63].

"*There are, of course, serious challenges inherent to this type of culture and country-crossing venture - particularly when conflict flare-ups decrease mobility across borders,*"[64] says Leah Koenig. She adds that "*...the growers and factory workers involved with producing Meditalia often feel pressure to keep their joint efforts quiet, lest they attract negative attention*"[65].

PeaceWorks donated a minimum of five percent of its profits to empower the voices of the moderates in the conflict regions of the Middle Eastern countries. "*I think business plays a very important role and has a big responsibility. If it plays an amoral role or an uninvolved role then we're missing out on a lot of the potential market,*" said Lubetzky[66].

60 https://www.fastcompany.com/3023368/kind-snacks-setting-a-high-bar, Accessed on September 24, 2017.

61 http://www.peaceworks.com/, Accessed on September 24, 2017.

62 http://press.onevoicemovement.org/2008/01/talking-to-daniel-lubetzky-founder-of-peaceworks-and-onevoice/, Accessed on October 4, 2009.

63 http://press.onevoicemovement.org/2008/01/talking-to-daniel-lubetzky-founder-of-peaceworks-and-onevoice/, Accessed on October 4, 2009.

64 http://forward.com/articles/154952/boycotting-israel-and-my-olive-tapenade/, Accessed on October 2, 2017.

65 http://forward.com/articles/154952/boycotting-israel-and-my-olive-tapenade/, Accessed on October 2, 2017.

66 http://press.onevoicemovement.org/2008/01/talking-to-daniel-lubetzky-founder-of-peaceworks-and-onevoice/, Accessed on October 4, 2009.

Questions

1. How do businesses contribute to maintaining cordial relationships between neighbouring countries? Provide examples, supported by economic data.

2. Read through the criteria document related to 'Peaceworks Partners of Peace' (available at https://peaceworks.com/bizWithUs/partnersForPeace.html). In addition to Peaceworks, are you aware of companies that consider similar parameters while engaging with other business organiations? If yes, share details about such companies.

'LENTIL AS ANYTHING' RESTAURANTS, AN IDIOT'S VISIT TO THE MARKET, AND, A KING'S PROCLAMATION

"Food responds to our soul's dream, as to our stomach's appetite"
—Joseph Delteil[67] (1894-1798)

'Lentil As Anything' (Lentil) is a chain of not-for-profit vegetarian restaurants. In mid 2018, the restaurants operated in the city of Melbourne and Sydney.. The restaurants operates through an honour-system where visitors can choose how much they would like to pay. *"The Australian pay-as-you-feel restaurant chain Lentil as Anything is a brilliant lighthouse shining hope to the rapidly-growing global village of people who value people over profits,"* says an article[68]. Lentil has been ranked amongst the top restaurants in Australia that considers ethical, social and environmental responsibility parameters[69].

'Lentil As Anything' was started by Anthony Fernando ('Shanaka Fernando'[70], who spend his childhood and teens in Sri Lanka[71]. He opened the first restaurant at St Kilda, Australia in 2000. Through the years, the services of the organisation have increased. Lentil unit at Thornbury offers a community hall, named 'Common Ground' on the 'pay-as-you-feel' donation mode. The organization has also been recognised by the community. The restaurant at Newtown has won an award for sustainable innovation and was commended for community leadership[72]. Lentil has also been considered an apt setting to converse on human values. Many educational institutions arrange student visits to Lentil[73].

67 A French poet. It is said that, at the facade of his house at Languedoc, it was inscribed "Live Humbly", probably, a Confucian influence on the poet. However, later searches, in the years following his death, has not yet been able to unearth these.

68 http://www.sparklingadventures.com/index.php?id=2060, Accessed on October 10, 2016.

69 https://www.unisa.edu.au/Global/business/management/CTLM/Sustainability_report_FINAL_22-9-15.pdf, Accessed on October 16, 2016.

70 https://www.magistratescourt.vic.gov.au/sites/default/files/fernando%2Bdecision.pdf, Accessed on October 15, 2016.

71 http://lentilasanything.com/about/, Accessed on October 9, 2016.

72 https://www.marrickville.nsw.gov.au/Global/Council/News%20and%20notices/Marrickville%20Matters/Autumn%202015/MMAutumn15.pdf, Accessed on October 15, 2016.

73 http://www.mercy.edu.au/_uploads/rsfil/000739_adee.pdf, Accessed on October 15, 2016.

Lentil is driven by volunteers. Paid staff is lower in number. The Lentil restaurants invite volunteer participation in various roles. One of the volunteer says, "*The staff was extremely friendly and grateful that I was there to help out, as were the rest of the volunteers, whose ages varied greatly, along with their countries of origin. One gentleman was around 65 and lived just up the street, and another girl around my age was from France. All of us were there for the same reason: to dedicate our time to assist those who were experiencing hardship in their lives.*"[74] The 'pay-as-you-wish' concept has attracted many to this restaurant. "*There are no cash registers here - no waiters handing out bills. There's just a little wooden box asking for donations - whatever you feel your meal is worth.*" mentions a posting in a blog referring to a volunteer comment.[75]

Some of the ways through which the organization attempts to raise revenue is through offering catering services for external events. It also sells merchandise such as T-shirts, books, bags, clocks and mugs. Lentil also charges for an advanced table reservation. Various organisations also conduct their informal gatherings at Lentil[76].

Lentil restaurants offered a mix of 'a la carte' and buffet option, depending on the time and the day of the week. Lentil offered vegetarian cuisine that included preparations from various regions of the world. Shanaka Fernando considered a vegetarian or a vegan menu as a representation of inclusiveness. He said, "*Jewish people can come and eat without having to worry about (the food not being Kosher); Muslims can come and eat without having to worry about Halal, and anyone can enjoy a vegetarian meal...*"[77] The restaurants also provided food options that were fully plant-based. It also offered gluten-free options.

Visitors have generally been appreciative of the restaurant. A lady donated a portion of her 35 hectare farmland to Lentil towards growing and providing food ingredients. However, through its history, some of the Lentil units have closed due to financial non-viability. These include the Brunswick, Belgrave, Collingwood, Lentil as Africa, and Lentil at Fed Square units. The life span of these eateries ranged from one year to eight

74 http://capaworld.capa.org/lentil-as-anthing-volunteering-abroad-in-sydney, Accessed on October 15, 2016.

75 https://themelbournelocal.wordpress.com/2014/05/08/lentil-as-anything/, Accessed on October 10, 2016.

76 http://www.cimaglobal.com/Documents/Our%20locations%20docs/Australia/Events%202015/20151107VICXmas.pdf, Accessed on October 15, 2016.

77 http://www.moustachemagazine.com/2014/02/one-big-fat-international-family-lentil-as-anything/, Accessed on October 10, 2016.

years. There have been references to instances where people who can afford to pay, chose not to[78].

"If people can afford to give, they should - if customers can pay, we need them to donate." said the restaurant manager at the Newtown outlet[79]. Such assertion has helped in drawing attention to the necessity of financial support for sustenance of these restaurants, which has been helping the migrants, refugees, people with disabilities and the long-term unemployed[80]. *"There's no pressure for anyone to pay a certain amount. People pay what they can afford. People come in with a $50 note and ask for change and we say don't worry, pay another time,"* says a volunteer at the Sydney outlet[81]. The restaurant has been trying to communicate that the diners should not just calculate what the food costs at the restaurant will be. *"What we say is, 'Pay what you feel the whole experience is worth' – the food is part of that, but so too is the music, the shelter and the smiling faces,"* said the operations manager at the Footscray unit[82] (**Refer figure 7.2**).

Lentil has been a theme included in educational materials[83][84][85][86]. In a talk given in 2012, Shanaka Fernando mentioned, *"I want to submit myself to the people around me... We fight for freedom. We sent armies overseas - to protect our freedom... But do we recognise freedom when it is presented to us? Do we value it, do we treat it with care and responsibility?"*[87]

78 http://www.goodfood.com.au/eat-out/news/lean-takings-as-tightwad-diners-exploit-lentil-as-anythings-philosophy-20150208-138wvk, Accessed on October 9, 2016.

79 http://www.dailytelegraph.com.au/business/small-business/lentil-as-anything-in-trouble-as-cheapskates-take-advantage-of-restaurants-charity/news-story/1973fd606b162b0ff091fae0e4af76cd, Accessed on October 9, 2016.

80 http://www.multicultural.vic.gov.au/images/stories/documents/awards-for-excellence-book-2011.pdf, Accessed on October 15, 2016.

81 http://www.notquitenigella.com/2014/05/27/lentil-as-anything-sydney/, Accessed on October 10, 2016.

82 http://www.starweekly.com.au/news/lentil-as-anything-facing-tough-times/, Accessed on October 10, 2016.

83 https://www.border.gov.au/Citizenship/Documents/secondary_school_teaching_resourceV2.pdf, Accessed on October 15, 2016.

84 http://www.parade.vic.edu.au/Documents/Newsletters/Archive/NL%207%20-%202015.pdf, Accessed on October 15, 2016.

85 http://www.dlscronulla.catholic.edu.au/Documents/Document%20Library/Newsletters/Issue%2015.pdf, Accessed on October 15, 2016.

86 http://www.msj.vic.edu.au/_uploads/rsfil/000277_dafc.pdf, Accessed on October 15, 2016.

87 http://tedxtalks.ted.com/video/Universal-pay-as-you-feel-Shana, Accessed on October 18, 2016.

Figure 7.2

LENTIL AS ANYTHING

FOOD • CULTURE • COMMUNITY

HOW MUCH SHOULD I CONTRIBUTE?

Did you know that the money you contribute is our **sole source of income**?

We receive **no external funding**, buy the majority of our ingredients and have all the **usual running costs of a restaurant.**

$5 or under — This doesn't cover the cost of your meal and drink but we have many other ways you can contribute...

What about volunteering for a shift to help cover the rest?

$12 — Your meal and drink are covered, and with your contribution we can also pay our **wages** and running costs such as **gas, electricity and rent**

But we still have many other overheads such as **equipment servicing**, administrative fees, **maintenance**, and delivery and vehicle costs

Are you an artist, musician or handy-person? We have an endless list of projects we need help with

$15 — We made it! All our expenses are covered.

Lentil can continue to smoothly run for years to come!

But you know what we say ***"Everybody deserves a place at the table"***

$20.. - Offer someone who can't afford it a **place at the table** by paying for their meal

$30.. - Help an **asylum seeker** find their feet in a new country and find a new chance in life

$50... - Offer the disadvantaged and **long-term unemployed** a community, valuable training, experience and a job

Thank you so much for your contribution....

No matter what form it takes.

KUKURI AND HIS EXPERIENCE AT THE MARKETPLACE

Nodar Dumbadze (1928 – 1984) was a writer from Georgia. In one of his writings, he introduces Kukuri, a youthful character. It is not known whether Dumbadze has known Kukuri in person or whether Kukuri is a fictional character. The writings of Dumbadze mentions, *"In the autumn of 1941, Kukuri and his horse were drafted into the army"*. The narration refers to the second world war, and many youths were enlisted into armed forces. Dumbadze's writings mentions that a month before the enlistment of Kukuri and his horse into the army, an interesting incident had occurred.[88]

One Sunday morning, Kukuri drove his only cow to the market. He tied her to a plane tree and then sat down on a boulder. His barefoot sister Natela sat down next to him.

No one was interested in buying the animal, but there was no end to the questions.

> *"How much do you want for the cow, Kukuri?*
> *"How much milk does she give?"*
> "Is the cow's milk rich, Kukuri?"
> *"What's her name?"*

Some of the questions Kukuri answered, others he ignored.

Finally Anania Nibladze arrived, a man who, if he so desired, could have purchased the entire market, much less the cow.

"Is she for sale, young man?"

"Yes, Respected Anania." Kukuri answered, rising.

"How much are you asking for her?"

"Three thousand, Respected Anania."

"That's a lot"

"I know"

"If you know, then lower the price"

"Respected Anania, money is only paper to you, but to me this cow is my entire fortune"

88 This excerpt is an English translation from the original and the translation was published by Raduga Publishers, which ceased to exist with the dissolution of Soviet Union. The translation to English was done by Tracy Kuehn.

"Why are you selling her?" Anania asked smiling, and looked complacently at those who had gathered.

Kukuri did not answer.

"I asked you a question!"

"Do you see that little girl in rags, Respected Anania?" Kukuri asked, indicating Natela.

"Two thousand five hundred"

"She hasn't gone to school for a month because she doesn't have shoes or a decent dress."

"Sell it to him. He's offering a good price!" Someone advised.

"A good price? Will you feed my mother and sister after i leave for the army?" Kukuri snapped at the man.

"Two thousand eight hundred!" Anania said, pulling a wad of bills out of his pocket. Kukuri stared at the huge hundred-ruble notes as if bewitched.

"Take her", he said.

Anania quickly counted out the money and handed it to Kukuri. The young man counted it carefully and then wrapped it neatly in newspaper and put it in his pocket. Anania untied the cow and turned to his neighbour standing next to him.

"What do you think, Akaky? Will it be enough for sixty people? We're going to put a new roof on my house tomorrow."

"I doubt it, Respected Anania"

"But we're also having suckling pig and turkey."

"Then of course it's enough"

"It's a cow, after all", Anania said, slapping the animal's back.

Kukuri looked at Anania and then at his neighbour in astonishment. Suddenly his lips paled and his nostrils flared.

"Why are you buying a cow, Respected Anania?"

Anania burst out laughing.

"What do you mean, why? To butcher!" His neighbour answered for him.

"To butcher?" Anania asked, surprised.

Kukuri immediately pulled the bundle out of his pocket.

"Here is your money, Respected Anania. I'm returning it. How could you butcher a cow?"

"Have you gone crazy?"

"No, Respected Anania, but I'd sooner let you butcher me than my cow!"

Kukuri cautiously took the rope out of Anania's hand, stuffed the money in the man's pocket, and turned to his sister, *"Take the cow home."*

"I'll give you three thousand!" Anania said.

"I said take her home"

"Three thousand two hundred."

"I won't sell her, Respected Anania."

"Three thousand five hundred!"

Natela stopped. Kukuri looked at her bare feet, then at the money, then at Anania, and finally at the cow, He did not utter a word. People anxiously awaited the outcome.

"Didn't you hear me?" Kukuri suddenly exploded. *"Go home this minute!"*, he shouted at his confused sister and shoved the animal.

And the cow started for home, with Kukuri behind her.

"What a dolt!", Anania said.

"He's simply an idiot!" someone else added.

Dumbadze also mentions about the enlistment process to the war. *"A meeting was held in the yard next to the office. People gave patriotic speeches, waved small flags and banners, and recited poetry. A local poet recited a poem by the great Akaky Tsereteli, claiming it was his own. That poet also went to war with Kukuri and his horse, and none of them returned."*

THE PROCLAMATION OF KING BIMBISARA

One of the works of Edwin Arnold, a poet and journalist[89], is *'The Light of Asia'*. The below is an excerpt from this book, and is in the contextual reference to Buddha, when during his wanderings in one of the kingdoms of northern India (Magadha), visits the king of that region (Bimbisara[90]),

89 Edwin Arnold (1832-1904) was also a school teacher in Birmingham, and the principal of a college at Poona (Pune).

90 Bimbisara (approx. 500 BCE) was the king of Magadha, a region in the state of Bihar in India. He lived during the times of Gautama Buddha and Vardhamana Mahavira,

during a sacrifice that was to result in the death of many four-legged beings that provides "milk and wool", as mentioned in the passage.

> ...But Buddha softly said,
> "Let him not strike, great King!" and therewith loosed
> The victim's bonds, none staying him, so great
> His presence was. Then, craving leave, he spake
> Of life, which all can take but none can give,
> Life, which all creatures love and strive to keep,
> Wonderful, dear and pleasant unto each...
>
> ...Unto the dumb lips of his flock he lent
> Sad pleading words, showing how man, who prays
> For mercy to the gods, is merciless,
> Being as god to those; albeit all life
> Is linked and kin, and what we slay have given
> Meek tribute of the milk and wool, and set
> Fast trust upon the hands which murder them.
> Also he spake of what the holy books
> Do surely teach...
>
> ...The fixed arithmic of the universe,
> Which meteth good for good and ill for ill,
> Measure for measure, unto deeds, words, thoughts;
> Watchful, aware, implacable, unmoved;
> Making all futures fruits of all the pasts.
> Thus spake he...,
>
> ...Which when these heard,
> The might of gentleness so conquered them,
> The priests themselves scattered their altar-flames
> And flung away the steel of sacrifice;
>
> And through the land next day passed a decree
> Proclaimed by criers, and in this wise graved
> On rock and column: "Thus the King's will is:
> There hath been slaughter for the sacrifice,

And slaying for the meat, but henceforth none
Shall spill the blood of life nor taste of flesh,
Seeing that knowledge grows, and life is one,
And mercy cometh to the merciful."

Questions

1. Have you visited any 'Pay-as-you-wish' restaurants? If so, share experiences of your visit.
2. "Valuing people over profits". Have you noticed examples of this principle in practice in your surroundings? If so, share details.
3. If you happen to visit a 'Pay as you wish' restaurant similar to 'Lentil as Anything', how will you decide on the payment?
4. Shanaka Fernando mentions about the importance of connecting freedom with care and responsibility. List out any three instances where you had the freedom to make choices. What are the ways through which those instances may be improvised by connecting to care and responsibility?
5. The article mentions that volunteers contributed significantly to 'Lentil as Anything'. Volunteering is a non-paid activity. What are the ways through which volunteers contribute to (a) family, (b) nation-building, and (c) strengthening values such as honesty, integrity, service and compassion?
6. Examine, ponder, introspect and contemplate on the ethical and moral values, principles and dilemmas that you were introduced to, evolved or learned from the three sections of the caselet.

	Ethical Dilemma	Principles and Values	Application to one's life
Lentil as Anything			
Kukuri's Cow and the Nature of Market-place			
Proclamation of the king			

PATANJALI'S EMERGENCE AS AN FMCG MAJOR

Patanjali Ayurved, based in Haridwar, has been a late entrant into the consumer goods market in India. The popularity of the company rose in mid 2010s with the launch of a number of consumer food products including *atta* noodles (which used less refined flour (*maida*) and more whole wheat flour (*atta*)) and biscuits (that avoided *maida).* The organisation's portfolio covered personal care, oral care, home cleaning, food products and Ayurvedic products. One of the reasons for the growth and success of the company has been attributed to its social responsibility outlook.

The name 'Patanjali Ayurved' has been attributed to the yogic saint from India, Patanjali, and to the traditional medicinal system of India, Ayurveda. It was founded in 2006 by Baba Ramdev and Acharya Balkrishna. Prior to that, they had founded a charitable trust in 1995, and distributed Ayurvedic and herbal medicines. The yoga classes held by Baba Ramdev had been attracting a mass following, in India and abroad. Participants were also able to seek counsel from Ayurvedic doctors in these camps and Ayurvedic medicines were distributed. In 2018, it was announced that Patanjali Ayurved is registered as a non-profit charitable trust[91].

The print advertisements from Patanjali communicated a swadeshi and patriotic theme (**Refer Figure 7.3**)[92]. Patanjali exhorted people to start business enterprises that contributes to the well-being of nation. The organisation's newspaper advertisement inviting franchise application also communicated a swadeshi and patriotic theme. "*Not just as consumers but also as entrepreneurs, they prefer our stores and products,*" said the department head - swadeshi vibhag, Patanjali Ayurved[93]. Patanjali franchise store outlets had a minimum area of 300 square feet and went up to 2000 square feet. "*It is one of the rare franchise brands which touch the rural as well (as) urban masses with same zest*", said a news article about Patanjali[94].

91 https://www.thehindubusinessline.com/news/patanjali-ayurved-to-expand-presence-in-dairy-segment/article23446400.ece, Accessed on May 15, 2018.

92 Page 18, Mathrubhumi, Palakkad Edition.

93 http://www.franchiseindia.com/content/Invest-in-Patanjali-franchise-for-best-revenues.6037, Accessed on April 24, 2017.

94 http://www.franchiseindia.com/content/Invest-in-Patanjali-franchise-for-best-revenues.6037, Accessed on April 24, 2017.

Figure 7.3

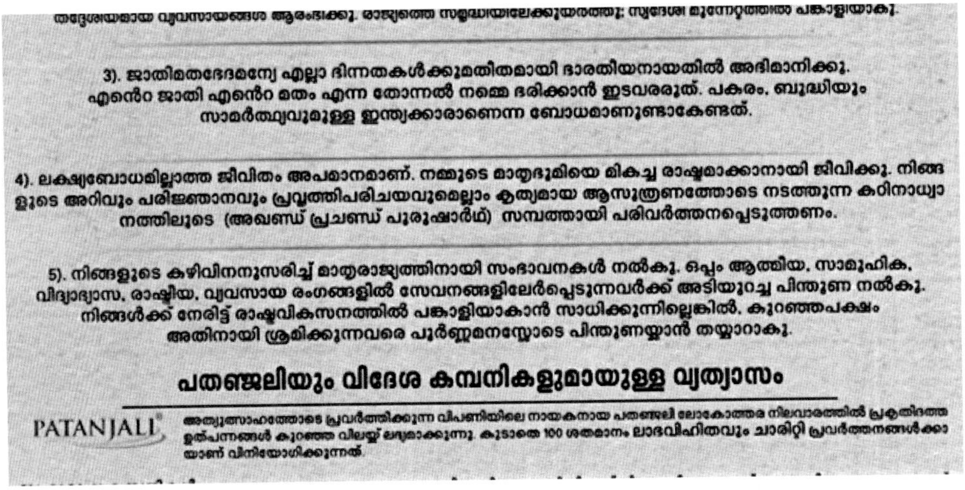

A part of the print advertisement released by Patanjali Ayurved in a regional daily on August 15 (India's Independence Day), 2017.

Patanjali has been communicating to people that multinational companies have been making excessive profits and did not focus on charitable and philanthropic endeavors. Baba Ramdev has been communicating that profits made by Patanjali will be used for charity. In the context of starting a food park in Assam, Baba Ramdev said, "*The complete profit from the Food Park will be dedicated for the welfare of Assam by setting up school and skill development centres in each district.*"[95] In another interview, Baba Ramdev mentioned, "*World-class quality, low price and giving away our entire profit to charity are the three main reasons for the boom seen in Patanjali products.*"[96] He has also invited attention to the employment generation by Patanjali. "*I am an unpaid brand ambassador and Acharya Balkrishna is an unpaid CEO, MD and shareholder of the company, with a model of no dividend or no profit sharing. The 100 per cent profit earned by the Patanjali is used for charity to provide world-class quality and affordable products. We have provided one lakh direct employments and indirect employment opportunity to one crore farmers. In the next five years, our target is to provide direct and indirect employment to five crore farmers,*" mentioned Baba Ramdev[97].

95 https://thenewsmill.com/rs-1300-crore-patanjali-herbal-mega-food-park-come-near-tezpur/, Accessed on April 24, 2017.

96 http://www.littleindia.com/business/22583-the-yoga-gurus-behind-india%E2%80%99s-hottest-consumer-products.html, Accessed on April 24, 2017.

97 http://www.asianage.com/opinion/oped/130117/note-ban-is-a-step-to-bring-transparency-and-reforms.html, Accessed on April 24, 2017.

QUESTIONS

1. What parameters do you consider while purchasing products for personal purposes? Would you consider an organisation's environmental-friendliness, participation in humanitarian activities etc. as parameters while make decisions on purchasing a product?
2. List any ten brands that you use for personal and household purposes. Name the companies that own these brands. How much percentage of profits are shared by these companies to charitable/ philanthropic/ CSR activities?

NARAYANA HEALTH

Narayana Health is a Bengaluru based hospital chain that has been known for providing high quality health care services at a pricing that is lower in comparison to various privately managed super-specialty and multi-specialty hospitals in India. Operating 23 hospitals across India, it has more than 30 medical specialties and is visited by more than two million patients annually.

The hospital chain was founded by Dr Devi Shetty, who started a hospital in the city in 2001, with the name of *'Narayana Hrudayalaya'*. Dr Shetty has been known for conducting paediatric heart surgeries, and has performed more than 20,000 major heart surgeries in India. Through the years, the hospital has expanded across India. By May 2018, the number of operating beds in the Narayana Health hospitals were more than 6100. For hospitals that had been in existence for more than five years, the occupancy rate approximated 65%, while the hospitals with an existence of 3-5 years had an occupancy rate of 57%. The hospitals had permanent staff of more than 10,000 people, while more than 3500 people were hired on a temporary or contractual basis[98]. The company has also been promoting information campaigns related to healthy living through its social media platform **(Refer Figure 7.4)**

Figure 7.4[99]

98 Annual report 2017-18.

99 Image included with permission. Courtesy: Narayana Health

For a particular surgery/procedure that required a stay in the hospital, the patient was offered a variety of "packages" with variable pricing. Dr Shetty believes that a "sound business model" is necessary for reaching more number of people. The hospital chain has been able to provide a lower pricing, as compared to some of the other specialty hospitals. This was managed in a number of ways, including doing high volume business. It conducts approximately 400 surgeries and procedures daily. *"A bypass surgery typically takes about five hours. The critical part, which is the actual grafting, takes only an hour. The specialist does that while harvesting of the veins/arteries, opening and closing of the chest, suturing and other procedures are done by junior doctors. The preparation of the patient is handled by nurses and paramedical staff,"* says the COO at Narayana Health[100].

Higher volumes enabled the hospital to negotiate lower prices for the various medical related products that they purchase from suppliers. Standardisation was done for the purchase of consumables and devices. A central buying unit was set up that purchased almost 80% of all consumables and devices. The hospital group's search for efficiency has been visible in various endeavors including developing its information management system, which was based on a "cloud" based enterprise platform to analyse the medical history of its patients[101]

"We will keep our model predominantly asset-light; we will reinvest our accruals; we will engage with governments for land and help them achieve affordable healthcare promises made to their constituencies; we will rent premises from private owners and create small-to-large clinics within existing hospitals," says Dr Shetty[102]. Of the 23 hospitals it operates in India, it owns and operates only four. Seven hospitals are under a lease and operating agreement. In another six hospitals it paid a share of the revenue to the owner of the premises, while another two hospitals were operated in a public-private partnership mode.

In 2013, Narayana Hrudayalaya Pvt. Ltd. changed its name to Narayana Health. In January 2016, Narayana Health was listed in BSE at a 35 percent premium on its issue price of 250 rupees and had a market capitalisation of more than one billion dollars on its listing. While the revenues of the hospital chain increased from 480.2 crore rupees in 2010-11 to 2,280.9 crore rupees in 2017-18, its profit margins remained modest through the years (2.8%, 3.9%, 2.9%, 2.8%, -0.8%, 1.2%, 4.3% and 2.4% for the eight

100 http://www.businesstoday.in/magazine/cover-story/biggest-india-innovation-narayana-health/story/205823.html, Accessed on June 27, 2017.

101 http://www.hclinfotech.in/wp-content/uploads/2014/04/Narayana-Hrudayalaya.pdf, Accessed on June 27, 2017.

102 http://www.narayanahealth.org/about-us/chairmans-message, Accessed on June 27, 2017.

years ending 2017-18). The hospital's attempt to keep its pricing relatively lower has not eroded its endeavors to provide high quality health care. The mortality rate and infection rate for a coronary artery bypass graft procedure, and the incidence of bedsores after a coronary surgery is on par with some of the best hospitals in the world. "*India is in a phenomenal position to make a difference and show the world a new way of delivering affordable healthcare,*" says Dr Shetty[103].

Questions

For Discussion:

1. Narayana Hospitals have a policy document that mentions about 'zero-tolerance' towards bribery and corruption (http://www.narayanahealth.org/Anti-Bribery-Corruptio-Policy.pdf). What could be the ways through which a healthcare organisation can embody the values of honesty, integrity, service and compassion?
2. The article indicates that Narayana Hospitals have modest profit margins. What could be an optimum profit margin for a private organisation offering healthcare services? What are the criteria that you will consider for your decision, and state the reasons for selecting such criteria?

For Conversation:

1. What are the ways through which you can help in making healthcare affordable to all?
2. How can you create and contribute to a world where people are not affected by diseases?

For Contemplation:

1. Air, water and food – they are outside us, while being inside too. Pollute them outside, the inside gets polluted. Pollute them inside, the outside gets polluted. How can we keep them serene?
2. In the tradition of Ayurveda, the doctor does not charge a fee from the patient. In the present day India too - in small towns and rural areas - Ayurvedic doctors do not charge a fee from the patient for consultation, while they charge a fee for the medicines provided, with the patient having a choice to buy or not to buy those medicines. What could have prompted the Ayurvedic tradition to follow such a practice?

---

103 http://indianexpress.com/article/business/business-others/rs-600-cr-narayana-hrudayalaya-ipo-balancing-affordable-healthcare-and-the-impending-pressure-for-profits/, Accessed on June 27, 2017.

ZED HOMES: HABITATS OF HARMONY

Zed Homes is an initiative of BCIL, founded by Chandrasekhar Hariharan in 1994. BCIL has been known for earth-friendly buildings and all ZED projects are carbon-neutral. ZED stands for Zero Energy Development. "... *we believe in zero water from government board or tankers, zero borewells, zero waste water export, zero solid waste export and we take only 30% energy from the grid. No waste should go out of residential enclaves,"* says Hariharan[104]. Every ZED project is platinum rated - the highest standard accorded to a green building project.

ZED Home projects are in Bangalore, Chennai and Mysore, and offers luxury villas, 2BHKs and 3BHK dwellings. The company has constructed TZED Homes in Bangalore. This project, consisting of 80 apartments and 15 independent homes, attempted to ensure that there is environmental-friendliness through the entire life-cycle of the building. For this, assessment was done primarily on the six areas of design and planning, building material, water, waste, quality of air and energy management (**Refer Table 7.2**).

Table 7.2

	Areas	Features/ Impacts
1	Design/ Landscape Planning	Ascertain the carrying capacity of the area, and decide on the number of apartments that can be build there
2	Building Material	Usage of stone, mud, fly ash blocks, green roof
3	Water	Self-sufficient water supply system, rainwater harvesting, recharge wells, solar water heaters, solar pumps, waste-water treatment, waste-water re-used in gardens
4	Waste	Waste segregation, vermi-composting pit, sewage treatment plant
5	Quality of Air	Centrally air-conditioned, Air-conditioners that bring 100% fresh air
6	Energy Management	LED, CFL, motion sensors and ambient light sensors

104 http://www.thehindu.com/features/homes-and-gardens/wake-up-theres-a-crisis/article5844013.ece, Accessed on June 28, 2017.

Elements of harmony between construction and nature can be observed in ZED projects (Refer **figures 7.5 and 7.6**). The design may be in alignment with the flow of wind, water and sunlight. The buildings constructed by the organisation do not use bricks, concrete blocks, clay blocks and clay tiles, considering that they use significant amount of top soil, which has a high fertile nature. With a similar perspective, vitrified and ceramic tiles are not used, considering the high energy requirement needed to manufacture these tiles. Flooring is made with natural stones. The projects avoid toxic paints. Chemicals are not used for water-proofing. Mortar is avoided for construction of walls. The gardens at Zed projects use micro-irrigation systems. In these gardens, vegetables and greens are grown, with manure coming from composting. This contributes to making available fresh produces, with the least transportation involved[105].

Figure 7.5[106]

This open air theater was a dumping place for construction debris. The debris was used to make the top deck of the seating area (foreground left), while flattening the area that is now the stage. Construction waste materials were also used for retaining the edges and for making the seating arrangements.

105 http://www.mybangalore.com/article/1210/interview-with-chandrashekar-hariharan-ceo-of-biodiversity-conservation-india-ltd-bcil.html

106 Included with permission.

Figure 7.6[107]

Breathing and porous ground surface areas helps in water percolation, and charging of the shallow aquifers[108].

Questions

1. If you are living in an apartment, ascertain the sources of the following, for the inhabitants of the apartment:
   (a) drinkable water
   (b) safe food ingredients
   (c) clean air

2. Reflect on the ways through which earth-friendly apartment designs and earth-friendly architecture can lead to improving the quality of living in the cities and towns.

107 Included with permission.

108 During the floods of 2018 in Kerala, a state in India, the district of Palakkad was amongst the two districts that received the highest percentage increase in rainfall as compared to previous years. Yet the negative impact of excessive rainfall in the district was lower as compared to other districts of the state of Kerala. This was because the district had the existence of porous ground surfaces and water bodies allowing for water percolation, storage and flow. However, the district headquarters of Palakkad, where such areas where converted for developmental purposes, witnessed floods.

3. Read through news articles and reviews about the company. What are the areas where Zed Homes can be considered as setting higher standards in environmentally and socially responsible apartment designs and constructions?
4. Provide examples of architectural structures, designs and styles that are efficient and effective in:
   (a) management of water resources – its conservation, replenishment, reuse, drainage, etc.
   (b) usage of natural lighting
   (c) usage of natural and locally available materials
   (d) natural and pollution-free methods of cooling and warming

FAIRPHONE – THE REAL SMART PHONE

Fairphone is an Amsterdam based company that designs modular smartphones - smartphones that has components that can be replaced or upgraded individually. Fairphone 2, launched by this company, won a 10/10 score in the 'repairability' criteria by Ifixit.com[109]. The company has set industry standards in avoiding the usage of 'conflict minerals' in its phones.

Fairphone started in 2013. *"We didn't start as a company...We started as a campaign. And the campaign question was how can we give visibility to the situation in eastern Congo."*[110] Congo has become (in)famous for its role in 'conflict minerals', a term used in the context of how money made from mineral extraction is used to fund conflicts in the region. A review says, *"Most of us don't know how to open up our smartphones, much less what's inside. Believe it or not, even phone makers can't account for the origins of every ingredient. Behind the glossy surface are dozens of minerals, processed in hundreds of factories, touched by thousands of hands. The more I ask about my phone's roots in African mines and Asian assembly lines, the more uncomfortable I become."*[111]

The company has attempted to create a 'fair phone' through processes aiming at *"positive social and environmental impact from the beginning to the end of a phone's life cycle"*[112]. Towards this, Fairphone has listed its goals and objectives (**Refer Table 7.3**). Traceability and transparency in supply chain has been one of the key focus areas (**Refer Figure 7.7**) for Fairphone. The company has set up traceable supply chains for the four conflict minerals – tin, tantalum, gold and tungsten[113]. Fairphone is also a signatory to an agreement related to responsible business conduct for Netherlands based companies that have gold or gold-bearing materials in their value chain[114][115].

---

109 https://www.ifixit.com/Teardown/Fairphone+2+Teardown/52523, Accessed on July 9, 2017.

110 http://www.bbc.com/news/business-35094050, Accessed on July 11, 2017.

111 https://www.wsj.com/articles/how-was-your-smartphone-made-nobody-really-knows-1467832310, Accessed on July 11, 2017.

112 https://www.fairphone.com/en/our-goals/, Accessed on September 24, 2017.

113 https://www.fairphone.com/en/2016/06/20/fairphone-2-good-vibrations-with-conflict-free-tungsten-2/, Accessed on September 23, 2017.

114 http://www.internationalrbc.org/gold/news/2017/6/child_labor?sc_lang=en, Accessed on September 23, 2017.

115 http://www.fairtrade.org.uk/Media-Centre/News/June-2017/Fairphone-joins-forces-with-key-players-to-source-gold-responsibly, Accessed on September 23, 2017.

Table 7.3

	Criteria	Objective 1	Objective 2	Objective 3
1	**Long-lasting design**	Focus on modularity and easy repair	Usage of open software	Engineering and production decisions that reduce environmental footprint and support longevity
2	**Fair materials**	Sourcing of materials that are less hazardous/ toxic	Increasing the usage of recycled and/ or renewable resources	Usage of materials from mines that support vulnerable communities or have better sustainable performance
3	**Good working conditions**	Improve working conditions and worker satisfaction	Worker engagement and dialogue	Transparency, Responsible business practices, Skill enhancement
4	**Reuse and recycling**	Encouraging Fairphone users to donate their old phones	Support the collection of used phones in developing countries	Research on optimization of recyclability in smartphones

Figure 7.7

Traceability Tags on Tungsten bags from Rwanda[116]

116 Included with permission from Fairphone. Image available at https://www.flickr.com/photos/fairphone/15027670598/, Accessed on September 23, 2017.

Fairphone 2 has six modules that users can replace by themselves – display module, camera module, battery, core module, top module and bottom module[117]. It has been reported that DIY (Do-It-Yourself) repairs for Fairphone have scored a 95% success rate[118]. *"This is the first and only smartphone to receive a perfect score from us, and the modular design is a major factor. It was very impressive to be able to replace the display in seconds without any tools,"* mentions the Director, iFixit[119] (**Refer Figure 7.8**).

Figure 7.8

Fairphone 2 Modular Design[120]

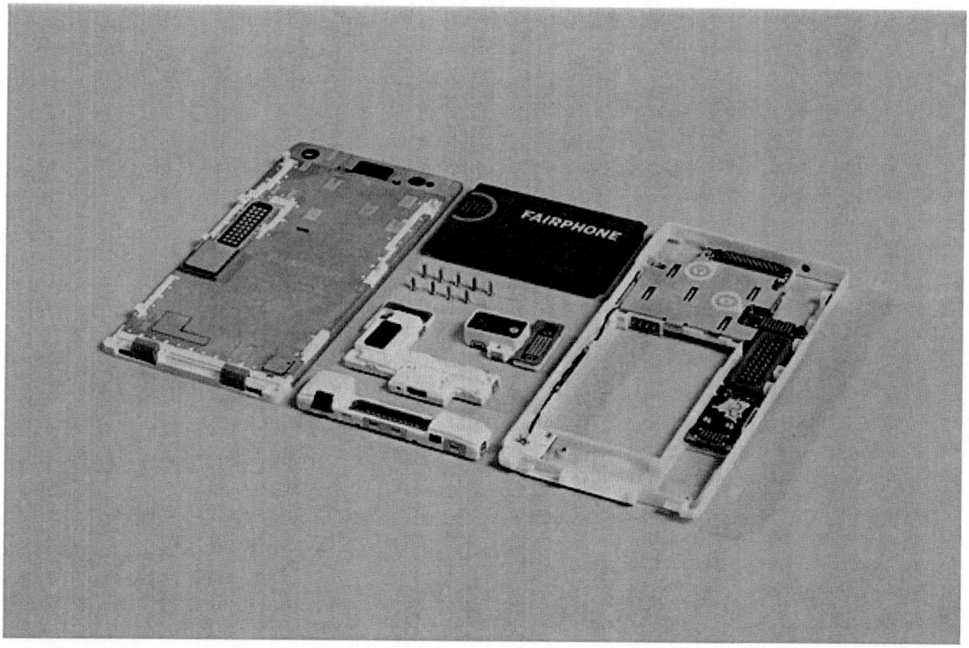

While media has critiqued on Fairphone's technology lagging behind the globally popular mobile phones, they've been acknowledging Fairphone's high standards on sustainability parameters. *"...people will likely buy the*

117 https://shop.fairphone.com/en/spare-parts/filter/choose-your-fairphone/fairphone-2, Accessed on September 23, 2017.

118 https://www.digitaltrends.com/mobile/fairphone-mwc17/#ixzz4aoyFRns5, Accessed on July 11, 2017.

119 https://www.digitaltrends.com/mobile/fairphone-mwc17/, Accessed on July 11, 2017.

120 Included with permission from Fairphone. Available at https://www.flickr.com/photos/fairphone/23624799326/, Accessed on September 23, 2017.

Fairphone 2 not because of its software, but because of how it was designed to reduce the environmental impact of mobile devices." says *Digial Trends*[121]. Rankabrand.org has given the highest grading for Fairphone in the category of smartphones[122].

"We haven't created the 100% fair phone...We are showing through our own supply chain what's wrong with the supply chain," says Bas van Abel, CEO, Fairphone[123]. He says, *"The mechanism we use to change things is a commercial model. By being part of the economic system and a market mechanism we are able to actually put idealist values into the core of what moves the world."*[124]

It has been reported that Fairphone has reused minerals from more than 1,00,000 disposed phones to be included in the phones that the company manufactured[125]. Many of these phones were collected from countries in the African continent such as Ghana, Uganda and Rwanda[126].

Questions

1. Do you own a mobile phone? If yes, how important is repairability and modularity to your mobile phone? What are the advantages of repairability and modularity? How has Fairphone contributed to these two aspects in the mobile phone industry?
2. Where does your phone come from? Where does your phone go? Trace the origin of the various metals used in your mobile phone. Do a 'life-cycle-analysis' of your mobile phone – from collection and extraction of raw materials, to the post-disposal processes.
3. What percentage of your mobile phone is recyclable, and what percentage of your phone is made from recycled materials?
4. Visit the website of Fairphone. Comment on three significant/ inspiring/ positive contribution that Fairphone has made?

121 https://www.digitaltrends.com/mobile/fairphone-2-camera-module-news/, Accessed on September 23, 2017.

122 https://rankabrand.org/electronics/Fairphone, Accessed on September 23, 2017.

123 https://www.wsj.com/articles/how-was-your-smartphone-made-nobody-really-knows-1467832310, Accessed on July 11, 2017.

124 http://www.bbc.com/news/business-35094050, Accessed on July 11, 2017.

125 https://www.digitaltrends.com/mobile/fairphone-mwc17/, Accessed July 11, 2017.

126 https://www.fairphone.com/en/2017/08/01/collecting-used-phones-africa-europe/, Accessed on September 23, 2017.

NOTES:

Caselets/Case-studies completed

A road shaded with trees in Sadki, Nakło County, Poland. This 'avenue of trees' consists mainly of chestnut and common ash trees[127].

127 https://commons.wikimedia.org/wiki/File:Bdg_aljarzebow_10-18_5.jpg, Accessed on August 17, 2019, Image available in public domain.

A road in Queensland, Australia, shaded by mango-trees[128].

Trees providing the solace of shade to a road, in the state of Tamilnadu, India.

128 https://commons.wikimedia.org/wiki/File:Mango_Trees_along_Anzac_Avenue_at_Mango_Hill,_Queensland.jpg, Accessed on August 17, 2019, Image available in public domain.

The above photo was taken by Captain Linnaeus Tripe (1822-1902) of the 12th Regiment Native Infantry at Bangalore. For four years, beginning 1856, he was government photographer to the Madras presidency of British India. The photo is titled "Photographic views of Ryakotta and other places in the Salem district, pl. IX: Avenue of the Banian Trees, Seringham, India"[129].

Referring to the stone edicts of Asoka, who lived two centuries prior to Jesus, and was also the third king of the Mauryan kingdom, E Hultzsch[130], mentions, "*Aśóka arranged for medical treatment of men and cattle not only in his own dominions*[131]*, but among his borderers, and caused medicinal herbs, roots, and fruits to be cultivated. Along the roads he had trees planted and wells dug for the benefit of cattle and men. The Delhi-Topra pillar-edict VII, which was issued twenty-seven years after the abhisheka, states that he planted banyan-trees and mango-groves along the roads, that at intervals of eight kós*[132] *he had wells dug...*".[133]

---

129 Image Source: https://commons.wikimedia.org/wiki/File:Captain_Linnaeus_Tripe_-_Avenue_of_the_Banian_Trees,_Seringham,_India_-_1994.18_-_Cleveland_Museum_of_Art.tif, Accessed on March 4, 2020..

130 "Epigraphist to the Government of Madras, Retired".

131 The Eastern land frontiers of the Ashokan empire included regions from Baluchistan and Afghanistan. The Himalayan mountains remained the northern boundary, while, to the south, the empire covered almost half of the present "South India". It was during the 3rd - 2nd century BCE that the Mauryan empire flourishes in the Indian sub-continent. King Ashoka issued decrees that provided protection to forests, and many animals and birds. After the war of Kalinga and his adoption of Buddhism,."conquest" acquired a new meaning for Asoka - the king sends messengers (*bikku* or *bhikshu*), to regions beyond the sub-continent, to live and communicate the message of Buddha.

132 Various measurements have been provided for a '*kos*' - "approximately a kilometre", "a mile", "the greatest distance, at which the bellowing of the cows can be heard", four miles, approximately three kilometre or 1.9 miles, etc. are some of them. Hiuen Tsiang mentions in his travel diairies, "In the subdivision of distances, a *yojana* is equal to eight *krosas* (*kcu-ln-she*); a *krosa* is the distance that the lowing of a cow can be heard; a *krosa* is divided into 500 bows (*dhanus*); a bow is divided into four cubits (*hastas*); a cubit is divided into 24 fingers (*angulis*); a finger is divided into seven barleycorns (*yavas*) and so on to a louse (*yuka*), a nit (*liksha*), a dust grain, a cow's hair, a sheep's hair, a hare's down, copper-water, and so on for seven divisions, till we come to a small drain of dust; this is divided sevenfold till we come to an excessively small grain of dust (*anu*); this cannot be divided further without arriving at nothingness, and so it is called the infinitely small (*paramanu*).

133 Inscriptions of Asoka, Clarendon Press (for Government of India), 1925.

स्वस्तिप्रजाभ्यः परिपालयंतां
न्यायेत मार्गेण महीं महीशाः।
गोब्राह्मणेभ्यः शुभमस्तु नित्यं
लोकाः समस्ता सुखितोभवंतु।।

Swasthiprajabhya Paripalayantham
Nyayenamarghena maheem maheesha
Gobrahmanebhya shubamasthu nithyam
Loka samastha sukhino bhavanthu

Let there be well-being among all, and those who care for and protect them,
Let righteousness be the path chosen by the great and the supreme,
Let there be auspiciousness eternal, for the living and the learned,
Let all in the world be happy.
(Let all worlds be happy.)